W9-DIJ-911

TO

George W. Chambers

LiA lynn Rosen

PREHISTORIC
SOUTHWESTERN
CRAFT ARTS

Fig. 4.28   Kayenta polychrome styles.

CLARA LEE TANNER

Author of *Southwest Indian Craft Arts* and *Southwest Indian Painting*

PREHISTORIC
SOUTHWESTERN
CRAFT ARTS

THE UNIVERSITY OF ARIZONA PRESS
Tucson, Arizona

About the author...

CLARA LEE TANNER, acknowledged expert, lecturer, and student of Southwest Indian crafts, arts, and religion, is the author of two other highly acclaimed books, *Southwest Indian Craft Arts* and *Southwest Indian Painting,* as well as countless articles. A member of the University of Arizona faculty of anthropology since 1928, she has done continuous research in her extensive travels among the Southwest tribes with her husband John, a long-time Indian trader. Professor Tanner frequently is called upon to judge craft and art exhibitions. In 1974 she received First Award from the National Federation of Press Women for *Southwest Indian Painting.* Mrs. Tanner is a Fellow of the American Anthropological Association and member of the Society of American Archaeology, Delta Kappa Gamma, Society of the Sigma Xi, and the National Federation of Press Women.

THE UNIVERSITY OF ARIZONA PRESS

Copyright © 1976
The Arizona Board of Regents
All Rights Reserved
Manufactured in the U.S.A.

I.S.B.N. 0-8165-0582-9 cloth
I.S.B.N. 0-8165-0416-4 paper
L.C. No. 75-19865

Credits for Use of Illustrations

Grateful acknowledgment is given to the Arizona State Museum and the Peabody Museum of American Archaeology for permission to reproduce numerous illustrations within this book. Credits are listed by figure numbers as follows: Arizona State Museum —1.1; 1.8–9; 2.1; 2.2j; 2.3; 2.9b, c; 2.11; 2.14a; 2.15p; 2.16; 2.18; 2.20e, f, j; 2.22b; 2.23b; 2.24c; 2.27a; 2.40; 3.1; 3.2a; 3.4b; 3.10b; 3.13; 3.14f–h; 3.15–16; 3.17a, d; 3.18; 3.19a, f; 3.20; 3.21a, b, d; 3.22–23; 3.25–27; 3.28b; 3.29a, b; 3.31–32; 3.34; 3.35b; 3.36–38; 3.40b, c, d; 3.41–42; 4.10–11; 4.13–14; 4.16–38; 5.6; 5.7t; 5.8b, c; 5.9; 5.12b; 5.13c; 5.14; 5.19; 5.20b, c; 5.21; 5.23; 5.24b; 6.9b; 6.13; 6.15–16; 6.18c; 6.21b; 6.22c; 6.23e; 6.24; 6.26; 6.29–30; 6.32. Peabody Museum of American Archaeology—2.2h; 2.19; 2.23a; 2.24; 2.27e, f; 2.30b; 2.41; 3.3b–v; 3.11; 3.14a, b, d; 3.21c; 3.24c; 3.30; 3.39; 3.40a; 4.6b, c; 4.7d; 4.39–40; 5.4a, c; 5.7f–m; 5.25–28; 6.1–3; 6.9a; 6.12; 6.17; 6.20a; 6.23d.

Contents

Illustrations

Maps

Foreword

The prehistory of the southwestern United States is probably better understood than the prehistory of any comparable region in the world. For more than 100 years, archaeological research has been carried out, and the broad outlines of cultural development over the past 12,000 years have been worked out. One legacy of these thousands of years of cultural growth and change is the artistic traditions of the modern descendants of the prehistoric American Indians of the Southwest.

In contemporary America there is growing interest in and appreciation of Southwest Indian art. Much of this modern artistic tradition has deep roots. Yet, until now, no one has undertaken an in-depth study of its prehistoric background. No one has explored in detail the emergence of major art forms and styles of prehistoric Southwestern peoples.

Perhaps no one is better qualified to undertake such a project than Clara Lee Tanner who has devoted a lifetime to the study of Southwestern Indian craft arts, both contemporary and prehistoric. Her many articles and books on the subject reveal painstaking research. Although she has briefly summarized the prehistoric background in her books on contemporary Indian art, we have had to wait until now to have her expertise applied to the subject in book form. Mrs. Tanner has produced an interesting and a useful book that will be valued by both laymen and professionals. It is highly readable and enjoyable, yet rich in detail and reference.

The work traces the development of the major craft arts, including basketry, pottery, and textiles through the millennia of Southwestern prehistory. Through the author's careful analysis and presentation, one sees the emergence of artistic traditions and their relationships to other aspects of culture. With Mrs. Tanner's help, one can begin to see the rich heritage of the modern Southwestern Indian artist.

Anthropologists, art historians—anyone interested in Southwestern Indian art—will profit from a careful reading. We are fortunate indeed that Mrs. Tanner has taken the time and devoted the energy to produce this valuable study. The work as it stands, representing the culmination of fifty years of research and study, is an immensely important contribution.

WILLIAM A. LONGACRE

Preface

Hundreds of archaeological sites in the American Southwest excavated in the past century have revealed a wealth of craft arts of the prehistoric peoples of this area. Reports on excavations have concentrated on sites and architecture, and, in varying degrees of coverage, the crafts. The latter include more complete discussions of pottery; intensive study of this material has long served as a basis for relative dating of sites. Varying emphases on the remaining materials often reflect the quantity of preservation, for in different areas baskets, textiles, and other perishables may occur in considerable abundance, rarely, or not at all. Stone tools, articles of personal adornment, and other non-perishables are apt to occur more generously; often these are discussed in considerable detail in archaeological reports.

It is from these rich written sources of craft materials, plus research of museum collections, that the information for this book has been drawn. Basically, an effort has been made to survey each of the major arts, namely baskets, textiles, pottery, jewelry, and some lesser miscellaneous crafts, in broad perspectives of their production and artistry. A brief presentation of materials, techniques, and forms for each craft serves as a basis for discussions of design styles and artistic development. In addition, thirty-five years of teaching a course in Prehistoric Southwest Indian Craft Arts has contributed to the organization of this book.

Acknowledgments

Appreciation is expressed for two generous grants from the Graduate Committee for Support of Faculty Research in the Humanities and Social Sciences. These made possible the wealth of drawings without which much of the value of this book would be lost. In particular do I wish to commend the magnificent work of Christine Walsh who produced the majority of the drawings. Valerie Clark also did some of the drawings.

To Raymond Thompson, head of the Department of Anthropology and Director of the Arizona State Museum, I wish to express my indebtedness for his thoughtfulness and cooperation at many points in the development of the manuscript. Thanks, too, to the Arizona State Museum staff, always pleasant and cooperative, and most particularly to Helga Teiwes whose superb photography adds dimension to this publication. And to many of the staff of the University of Arizona Press whose ready cooperation in all stages of the book's production made burdensome chores lighter, my sincere gratitude.

Always, in writing a book there are many who stand by to perform those thankless tasks which shine through, perhaps more to the author, but which contribute mightily to the finished product. Thanks to Barbara Robinson and Dorothy Inslee who brought to light material buried in a morass of corrections, over corrections, erasures, pinched-in additions, and subtractions. Thanks, too, to those whose names are not mentioned, but whose efforts are not forgotten.

Last but not least in the heart of the author is deep appreciation for her patient and understanding husband, John, whose encouragement kept pen to paper at many a low-ebb point.

CLARA LEE TANNER

Chapter 1

Cultural Background

THE FOUNDATION STONES of Southwest Indian culture were laid by men and women who were well established in the area some 10,000 or more years ago. All were basically hunters and/or gatherers. Nonetheless, these Indians established distinctive cultures, cultures with technological differences that set each apart from the other. Archaeologists have labeled these people "Paleo-Indians" or "Early Man." Paleo-Indians persisted for millennia with a minimum of change, each group following its own pattern of culture for its respective span of time. Eventually one group made contact with corn cultivation; in time it passed to all. Several thousands of years, perhaps, were spent in experimentation and adaptation to a new way of life based on this great discovery. Out of it all emerged sedentary people who eventually built permanent residences, lived by an agricultural economy to a greater or lesser degree, and developed relatively simple village life-styles. These prehistoric Indians are called Anasazi, Hohokam, and Mogollon by archaeologists.

Paleo-Indians

Wormington has established a minimum of three basic and differing Early Man cultures in North America: the Paleoeastern, Paleowestern, and Paleonorthern.[1] Variation and distinctiveness in the ways of life of these three groups can be attributed in some measure to varying environments and times. This was the time after the recession of the great glaciers, the postglacial period. Alaska was much as it is today except

that some life forms differed—for example, there were mammoths still roaming the area. Paleowesterners lived in the Great Basin and adjoining areas, from the Rockies on the east to the Coastal Range on the west, and extending from Oregon-Washington on the north to southern Arizona. Environmental conditions in the area were gradually assuming their present state, going through earlier stages of greater moisture, which were characterized by many lakes, some even in southern Arizona, and later phases of growing aridity, with the establishment of modern, semiarid conditions several millennia before the opening of the Christian Era. Plant and animal life varied throughout this region, but it did not differ too greatly from present life except for more abundant grasses in the wet areas. Foods for the inhabitants of this area included small game such as rabbits, rodents, and occasional deer, plus vegetal foods such as nuts, berries, grass seeds, and other local plants in season.

Contrarily, big game was fairly abundant in the area occupied by very early (10,000 years ago) Paleoeastern men, from the eastern seaboard to the Rockies, with some wedging into southern Arizona, and from the Great Lakes to the Gulf of Mexico. Over much of this territory roamed mammoths, mastodon, a bison larger in size than the historic species, deer, horse, and a few other larger creatures. Many of these, but definitely excluding the mastodon, served as sources of food for coexisting Early Man. That the environment of these early Paleoeasterners contrasted with that of contemporary times, at

Fig. 1.1   Diorama showing both plant and animal life of ten thousand years ago, southern Arizona. Vegetation was lush; many of the animals were large and there was a great variety of them.

least in parts of this vast territory, is obvious in the great size of many of the animals. In southern Arizona, where these creatures were found, not only did the grass grow more abundantly than now, but also there were more luxuriant trees and more brush. Toward the end of the Paleo-Indian period a number of these animals disappeared, particularly the mammoth, mastodon, horse, and large bison.

PALEONORTHERN CULTURE

In Alaska, both small and large game were hunted, including the mammoth. It is likely that both man and mammoth (plus other animals) made the trek across the Bering Straits from Asia simultaneously; undoubtedly man brought with him already-established hunting techniques and tools. At any rate, there have been found in this and adjoining areas many tools large and small and made in specialized techniques. In size, they ran the gamut from microliths (very tiny stone tools) to larger points. The latter are sometimes worked in the manner of Eurasian Solutrean types, beautifully chipped and flaked points of great symmetry and perfection.

PALEOEASTERN CULTURE

The Paleoeastern people were big game hunters. They were widespread in distribution, as their remains have been found in the same area occupied by the animals from the Eastern Seaboard to the Rockies, with some penetration into the Southwest, and from Canada to the Gulf of Mexico. Frequently found in these

regions in very early years were the mammoth, mastodon (not hunted by these Paleo-Indians), the large bison, horse, deer, antelope, and a few other creatures (Fig. 1.1). Seemingly, the most important game hunted by these early men included the mammoth and bison. Obviously, hunting such large animals necessitated the production of weapons efficient enough to kill and prepare them. Not only did sizes of Paleo-eastern tools and weapons exceed those of the Paleowesterners, but also there was far more specialization in form and workmanship. Hand-in-hand with better tools went the selection of finer materials, such as obsidian, chalcedony, and other flintlike stones.

The most common evidences of Paleo-easterners include kill sites, where the animals were brought down and often where they were butchered; industry sites, where the men of this culture produced their many tools and weapons; and, less frequently, hearth sites, where man probably cooked and ate the animals, and possibly spent some time. Sites were located either in caves or in the open. At the kill sites are found the finished weapons, such as projectile points, with which animals were hunted, and the variety of knives, scrapers, and other tools with which animals were skinned, cut up, and otherwise prepared for removal. At the industry sites archaeologists frequently find the raw materials of production, chips and flakes knocked off in the manufacturing process, and tools in various stages of manufacture. Bones of animals hunted and sometimes tools and

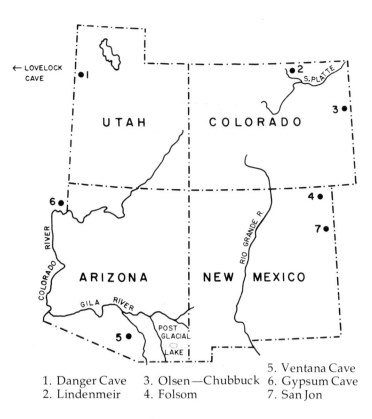

5. Ventana Cave
1. Danger Cave   3. Olsen—Chubbuck   6. Gypsum Cave
2. Lindenmeir   4. Folsom   7. San Jon

MAP 1.1   SITE LOCATIONS OF EARLY MAN.

weapons made and used by these men are found about the hearths and in caves.

Map 1.1 locates some of the many sites where Paleoeastern materials have been recovered. In northeastern New Mexico (near Folsom, for which the points were named) were found remains of bison which had been killed as they came to drink at a site where it was difficult for the animals to get away from the hunters. Apparently the animals had been skinned right on the spot, for no tail bones were found. At a site in eastern Colorado, Lindenmeir, an apparent workshop was located, complete with quantities of waste materials and some worked fragments. In a cave in the Sandía Mountains, near Albuquerque, New Mexico, were found points associated with the same levels in which bones of now-extinct animals were located. Near the eastern border of Colorado is one of the most interesting of all Paleoeastern sites, Olsen-Chubbuck.[2] Recovered here were the remains of a large number of bison that apparently had been stampeded by the early hunters; many were killed as they fell into an arroyo, stacking up one on top of the other. The hunters closed in, putting an end to those that had survived.

Then they worked their way down the piled animals, dragging individual carcasses away to skin and cut up, seemingly feasting on the newly cut meat or drying it for future use; or retrieving internal organs; preparing skins, probably for shelter and clothing; or removing horns for containers. Fine points used in killing these animals remained, along with the stacked bones, to tell another story about these early men.

Paleoeastern tools were generally made of obsidian or flintlike materials which were readily worked by the pressure methods of chipping and flaking (Fig. 1.2). Folsom points are short and broad, and characteristically have a groove down one or both sides (Fig. 1.3a); they are beautifully chipped and flaked. The Yuma point, first found at Lindenmeir, is long, slender, narrow, and is also marked by fine chipping and flaking (Fig. 1.3 b,c). The Sandía point (Fig. 1.3d), first identified at the site of the same name, was less well made: it is large, crudely worked, and has a slight inset extending on one side from the base. Scrapers were recovered from many locations (Fig. 1.4). From the Olsen-Chubbuck site were recovered scrapers with working ends or sides, knives, and points. The latter were basically of two types, one like the San Jon style from eastern New Mexico, with a short and narrow body, and the other, called Firstview, with some features

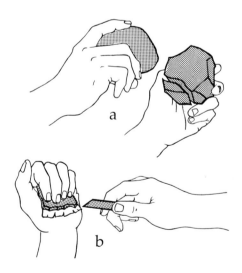

Fig. 1.2   Methods of working stone tools. (a) Percussion flaking, or striking a blow to remove a piece of stone or a flake in forming a tool. (b) Pressure method: placing a bone or horn tool on the stone then applying pressure to remove flakes. The latter is obviously a more controlled method of working stone.

not unlike the Yuma point in long and slender proportions, but with most of them thicker in width. These projectile points were probably attached to a long handle or spear and thrust from the hand or from a spear thrower called an atlatl.

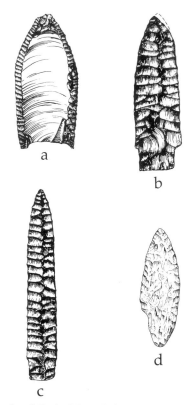

Fig. 1.3   Tools of Early Man, Paleoeastern types. (a) General style of Folsom fluted point; original point from Folsom site, northeastern New Mexico. (b) One variety of Yuma points, the Eden, with collateral flaking (Wormington 1957, Fig. 40, top row, no. 2); (c) Scottsbluff (Eden) point, with collateral flaking (ibid., Fig. 40, top row, no. 1). (d) Sandia point, one of two types found at Sandia Cave, New Mexico (ibid., Fig. 68).

Fig. 1.4   End scraper, used by Early Man (Wormington 1957, Fig. 25, top center).

PALEOWESTERN CULTURE

Paleowesterners, who were later than the Paleoeasterners, were widely scattered from Washington-Oregon down through the Great Basin, south into desert areas, and on beyond the United States-Mexican border into the Valley of Mexico. It is possible that these people were not entirely nomadic as they seem to have spent some time in certain areas where they gathered seeds, nuts, and other edibles on a seasonal basis. Paleoeastern men seem to have lived more in the open, while some Paleowesterners sought at least temporary shelter under overhangs and in cavelike protected spots. Fortunately for the archaeologist, the caves are responsible for the preservation of more perishable materials both produced by and/or used by these simpler folk. In addition to gathering, Paleowesterners hunted small game. Thus it is likely that they were loosely organized into small, cyclically wandering groups, seasonally moving into those areas where the vegetal foods were ripening, and at the same time hunting rabbits, birds, and other small animals. Basically, their stone tools were small and not too well made.

Some regional variation is to be noted in these western cultures. Jennings feels that there are two common denominators in what is designated the Desert Culture of Utah, Arizona, and some adjoining areas. These "twin hall marks" are identified as baskets and grinding or milling stones.[3] Baskets were of several varieties and were made by several techniques; they were used for gathering and transporting seeds, for containing water, and for parching and cooking. Milling stones were employed in grinding and crushing the vegetal foods.

Stone tools were made by Paleowestern men but they were far cruder than those produced by the Paleoeasterners (Fig. 1.5). A few larger points, such as the one from Gypsum Cave, southern Nevada, have been found; this one was poorly shaped and equally poorly crafted. Many more western weapons and tools were small in size, crudely made by percussion chipping (striking a blow to remove flakes, in contrast to Paleoeastern pressure chipping), and

Fig. 1.5   A tool type used by Paleowestern man: Gypsum Cave point, from cave of the same name, southern Nevada (Wormington 1957, Fig. 72).

they were made of poorer stones such as quartzite, andasite, and basalt. Points, scrapers, and knives were the most common pieces produced.

In addition to stone tools, Paleowesterners made a variety of other objects, perhaps no more than the Paleoeasterners, that were preserved because their craftsmen lived in protected spots. From caves in northern Utah, Jennings identified a variety of wooden and fibrous materials, including hunting sticks of various sorts (fire-pointed "spears" and curved sticks; the latter may have served like similarly shaped pieces used by the historic Hopis for rabbit hunting), baskets, mats, and crude fabrics. Both twined and coiled baskets were produced (see Chapter 2), plaited mats were apparently made, and fragments of rabbit fur cloth have been found that originally may have been parts of robes (see Chapter 3).

The culture of Paleoeastern man is thought to go back as far as or beyond ten thousand years ago. The western manifestation of Paleo-Indian expression is later. Then there evolved, particularly in southern Arizona and southwestern New Mexico, the Cochise Culture, probably an adaptation of the Paleo-Indians to semiarid conditions. In southern Arizona there were remnants of postglacial lakes about which grasses seemingly grew in considerable abundance. Evidence for the utilization of the seeds of these grasses is found in the fair abundance of grinding stones, consisting of a combination of an irregular, larger piece, with a basin-shaped grinding area on which the seeds were placed, and a small, rounded hand stone with which the grinding was done. Not only did this stone complex suffice for the Indians' immediate needs but also it prepared them for the development of the still more important metate-mano combination which was essential to the preparation of corn. In fact, it is quite likely that the users of this device were better prepared to receive and utilize corn than the hunters who seemingly had no familiarity with grinding. Whatever the situation, it is the concensus that some hundreds of years before the opening of the Christian Era corn appeared in the Southwest; in the late phase of an early, widespread, simple culture called the Cochise, it was cultivated, causing people to settle down more permanently in small villages. At first they built pit houses; later they made pottery. Continued diversification and intensive exploitation that characterized the

post-Paleowestern period eventuated in three basic prehistoric sedentary cultures, earlier the Hohokam and the Mogollon, and later the Anasazi,[4] and two lesser cultures, the Sinagua and the Patayan. It is apparent from the excavations at Snaketown that the Hohokams were well established by 300 B.C. It is likely, too, that Mogollon culture was equally early, but, seemingly, Anasazi folk did not settle down until close to or several centuries after the opening of the Christian Era.[5]

Sedentary Cultures

These three major sedentary cultures existed in the Southwest from the time just prior to or just after the opening of the Christian Era to the end of the prehistoric period, 1540. All three cultures had certain traits in common and others that set them apart. Archaeologists have located these cultures as follows (Maps 1.2, 1.3, 1.4): the Anasazis in the high plateau country of northern Arizona and New Mexico and in southern Colorado and Utah; the Hohokams in the southern Arizona desert area; and the Mogollones in mountainous eastern Arizona and southwestern New Mexico. All were more or less simple agricultural folk, raising corn, beans, and squash; all lived in larger or smaller villages; all were nature worshippers; all lived by their own efforts, producing practically everything that they needed to get along in life.

Basically, the Anasazi, Mogollon, and Desert Hohokam people were dry farmers who diverted rain-swollen washes to water their fields; River Hohokam and a few Anasazi, such as those in Chaco Canyon, developed irrigation canals. Cultivation and maturation of crops were of deep concern to these people; this is reflected in many of their designs wherein clouds, rain, lightning, and life forms associated with water are represented. The complex pueblos of the Anasazis, consisting of multi-roomed and multi-storied, joined homes, certainly placed people in close association. Surely this was reflected in their social order. As the prehistoric people have living descendants today in the Hopis of Arizona and the Zuñis and Rio Grande Indian villagers of New Mexico, it can be suggested that the following aspects of contemporary puebloan organization applied to the prehistoric people. Some probably had matrilineal clans, with several in each village

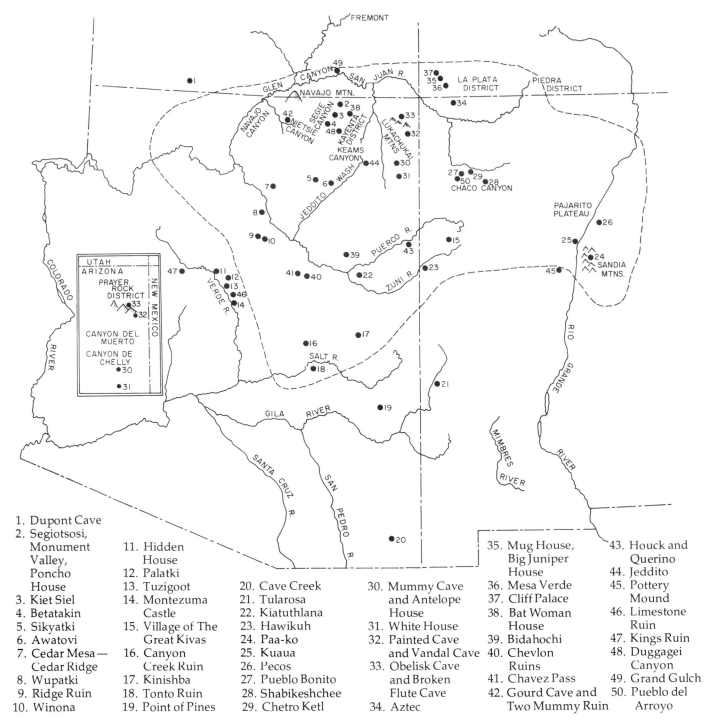

1. Dupont Cave
2. Segiotsosi, Monument Valley, Poncho House
3. Kiet Siel
4. Betatakin
5. Sikyatki
6. Awatovi
7. Cedar Mesa— Cedar Ridge
8. Wupatki
9. Ridge Ruin
10. Winona

11. Hidden House
12. Palatki
13. Tuzigoot
14. Montezuma Castle
15. Village of The Great Kivas
16. Canyon Creek Ruin
17. Kinishba
18. Tonto Ruin
19. Point of Pines

20. Cave Creek
21. Tularosa
22. Kiatuthlana
23. Hawikuh
24. Paa-ko
25. Kuaua
26. Pecos
27. Pueblo Bonito
28. Shabikeshchee
29. Chetro Ketl

30. Mummy Cave and Antelope House
31. White House
32. Painted Cave and Vandal Cave
33. Obelisk Cave and Broken Flute Cave
34. Aztec

35. Mug House, Big Juniper House
36. Mesa Verde
37. Cliff Palace
38. Bat Woman House
39. Bidahochi
40. Chevlon Ruins
41. Chavez Pass
42. Gourd Cave and Two Mummy Ruin

43. Houck and Querino
44. Jeddito
45. Pottery Mound
46. Limestone Ruin
47. Kings Ruin
48. Duggagei Canyon
49. Grand Gulch
50. Pueblo del Arroyo

MAP 1.2   SITE LOCATIONS OF ANASAZI CULTURE.

and with some more important than others; other Puebloans, and possibly the Hohokams, may have been organized on a moiety basis, with each half of the community charged with directing the socio-religious organization and enactment for specified periods of time, such as summer or winter. It is likely that there was general socio-political rule or direction under a theocratic head or body. Whatever the order, there was a rigid adherence to established mores and customs. Precise order is reflected in the exact decoration in the Anasazi craft arts; a freer art suggests a somewhat looser organization among the Hohokam.

Not only did these prehistoric people cultivate or hunt whatever food they had, but also, they produced everything they needed and used, their pots and pans, their clothing and ceremonial paraphernalia, their tools, weapons and implements, and their jewelry. The immediate environment was exploited to the fullest, yet occasionally they traded with other folk for additional raw materials or finished products. Ideas also were exchanged between cultures.

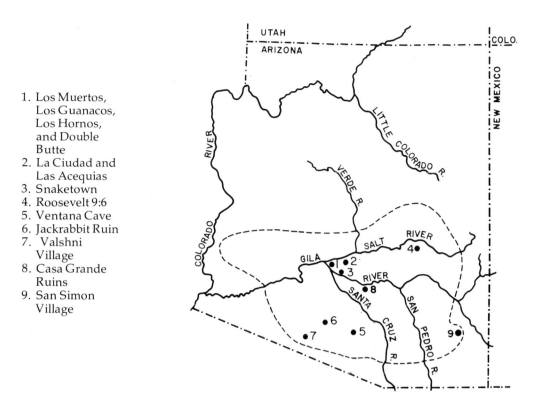

1. Los Muertos,
   Los Guanacos,
   Los Hornos,
   and Double
   Butte
2. La Ciudad and
   Las Acequias
3. Snaketown
4. Roosevelt 9:6
5. Ventana Cave
6. Jackrabbit Ruin
7. Valshni
   Village
8. Casa Grande
   Ruins
9. San Simon
   Village

MAP 1.3   SITE LOCATIONS OF HOHOKAM CULTURE.

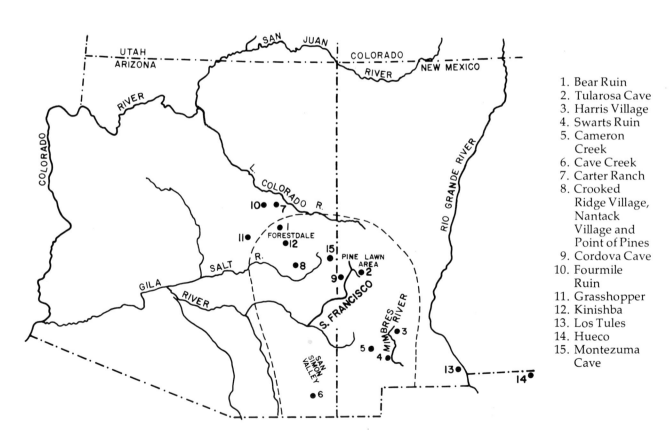

1. Bear Ruin
2. Tularosa Cave
3. Harris Village
4. Swarts Ruin
5. Cameron
   Creek
6. Cave Creek
7. Carter Ranch
8. Crooked
   Ridge Village,
   Nantack
   Village and
   Point of Pines
9. Cordova Cave
10. Fourmile
    Ruin
11. Grasshopper
12. Kinishba
13. Los Tules
14. Hueco
15. Montezuma
    Cave

MAP 1.4   SITE LOCATIONS OF MOGOLLON CULTURE.

SEQUENCE OF SOUTHWEST CULTURE PERIODS

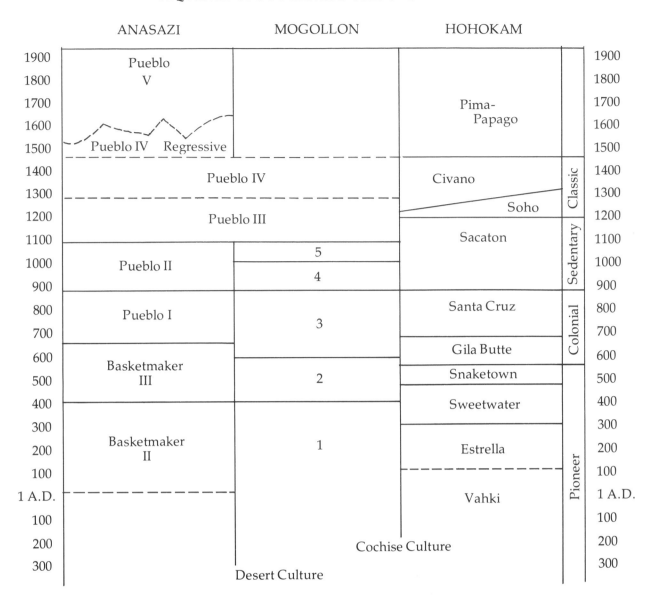

Fig. 1.6   Chart of developmental stages in the three main culture areas of the Southwest.

A period by period survey of more specific developing trends for the Anasazi, Mogollon, and Hohokam people follows, to set the stage for the craft expressions discussed in the following chapters. Figure 1.6 gives the relative time developments for the three major cultures of the prehistoric Southwest. Also it points out the probable rise of all three out of Cochise Culture.

ANASAZI

The Anasazi went through two periods of development, the Basketmaker and the Pueblo. Not given in the chart is the probable hunting-gathering Basketmaker I Phase, while Basketmaker II and III are included as the time of the more or less settled folk. There are evidences of

Basketmaker II occupations of caves, sometimes with no structures in them beyond excavated cists used primarily for storage and burial, and, perhaps in colder weather, secondarily for temporary residences. The presence of corn and squash would testify to at least a semipermanency of residence in and about the cave areas. Much perishable material has been found in the caves. In southern Colorado there are saucer-shaped floors and indications of wood-in-mortar walls of domestic structures that indicate slightly more permanent residence.

There is no question regarding Basketmaker III permanency—there are slab-lined pit houses, generally of circular form and fairly deep, arranged in villages. Beans found at these sites are thought to have required more attention on the part of cultivators than corn and squash; therefore it may be that beans contributed to the further settling down of this last Basketmaker phase. New varieties of corn were also encountered in Basketmaker III times. It was at this time, too, that pottery was first made by these people. Possibly by the end of the period, the bow and arrow replaced the atlatl, or spear-throwing complex. During the Basketmaker Period the Anasazis spread out both to the west and south, the latter distribution possibly bringing them into contact with the Mogollones who, in turn, may have introduced them to the pit house and pottery.

Pueblo I people continued living in pit houses, which were usually rectangular in form, and some built simple beginnings of houses on the ground level, consisting of one or several rooms, and constructed of masonry. Cotton and the loom probably came to the Anasazi at this time. In Pueblo II times, pit houses went out of style except possibly in fringe areas, and true but small pueblos appeared. They included rows of joined masonry rooms one or two stories in height, with an associated kiva. The kiva (Fig. 1.7) was generally a semisubterranean, circular

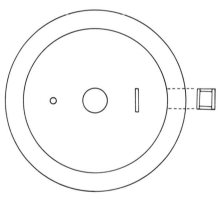

Fig. 1.7 Ground plan of a kiva, with a central fireplace, small hole to left, deflector to right, ventilator to far right, and passage under encircling bench.

chamber used for ceremonial purposes, with more or less standard internal features consisting of a central fireplace and a small, sand-filled hole in the floor off to one side, an upright stone (deflector) on the opposite side, and an opening to the ground level through the wall beyond the deflector. With the growing production of pottery, basketry declined but it never died out.

Pueblo II (or the end of what is sometimes called Developmental Pueblo) merges into Pueblo III, at an earlier date in some parts of the

Anasazi area, later in others. Actually this shift was in the direction of larger, or true, pueblos and high level expressions in a majority of the culture traits of these people. Villages were now made up of great pueblos of two, three, or more stories in height (Fig. 1.8). Fine masonry of coursed stone with little or no mortar, was used in the construction of some of these, such as Pueblo Bonito in Chaco Canyon of western New Mexico. In others, for example Betatakin in Segi Canyon of northern Arizona, rough stones were set in a mass of clay. Degree of exposure to the elements often dictated such matters. High levels of attainment were expressed in many ways in the crafts during this period; pottery not only peaked in white wares decorated with black designs, but also three- or four-color styles were outstanding. Baskets were inferior in decoration but some fine weaving persisted. Textiles reached a high level in a variety of forms, in outstanding technologies of weaving, and in a number of styles of decoration. Jewelry kept up with the other crafts, for the Anasazi produced some of its finest turquoise work at this time. Perhaps the greatest attainment of Pueblo III times was regional specialization, particularly in pottery. Another significant trend in this period was expansion into other areas, the Hohokam and Mogollon territories.

Pueblo IV witnessed the abandonment of many of the more northerly pueblos, but it also enjoyed growth in size of villages. It is likely that there were climatic changes in the north; it is possible also that incoming Athapascans (represented by Apaches and Navajos) created some problems for the settled Puebloans. Whatever the reasons, the shift was made, with a drawing in of populations to a final settling down in the upper Rio Grande and in the contemporary Zuñi (western New Mexico) and Hopi (north-eastern Arizona) areas. Although this last prehistoric period has frequently been referred to as Regressive, some of the high peaks of earlier times were preserved and new ones realized. Excellent pottery was produced at Sikyatki, some with dramatic life forms reflective, possibly, of Mexican influence. Brilliant kiva mural decoration was executed in the Hopi and Rio Grande areas; much of this art reflected high religious attainment, plus customs and costumes of the people. When the Spaniards arrived at the end of this period (1538-40), they found Puebloans in these areas, expressing a wealth of artistry in many ways.

Fig. 1.8 Prehistoric pueblo, Betatakin Ruin, Segie Canyon, northern Arizona. Many such cliff dwellings are well preserved because of obvious protection from the elements.

HOHOKAM

Hohokam peoples lived on the desert of southern Arizona, eventually extending their occupation into the Anasazi area to the north and possibly into Mogollon territory in the southeast. Most important in their distribution was the Gila-Salt River drainage along which they settled, and here is found their most intensive occupation. It is quite possible that population increases here caused an extension of these people into the Santa Cruz and San Pedro valleys to the south and southeast. The prehistoric Indians dwelling in the almost waterless and dry desert to the south and southwest had a much simpler version of Hohokam Culture, and may have been influenced by the Gila-Salt folk only slightly, if at all.

Perhaps the most important excavated site of the Hohokam is Snaketown, close to the Gila

River. Here this culture evolved to its full-blown expressions, starting on its way not later than 300 B.C., and culminating in its development into the 1200s. Canals appeared in the earliest levels that have been excavated; in the Gila valley canals reached such proportions and extent as to suggest that the Hohokams may have been governed by strong chiefs who controlled not only their own village but also, possibly, surrounding villages. It seems quite feasible that such power and control would have been necessary for the construction and maintenance of the great water system of these agriculturists. Other developments were on a par with this accomplishment.

During their years of growth there were several significant outside influences that channeled Hohokam Culture. The first evidence appears in strong Mexican traits of the very early years of this culture. The great spurts of cultural expression, such as canals, figurines with Mexican features, and other traits definitely came from the south; their influence is strongest in the heart of the Hohokam area. Much later, toward the end of the high Hohokam culture, an Anasazi group literally moved in with these southern dwellers, living peacefully with them for several centuries. These were the Salado people who originated in the upper Gila drainage. With their entrance, it was more a matter of living peacefully with the Hohokam rather than forcing their culture onto them; the latter borrowed what they liked and left the rest, while the Saladoans continued to express their own culture. Nonetheless, Salado influence was felt throughout the Hohokam area except for the dry desert to the south and west of the main villages; certainly this desert land was not intriguing to newcomers who could occupy the more desirable river valleys.

Typical Hohokam villages consisted of a small or sometimes larger, number of pit houses (Fig. 1.9), with later surface structures influenced by the Saladoans. The earliest known house was a very large one, about 40 feet on each of its four sides, found at Snaketown. This structure might suggest that several families lived together in such a generous-sized room. It was not long, however, before these people settled down to small, one-family, shallow, single pit houses, often shaped like a kidney bean and with a covered vestibule entryway. Walls and roof were of wattle construction, often with mesquite poles set at intervals, with small elements such as sahuaro ribs or ocotillo branches in between and close together, covered with mud or adobe plaster over the entire structure. There were variations on all these aspects of plan and construction, but no great deviation from this general type of domestic house. After the Saladoans entered Hohokam country, a distinct and different village type developed called a compound—a habitation area enclosed by high walls within which is a combination of Salado multistoried, heavy-walled communal structures and typical Hohokam single houses.

The kiva of the Anasazi area never appeared among the Hohokams; however, they did have

Fig. 1.9   Hohokam pit house, Snaketown, Sacaton Phase. Mesquite posts are in position. Average size of these houses is about 10 feet wide and 15 to 20 feet long.

a ball court that probably served some religious purpose. Courts were oval in form, larger in earlier years (some 200 feet long), and smaller later on. Seemingly, they had high earthen walls and were uncovered. In the center of the "floor" was a marker, with additional ones at each end. Whether or not the game of ball, with religious overtones as played in Mexico and the Mayan area, was enjoyed in these courts cannot be more than suggested. At least two rubber balls have been found in southern Arizona, but not in association with the courts. Also, it is possible that some platform mounds found at Hohokam sites may have been centers of religious dancing; too, some larger structures following the domestic house plan may have been used for ceremonies, as comparable houses were so used by the later Pimas and Papagos, who are the probable descendants of the Hohokams. Village size varied from a half dozen pit houses to as many as a hundred.

There are several convincing evidences that highly organized people inhabited the Gila-Salt valleys. The great canals, some of which measured as much as 30 feet across, extended for more than 150 miles, including mains and laterals. Larger ditches took off from the rivers, while smaller ones diverted the waters from them to the fields. This network made possible the support of a sizeable population; by the same token, it took many people and an overall organization to construct them. That there were large villages and that several of them may have come together for special occasions, work, ceremonies, or festivals, is indicated not only in canal building but also in such items as large jars and huge bowls, which could have been used for storing food and serving vast numbers of people. Too, the ball courts and dance platforms might attest to the same possibility. Certainly the immense jars could have been used merely for storage of excess corn and, possibly, beans. Recent and contemporary Papagos, despite their limited resources, have used huge baskets for storage of surplus from their fields; surely the same could have been true, and undoubtedly on a large scale, for the Hohokams of the Gila-Salt valleys.

There is a continuity in culture throughout the complete Hohokam, with a rise in certain traits to peaks in the Colonial Period, in palettes, mosaic mirrors, and carved stone dishes, and in other traits in the Sedentary Period, for

example, in fine carved and etched shell and in modelled heads which may have been portraits of these people. Red-on-buff pottery appears in all three major periods as the typical Hohokam ware; these wares are characterized by a free style of painting not found elsewhere in the Southwest. With a quick flip of the brush these decorators could create recognizable creatures of the desert on distinctive forms of vessels; in both of these characteristics Hohokam pottery cannot be confused with other Southwestern wares. Other developments among these folk labelled them Hohokam: paint palettes made of a schistose material and frequently decorated with either geometric or life forms, small stone dishes with human or animal forms carved on them in bas-relief, and the etching of shell. Furthermore much of the subject matter of all this decoration is distinctly desert, for these artisans featured the Gila monster, horned toad, rattlesnake, and a few other creatures found most frequently or exclusively in the desert.

MOGOLLON

Mogollon culture evolved out of the basic Cochise culture of the southern desert regions and appeared by 300 B.C. Wheat proposes five stages of development in this culture, and simply assigns them the numbers 1 through 5.[6] The first four phases are true Mogollon culture, while the fifth seems to have been heavily influenced by the Anasazi. The southwestern New Mexican expression of this mixed culture, the Mimbres, presents one of the outstanding ceramic developments of the Southwest.

Phases 1 through 4 of the Mogollon are characterized by the construction of deep pit houses. Although there are some differences from time to time, the major ones are more concerned with village size than with pit house styles. Two to 5 feet in depth, the house did tend to move from a circular form to a rectangular one; also, the round type generally had a sloping roof supported by a central pole, while the later structures featured a flat roof upheld by four corner posts within the room. Firepits and storage bins were commonly built within these structures. It is possible that a larger pit house in some of the villages may have been a primitive form of kiva. Anasazi influence, which came into the Mogollon area around the year 1000, seemingly caused the Mogollones to construct pueblos. Characteristically, the pueblos were smaller in size in this southern area; seldom were they more than two stories in height and with fewer rooms than in many of the Anasazi villages. Some attribute the Mogollon kiva of this later date to Anasazi influence; however, it was a large rectangular or almost-square structure with a wide ramp entrance way, the latter a feature that was not Anasazi.

It is quite possible that the Anasazis influenced the Mogollones in pottery too, at least in color. Mogollon ceramists started out with plain brown wares, which were later decorated with red paint, a color combination that allowed for little contrast. Later they developed red-on-white ware; this was not borrowed from the Anasazi. Still later a black-on-white decorated ware might bespeak such contacts, but it might also reflect an end product of experimentation on the part of the Mogollon themselves. The Mimbres folk distinguished themselves in their life-decorated wares, whether the idea was their own or borrowed from elsewhere.

In expressions other than ceramics and houses, the Mogollon followed the general patterns of the other two cultures. Stone tools and weapons, jewelry, baskets, and textiles... none was particularly outstanding, in fact their crafts, except pottery, were rather pedestrian. What happened to the Mogollones is not fully known. Some believe that at least a segment of this population went into the Rio Grande to join forces with some of the Puebloans there. Some believe that perhaps another segment of this population may have gone to Mexico, where they would have been absorbed by native tribes.

Area and Site Locations

A long and unique time span is represented in the Southwest, from 10,000 or more years ago to the present. The Paleo-Indians, or Early Man, left scattered remains throughout this area, largely in the form of tools, weapons, and implements, with many of them in direct association with animal remains. Early Man was followed by settled populations who lived from approximately the opening of the Christian Era to the time of the arrival of the Spaniards in 1540. The sedentary Anasazis, Hohokams, and Mogollones occupied small territories at first, then spread out over vaster portions of the American Southwest, and finally withdrew into the smaller land areas they occupied at the time of the arrival of the Europeans.

Several deviations or extensions from the mainstreams of culture occurred in the Southwest; these were largely related to the three main groups, and although closely related, they reflect certain differences. In addition to the Hohokams, Anasazis, and Mogollones, there were the Sinaguas and Patayans (both lesser cultures). Located to the northwest and particularly around Flagstaff and in the Verde Valley were the Sinagua, with the Patayans occupying a much larger area farther northwest and west, particularly along the Colorado River. As a whole these two cultures were relatively simpler than the other three and, hence, they have not been separately described. These areas are described in contemporary archaeological literature, and for purposes of this craft survey, they should be kept in mind. Several sites are located within one or the other of these two culture areas, for example, Montezuma Castle and Tuzigoot, both in the Verde area. No issue is made of their older classification as Anasazi.

Although earlier concentrated in the Four Corners area (where Colorado, Arizona, Utah, and New Mexico meet), the Anasazi enjoyed a later widespread distribution into each of these states (see Map 1.2). Remains of these early folk have been found in mountain caves such as the Lukachukais (Painted Cave and Vandal Cave) or close to the mountains, such as the Sandías (Paa-ko). Or they lived in caves located in canyon walls, such as the red sandstone, pocketed walls of Canyons de Chelly and del Muerto (White House and Antelope House) in northeastern Arizona; the ancients also found desirable homesites in the flats of wide canyons such as Chaco of northwestern New Mexico (Pueblo Bonito, Chetro Ketl, and Pueblo del Arroyo). Many homes are found in Nitsie Canyon and in the Segie (Betatakin, Kietsiel, and Bat Woman House) in northeastern Arizona and in Navajo Canyon to the west. They built early homes in or near the cliffs of the Prayer Rocks District (Obelisk Cave) in the colorful red rock country north of the Lukachukai Mountains. They also built homes in beautiful Monument Valley; some lived on the mesa tops or in the limestone cliffs of the Mesa Verde of southwestern Colorado (Wetherill Mesa, Cliff Palace, and Mug House), and in La Plata country to the east. North of Santa Fe, in the Rio Grande country is the Pajarito Plateau and adjoining canyons, which offered desirable homesites; farther down this important river and between Santa Fe and Albuquerque is Kuaua; still closer to Albuquerque is Pottery Mound. The Kayenta area of northeastern Arizona contains many sites of importance, among others, those in the Jeddito region including Awatobi and Sikyatki. There are, of course, hundreds of other sites in the San Juan drainage, hundreds more in the Little Colorado, with fewer and often later sites in the Rio Grande. Other sites and areas include Du Pont Cave of southwestern Utah and the Fremont River to the north in the same state; the Village of the Great Kivas and Hawikuh of northwestern New Mexico; Kiatuthlanna in eastern Arizona, and to the west in this same state, Chavez Pass and Four Mile Ruin, and much farther west, Navajo Canyon, and others along the Little Colorado River; Winona, Ridge Ruins, and Wupatki in the vicinity of Flagstaff; and, in central Arizona, Grasshopper and Kinishba, and to the east, Point of Pines, and slightly to the south, Tonto Ruins and Canyon Creek, in the Gila drainage.

The Mogollon culture centered in southwestern New Mexico and southeastern Arizona particularly along the Mimbres and Upper Gila Rivers (see Map 1.4). Sites and areas would include, among others, Hueco, Tularosa, and Cordova Caves; Forestdale, Bear and Bluff Ruins; and Swarts and Cameron Creek villages.

Desert Hohokam sites include Ventana, Valshni Village, and Jackrabbit Ruins (see Map 1.3). Along or near the rivers of southern Arizona are Snaketown, Arizona 9:6, Tonto; and in or near Phoenix are Los Guanacos, Los Muertos, La Ciudad, Las Acequias, and a cave site, Double Butte.

Thus, a long time span and a wide distribution both were enjoyed by the prehistoric Southwesterners. Concern here is largely with the Indians who lived from the opening of the Christian Era to the arrival of the Spaniards in 1540, and who, with rare exceptions, occupied areas from Four Corners south to the Mexican border, including a large part of Arizona and New Mexico and the southern portions of Utah and Colorado.

Chapter 2

Baskets

BASKETRY IS PERHAPS the most important of the craft arts as it is, apparently, the oldest of all with the exception of tool making. Certainly baskets set the pace for artistic expression in many parts of the world, both in form and decorative design. Among the Anasazi of the Southwest, some of the earliest ceramic pieces were formed inside baskets, thus effecting form. Also, many of the earliest pottery designs were taken directly from baskets.

Jennings maintains that basketry items represent one of the "twin hall marks" of Desert Culture, as previously indicated; they were a natural accompaniment of the basic seed culture that was well established by 7,000 B.C.[1] This would make basketry older in the New World than archaeological evidence would indicate for the Old World. It is probable, despite certain technological features to be discussed, that early Anasazi culture was derived out of some of these Desert cultural patterns, including certain aspects of basketry as well as other traits.

Among the pieces of basketry from the ancient levels at Danger Cave, and from other sites equally old, are examples of complete or nearly complete objects and many fragments that can be identified as baskets (or possibly mats). Several techniques are represented and some forms can be reconstructed, but decoration other than in structural variation is lacking. Perhaps one of the best arguments for the importance of these and other early efforts is the high level of both technological and artistic attainment in the earliest known Basketmaker materials.

In discussing baskets found at Danger Cave and other neighboring sites, Rudy, in Jennings,

posits that twining is the oldest basketry technique at these sites; it appears early and becomes better through time, although it diminished in quantity in later years and does not appear in Basketmaker levels.[2] Coiling appeared after twining on the more ancient level, but coiling neither developed nor supplanted twining. Some plain wicker was known fairly early. Willow seems to have been the most common material in these first baskets, although other materials were used.

Unfortunately, and probably because of the damp conditions, no basketry was found in the first levels of Ventana Cave, the most important of the early sites in southern Arizona.

"A container made of interwoven osiers, rushes, splints, or other flexible material" is a dictionary definition of basketry; it indicates shape, elements used, and technology in the broadest sense for this craft. However, this definition should be extended and elaborated, first, for basketry proper, and second, to include or exclude other objects produced essentially in the same way with the same or comparable materials. In the following discussion, basket weaving will be referred to as a craft expression executed in relatively coarse materials for the production of fairly rigid or rigid containers; forms will range from nearly flat to shallow to very deep, and from open- to very constricted-mouthed; techniques include coiling, wicker, and plaited; and baskets are made without benefit of any artificial device such as a loom.

Another class of weaving, including mats, some bags, and small noncontainers, will be discussed in the following chapter on textiles, despite close resemblance to basket weaving in certain features. Some were produced in the same or similar materials; some were made without any artificial aids, while others utilized simple devices in the weaving process; some employed the same weaving techniques found in basketry, while others reflected different technologies. As noted, baskets were made of relatively coarse materials, while some small weaving demonstrated the first use of refined elements. Almost all prehistoric baskets are cupped to a degree while small textiles, with one exception, are flat. Some baskets (plaited) are identical to mats in weave; some woven bags are broadly comparable in shape to some burden baskets, but the former are flexible, the latter rigid. The sandal may be either rigid or slightly flexible, yet the weaves of both bags and many sandals are more textilelike than basketlike. Many small pieces of weaving may be considered transitional between basketry and true loom weaving.

Like so many other craft arts, basketry was born and prospered in response to the environment in which the producer lived. This includes both cultural and natural surroundings. The Southwest is blessed with quantities of native materials usable for this particular craft. Primitive man, fraught with problems of producing all of the containers for collection and storage of seeds, or later, produce of the fields, with cooking and carrying, missed few of the materials that could be manipulated in the production of necessary containers. After supplying the essential forms, he then went beyond necessity to satisfy the ever present urge in all men to ornament his objects of utility. Again he looked to his resources and found vari-colored plants, and, with a little experimentation, minerals with which to color the weaving elements and satisfy

his yearning for a bit of decoration; these colors were added to the basic white or tan of which baskets were woven. In addition, the early Indians gave variety to methods of weaving, again expressing artistry.

By far most basket remains come from cave sites in the Anasazi area, since many Mogollon and most Hohokam sites are in the open. Basket impressions in clay (Fig. 2.1) and occasional burned fragments aid in telling the story of this craft; Carlson[3] reports that in southwestern Colorado such well-preserved clay impressions of coiled basketry were found that he could count the stitches and coils per inch.

Materials and Technologies

Materials used by these prehistoric people in the production of their baskets were carefully chosen to fulfill many specific requirements. In contrast to basketry, bags, sandals, and bands were coarsely woven of wide strips of soft and flexible cedar bark, or of the fine fibers of apocynum or yucca, which were twisted into cordage for the best of these pieces. The basket weaver, on the other hand, used wide or narrow strips or whole elements derived from a number of sources: among others, willow, broad and narrow leafed yucca, beargrass, desert willow, bullrushes, cattail, squawbush, sages, rabbitbrush, the outer bark from several plants such as devil's claw (Martynia), and various other grasses and rushes. No fiber cordage was ever used in the making of a true basket. It is possible that not all materials have been identified yet, but all of the named plants, and some others of local and limited use, have been recognized in a number of individual pieces.

Undoubtedly, the preparation of basketry materials was relatively simple and was probably achieved in a manner comparable to the methods employed by recent and contemporary Indians of the Southwest. Quite likely some of the stone knives (Fig. 2.2a) frequently found in prehistoric sites were used in cutting materials from the original plants; or the leaves or stems — perhaps sometimes the entire plant — were gathered by breaking or pulling with the bare hands. Surely stone knives were used in removing the jagged edges of certain leaves, in surfacing twigs, and, often, in splitting elements lengthwise in preparing the narrow sewing splints. Undoubtedly prehistoric women also used finger nails and teeth for the latter pro-

Fig. 2.1 Basket impression on clay. Where baskets are not preserved, these impressions can be very important. The larger example shows a coiled technique.

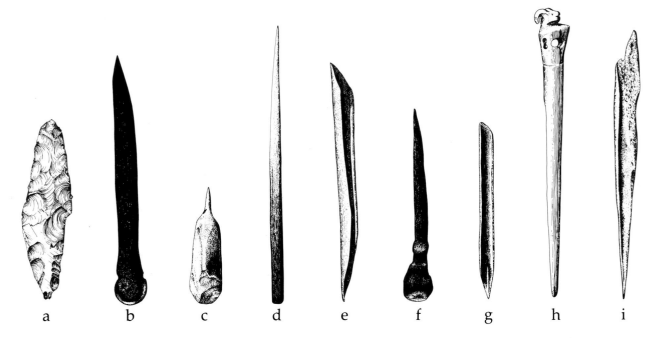

a   b   c   d   e   f   g   h   i

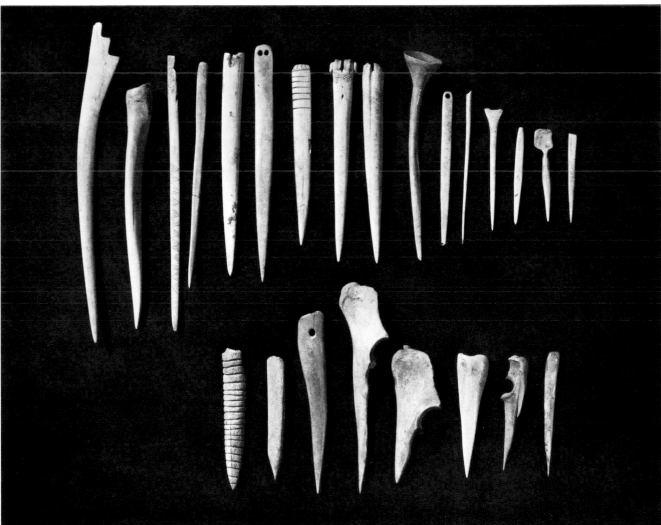

j

Fig. 2.2 Tools of the basket weaver. (Illustrations b,c,d, and f are from Elizabeth Morris 1959a, while e,g, and i are from Kidder 1932. Figure numbers only will be given for these.) (a) Stone knife. There are many shapes and sizes of these and probably their uses were multiple, including cutting and preparing material for baskets. (b) Bone awl from Broken Flute Cave, a tapered style (63k). (c) A short tip on a more blunt bone awl from Broken Flute Cave (63c). (d) An awl made from a splinter of a long bone, Broken Flute Cave (63j). (e) Splinter awl from a bird bone, from Pecos (184a).

(f) A wooden awl with a knob on the head, Obelisk Cave (110g). (g) Splinter awl made from a bird bone, from Pecos (184c). (h) A bone awl (maybe a hair ornament) decorated with the head of a mountain sheep, from Swarts Ruin (Cosgrove and Cosgrove 1932, pl. 59b). (i) Splinter awl made from a sharp fragment of bone by grinding down the point (178b). (j) Photo of bone awls showing thin and thick ones, short and long ones, very crude and very refined styles of workmanship.

Fig. 2.3   A bundle of grass elements which could be material prepared for basket weaving.

cedure as have so many basket weavers of historic years. Seemingly, the only other tool used in basket making was the awl; these are found by archaeologists in great abundance, usually made from bone, in a wide variety of forms. (Fig. 2.2b–j).

Bundles of prepared splints (Fig. 2.3) have been found tied together either in burials or in or around prehistoric ruins. This suggests that perhaps the women of ancient days followed practices common today: gathering materials at the proper season, preparing them, and storing them for future use. Today the weaver takes out the splints and subjects them to a moisture treatment such as soaking them in water or burying them in damp earth; comparable practices must have been pursued in the past. If natural colored splints were not used, such as black devil's claw, then the splints had to be dyed in examples where color decoration is encountered.

Reference is made to the woman as the probable weaver of baskets since the woman is generally the producer of this craft in many parts of the world. There are rare exceptions to this statement among the contemporary Indians of the Southwest; for example, in one modern pueblo an Indian man is responsible for the basket production; however, throughout recorded time predominantly women have been, and are today, the basket weavers in the Southwest.

TECHNOLOGIES

Two basic elements are used in the production of a basket, a warp and a weft. Warps are called foundations, wefts are fillers (or woofs). The warp is usually stationary; it is the base over which or about which the moving weft is sewed or intertwined in one way or another. Generally, warps are heavier and/or stiffer; wefts tend to be more pliable; both warps and wefts may vary in number, from one to many (i.e., a warp rod or bundle or a triple weft). Warps and wefts may be the same or vary in size and composition. A few exceptions to these general statements will be explained in relation to specific techniques.

The three basic basketry techniques are plaited, wicker, and coiled (Fig. 2.4). Fundamentally, plaited and wicker products are woven, while coiled work is the result of a process of sewing. For the most part, these three methods were practiced by the ancients in their simplest forms, particularly in earlier years; however, as time passed, interesting experimentation occurred with resulting variations in each technique. Some classifications deviate from this three-fold system, adding other basic techniques, but justification for the use of the simpler divisions will be defended in the descriptions of certain methods as variations of the basic types rather than completely different technologies.

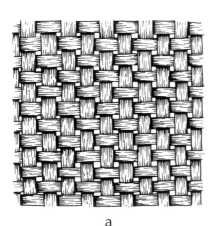
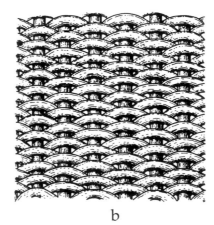
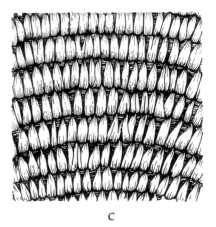

a   b   c

Fig. 2.4   Basic types of basket weaves: (a) plaited, warps and wefts are indistinguishable; (b) wicker, warps are vertical and wefts horizontal; and (c) coiled, warps are horizontal, wefts vertical.

The simplest technique developed in this craft was plaiting (Fig. 2.4a). Generally both warps and wefts are of equal size, shape, weight, and pliability; this posits one of the exceptions to variation in the two basic elements of weaving, warps and wefts. Actually, the terms warp and weft are used in this reference to plaiting in a very broad sense, simply to indicate two separate elements. There is no way to distinguish between the two in this particular process, for the weaver is constantly turning her work about so that there is no established direction for the elements as they are woven. This is contrary to the other two techniques in which direction in relation to the weaver is established for each element and so maintained throughout the production of the basket. In plaiting, elements range in size from about ⅛ to ¼ inch in width, and they are flat or nearly flat in form. Reeds, yucca leaves, beargrass, rushes, and sedge were used in the prehistoric Southwest for plaiting.

This weaving process can be divided into two basic types, plain and twilled plaiting. Plain plaiting is the simple process of weaving one element over the other in an over-one-under-one alternation (Fig. 2.4a). On the other hand, twill plaiting varies this rhythm, stressing over-two-under-two (Fig. 2.5a), over-three-under-three, or over-three-under-one (Fig. 2.5b), with each row offset from the one preceding and the one following, thus creating diagonals which, in turn, produce other patterns. Plain plaiting is creative of no artistry other than the repetitive regularity that results from evenness of element size and rhythmic repetition in the work. In contrast, twilled plaiting produces a variety of simple geometrics, such as meandering or diag-

onal lines, plain or nested chevrons, crosses, and simple or complex diamonds, squares, and zigzags. All of these were explored by the ancient Southwesterners. The monotony that resulted from the use of fairly large elements and the repetitive nature of the work, which generally characterizes patterning in twill plaiting, was relieved by the imagination of the weaver who created great variety in these few basic motifs. In the prehistoric pieces, patterning was produced in three ways: in weave alone in self, or natural, color; in varied weaves; or in color in the form of natural or dyed elements used in part or in all of the pattern.

Wicker (sometimes described as similar to plaiting) is a term used to cover several varieties of basket weaves (see Figs. 2.4b and 2.6a,b,c). It is in relation to this weave that considerable variation in classifications exists; however, as all of these varieties are related technologically to a fundamental type of weaving, all will be considered under wicker in this discussion. In all varieties, during the process of weaving, the warp is held in a position vertical to the weaver, the weft horizontal; the warp is stationary, the weft is the moving element. The following additional traits are basic. Both warp and weft may be of whole elements (rods), or the warp may be of a whole element and the weft a split one. Both may be of the same material or of different materials. If both elements are rods, the warp may be the same or of a heavier material; the latter is particularly true, for in the weaving of certain baskets it is desirable to have a more rigid and substantial warp. As working entities, both warps and wefts may be single or multiple in the same basket; if several warps are

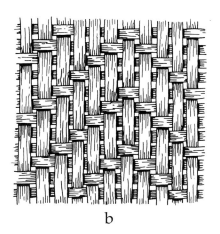

a b

Fig. 2.5   Two types of twill plaiting: (a) over-two-under-two; (b) over-one-under-three.

used, they may be manipulated as a single element. Considerable virtuosity in basketry surface and design may result from varied handling of a single or of multiple wefts.

Differences in the particular type of motion in handling the weft create differences in the end product of wicker basketry; herein is the most important base for variations in the actual weaves of this technique. In plain wicker (Fig. 2.4b) there is a regular alternation of one weft over one warp; this "one" may include more than one element (Fig. 2.6a), but each is manipulated as a single constituent. Twilled wicker is like twilled plaiting in that there is a variation in the rhythm of alternation, although in the former weave there is seldom more than an over-two-under-two or over-two-under-one variation in prehistoric baskets. Diagonal wicker results from these alternations. Plain wicker produces no design in itself unless color is introduced; the prehistoric people explored this potential little beyond simple banding. In addition to this color patterning, diagonal wicker can produce small geometrics.

Another variation of this weave is twined wicker (sometimes called twinedwork) in which two (Fig. 2.6b) or three wefts are used; for example in the process of weaving, two wefts are carried, one over and one under a single warp, then given a half twist on each other between this and the next warp. After each half twist, wefts exchange over-under alternations. This process secures the warps in position and also gives greater strength to the basket. In diagonal twining, wefts pass over two or more warps in the manner described for other diag-

onal weaves, with half twists between warps. In a single piece, combinations of two- and three-element twining can give a banded effect. If color is introduced in most varieties of wicker, bands and simple geometrics are possible. Prehistoric Southwesterners used both plain and twined wicker techniques.

Still another variation in this technique is called wrapped wicker, or wrappedwork (Fig. 2.6c). A single weft element is employed: it is simply wrapped about each warp as it is moved along.

The coiled basketry technique (see Fig. 2.4c) is unquestionably the most important and most sophisticated from the standpoint of art, for it is the most productive of design. Coiling is referred to as sewing, for the vertical weft is first wrapped about the horizontal warp, then secured by sewing it into the coil below. The coil or warp is a continuous spiral. Variations occur in the nature of the warp and weft and in the types of stitching.

Foundation coils are made up of rigid or nearly rigid elements. Figure 2.7a and b illustrate coils used in prehistoric times: a single rod; three rods, or two rods and a bundle of shredded grass arranged in pyramidal form; a rod core with a bundle around it; a bundle of shredded grass alone; two half rods, a rod and slat, or one rod or half-rod and bundle, each in vertical arrangement; or rarely, other coil composition. Interesting in the latter category are the single rod which is sometimes split for sewing and the Hueco half-rod with a lateral bundle. The latter was also reported by Morris as a foundation like no other in a piece from

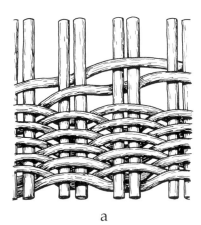 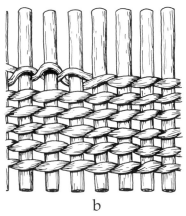 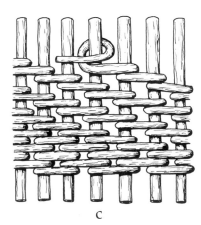

a   b   c

Fig. 2.6 Wicker weave techniques: (a) In plain wicker, wefts are passed over and under one (see Fig. 2.4b) or two warps at a time, then alternated in the next row. (b) In twined wicker, two wefts are woven one over and one under single warp elements, twisted over each other between warps, and alternated in the next sequence. (c) The process in wrapped wicker is a literal wrapping of the weft element about each warp.

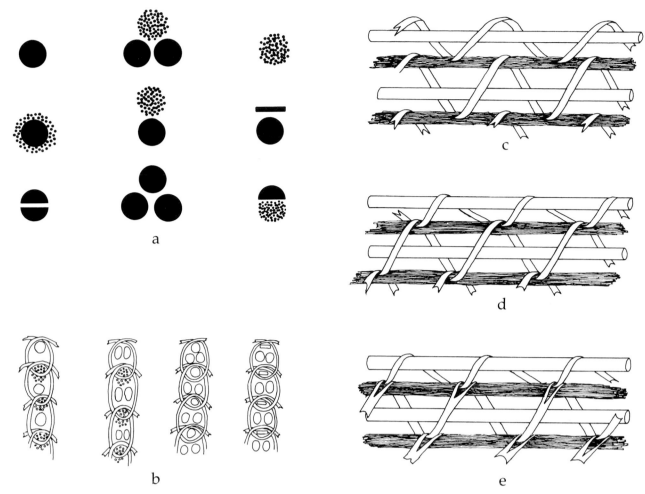

Fig. 2.7 Types of foundation and stitching for coiled basketry: (a) Top row: single rod, two rods and bundle, bundle; second row: rod surrounded by bundle, single rod and bundle, rod and slat; third row: two split rods, three rods, and bundle plus half rod. (b) Cross sections showing vari-

ety of methods of sewing in using different types of foundations. Simplified sketches to illustrate methods involved in coiled weaving: (c) non-interlocked stitching, (d) interlocked stitching, and (e) split stitch (adapted from Morris and Burgh 1941, Figs. 3d,h, and 4e).

La Plata area.[4] The height of the foundation dictates the length of the stitch, for over this is sewed a wider or narrower and very flexible element, the sewing splint. This is accomplished in one of several ways: the stitches are close together (Fig. 2.4c), slightly apart, or far apart. Vertical stitches result from close sewing, but spaced wefts result in diagonal lines in the stitching. The latter is called open stitching. A split stitch is simply the result of sewing, intentionally or accidently, into the middle of the stitch below, thus splitting and splaying it into a V-shape (Fig. 2.7e). If sewing combines this and open stitching, the technique is called open-split stitch.

There are also two other terms which describe stitching, interlocked and noninterlocked (Fig. 2.7c,d). Interlocked is a term applied to sewing in which the current stitch is actually inserted into the coil below and under the top of the

stitch below, thus locking with the latter; the noninterlocked, or uninterlocked, style simply passes through the top of the coil below, between two stitches, without engaging in any locking process. Most Southwest basketry of pre-Columbian time used the latter technique, although some local areas, such as the Hueco, produced a great deal of interlocked stitching.

Another important detail is the nature of the finish at the rim of the basket. Certainly the majority of baskets of ancient times were finished off in the simple sewing stitch like the rest of the piece, or in a self stitch. However, there is a false braid or herringbone stitch (Fig. 2.8) which is encountered on coiled basket rims, on either the total rim or at the very end of it. It is accomplished by manipulating the sewing element in a figure-8 fashion; there are both simple and complex versions of this. Morris and Burgh say that about 75 percent of the Anasazi

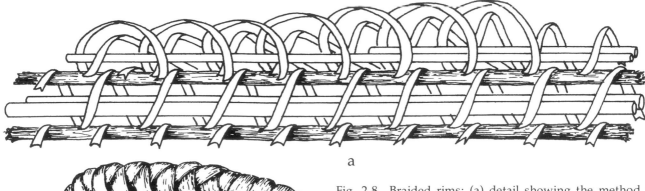

a

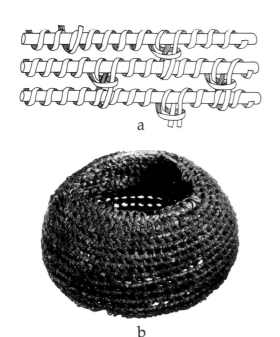

b

Fig. 2.8 Braided rims: (a) detail showing the method of producing a braided rim (Morris and Burgh 1941, Fig. 7g), and (b) the end or finishing off of the rim in braiding.

basket rims of the Four Corners area terminate in this false braid, most of it at the last bit of the rim end.

In sewing the coils together, some variation occurs. The normal process is to sew close together and to catch each coil to the one below with every stitch. This is plain or tight coil (see Fig. 2.4); deviations from this include the following. In stitch-and-wrap coil, the current foundation is wrapped several times, then a stitch is caught into the coil below, still keeping the coils close together, then back to wrap the current coil, and again the same is repeated. In sifter coil this process is repeated, but after wrapping the current coil, a loose stitch is caught into the coil below, and as the sewing splint is brought back up, it is wrapped about

itself before it again encloses the current coil, thus holding the coils apart (Fig. 2.9). As this is usually repeated every few stitches, it makes for an open effect, thus creating a basket that surely could have been used as a sifter.

The beginning of a coiled basket is usually a wrapped foundation formed into a circle (Fig. 2.10b,c); the second coil curls tightly about this and is sewed into it. The second procedure continues to the rim of the basket. An oval foundation was rarely used prehistorically (Fig. 2.10a); it was effected by wrapping a straight line of foundation, then bending the continuing coil abruptly back and sewing it into the wrapped section. If coiling is to the right of the worker, it is called clockwise (Fig. 2.10b), but if it moves to her left, it is counterclockwise

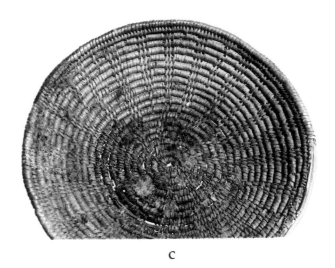

a

b

c

Fig. 2.9 Sketch showing (a) technique of sifter coiling (Morris and Burgh 1941, Fig. 6h) and two photographs of baskets done in this method: (b) bowl in plain sifter, and (c) tray in designed sifter coiling.

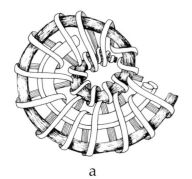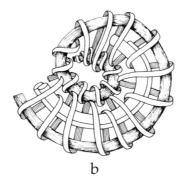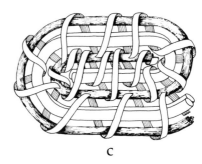

a   b   c

Fig. 2.10   Methods of starting coiled baskets: (a) Beginning of a circular coiled basket, with a two rod and bundle foundation, counter-clockwise sewing (Morris and Burgh 1941, Fig. 7d). (b) Beginning of a circular coiled basket, two rod and bundle foundation, sewing clockwise. (c) Beginning of an oval coiled foundation, two rod and bundle, sewing counterclockwise (Morris and Burgh 1941, Fig. 7a).

(Fig. 2.10a,c). Most Southwest coiling is counterclockwise.

As sewing splints can be introduced or dropped at any point, coiling is highly productive of designs in color. When sewing elements are fine and coils small, these are added potentials for design elaboration.

Much patterning in coiled basketry has a stepped edge to any elements built up from the basket interior and extending toward the exterior. Obviously this is related to the fact that stitches are not absolutely directly one above the other and in a straight line, even though the weaver may make an effort to arrange them in this fashion. However, in some fine sewing, there is not only an almost-even line, but also the attainment of a gentle smooth-edged curve in building the motif upwards and outwards. To be sure, the weaver could retain and emphasize the angular stepped effect most readily if she so desired just by skipping or adding several stitches in color in each successive coil.

Patterning in prehistoric coiled basketry was varied by and closely tied in with technology. Each element of design was made up of color added in one or more coils and/or one or a number of stitches, or built up from one coil to another, thus creating lines, squares, triangles, and other geometric elements or units. Angular life forms were possible in this weave also, although the prehistoric Southwesterner explored this potential only slightly. Any element, geometric or life, could be large or small; each could be executed in a solid or outline style, all relative not only to stitch size and quality, but also to the weaver's ability and imagination. Great diversity existed in the variety of motifs built up from the simple geometrics possible in coiled weave.

Form

As technique and artistry are intimately related, so too is there a close connection between form and decoration. This is particularly true in the coiled technique where the greatest diversity in contour existed. Man created shapes in baskets for specific purposes, refining but never changing a form beyond the use value for which it was originally created. Refinement of form assumed an artistic quality in itself, both in outline and in regularity and evenness. Somewhere along the way, decoration was added; it too was subject to the controls of use value. In the prehistoric Southwest, the basket weaver never descended to the level of the production of gadgets; decoration followed the same high standard. Miniatures of large utility forms existed; seemingly they were children's toys or objects of ceremonial use.

A general view of basket forms from prehistoric times would indicate considerable variety (Fig. 2.11). Included are flat or nearly flat styles called plaques, trays and bowls, deep burden or carrying baskets, water jars, and a miscellaneous category of limited numbers of "shields," dippers, wristlets, and cylindrical and rectangular pieces. The tray form was the most popular basket; it was produced in sizes from three inches to three feet in diameter. Circular in form (although a few oval pieces have been excavated), it varied in depth, although it tended to be on the shallow side and side walls tended to be gently sloping. Its use was probably as varied as its size; as in later historic times, it may well have served for washing, mixing, parching, and serving food, in addition to many other everyday purposes. Often a large tray basket is found by the archaeologist placed over part or all of a skeleton, or somewhere in a burial; these were used baskets—rarely was a new one placed in a grave. Although the tray basket decreased in size and apparently in numbers from Basketmaker to classic Pueblo times, it did persist to the end of prehistory; furthermore, trays have remained popular among many historic tribes into the twentieth century.

Burden baskets were fairly abundant in quantity. They, too, appeared early and continued into the historic period. Much variety is to be noted in the form of this basket, although the basic requirements of a large orifice and a smaller base characterized all carrying baskets.

The earliest Anasazi style was a deep or medium-deep cone-shaped basket with generous proportions. The rim was rounded, and the base was either a rounded almost-point or it was of slightly rectangular form. The cone-shaped burden basket remained one of the popular forms all through prehistory, with deeper styles more apparent in later Pueblo years, but with widely outflared rims not uncommon. A strange bifurcated style with an oval cross section first appeared in late Basketmaker times and reached an exaggerated expression in Pueblo III. Small and miniature clay effigies of this style were

Fig. 2.11 Basket forms from various prehistoric sites: *top row*: coiled tray, jar (could be an old Apache water jar, but is like ancient ones) and bowl; *middle row*: coiled trinket basket, plaited yucca plant basket, coiled deep bowl; and *lower left*: plaited ring basket.

found at Pueblo Bonito, supporting the basket's probable ceremonial use.[5] Deep bucket-shaped forms also were produced as burden baskets.

Bowl forms were fairly common. They can be distinguished from tray baskets by a base proportionately much larger in relation to the rim, or in fact, sometimes of nearly the same diameter. Some form variation can be noted, although the most common was a bowl with a simple and continuous line from rim to base; in others, walls were straight- or nearly straight-sided. Frequently bowls were flat based, and perhaps this trait was more common in later years. The circular style dominated, although a few complete pieces and many more bases alone of oval form have been excavated in various ruins. Several nearly complete oval bowl baskets were found at Pueblo Bonito.

The short lives of a variety of miscellaneous forms may be explained in part by the fact that their use value died. For example, a generous-sized water jar (probably for storage), with small orifice, full body, and smaller base, disappeared apparently with the development of a pottery substitute. In like manner, pottery replaced the many and varied small baskets so popular in Basketmaker II and III times that were often called trinket baskets. Obviously, clay counterparts also replaced a few large, globular-bodied, small-to-wide-mouthed storage baskets (possibly for foods), which appeared less frequently after the end of Basketmaker times; they were not to become popular again until well within the historic period. Prehistorically, flat plaques seem to be late in their appearance; it is possible that they persisted into historic time, although a clear-cut continuity cannot be established. The cylindrical vase from Chaco Canyon, some covered with turquoise mosaic, could have had a limited, local ceremonial value; thus it may be that this specialized form lived and perished in Pueblo III days. A so-called "shield," a very shallow tray-type basket with a handle on the inside, was another late prehistoric piece which left no descendant form. From Aztec ruin a one-of-its-kind dipper, complete with handle, was very likely a copy of a clay form. Needless to say, the burden basket was not replaced by a clay counterpart.

One other particular form should be mentioned for it, too, persisted into the present time. This is the plaited ring basket. Basically, it is a bowl form, but often it is distinguished by a heavy withe formed into a ring, which holds the rim in position and rigid and gives the basket added strength. Usually it is shallow and has a curving line from rim to flatter base. When excavated, the ring basket is usually very flat-bottomed from use. In all probability, prehistorically as now, it served as a sifter (as well as for other purposes), hence no ceramic piece replaced this popular basket. As a matter of fact, the ring basket was actually developed in Pueblo III times. A few examples of clay colanders have been found, and conceivably they might have served, in small part and in a limited area, in place of the ring basket.

Decoration

Methods of decorating all baskets centered in the use of colored splints woven into the piece. Generally, these were black, brown, or red combined with the natural or white of the basic material. If these colors were not natural they were dyed. Rarely, other colors were used, such as yellow, blue-green, and pink. Painting of the finished basket was known, but uncommon, and usually utilized both plain washes and designs in color. Turquoise mosaic has been mentioned as a decorative style embellishing several basketry forms. Feather quills have been found woven into baskets, thus reflecting still another method of decorating this craft item.

LAYOUT

Entering into a discussion of basketry decoration as it developed from Basketmaker through prehistoric Pueblo times, a first matter to come into focus is design layout. As basketry layouts are not as complicated as those on pottery, a more limited discussion is given here; the subject will be elaborated upon in the chapter on ceramics.

The general contour of a basket controls the area of decoration to some degree. Certainly form sets the limits of decoration, and, for the most part, will control where the design appears. Too, any natural divisions in form, as a neck, or an abrupt inturn of a side wall, would tend to further position the placement of design.

Layout is a term used to describe the placement of or place chosen for the total design in relation to the total form; further integration of the design into this chosen space for decoration is an additional aspect of layout. Primary layout involves the larger scheme of total space chosen to be decorated; any further subdivision within this space is termed secondary layout. For example, a band would be the primary layout while vertical lines within the band serve as a secondary division of the area into panels. Of course, there may be no secondary layout as design may be adjusted to primary layout.

In basketry, there are few layouts because technology not only limits forms but also further restrains variation within a given form. Too, technology limits variety of layout on any form, for it is more difficult to weave a pattern than it is to paint one. For these reasons pottery, with its tremendous variation in form and the ease with which painted design can be varied, offers far greater variety in layout than is found in basketry. Wide and open forms, such as trays, plaques, and some bowls invite layouts viewed from the interior, while almost all other forms feature layouts observed from the exterior.

The basic layouts (Fig. 2.12) found in basketry include divided styles, either banded or half-banded; and undivided, including repeated, allover, centered, organizational-banded; and composite, which is any combination of two of these layouts (Fig. 2.12g). The obvious distinction between divided and undivided layouts is

that: in the former, woven or colored lines, or other recognized natural features such as the rim, mark off the area to be decorated, while in the latter there are no specific area controls other than the size of the basket itself and the scheme in the mind of the weaver.

Banded layouts are those in which two parallel bordering lines, indicated by variation in weave, or by color, or, in part, by the rim of the basket, enclose a design that is almost always geometric in nature (Fig. 2.12a). An organizational band is one which looks like a band but lacks the bordering lines (Fig. 2.12f). Any form could use either of these styles; at one time or another, the banded layout was employed on almost all decorated forms in the Southwest, while the organizational band seemingly was used basically on the burden basket, particularly the wide-mouthed, conical-based style. If design appears over the entire surface of a basket, it is an allover layout (Fig. 2.12e); plaited ring baskets were most frequently decorated in this fashion, and coiled trays were occasionally, while other forms did not employ this style. The repeated layout is characterized by the repetition of a motif two, three, or four times, usually on the wall of the basket (Fig. 2.12d); it is found on trays, bowls, and rarely on jars. With a stretch of the imagination, repeated layouts could be considered organizational-banded; however, in many cases the designs are wide-spaced and sometimes a bit irregular in position, and thus should not be called bands of any sort. The centered layout is rare; it features a single large or small motif placed in the center of a tray (Fig. 2.12c). The best example of this is a frog in the middle of a shield (or game?) tray, with its body, legs, and head extending some distance toward the rim (see Fig. 2.38). A half-band is a layout wherein the design is pendant from a line, usually close to the rim, or rarely, from the center band (Fig. 2.12b). The half-band layout had limited expression in the prehistoric Southwest.

Whether large or small toward the base, burden baskets invite banded decoration. This may be in a single or double, regular, or organizational band; whether one or two bands are used depends upon the relative depth and neck-base proportions of the piece. Usually any decoration is on the wider part of the basket, close to or above the center. Deeper and more straight-sided bowls likewise may be decorated with banded patterns, although a repeated motif may

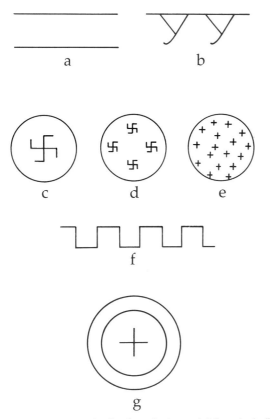

Fig. 2.12 Layouts for basket designs: (a) banded; (b) half banded; (c) centered; (d) repeated; (e) allover; (f) organizational banded; (g) composite (centered-banded).

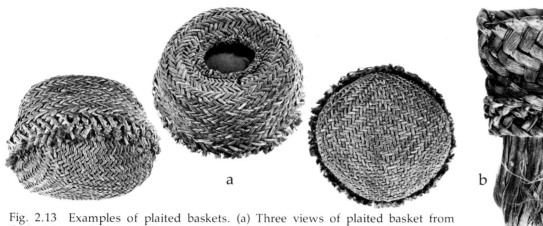

Fig. 2.13 Examples of plaited baskets. (a) Three views of plaited basket from Cedar Mesa, which started out as a ring basket but was woven up and inward to a small hole in the center top. (b) Another unusual piece, made from a whole yucca plant. (Photos by Marc Gaede, courtesy of the Museum of Northern Arizona).

be spotted at intervals on the wall without benefit of any bounding lines. Bottle or jar forms were decorated on the wider portion of the piece usually with a line or simple band; this is one shape which was not highly developed, and, therefore, there was not the same perfection in the relation of form and decoration which is so frequently found in other pieces. The most versatile adaptations are found on tray baskets: here are encountered single- or double-banded layouts; allover layouts, which may radiate from the center to the rim in a static or dynamic fashion or are comprised of allover bands with a blank circular center; repeated layout; or occasional other arrangements.

Examples of design on pieces in each weave and of specific baskets will be given, with illustrations of some of the decorative styles in accompanying drawings and photographs. There seems to have been no decoration of the pre-Basketmaker pieces previously described except for a wicker basket with a 3-strand line on a 2-strand base and a few other structural patterns. However, some day decorated pieces may be found, for there are relatively highly developed as well as simple patterns in Basketmaker II times that could hardly have been "beginners' work." In this discussion, the most common types of basketry decoration will be presented. First, in plaited baskets, design is in the weaves or the pattern is emphasized in dyed splints that are used during the process of weaving. Variation in weave is more significant in relation to design in both plaiting and twining than in coiling. Most important in coiling is color, which is woven in; other styles of decoration in this third weave include painting and mosaic. Likewise, the time factor will be brought into focus relative to decorative changes.

PLAITED BASKETS

Sizes of plaited baskets varied according to their uses. At Canyon Creek, they ranged from 8 to 10 inches in diameter. At Pueblo Bonito they are found largely in fragments, but one better preserved example measured 12 inches in diameter.

Form in plaiting is greatly limited by mechanical problems imposed by the use of large and relatively stiff elements. Frequently these are of yucca, the whole leaves or large portions thereof, or sometimes rushes, beargrass, grasses, or cane. Several odd forms, such as one with a square base and a round or elliptical rim, were made but were not common. Bowls were produced with considerable frequency. One from Hueco Caves was a plain weave piece, with an 8-inch by 8-inch base, an elliptical top which measured 7½ inches by 3¼ inches, and was 6 inches high. Bowls, of course, enjoyed a wide distribution, with the exception of the square-based type. An unusual form from Cedar Mesa (Fig. 2.13a), and in the Museum of Northern Arizona, appears to be a ring basket onto which a top was woven; in the center of this top is a small circular hole. Another rare form is an elongate piece woven from a whole yucca plant (Fig. 2.13b).

Some bowls, or trays as they are more commonly called, were shallow or deep, and they were either formed by plaiting from start to finish or were woven as small mats that were then forced into a stiff and sturdy ring. The ring was made of a heavy withe formed into a circle and secured by binding its overlapping ends. When pushed through the ring, the borders of the small mat were left hanging over the outer edge (Fig. 2.14a); they were then sewed to the body of the basket by a twined stitching all the

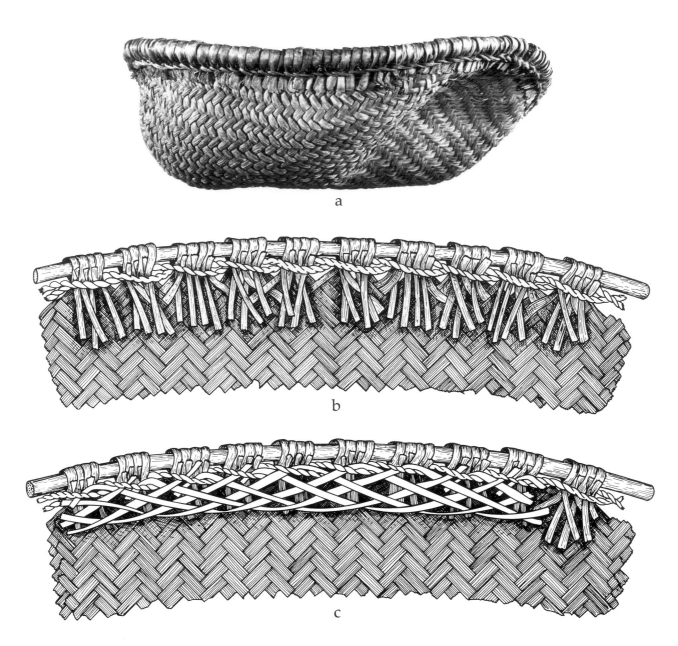

Fig. 2.14 Details on plaited baskets: (a) Profile of a plaited ring basket showing how the edge of the basket was sewed beneath the ring and cut off fairly evenly just below the sewing. (b) Detail showing the manner of cutting off the ends in a plaited basket (Morris and Burgh 1941, Fig. 8b). (c) The second drawing shows the ends woven into a fancy border (Morris and Burgh 1941, Fig. 8c).

way around the piece. Then the uneven ends were cut off evenly, leaving about one quarter of an inch hanging below the stitching (Fig. 2.14b). Sometimes this outside fringe of the leaves was woven back into the basket proper, thus lending a more finished appearance to the basket. Most often this was done in the form of an ornamental braid or band (Fig. 2.14c).

These ornamental braids on plaited bowl tops have been found in the Mogollon,[6] at the Carter site in east central Arizona, in the Glen Canyon area, and at Pueblo Bonito, to mention a few sites. A concentration of the twilled basket with the hoop in the rim has been found in the

Anasazi area, with the following sites illustrative of this general distribution: Mesa Verde on the north, Pueblo Bonito and the Chaco Canyon on the east, Betatakin to the west, and Canyon de Chelly on the south. The style appeared farther south occasionally, and is represented at Canyon Creek[7] and in the Gila-Salt. Historically, the woven rim style has been again picked up among the Pimas and Papagos.

In the decoration of plaited baskets, layout and design are related, first and foremost, to the weave itself; second, to the use of dyed elements that, in essence, followed and emphasized the woven theme; and third, to a combination of the

Decoration

two. Layouts are predominantly allover, with some banded or cross-banded styles. The arrangement of the pattern can be straight or diagonal across the basket, in quarters, or it can be allover and organized, or wander aimlessly over the entire surface. Despite the fact that there was much plain plaited, there was also a high development of decorated pieces of twill plaited. The latter style will be discussed for its artistry.

Basketmaker III twilled ring baskets, which are often large trays, were produced in the under-two-over-two rhythm, with one under-three-over-three as exemplified in the Prayer Rock pieces.[8] Morris and Burgh claim that design is totally lacking in the baskets of this period, but how could they be when these rhythms were employed?[9]

Inasmuch as plaited basketry was so prominent and widespread in Pueblo III times, it is to be expected that it would be exploited in terms of technique and design. And so it was. Technique involved not only the earlier over-two-under-two but also a development of the over-three-under-three, with some other variations and combinations. Forms were quite the same, basically the bowl or tray ring basket. Weave alone, or weave and color were used for designs; on rare occasions the two appeared in combination, each producing a different pattern. Interestingly, a comparison was made of these baskets and modern Hopi work of the same type, with results revealing many identical patterns.

For a summary of pattern variety (Figs. 2.15 and 2.16) the twilled baskets in Morris and Burgh will serve as a basis of discussion for Pueblo III designs.[10] Other examples will follow. Meander patterns were quite common in plaited baskets. They varied from simple single lines beginning in the center and moving in a regular, continuous fashion to the edge of the basket, to more elaborate labyrinthian styles in which single lines (Fig. 2.15a) or double lines (Fig. 2.15b) became more involved, or there were more complex line forms (Fig. 2.15c). And there were diamonds; they were single and concentric (Fig. 2.15d), or they were of double arrangement (Fig. 2.15e), or quadrate and concentric (Fig. 2.15f,g). Chevrons or chevronlike figures were fairly popular and were presented crossing the center of the basket in one band (Fig. 2.15h), or in two bands at right angles each to the other (Fig. 2.15i). This latter is a good example of a combination of a design in both weave and color, inasmuch as there is a subtle background of concentric diamonds in the weave alone, against which the black chevrons stand out. Frets were popular also and were of simple nature or they were interlocked; they were single (Fig. 2.15j) or double (Fig. 2.15k) or quadrate (Fig. 2.15l). Plain zigzags (Fig. 2.15m) or diagonal lines across the entire basket were not uncommon. There were a few composite styles (Figs. 2.15n,o,p).

Judd reported that at Pueblo Bonito the only design in over-three-under-three rhythm in ring baskets, made of narrow strips of yucca, was the interlocking meander. Pepper reported a twilled ring basket from the same site with the "design in the bottom," a series of concentric rectangles; the weave is an over-two-under-two alternation; the size is about 7½ inches in diameter and about ¾ inch deep.[11] Concentric diamonds were popular at Painted Cave.

One very interesting feature about a great many of these plaited baskets is the presence of the braided or woven section at the rim. In these pieces the section may be simple or elaborate (see Fig. 2.14c). These added a finished quality and decorative detail not found in the pueblo basket today; a few years back, however, Papagos did feature this finishing touch. To be sure, some of the baskets were simply twined beneath the ring, with the ends of elements trimmed evenly.

A twill ring basket woven in an over-three-under-three technique was excavated at Carter Ranch Ruin. Near the rim was an ornamental braid. This same type was also found in the later stages of Mogollon Culture.

Only a few pieces of this plaited basketry have been found in the Hohokam area. Haury noted limited fragments at Ventana Cave;[12] these were in a two-two-two rhythm and made of sage. It could not be determined whether the pieces were from mats or baskets. At Snaketown, impressions of matting (for mats or baskets?) of a coarse nature were found. From Los Muertos, near Phoenix, come impressions of plaiting, apparently of narrow cane or grass stems, and woven in an over-two-under-two style.[13] Although seemingly for mats, it is quite possible that baskets were made in a comparable manner; again, later Pima-Papago pieces might support this idea.

Canyon Creek Ruin presents a rather different type of twilled basket, one with reinforcing at

Fig. 2.15   A series of plaited basket designs showing great variety. (Figs. 15a through 15o from Morris and Burgh 1941, figure numbers only given.) (a) Single line patterns (37k, m). (b) Double line themes (37d). (c) Complex, joined lines (37o). (d) Concentric diamonds (37c). (e) Double concentric diamonds (36l). (f) Quadrate division with four diamonds in concentric arrangement (36m). (g) Four concentric diamonds with the innermost checked (38i). (h) Chevron-like figures crossing the field of decoration (35f). (i) Double arrangement of nested chevrons (35d). (j) Single arrangement of interlocked frets (35o). (k) Double arrangement of interlocked frets (36f). (l) Quadrate fret scheme using both single and interlocked frets (38l). (m) Simple zigzags crossing the field of decoration (38j). (n) A composite design arrangement, with a central fret and double lines (35j). (o) Composite design including line and fretlike themes (36g). (p) Zigzags and centered diamonds crossing the basket, another composite style.

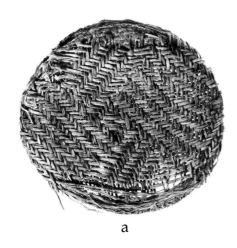

a

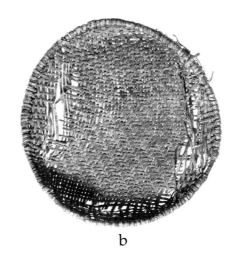

b

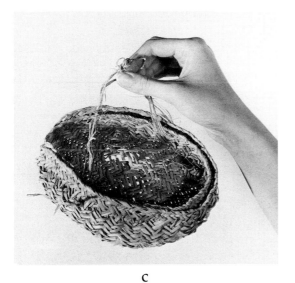

c

d

Fig. 2.16 Additional examples of plaited objects: (a) An interesting quadrate design on a twilled tray. (b) A simple over-two-under-two weave. (c) An unusual and simple handle on a double-rimmed and woven-edged bowl. (d) Two plaited rings, used as pottery supports.

the rim and two with almost-square bases.[14] Made of beargrass, the latter two are only about 2 inches in depth, and one is about 10 and the other 12 inches in diameter. Bottom corners are nearly square. Each basket begins with a cross in the bottom.

WICKER BASKETS

Wicker weaving was a basketry technique that did not receive too much attention from prehistoric Southwesterners. Perhaps this is due to the fact that it is productive of neither a great variety of forms nor an abundance of creative design. Too, it may be that the popularity, as well as longevity, in Basketmaker-Pueblo culture of the other two techniques and of woven bags, as well as the development of pottery, fulfilled most of the needs of the ancients; therefore there may have been little need or inspiration to develop this style. It might also be mentioned that wicker was neither very popular nor effectively developed artistically in historic times except by the Hopis, and to a lesser degree by the Apaches.

As to the age of the wicker technique, it has been noted that it was the earliest at Desert Culture sites. These first pieces were of close, simple twining primarily, but there was some work in plain wicker and diagonal twining combined. Later, in the Pueblo Period, some of the most decorative wicker of prehistoric times was developed at Lovelock Cave, in west central Nevada.[15] Although most of the pieces are small, there are some indications of shape, for example, in converging warp rods in every fragment; apparently, these were parts of conical burden baskets. Unfortunately, of the more than 1,000 pieces recovered, not one is complete.

Wicker has not been found in many sites, and, generally speaking, it is limited in quantity wherever found except for the Lovelock example. Most of the designs in the wicker baskets from Lovelock Cave were created by using a split weft splint with the bark left on one side; the latter was generally a dark brown color. A quick twist in the weaving of this element

Fig. 2.17 Sketches of designs found in wicker burden baskets from Lovelock Cave, southern Nevada (Loud and Harrington 1929, Fig. 13).

would either expose the brown to the desired surface and spot in the design or it would conceal the brown and expose the light color of the inner part of the weft splint.

Almost all of the patterning in this collection of wicker is in horizontal bands of simple nature (Figs. 2.17 and 2.18). Included are the following elements and units, most of them made up of tiny lines or squares, as is frequent in modern Southwest Indian wicker baskets: triangles, zigzags, checks, cogwheels, diagonals, parallelograms, and bands. Bands and zigzags seem to be the most common. Both equilateral and right-angle triangles were created. Spacing in the combinations of several elements in one design is pleasing and effective.

All of the Lovelock baskets are in plain or twined wicker weave. Much less twined work seems to have been done at this site. The only designing in the weave itself is in the use of

Fig. 2.18 A wicker basket with vertical bands resulting from the weave.

three-strand twining along with plain twined to give a different surface effect at limited points. Both open and closed wicker weaves were produced.

Technologically of interest is a basket from Palatki Ruin, central Arizona. Fragments of a conical burden basket are woven in a twill twine almost to the rim; then three-strand twining is done. At the rim proper are two finishing rows of a loose and poorly executed coil. The use of several types of wicker in a single piece is common, with this variety adding a decorative note. Incidentally, the modern Hopi wicker basket rim is finished off with a poorly executed coil at the rim. Also there are examples of prehistoric wicker weave exactly like the Hopi wherein multiple strands are held together by double plain weave twining.

Pieces of twining from upper levels in Cordova Cave may represent baskets; the rhythm is over-two-under-two. Twined material from Carter Ruin, in east central Arizona, may be basketry also. Seemingly, it is made from yucca leaves, or some similar material, twined in an over-one-under-one technique over a thin twig or rod foundation.

At Canyon Creek ruins, wicker weave seems to have been favored, for baskets of this type were fairly common. Some pieces, particularly plaques, resemble Hopi types. One piece, which was incomplete, measured 15 inches in diameter. In preserved centers, "weaving was begun with sixteen warp elements consisting of rigid sticks arranged by fours in a checker pattern."[16] Then they are splayed out and a plain wicker weave proceeds to the edge. A coiled rim was wrapped with beargrass leaves. Apparently there was no patterning in these pieces. These pieces support the concensus that plaque weaving was a Pueblo IV innovation in the Anasazi area.

COILED BASKETS

Basketmaker III baskets reached a peak of sophistication in the decoration of coiled pieces not again attained until late in the historic period. Even in Basketmaker II times there are fairly well-developed patterns; there is still an unknown background to the known sequence in these earliest decorated pieces, that is, between the last Desert Culture material and those of Basketmaker II. There is no comparable development in design in plaited baskets in early years; rather simple plain plaiting was the rule.

And, seemingly, there was no wicker work in the Basketmaker Period of development.

In Basketmaker times, the two-rod-and-bundle type of foundation prevailed, although the use of some bundle warps or a single rod was practiced in coiled basketry. Sewing splints were generally of wood, but yucca was noted at DuPont Cave. Five coils and about 9 stitches to the inch represent average work; however, on the finest pieces, the count runs to 7 coils and 12 stitches to the inch. Better sewing appears in some Pueblo III coiled baskets. Trays, bowls, and carrying baskets were made throughout this time, with Basketmaker III additions of globular (for storage?), large, constricted-mouthed bowl forms. A water-carrying basket with a small lower section and a large, globular upper section is found in Basketmaker II times, but such pieces have not been reported for upper levels. A slight depression in the bottom of some burden baskets anticipates the deeply bifurcated form of Pueblo III. Black design alone prevailed in the earlier phase, while red was a common addition to this in later Basketmaker years. Design and layout were simpler in Basketmaker II and much more complex in Basketmaker III times. There is a symmetrical arrangement of pattern throughout the period.

A cluster of traits characteristic of Basketmaker II and another for Basketmaker III coiled baskets follows. In general, Basketmaker II baskets were fairly well made; some from DuPont Cave had 5 coils and 11 stitches to the inch. Some trays were as much as 18 inches in diameter. Almost all were sewed with wooden splints. In these features, the Basketmaker II product set high standards for centuries. The area occupied by the design in relation to the total space is more limited, and this decorative field or layout is set off by framing lines (Fig. 2.19). If there is a solid black area, it is apt to

have a line or other secondary treatment at its margins. There is no discrimination in terms of design or layout on different forms. Design elements and units are well integrated, and they are predominantly black, with red added rarely. Characteristic elements include line and solid zigzags both plain and fancy, fringed lines and bands, diamonds, steps, and ovoid forms. Compared to later work, these are combined into relatively simple motifs.

In the Basketmaker III Phase, framing lines were frequently used to mark off the decorative field which often occupied at least one-third to one-half of the total basket area. Design remained the same in plan and treatment on all forms, but here the similarities end (Fig. 2.20a–j). The later style frequently featured the addition of red to the black designs, and these colors were handled in a variety of ways. When juxtaposed, elements in black and red were alternated and were usually separated by a plain coil or coils or by a line of plain stitching (Fig. 2.20a–c). Frequently, the same element or motif was repeated in the two colors, either in left-right balance (Fig. 2.20c) or reversed and inverted in position (Fig. 2.20d,e). Also, a solid black mass might be edged in red or a red mass outlined in black (Fig. 2.20c,h). Occasionally, one motif in black was opposed by or alternated with a different theme in red (Fig. 2.20i,j). Diversity in patterning was expressed in repeated motifs, the addition of new elements, or larger and more complex motifs. The latter contributed to the melting of elements into the whole pattern. There are also great numbers of spiral and radial arrangements as well as static radii, the former giving great dynamism to patterning as a whole. There was a wider variety of design as a whole and more complicated arrangements of elements, the latter often resulting in the loss of identity of individual units of design.

Although the best preserved and the greatest abundance of coiled baskets are related to the Four Corners region, many pieces have come from other parts of the Anasazi and some from the other two major culture areas; examples of coiled baskets from all of these regions will be cited.

Coiled baskets of the Pueblo Period present quite a different picture from those of Basketmaker times. In the first place, far less is known about this craft in the Pueblo I and II Phases, since during these years homes were small sur-

Fig. 2.19 An example of Basketmaker II coiled basket, showing sparse design in relation to total space (Guernsey and Kidder 1921, pl. 24j).

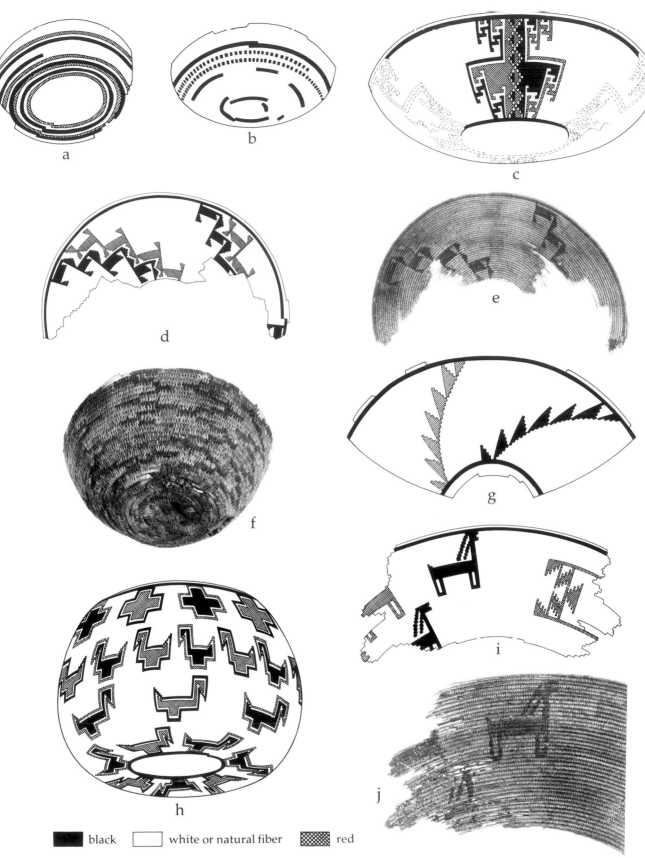

black ▮   white or natural fiber ☐   red ▨

Fig. 2.20 A series of Basketmaker III coiled baskets showing various methods of handling color and design (Morris
and Burgh 1941, except photographs *e*, *f*, and *j*; figure numbers only given). (a) and (b) Two coiled basket bowls with
simple alternation of black and red. The first has continuous bands of color, the second has outer bands but broken
squares in the two inner rows (13e,h). (c) In this example
there is repetition of the same element in red and black, in
left-right balance (13f). (d) Design reversed and inverted, in
opposed colors, red and black (16d). (e) In the photo is a
comparable but simpler version of *d* done in black and
maybe red. (f) A deep bowl, with an allover line pattern in
steps forming almost-chevrons. (g) Simple repetition of
identical pattern, in alternating black and red (13a). (h) Figures of ducks (?) in red, outlined in black, and in black
outlined in red (16f). (i) Alternation of totally different
designs, one in black, one in red (16a). (j) Photograph of
a fragment of basket showing the same mountain sheep
(goat?) as in the drawing.

face structures usually built in the open; neither size nor location was conducive to the preservation of perishable materials. There are some examples of coiled work from Pueblo I times, but still fewer from the following period, Pueblo II.

Some of the decorated pieces of basketry from Pueblo I would indicate that many of the traits of Basketmaker III carried over into this later period. In turn this would indicate that basket making and decorating were still at a high level, although probably not as high as in Basketmaker III times. Two-rod-and-bundle triangularly arranged and one-rod foundations have been reported. Oval and round bowl forms and carrying baskets with a larger orifice and a smaller base are three known forms; it is probable that trays were still made for they are found in such abundance in Basketmaker villages and later in Pueblo III sites.

The limited samples of Pueblo I decoration reveal at least the following traits. Encircling bands and radial styles are found, and in the former, framing lines are sometimes far apart; apparently, these features apply to all known forms. Small-unit designs in black and red tend to lose their identity in fairly complex arrangements, with equal parts of the background showing through. The effect is mosaiclike, with the natural color of the basket of equal importance in the pattern along with the black and red. A given motif in black may or may not be balanced by the same in red; this offers further diversity in patterning.

Pueblo III coiled basketry shapes are perhaps equally as varied as those in Basketmaker III times, for there is not only the continuation of older forms, such as trays (diminished in size), bowls large and small, carrying baskets, and miscellaneous small items, but also the addition of such new shapes as cylindrical and rectangular forms, plaques, shields, and variations on burden baskets. Probably the quantity of basketry had diminished in this later period, since through the years pottery had replaced basketry prototypes in many individual forms. Certainly vessels of clay were more desirable than baskets for specific utility purposes such as cooking, water and seed storage, and serving food. Technically, Pueblo III baskets are often the best woven examples of all prehistoric times, with stitch counts sometimes as high as 24 per inch and coils counting as many as 8 to the inch.

In general, basket designs and layout are quite different in Pueblo III times; too, there was some

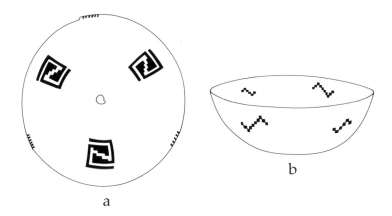

Fig. 2.21 Simple and limited patterns, usually black, characterize Pueblo III coiled basket designs, as illustrated in these two examples: (a) tray and (b) bowl (Morris and Burgh 1941, Fig. 18a,b).

degeneracy in decoration from the peak attainments of Basketmaker III, although some of the individual pieces of the later time are beautifully ornamented. Seemingly, more effort was applied in the direction of using particular layouts for certain forms; trays (Fig. 2.21a) and shallow bowls (Fig. 2.21b) were decorated with scattered designs or panels of design, while on deeper bowls, flat plaques, and carrying baskets encircling bands of several types were favored. Concentric framing lines are not common. Frequently, decorated areas are small. Design is generally in black alone and of dyed sewing elements or bird quills; if red is added, motifs are identical and opposed. Although integrated designs do occur, the predominant style was to space out relatively simple and identical motifs, with one theme repeated two, three, or four times.

Pueblo IV basketry suffered a fate similar to that of the early Pueblo periods, for the Indian again turned to more open sites for the location of his villages. Consequently, there are very limited remains of basketry. In general, weaving degenerated technically and artistically, if judged by the few pieces actually recovered; however, it can be suggested on the basis of kiva murals and what appear to be baskets therein, that much more has been lost than preserved. In form, straight-sided bowls have been found, with coarse and large coils and stitching, and in two instances, negative patterning (Fig. 2.22a,b).

Before turning to decorated types of coiled baskets, it might be pertinent to mention briefly several undecorated pieces of very coarse coils (Fig. 2.23a,b). A fine specimen of this work was excavated at Canyon Creek Ruins; it is 8 inches high, and has a coil count of 2 to the inch and

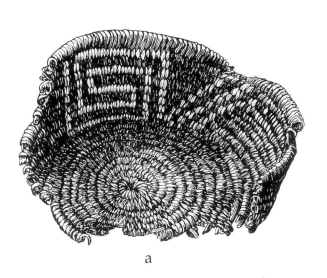

a

b

Fig. 2.22 Negative patterns on coiled baskets. (a) Fragment of a Pueblo IV basket, coiled weave, and designed, from Chevlon Ruin. This pattern appears in white against a dark background (Fewkes 1904, Fig. 63). (b) A second negative pattern with frets and stepped zigzags in the light color of the sewing splints against a dark ground.

wide-spaced sewing (Fig. 2.23a). In general appearance it resembles the huge storage baskets made by Pimas and Papagos about the turn of the century. Another coarse weave basket from the same site, which is larger in size, measured about 45 inches at the base; it is a true granary piece and was built into a room. Coils measured from 1 to 1½ inches in diameter and were formed of bundles of twigs; the piece was sewed with "small pliable branches before being built into the structure."[17] It was covered inside and out with clay. Another example seems to be a basketry lid (Fig. 2.23b). It would seem that this style of coarse coiled basket weave was more peculiar to the southern part of the prehistoric Southwest, with a few large examples from the middle area. Tuzigoot provided pieces which

are wide-coiled (coils 1 to 1½ inches thick); several of these baskets are made of beargrass.

Turning to specific decoration of coiled baskets, emphasis will be placed on the high development of decorative styles in this technique. All forms will be considered, trays, bowls and burden baskets—all forms which are most important decoratively—and a small selection of varied forms that have less significant decoration. Adaptation to changing forms as well as specific designs will also be treated. The Basketmaker Period will be considered first, then the Pueblo Period, with emphasis on Pueblo III because of the dearth of Pueblo I and II decorated basketry products.

An unusual shape is a water jar with a large upper portion and a smaller base; Guernsey and Kidder report a Basketmaker II water jar of this type that is 17 inches high, 14¾ inches at its greatest diameter, and 4½ inches at the orifice.[18] The elongate base is oval. Human hair cord loops for the carrying strap are in place on the large part of the basket. The interior of the basket was covered with piñon pitch. A faint pattern made up of stepped units can be seen on the upper part of the basket.

Banded patterns predominate in Basketmaker II pieces for several reasons. In trays, there is generally a single (Fig. 2.24a) or double (Fig. 2.24b) circle near the center; with the rim or another line serving as a second and natural boundary line, a banded area is created that seemed to invite decoration. In burden baskets, which were basically conical at this time, the

Fig. 2.23 Coarse weave and open stitch coiling. (a) Although this example is but 8″ high, the weave is of a type used for large storage baskets (Haury 1934, pl. LId). (b) Photograph of a probable basket lid made of coarse grasses.

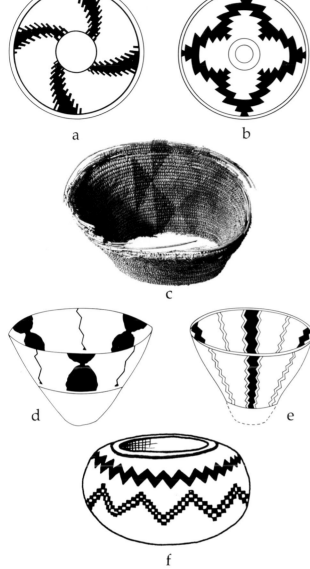

Fig. 2.24 Basketmaker II basket designs. (All baskets except c are from Guernsey and Kidder 1921. Plate numbers only will be given.) (a) The short lines at the edges of the radiating bands are quite common (24a). (b) As in so many early baskets, this encircling design is dynamic (24h). (c) Photograph of another simple design in a burden basket from Obelisk Cave, woven in red and black. (d) The rim and a woven black line create a band used for decoration in this burden basket (24e). (e) Narrow and broad zigzags are effectively combined in this burden basket design (24f). (f) A small bowl basket which shows variety in the use of a solid zigzag and a second zigzag made up of checked squares (24d).

rim, or an encircling black band close thereto, plus a black line low on the vessel, created a similar banded area (Fig. 2.24c,d,e). The same tended to be true of bowls, particularly those with flat bottoms, for the shape itself invited banded patterning on the side wall (Fig. 2.24f). Guernsey and Kidder report that trinket baskets from northeastern Arizona are very small and that they have black—but no red—designs on

them.[19] They add that some of these baskets had trinkets in them, hence the name of this small bowl. With very few exceptions, Basketmaker II designs were radiate or encircling; they were both static and dynamic (Fig. 2.24a,b). Wide or narrow line zigzags were popular (Fig. 2.24b,d); sometimes both were combined in a single basket design. One example shows four dynamic bands radiating from close to the center, increasing slightly in width from the inner to the outer edge; short, straight lines emanate from both sides of these bands (Fig. 2.24a). In a burden basket, three solid units of double or joined half-rounds alternate with three simple and slender zigzags (Fig. 2.24d). A four-times-repeated stepped zigzag encircles a tray basket (Fig. 2.24b); in this form also there are simple encircling or radiate zigzags. Occasionally other—and odd—design units were added in these tray forms (see Fig. 2.19). The majority of all patterns mentioned so far are repeated four times; however, a few repetitions of three motifs are to be noted in these earliest decorated baskets, as seen in Fig. 2.24d.

As indicated in the earlier part of this chapter, Basketmaker III baskets became more elaborate in all matters pertaining to decoration (see Fig. 2.20c–f). Traits common to this and the previous period would include a predominance of banded patterns and a 4-times repetition of major motifs. Following are the basic differences in the later period, largely additions or changes: greater use of red; greater diversity and complexity of motifs; and unbalanced placement of design as exemplified in an elaborate pattern on the face of certain burden baskets and a simple theme on the reverse side. The latter point was a concession to form and use, probably, for this is found on a style that is more oval in cross section, with one side of the basket probably against the back of the carrier. Two additional differences in the later period are double bands, rather than single ones, on flaring-rimmed burden baskets and the introduction of life forms in decoration. The former well illustrates how adaptation of design goes hand in hand with changing forms, increase in size, and other related matters. The second point, life forms, saw its highest development in prehistoric times in the Basketmaker III Phase.

In the large conical burden basket of this period, Fig. 2.25a, there is an abrupt turn from the lower portion into the wide and flaring rim; this turn formed a natural dividing line that was

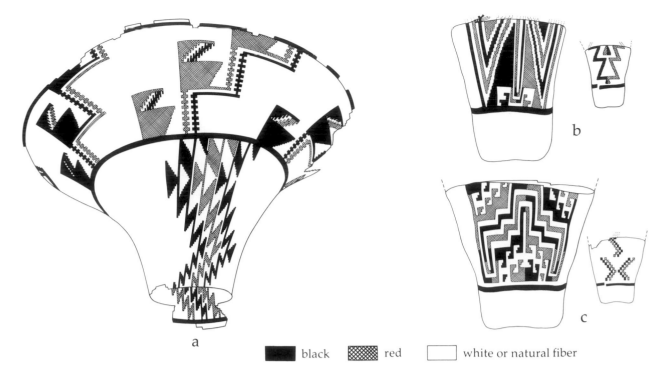

| ■ black | ▨ red | □ white or natural fiber |

Fig. 2.25 Burden basket forms and designs. (All from Morris and Burgh 1941; figure numbers only given.) (a) A large conical burden basket showing a different design on expanding rim and body, both patterns with interesting handling of red and black (15a). (b) One of the common features of the bucket-shaped burden baskets is the simple design on the side which rested against the back of the carrier and the elaborate pattern on the exposed side (14d). (c) Clever balancing of design and reversal of red and black colors resulted in sophisticated patterning in this piece (14c).

emphasized by the weaver as she wove a black line at this point. The two resulting areas invited banded decoration, a larger upper section and a more limited lower area. This lower part of the basket was also cone-shaped; perhaps these circumstances encouraged the weaver to put two repeated designs within this area, while in the upper section, which was considerably longer, she repeated a common motif four or six times. Here too, the weaver enjoyed playing with the two colors, red and black. In the lower section, designs were simpler, as illustrated in the basket in Fig. 2.25a that has a vertical arrangement of red and black geometrics and a few triangles with stepped edges framed on both sides by the same units in black, all joined by lines. Or the lower patterns were a bit more elaborate as another example shows: here are plain-edged bands plus bands with one straight and one zigzag side, with positive and negative geometrics within each, plus outer rows of joined triangles.[20] All motifs are balanced in right-left variations of red and black.

Patterns in the wide rim of these burden baskets also run the gamut from simplicity to complexity, as illustrated by the same two baskets. In the first, Figure 2.25a, there is a simpler, four-times-repeated arrangement of stepped triangles (or almost-triangles), with a solid line or

lines crossed with small elongate rectangles outlining or pendant from the main motifs. Repetition is a little different here in that there is mass red with black outlines alternating with mass black with red outlines. In the second basket there is greater complication in both design and color. There are opposed vertical rows of joined triangles, with stepped edges, black above, red below, then they are reversed in the next panel; there are three such sets, repeated and alternating to form the total design. A few small geometrics are added, also in balanced red and black. The size of conical burden baskets, 3 to 4 feet across the wide tops, may have inspired some of this fine decoration.

The bucket-shaped burden basket, with a slight concavity on the bottom outside, is the type which has a more complex design on the face and a simpler motif on the back. The two-unit face motif on one has deep stepped triangles with short triangles at their bases and line projections on the opposite side, plus two V-shaped lines and one diagonal line to the right and left of the triangles (Fig. 2.25b).[21] All of this is an elaborate arrangement within a band, with alternation of black and red within each unit, and with opposite alternation from the left to the right unit. Design on the reverse side consists of two joined outline-triangles, with a broken and heavy bordering and enclosing line below them. More elaborate is a second example of this bucket-type burden basket (Fig. 2.25c). Here there are left-right repeated motifs, each consisting of two basic units of design: steps with elongated stepped "hooks," and deep-stepped and plain broad lines. There is a left-right balance of these two themes, both in form and color, and an internal play of black and red within each motif. The back pattern is composed of much simpler stepped squares, but carries out the same color balance.

Bowls tend to be undecorated or to have relatively simple decoration. One of the latter, Figure 2.20a, has encircling and alternating black and red lines; a second, Figure 2.20b, expresses the same general idea but with black lines above and below, and with two inner rows of small repeated squares forming the "lines." Some bowls have life forms; one with a more incurved rim, Figure 2.20h, has three rows of birds (ducks?) and a top row of crosses; each figure is in black, outlined in red, alternating with the same in red, outlined in black. A feeling of an allover pattern results, for there is only a very small undecorated space at the bottom of the bowl. Bowls vary in size from small ones a few inches in diameter to larger pieces like the oval one found by Hough in New Mexico, which is 19½ inches by 16 inches and 6½ inches deep. Stepped figures in black dominate in the wall pattern. There are also oval bowls with vertical zigzags on side and end walls. A round bowl basket from Hidden House, Figure 2.26, is about 5¾ inches high, has diameters of about 9¼ inches at the rim and about 4¼ inches at the base. A ¾-inch false braid terminates the plain-sewn rim. It has a three-rod foundation, is coiled in counterclockwise fashion, and has 5 coils and 10 stitches to the inch. A black design, "probably of devil's claw" features three chevronlike arrangements of joined triangles outlined in a straight line, extended low on the basket.[22]

Since trays are the most abundant of all Basketmaker III forms, one would expect a greater variety in design also (Fig. 2.27). Such is the case. Encircling bands are narrow or broad; the majority have a single-coil inner black band or zigzag and some have the same near the outer edge (Fig. 2.27b). A few design layouts appear to be organizational-banded even though there is a close-to-the-rim black band. Such is a row of ducks and two butterflies on one tray or four butterflies on another (Fig. 2.27c,d), or simple zigzags between the rim and center of another (Fig. 2.27e). Rarely, a design is pendant, or nearly so, from a black rim band and is, therefore, a half-band (Fig. 2.27f). Some trays are decorated in simple geometric fashion; for example, one has four alternate red and black paired and stepped-edged triangles in a band (Fig. 2.27g); another has four pairs of black and red opposed and joined rectangles, swirling from the inner border of the band to the rim of the basket (Fig. 2.28). This same use of more or less identical and paired black and red geometrics appears in many other designs, usually repeated four times, or sometimes there are alternating and different motifs. One example of the latter has a geometric theme repeated on opposite sides of the tray with life forms in between. Much more elaborate is a tray with four repeated complex motifs, each made up of central opposed rows of stepped themes and more elaborate stepped geometrics on each side; everything is bordered with irregular and more or less stepped wide lines on the outer edges. There is a great deal of left-right opposition of color in these motifs: interestingly, each is repeated identically in this fine specimen with clear-cut exchange of color in the repetitions. This seems to be a common device.

The basket in Figure 2.29 is an excellent example of Pueblo I style of decoration wherein the light color of the basic natural material plays a part in design. The wide band on this bowl is made up of stepped joined triangles and other stepped geometrics repeated in this color alternation: black, natural, red, natural; motifs in all colors are approximately the same size, although there are some irregularities.

Several trends are outstanding in Pueblo III styles of decoration. One is overall greater simplicity, although some individual pieces are fairly elaborate. Whereas geometric patterning in bands is usually repeated four or six times in Basketmaker examples, a three-fold repetition is

Fig. 2.26 A fine example of a decorated coiled bowl basket, with a three-divisional design in black, from Hidden House, central Arizona (Dixon 1956, Fig. 28).

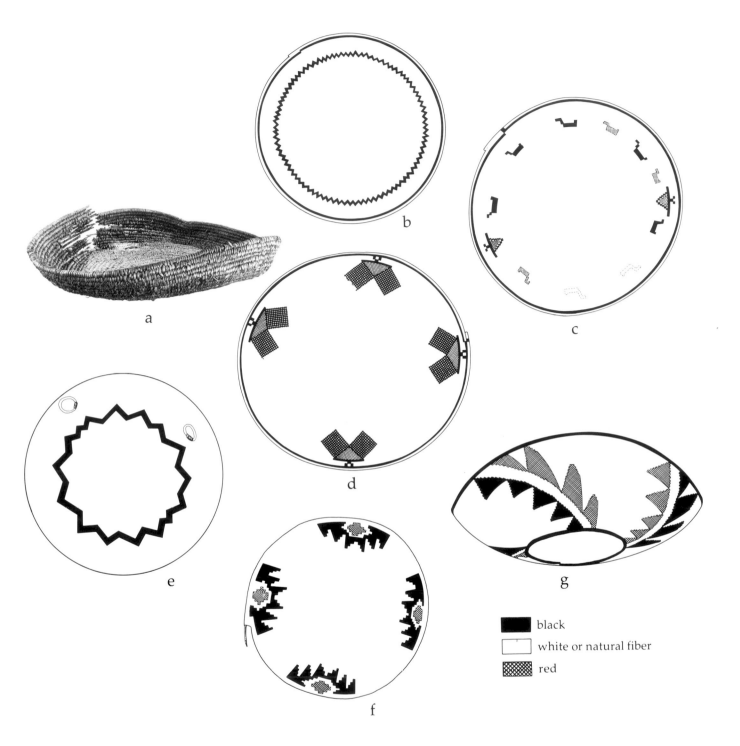

Fig. 2.27 Design styles on tray baskets. (a) The low open form of the tray (this one exaggerated by use) invited a quantity and variety of patterning. (b) Coiled basket of the Basketmaker Period, with an encircling design in black and a plain black line near the rim. Most of the simple designs of this type were earlier in time, although a few survived into much later periods (Pepper 1902: 10, center bottom row). (c) A tray decorated with butterflies and ducks (ibid., p. 15). (d) Another tray basket decorated with "butterflies," found over the burial of a child in southeastern Utah (ibid., p. 12). (e) A design on a coiled basket tray from White Dog Cave. Design is in black (Guernsey and Kidder 1921, Plate 23j). (f) Decorated coiled basket from Cave Canyon, Upper Gila, nine inches in diameter (Cosgrove 1947, Fig. 98b). (g) A dynamic pattern confined to a band delineated by broad lines. The design is balanced red and black (Morris and Burgh 1941, Fig. 13g).

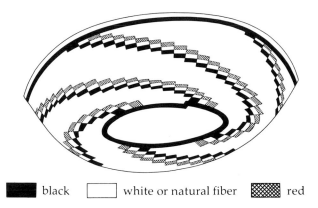

■ black ☐ white or natural fiber ▨ red

Fig. 2.28 A swirling pattern within a band. Balanced red and black rectangles are arranged in the usual four rows (Morris and Burgh 1941, Fig. 14e).

fairly common in Pueblo III trays and bowls. Four, of course, continues to be a popular number for design repetition in both carrying baskets and trays. In general, burden baskets are comparatively more elaborately decorated in Pueblo III times than are bowls and trays; this may reflect the possibility that they might have been more important since there was no clay substitute for them. In bowl and tray decoration, there is little variation from diamonds (Fig. 2.30a); or repeated, interlocked, or plain steps (Fig. 2.30b); or continuous motifs (Fig. 2.30c). Some of these are made up of tiny squares or zigzags repeated three times (Fig. 2.30a), or equally simple geometrics repeated four times (Fig. 2.30d). The greater simplicity of burden basket design as compared with earlier styles is exemplified in two rims or upper sections from deep, cone-shaped pieces; both present simple interlocked, stepped and opposed black and red meanders terminating in stepped triangles, with color

Fig. 2.30 Pueblo III baskets. (a) The great simplicity of design in this period is again emphasized in three simple diamonds made up of black squares (Morris and Burgh 1941, Fig. 18h). (b) Coiled basket from Water Canyon Cave, Upper Gila, with a design in black and red on natural (Cosgrove 1947, Fig. 35a). (c) Another triple division design of simple structure (Morris and Burgh 1941, Fig. 18c). (d) Typically Pueblo III in simplicity is this tray basket design of stepped elements repeated four times (ibid., Fig. 18d).

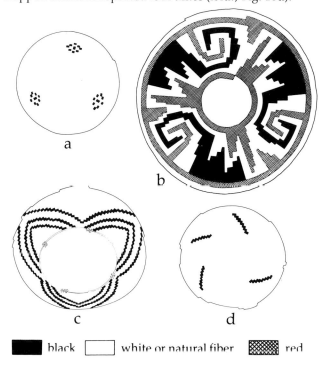

■ black ☐ white or natural fiber ▨ red

opposition alternating in each row in one example (Fig. 2.31), and, in the other, repeated exactly in each of the two rows, but different in top and bottom rows.

A perfectly preserved example of a burden basket with fairly elaborate decoration was found in a burial at Painted Cave, in northeastern Arizona (Fig. 2.32). It is rather bucket-shaped, is oval in cross section, and has a slight

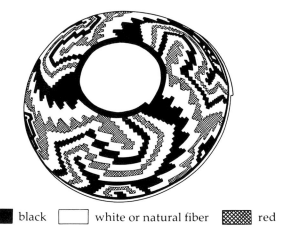

■ black ☐ white or natural fiber ▨ red

Fig. 2.29 A typical Pueblo I basket where there is quite equal balance between black, red, and natural colors throughout the design (Morris and Burgh 1941, Fig. 16g).

Fig. 2.31 Pueblo III burden baskets were decorated with simpler designs than in Basketmaker years, yet they are generally more elaborate than patterns in other contemporary forms (Morris and Burgh 1941, Fig. 17d).

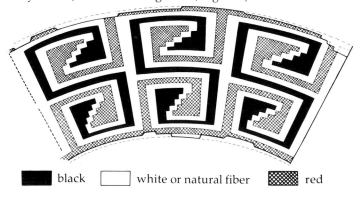

■ black ☐ white or natural fiber ▨ red

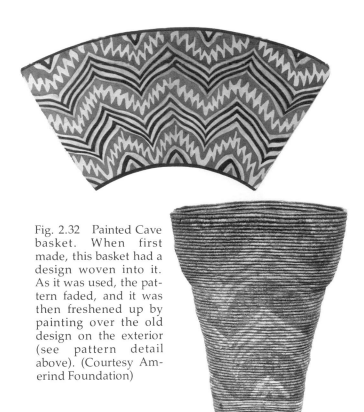

Fig. 2.32 Painted Cave basket. When first made, this basket had a design woven into it. As it was used, the pattern faded, and it was then freshened up by painting over the old design on the exterior (see pattern detail above). (Courtesy Amerind Foundation)

Fig. 2.33 Drawing of inside woven design of Painted Cave basket. Compare with Fig. 2.32.

dent in the base.[23] Originally a design had been woven into the basket, over most of the basket wall, in black and red on a background of natural tan material. The pattern was composed of zigzags of stepped lines (made up of tiny rectangles), in red, and stepped triangles, largely in black. Then, perhaps because the design faded on the outside, someone painted over the original woven pattern in green and red, and added yellow. Some interesting changes occurred in the painted design (Fig. 2.33): the zigzags made of rectangles became straight, narrow bands, and the stepped triangles became straight-edged, semi-triangles. However, the dynamism and general feeling of the original design were retained, despite the fact that paint on a brush smoothed out the angular lines which basket technology dictated in the woven pattern.

Deeply bifurcated baskets are sometimes referred to as the major burden type for Pueblo III times; they did enjoy a fairly wide distribution for they have been found at Pueblo Bonito, Mummy Cave (Utah), Bat Woman House, Segiotsosi, the Segi, and, as reported by Fewkes,[24] in one of the Navajo National Monument sites. However, the above two, the cone and the deep, oval forms, would indicate that the bifurcated style was but one of several popular burden baskets of this period. And, as a matter of fact, most bifurcated baskets come from the defined area, near the San Juan River

in southeastern Utah and northeastern Arizona, except for several examples from Pueblo Bonito in northwestern New Mexico. Another point to bear in mind is that this form became so specialized that possibly it lost its utility value and became a strictly ceremonial object. In fact, small clay copies of this form have been found at Pueblo Bonito (Fig. 2.34a,b). One Pueblo Bonito example of a basket (Fig. 2.35a), has a line design woven in black and red all over the main body of the piece, in half terraces attached to narrow bands. Of this design Judd says, "horizontal lines are one coil wide; vertical lines, two stitches in width."[25] At some later time, someone painted over the original design of this

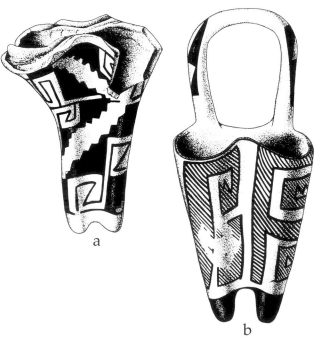

Fig. 2.34 Clay effigies of bifurcated burden baskets. It is likely that the basket was decorated on one face only, for the effigies are devoid of design on their backs. Design a more closely resembles a real basket pattern than does b (Judd 1954, Fig. 100a). (b) This clay effigy of a bifurcated basket reveals a typical style of Pueblo Bonito hatched ceramic decoration (ibid., pl. 88b).

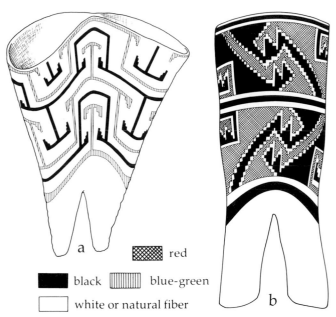

Fig. 2.35 Two bifurcated burden baskets. (a) The design was painted on this basket from Pueblo Bonito in black and blue-green on natural. Originally the black was a design woven in; the blue-green was added, perhaps as a balancing theme (Judd 1954, Fig. 99). (b) Basket from Moki Canyon. A Pueblo III, deeply bifurcated basket with two wide bands of red and black decoration. The natural color of the basket shows through like a negative pattern (Morris and Burgh 1941, Fig. 18f).

basket with black paint, then added balancing themes in a greenish-blue pigment.

This last design becomes even simpler in contrast with the pattern on another bifurcated basket from Moki Canyon, in southeastern Utah. The second example is decorated in a quite elaborate pattern in black and red, with heavy black triangles and other geometrics opposed by the same motifs in equally large areas of red (Fig. 2.35b). The two colors join in such a way as to suggest a negative pattern between them, which is made up of small, more or less joined squares

in the natural color of the basket. Heavy black bands separate two such treatments and border both of them above and below.

A deeply bifurcated basket from Navajo Canyon (Fig. 2.36) in the Museum of Northern Arizona, Flagstaff, has a double-banded pattern, each band in black and red, featuring diagonal wide lines, zigzags, and small triangles. Excessive wear on the back of this basket would seem to indicate that its purpose might have been for utility rather than ceremony; the latter has been suggested by some archaeologists.

Two other unusual forms found at Pueblo Bonito are elliptical trays and cylindrical vases. A few shallow, oval forms have been found elsewhere, but Judd believes that the straight-sided, flat-bottomed vase is peculiar to Pueblo Bonito.

In the four elliptical trays, weaving is superior; one example counts 7 coils and 22 stitches per inch, while the finest of these has 8 coils and 24 stitches per inch. An attractive and decorative false braid appears at the rim of the latter. Perfection of workmanship can be noted in the fine weaving and the unusual form, which combine to make these baskets of interest.

Equally interesting, although not as artistic, is the cylindrical form. Of the 5 measurable forms, the average height was 8.53 inches and diameter was 5.35 inches. Superior weaving is indicated in most of the 19 whole pieces and fragments of this form, with coils counting 5 to 7 per inch and with stitches running up to 20 per inch. Four pieces had false braid at the rim, an always subtle and attractive addition. Only two of the cylindrical vessels showed signs of additional color decoration, one with stained splints of black and red combined with the natural color of the base material in an allover but indistinct pattern, and the second with a design painted on the finished piece (Fig. 2.37).

Fig. 2.36 A deeply bifurcated basket from Navajo Canyon. The design in red and black is well preserved on the outside. (Photo by Marc Gaede, courtesy of the Museum of Northern Arizona)

Fig. 2.37 Reproduction of a small (3¾" in diameter and 5" high), well-woven basket. It was painted in successive, ascending and diagonal rows of diamonds, in black, orange, blue-green, and natural (Judd 1954, Fig. 98).

In an earlier excavation at Pueblo Bonito, Pepper found one of these cylindrical baskets covered with turquoise mosaic.[26] This introduces another style of decoration of baskets, which will be discussed, and posits a question relative to all baskets of this form: Were they produced for everyday use or for ceremonial purposes? Their abundance at the site of Pueblo Bonito only, their impractical shape, and their special decoration in several known instances are points that surely could be used as support for the suggested ritual purposes of such pieces. Judd advances a theory of their possible use in a women's secret society or other such religious group.

Another interesting way in which the prehistoric Southwesterners altered woven baskets was to cover them with clay, on one or both sides. Frequently this was done on the inside of tray forms for utility purposes; this use is merely stated here, but it is excluded in the following discussion which pertains more to a custom that seems to have been practiced for other and often decorative reasons. Rather ordinary clay was used for utility baskets, while a fine red clay was employed for the special baskets, seemingly either for decorative purposes or for some particular use in ceremonies. In some instances, the clay was merely smoothed with care, but in others it served as a base for the application of a design. Most of the latter specimens are confined to the Chaco Canyon or Flagstaff areas; this was not a wide-spread custom; however, occasional other examples have been encountered.

Several pieces of clayed basketry have been found at the two ruins, Pueblo Bonito and Aztec. One small fragment from the former site has either triangles or rectangles (only part of the theme remains) painted in black on the red surface. The other examples from Pueblo Bonito had the fine red clay surfacing, but no additional recovered pieces had any design preserved on them.

More abundant are decorated pieces of this nature from the Flagstaff region, recovered at or near Ridge Ruin.[27] On one piece are red and green geometric designs on the interior of the basket. On another piece, a deep, straight, sloping-sided, flat-bottomed bowl, is more elaborate decoration. The interior was painted green, while the entire exterior was given a base coat of light blue. On the exterior, meanders end in frets outlined in darker blue, balanced by comparable motifs outlined in red and filled with yellow. Fine weaving is indicated in these pitch-coated baskets, which, along with their rarity and unusual decoration, might well indicate their possible ritual use.

From Las Acequias, near Phoenix, comes one exception to the previously suggested distribution of this style, a bowl in the coiled weave with clay surfacing on the exterior. The foundation is three-rod stacked, stitches are non-interlocked, and coils are counterclockwise. Stitches count from about 10 and coils 5 to the inch. Over the exterior surface of one basket is "a heavy sizing of red paint," and apparently on this is "a painting of indistinguishable colors."[28] Other examples from La Cuidad, also close to Phoenix, have clear patterns in blue, red, yellow, and green.

Painting on the immediate surface of baskets is another matter, and a much more widespread custom; possibly it was one that had no ritual significance. In the two examples mentioned of painting over a woven design, the decorator followed more or less the original pattern. Then there are other instances where the weaver worked on a plain woven surface, creating a decorative effect in color alone. In general, this practice runs the gamut from putting washes of several colors on a basket, more or less in an aimless fashion or in banded effects, to carefully creating a specific pattern. An example of the latter type of painting comes from Pueblo Bonito (Fig. 2.37): on a cylindrical basket, a design was painted over the entire perpendicular wall surface. It consists of four rows of diagonally arranged parallelograms in black, orange, blue-green, and the natural tan of the basket material. This motif is repeated three times. Fragments of other baskets with bits of paint adhering to them were also found at Pueblo Bonito, indicating the further pursuit of this practice.

A design that is not as well preserved as some others is on a so-called shield (it has grip fastenings and holes for other attachments, with buckskin in position in some spots). On this basket is painted what appears to be a frog (Fig. 2.38). Despite contentions to the contrary, the outline of such a figure is surely indicated in the reproduction in Morris and Burgh, taken with a "red filter on panchromatic film" (a new process at that time) which "brings out the disputed figure more distinctly than it appears to the eye on the

Fig. 2.38 A traylike basket, called, in this instance, a shield. The frog was painted on the finished piece: the central circle in red, and the rest of the body and the legs black (Culin 1908, Frontispiece).

shield itself."[29] The use of a three-rod foundation labels this piece Pueblo III.

Unquestionably the most colorful of the unusual methods of decorating basketry is to cover the piece with mosaic. In a room at Pueblo Bonito was found what was apparently one of the cylindrical baskets that had turquoise beads and oval pieces of shell adhering to its surface. Beneath the floor of the same room was found a second piece, again apparently a cylindrical basket, with its surface covered with 1,214 fragments of turquoise embedded in a fixitive,

probably piñon gum. A turquoise and shell bead necklace wrapped about one of these baskets would seem to support its probable ritual use.[30]

Another small piece of basketry encrusted with turquoise might have been a bracelet (see Fig. 5.19b). It came from a cave near El Paso, Texas.

Mosaic on basketry was also found at Ridge Ruin, in the grave labeled "Burial of an Early American Magician." Apparently one piece was tubular in shape (Fig. 2.39), with the mosaic consisting of "1,500 pieces of carefully cut and fitted turquoise . . . as well as rows of orange rodents' teeth, square red argillite inlays, and elongated black stone inlays."[31] It is reported that there was no bottom to this piece, and if not, it is postulated that it could have been a large, elaborate arm ornament (about 4½ inches long). For those who argue the point, some recent Navajo bow guards measure over 4 inches in length. This piece is included because it is comparable in form to the vases at Pueblo Bonito, and surely there is the possibility that the bottom was merely missing in the Ridge Ruin example.

One last piece of basketry ornamented in a different fashion is from Aztec Ruin. It is a large basket shield from the "Warrior's Grave" at this site. Forty-eight coils were stained a greenish-blue, 5 were a dark red, while the outer 5 coils were coated with pitch and "thickly spangled with minute flakes of selenite."[32]

Fig. 2.39 Tubular basket, mosaic covered. Variety is to be noted in turquoise plus rodents' teeth, argillite, and black stone (McGregor 1943, pl. I, Fig. 1).

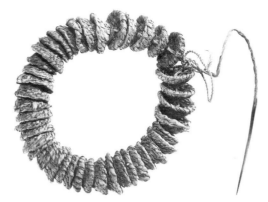

Fig. 2.40 A string of forty-one miniature baskets, each in coiled weave over a two-rod foundation.

Thus, it can be seen that the greatest variety and amount of decoration in basketry appeared on the coiled pieces. Most elaborately developed and most refined stylistically are designs woven into these baskets. Shapes varied greatly, and there was keen adaptation of layout and design to this variety. Design elements, units, and motifs also became highly varied and sophisticated through the years of their development. Some designs were simple and static, but many were dynamic and elaborate.

Miniature baskets have been found in a number of places in the Southwest (Fig. 2.40). Quite naturally they are made of the materials and in styles prevalent in the areas where they occur. There is some question as to why they were made; suggestions, which are not lacking, run the gamut from toys, to beginners' efforts, to ceremonial use. Some idiosyncrasies appear in these baskets and they too have been explained in various ways. A small twilled basket found at Painted Cave lacks the usual hoop in the top. In the Hueco area, the coarseness of several quite small pieces is explained as evidence that they were made as offerings and not for any utility purpose.[33] Two forms of coiled baskets were encountered here, one a straight-sided bowl, the second a carrying basket. Each of these had a bit of black decoration near the rim (Fig. 2.41). It is of interest to

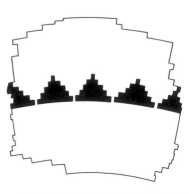

Fig. 2.41 Fragment of a coiled basket, with a simple design; from Chavez Cave, Hueco area, probably of Basketmaker times (Cosgrove 1947, Fig. 35b).

note that they were woven on a bundle foundation, the most common type in the Hueco region. Quite crude are two other baskets of the Mogollon area, from Tularosa Cave; each is about 1⅜ inches in diameter and roughly bowl-shaped. They are made on a yucca-bundle foundation, a type not too common in the Mogollon area but certainly practical from the standpoint of making such tiny coils. Stitches are wide apart and of wooden splints. There are 5 coils and 7½ stitches per inch in one, and 5 stitches and 2½ coils per inch in the second of these miniatures.

An example of a miniature carrying basket can be identified as Anasazi on a basis of some of its decorative features. The upper part of the piece is ornamented with stepped-edged, notched right triangles; there is alternate inversion and reversal, alternate use of black and red.

In Montezuma Cave, on the Blue River (tributary of the Gila), two miniatures were found. One measures 1½ inches high and 2½ inches in diameter. The second is very globular in form and its dimensions are 1 inch height and 1¼ inches diameter. The first has a dark red decoration, and both are of finer weave than any of those previously mentioned.

Some miniatures are found in caves with other objects which are obviously ceremonial; certainly the baskets could be so identified. Also, it is contended by some archaeologists that when pottery miniatures were made, those of basketry disappeared.

It is slight wonder that basketry influenced other craft arts. This is particularly true of ceramics, where the older expression, basketry, affected form and decoration in pottery, as can be so well illustrated in the Anasazi. In textiles, too, basketry had an influence on some layouts and design styles; this is especially true of those areas where common technologies were utilized in the two crafts.

Basically, basketry served prehistoric people for their everyday needs, with additional use for rituals, and who knows... perhaps for other still unknown purposes. There is no question that the Anasazi used them for many ends, probably for all household needs until pottery was introduced. Much of this specialized service on the part of basketry continued among the natives of the Southwest throughout the prehistoric

Decoration

period and of course some of it persists right up into the 1970s.[34]

In addition to basketry itself and its tell-tale shapes that indicate specific usage, there are many other sources for identifying use value for this craft. Open trays were probably all-purpose utensils then as they are historically, for example, among the Apaches. Small-mouthed bottle forms were undoubtedly used for conveying water; shapes are frequently similar to modern basketry water bottles. Carrying devices are invariably wide-mouthed, frequently smaller at the base; Havasupais used a cone-shaped burden basket; Apaches continue to use a bucket-shaped one. Most of these early baskets were water proof, either as a result of their close weave or because they had been pitched with some native substance such as piñon gum; Apaches still do the latter, using the identical water-proofing material. Pieces that are labelled burden baskets and water bottles frequently have loops on their sides through which tump lines were passed (and remnants of these may be noted in position); both tump lines and straps have been found in abundance.

To these specifics of construction for the various forms of baskets can be added other evidences for their exact uses. Burden baskets and the manner of their being "worn," or carried, can be proved in a large number of widely distributed pictographs or petroglyphs and in the decoration of Hohokam pottery. In these instances, the tump strap is over the forehead, with strings attached at the rear of the strap, and the strings in turn fastened to the loops in the basket, which is borne on the back of the carrier. In the kiva murals at Awatovi, there are bowl baskets piled high with various items. That baskets were made with the thought in mind that they would eventually be buried with the dead is indicated in an abundance of pieces found in graves, particularly from Basketmaker times. That baskets had ceremonial value is evidenced in their abundance in these burials; the presence of many and often specially decorated styles; their occurrence in kivas as well as their representation in kiva wall murals in apparent ritual situations; and, as reproduced at Pueblo Bonito in clay miniatures.

In the Southwest as a whole, temporal and regional trends exist in basket development, and, in the broad perspective of the craft, there are many small differences as well as similarities. Some of the differences are practical and merely reflect environment, for example, variation in materials, while others are reflective of art concepts, such as design differences.

Further, there are certain overall features: Anasazi emphasis was on two-rod-and-bundle foundation, wood sewing elements, noninterlocked stitching, and counterclockwise coils. The Hohokams and Mogollones shared some of these traits; however, the former favored the bundle foundation and the latter used the two-rod-and-bundle style as well as the half-rod-and-bundle type which appears throughout its history. Haury reports that in charred Mogollon pieces the two-rod-and-bundle style and non-interlocking stitches prevailed.

Basketry from smaller areas within the Southwest reflect interesting traits also. Both Upper Gila and Mimbres basketry are said to be one hundred percent Basketmaker-Pueblo, while the Hueco district leaned heavily away from the north and to the south and southeast in its interlocked stitches, bundle foundation, yucca and sotol sewing splints, and in true splitting of stitches.

Twilling was more important in the Anasazi than in the Hohokam and Mogollon areas.

Materials present differences that can be related at least in part to environment. In the Anasazi, woody substances were more commonly used for both foundations and sewing materials. Whole willow rods, alone or in combination with grasslike substances, formed the foundation, and willow shoots were split for the sewing material. To the south in the Hohokam area, and to the southeast, there was more emphasis on bundles of grass, split yucca, or like materials for the foundation; too, the sewing elements were more frequently of the same types of materials. Abundant use of yucca or beargrass in the Hueco area is a good example of this—in fact, almost all sewing is done in yucca in this southeastern section. In technology, there are environmental influences as well as dictates by the very nature of the method itself. For example, all preceding comments apply to the coiled technique. In plaiting, however, yucca leaves or comparable materials were used throughout the Southwest; rods would be almost impossible to use in this technique. Wicker is less frequently found where lighter rodlike materials are scarce; fine willow twigs and rabbit brush were and still are good materials to be used in this technique. Haury notes in his Canyon Creek report that the materials in wicker pieces were unidentified but that "their appearance is identical with those employed by the Hopi," which would mean, basically, rabbit brush. Perhaps this explains the more limited use of wicker to the south, for these materials are limited, if not lacking, near more southerly sites.

Certainly basket forms are dictated first and foremost by use, but materials, technology, and personal (or cultural, and, thus, regional) preferences are also important factors. Obviously plaited and plain wicker could not be used in the production of containers for liquids, but a tight twined wicker, which could be pitched, and coiled weaves were used for such purposes. Coiled work allows for the greatest diversity in form; therefore, it was the most popular technique for all the Southwest. More forms are found throughout the Anasazi area, perhaps in part because pottery as a utensil-producing craft was late in arriving there; in later years, the retention of basketry forms for ritual uses may explain a possible greater abundance of this commodity in the Anasazi area. Eccentric forms, such as the deeply bifurcated basket, may have been preserved solely for ceremonial purposes. Too, the seeming greater conservatism in the Pueblo area may well have contributed its share to the development of finer weaving in the classic period.

The majority of baskets were undecorated, but those bearing ornamentation are more important in this study; however, both plain and decorated styles reflect much of significance in this craft, particularly in such matters as form, stitch and coil counts, and foundations. Design was probably more of a regional matter than any of the just mentioned characteristics; it was also indicative of time. Because of the dearth of basketry in the Hohokam and Mogollon areas in general, and because of the limited decoration which has been found, little can be said for these two areas beyond the following. Decoration was simple; it was structural in plaiting; and it was limited in colors, usually black alone used in coiled work. Designs were made up of limited elements, and motifs were not as complex as they were on northern Anasazi basketry. In fact, even in the intermediate areas, the Upper Gila, the southern Anasazi, and the Patayan regions, there was less complex designing as a whole.

All things considered, the best temporal analysis can be made in the northern Anasazi. Beginning with Basketmaker II, quite sophisticated black designs appear on large conical burden baskets, trays, and bowls. This is one of the first important arts in the Southwest, along with earlier pottery decoration in the Hohokam area. Basketmaker III added a wedge-shaped burden basket and increased the size of trays. Also, in this period, more design elements and the color red were added. Designs became highly sophisticated, with repetition of the same (or similar) elements, which were frequently reversed and inverted. Pueblo I carried on Basketmaker III traditions, but to what degree is not known; in particular, there was complete balance of black, red, and the natural color of the sewing splints.

Little is known of Pueblo II basketry, but some degeneracy in designing can be postulated since patterns in Pueblo III became inferior and were greatly simplified as compared with those of Basketmaker III-Pueblo I times. One small diagnostic feature reflective of time is the rim braid which was, apparently, more complex in the Pueblo Period than in the Basketmaker; it is flat on top in the former and more tubular (around the coil) in the latter phase. However, the finest weaving, technically, occurred in Pueblo III times; also, a three-rod foundation was added to the two-rod-and-bundle style that prevailed from Basketmaker II times on. Pueblo IV saw further degeneracy in coiled weaving and designing alike. It seems that wicker became more important in Pueblo IV times as coiled became less so. However, all three weaves, coiled, plaited, and wicker seemed to have continued as links in the long chain from the beginning of basketry to modern Hopi work, and all three have continued into the 1970s.

Ventana Cave basketry would also support continuity from prehistoric times into the modern Papago period. In the Pajarito Plateau, impressions in clay would indicate a substantial background in basketry for some of the Rio Grande puebloans. Here stitch counts were 15 or better and 5 or 6 coils to the inch. Quite fine baskets have been made historically in this same area.

Thus, from many standpoints, it is not amiss to refer to basketry as the mother of the craft arts, in form, use value, and decoration.

Chapter 3

Textile Weaving

ONE OF THE GREAT CRAFTS that man has developed in his upward climb toward civilization is textile weaving. For the most part, it started in the stages before metallurgy and writing; in fact, weaving reached great heights before the time of these arts in several parts of the world. The Southwest was no exception in this matter, for there evolved a weaving technology and artistry of which any culture could be proud. So elaborate were some of the weaves and so sophisticated the designing that the Southwest prehistoric Indian can vie with any group of the same cultural level in the full scope of textile weaving.

Sources of information relative to textiles are basically the actual woven pieces themselves. As in the case of baskets, most of these have been found in the Anasazi area, due to preservation in protected sites. These pieces run the gamut from very small fragments which are important only as they reveal technology or a suggestion of design, to complete belts, blankets, and other garments which "tell all." Another source of textile information is the painted design on pottery or in kiva murals. For example, on a Mimbres bowl interior are represented a man and a woman wearing belts, his terminating in elaborate ends and hers in the rain belt long fringe (see page 74). Another bowl in the same report shows a man and woman dancing behind a blanket decorated with allover, diagonal, criss-crossing lines.

In the prehistoric Southwest, there were many objects which were produced in techniques and materials closer to the same in basketry than in true textiles. Also some were made of vegetal fibers reduced to fine cordage or thread ele-

ments, and employed techniques in their production more like those used in textile weaving. In essence, these woven pieces belong to neither basketry nor to true loomed textiles. They are, indeed, transitional pieces, and as such, they are included as part of the background on textiles.

Many stages of development from basketry to true weaving will be demonstrated. There is variation in material from whole yucca leaves to fine cordage, sometimes all used in one form alone, such as sandals. Weaves ran the gamut from plaiting in sandals, which sometimes was coarser than in basketry, to fine tapestry weave in bands and even in larger pieces. End products in the category of transitional pieces include many items, among others, sandals, mats, bast fiber textiles (which are all flat pieces), and finely woven bags which are more basketlike in form.

What, then, is a true textile? How do textiles differ from basketry? Are there really transitional pieces of weaving as mentioned? What is the real difference between bast fiber textiles and cotton textiles? These questions need to be answered in terms of specific examples in order to put the two major crafts, baskets and textiles, in proper perspective.

In general, a textile is a craft product resulting from the manipulation of materials so fine and flexible that some device is necessary to hold certain of the filaments in position during the process of weaving. This, of course, is not true of basketry, for all elements are sufficiently coarse to be manipulated by hand, without benefit of any controlling aids, throughout the entire process of the production of the piece. The awl is not a device fitting into this category, for it was used in a sewing process and not to hold any filaments in position during the actual weaving. Further, it seems reasonable to assume that some artificial contrivance was essential to the making of small and large pieces of bast and other early fabrics, for often the cordage, of which many of these pieces were made, was most flexible. Two sticks, with warps strung between them, sufficed in some cases. Also a simple weaving frame was probably used, with warps secured at top and bottom (or, if horizontal, at both ends), or at the top only, the latter perhaps true for making fur or feather cord robes. Probably tapestry weave sandals and woven bags also required some simple aid in holding warp threads in position as the weaver manipulated the wefts.

Then came the greatest change of all, the true or heddle loom, which was preceded in the Southwest by a belt loom. Seemingly, cotton may have predated this device, the true loom, by some centuries, and in its first usage apparently employed the mechanisms which had been worked out by the natives in handling bast fiber threads.

With this broad introduction in mind, a more detailed presentation will be made of the step-by-step development of textiles. In summary, there were baskets and some small pieces of weaving that were produced without benefit of any aids; also there were bands, some sandals, small and large bast and cruder cotton textiles that required some simple mechanical device to assist in the weaving process—these were transitional pieces; and there were true textiles, largely of cotton, that resulted from the use of the heddle loom.

Technology

MATERIALS

The type of material is significant in relation to the development of true weaving, both in a general and in a specific sense. Bast or woody fibers on the whole are coarser and seldom are or can be prepared to equal the fineness of cotton, flax, or other such materials. Even the very fine apocynum cordage does not equal the best cotton thread used in the prehistoric Southwest.

For the intermediate small woven products, a variety of materials were explored by the natives. Most popular throughout the entire Southwest were yucca and apocynum; the former grows widely and often abundantly. Whole or partial leaves of yucca (Fig. 3.1a) were used for mats, some sandals, and occasional other items. To remove the fiber from the leaf it is likely that it was soaked, beaten, and the pulpy mass scraped away, thus freeing the long, sturdy elements. These were then twisted into cordage, possibly by rolling between the palms of the hands or between the hand and the thigh; this cordage was of varying quality and weight. Cordage that was heavier was made from twisting diverse numbers of threads together. The result was material which varied from a sturdy fine string to heavy rope; these could be used for a multitude of purposes, from weaving to tying heavy bundles. Another native plant, apocynum (also called Indian hemp, or dogbane), is thought by archaeologists to have been processed and used in essentially the same manner as described for yucca. Fine apocynum threads have a softer feel to the touch than yucca; in fact, it is sometimes like cotton in respect to softness.

Thread and cordage were of extreme importance to man. In his earliest years, it was necessary to have some device for fastening points to shafts, to hold skin garments on the body, to carry food or other objects from place to place. Obviously, sinew or skin products sufficed for a time, particularly for the early hunter. The seed, nut, and fruit gatherer needed more. It was probably a gatherer who invented cordage, perhaps of twisted sinew first—which is found in prehistoric Southwest sites—and then he learned to use fibers of local bast materials. Human and possibly other animal hair came into focus as an important material somewhere along the way, either before or after bast fibers were used. Certainly the abundance and fine quality of human hair cords in many Basketmaker sites would suggest knowledge of its production for some time.

Prehistoric Southwestern Indians had a wealth of experience in spinning thread before the introduction of cotton. Of course, bast threads were prepared in far simpler fashion than the finer fiber, cotton (Fig. 3.1b); yucca fibers were probably spun between the hand and thigh for centuries without benefit of a spindle stick and whorl. Threads of bast fibers were largely two-ply, S-spun, Z-twisted (Fig. 3.1c). This means that the fibers were spun so that the filaments presented a diagonal line from upper left to lower right, comparable to the main line in the letter S, thus, it is designated S-spun.

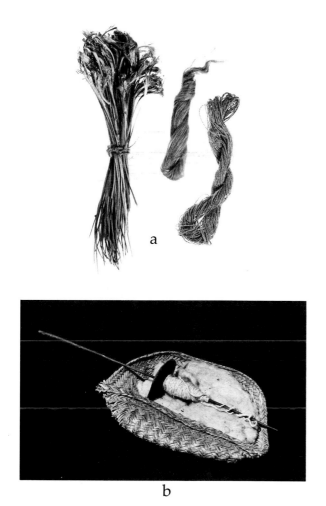

Fig. 3.1 Basic materials and threads used in textiles. (a) Bundles of splints (left) are found in prehistoric sites. They have been gathered seasonally, prepared, and stored against future use. Fibers removed from the leaves (center) are also prepared; so too was this hank of twisted yucca cord (right); the latter represents a common find in archaeological sites. (b) A prehistoric "work kit," showing raw cotton and spun cotton still in position on a spindle stick. (c) The seven vertical bits of cordage illustrate variety in sizes, twists, and materials. The second from the left is made of human hair. Seventh from the left is a cord wrapped with rabbit fur. The remaining cords are of miscellaneous types, some of yucca.

Two of these spun elements were then twisted in the opposite direction, with the result that the yarn presented diagonal lines from the upper right to the lower left throughout the thread. Again, as this line follows the main slant in the letter Z, it is called Z-spun. Early in their experience with thread preparation the Indians found out that in a single thread the combination of twisting fibers first in one direction, then in the opposite, caused them to stick together in far better fashion than if done all in one direction. Some believe the Indians worked the single filaments first down the thigh then the double (or multiple) elements up between thigh and palm of the hand (or vice versa) to produce these results.

Fur and feather cord were made and used by prehistoric Southwest Indians (Fig. 3.1c). In the 1970s, fur cord was still being produced for robes among the Hopis; feather cord was long-lived in the prehistoric period, persisting through Anasazi-Pueblo times. Rabbit skins were cut into narrow strips which were then joined; these were wrapped over or twined together with cordage of whatever material was available at the moment, that is, yucca most commonly, or agave, milkweed, or apocynum in earlier years, cotton later, and wool in the historic period. Skins of other small animals were used; if the strips were tough, like that of the badger, they were "sometimes merely twisted on themselves."[1] Feather cord was made by stripping the feathers down the midrib, then twisting the half piece in with or spirally around the cordage.

Materials used in this cordage in Basketmaker times, according to Kidder and Guernsey, were "narrow strips of the skins of small birds with downy feathers upon them";[2] these strips were wound upon the cord base. Later, in Pueblo times turkey wing and tail feathers were used. Both types of cord, fur and feather, were coarse, soft, and warm, and served for the making of robes and sleeping blankets and for smaller items or parts of them, such as sandals or sandal ties.

Apparently fur cord was used generously, particularly for blankets and robes in the Basketmaker Period. However, feather cord was used sparingly, for ornamental purposes, or for lashings for cradles in earlier years, and for whole fabrics in later years, particularly in Pueblo III times, for blankets large and small, as well as other pieces.

Other materials of less importance would include human and animal hair, but little or no wool until sheep were brought to the New World by the Spaniards after 1540. Human hair cord was used abundantly in Basketmaker times, less so but still much in evidence in Pueblo years. Dog hair was used, as well as hair from mountain goats and bear, and possibly buffalo. Hair was twisted into self cord or later combined with cotton thread. It is thought that, at certain times in prehistory, particularly in Basketmaker years, the women regularly cut their hair for this purpose. Some burials and figurines reveal women with unevenly bobbed hair and men with elaborate coiffures. It is interesting to note in passing that, in spite of the presence of mountain sheep and their popularity as subjects of pictographs and petroglyphs, this animal was never domesticated nor was its wool ever used to any great extent by the natives.

It may be that cotton came into the Southwest at about the same time as the belt loom, although it seems more likely that it preceded this device, perhaps by centuries. From Tularosa Cave, in southwestern New Mexico, comes the earliest report of cotton, a piece of one-yarn thread which dates back to a prepottery level, a time between 300 B.C. and A.D. 1, and another piece of the same dated about 500 A.D.; in the same cave but from a later level (500-700) were recovered a fragment of clay with a textile impression on it, a piece of cotton netting, and weaving equipment including a spindle stick and pottery spindle whorls.[3] Seemingly there is no further evidence of cotton in the Southwest prior to 700, but it had spread throughout the entire area by 1100. Seeds and matted fibers affirm its presence and perhaps its cultivation in the Hohokam area between 700 and 1100. From

Chaco and Aztec ruins come seeds and stalks, evidence to support the growing of cotton in northwestern New Mexico by Pueblo III times. Thus, because of the early and widespread occurrence of cotton seeds, thread, stalks, and fabric made in part or entirely of this fiber, some believe that there is the possibility of an earlier than Pueblo I appearance and, perhaps, cultivation of cotton in the Anasazi.

Cotton was apparently introduced into the Southwest from Mexico. "The only aboriginal species so far reported within the area is *Gossypium hopi*";[4] this is, according to specialists in the field, related to a southern Mexican and Guatemalan species, *Gossypium hirsutum*, with *var. punctatum* of eastern Mexico and Honduras, significant to the Southwestern species. *Gossypium hopi* was widely cultivated in both the pre-Columbian and historic Southwest; in the older period, this may have extended to the areas of present-day Colorado and Utah, for raw cotton has been found in the former state and cotton bolls in the latter. Also, a quick growing variety of cotton was developed, but it could not be raised in all locales, particularly where elevation and temperature or limited moisture, prohibited its cultivation. Fabrics found in these locations would testify to a developed trade in this commodity.

EQUIPMENT

After gathering the cotton bolls, the Indian removed the short fibers by hand. Cleaning or ginning and carding were necessary steps of preparation; exactly how these steps were taken is not known but several educated guesses would indicate possibilities something like the following. Some cleaning, or perhaps all of it in certain areas, was probably done by hand, the worker removing seeds and foreign substances in this way. Carding, of sorts, was probably done in one of two ways: the cotton was placed on clean sand and beaten with a stick (or several of them tied together at one end) (Fig. 3.2a,b); or the cotton may have been placed between two fabrics and beaten in the same way. These sticks, which have been found by archaeologists, were often willow, and were about two feet long. Both steps not only cleaned the cotton, but also had a tendency to align and mat the fibers together; these "pads" were then fed onto the spindle stick for the spinning process.

Reference will be made once more to the two basic elements used in weaving, the same as

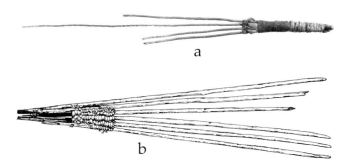

a

b

Fig. 3.2 Beaters for preparing cotton. (a) A photograph of a beater and (b) a drawing to show details of the same. Evident are variations in ways of securing the sticks in position.

referred to in Chapter 2 on basketry, warps and wefts. As for basketry, so too in weaving: the warps are stationary or nearly so, while the wefts are the moving elements. In the half loom or any device comparable thereto, the warps are fastened at the top but loose at the bottom, thus, not as stationary as in the true loom where they are secured at both ends. In the upright loom, the warps are vertical, the wefts horizontal; in the horizontal loom, the warps extend directly in front of and at right angles to the weaver, and are parallel to the ground, while wefts are simply at right angles to the warps. In one decorative weave, the warps are manipulated by the weaver; otherwise they remain in their vertical or perpendicular position throughout the weaving process.

In cutting bast materials, it is likely that a crude stone knife might have served the worker; the same tool, or a less sharp-edged one, or a stone scraper could have been employed to remove the pulpy matter from the yucca leaf or the apocynum stem, or this could have been done by pulling the leaf between the teeth. The manner in which spinning of bast fibers was accomplished has been suggested; there is, of course, the possibility that the spindle stick and whorl combination (Fig. 3.3a; also see Fig. 3.1b) was developed in this area, or introduced into the Southwest, and used to spin these local materials. It is also possible that cotton was twisted by hand at first, and later by using this device. The spindle stick is 10 to 30 inches in length; it is smooth, slender, and slightly pointed at one or both ends. Over it is slipped the whorl, a circular disc of 1 to about 2 inches diameter, and made in many forms of clay, wood, sheep's horn, gourd rind, or stone. Some are smaller in diameter and thick, others of a

wider dimension and thin (Fig. 3.3b–v). Kent maintains that the combination of spindle stick and whorl came in with cotton, was not used before this introduction, and, possibly, some whorls may have come into the Southwest sometime after cotton.[5] There is also the possibility that a simple cross-bar spinning device, a short stick bound low on a shaft, was used in the Basketmaker Period (Fig. 3.3w).

Although not too much work has been done on the subject of dyes, the consensus among archaeologists is that all dyes were derived from vegetal or mineral sources. The most common colors in order of frequency are brown, red, and black. Their probable sources are: brown is organic, black is usually from manganese or this plus trace iron, and red is from iron oxides, commonly hematite, or iron and manganese. Less frequently used are yellow, blue-gray, dark blue-green, and green; yellow is derived from yellow ochre, blue and blue-green are from copper sulphates, and green is thought to be derived largely from vegetal sources, with some possibly of mineral origin—iron plus a trace of manganese. The problem of fading of colors is significant; for example, some blacks undoubtedly faded into browns. Kent says that light browns, yellows, and pale reddish-orange tints may be natural colored fibers.[6] In the use of color, the natives generally dyed the threads; then they were woven into the fabric. However, both tie-dye and painted fabrics were decorated after the textile was removed from the loom.

Warp frames and other simple mechanisms preceded the true loom, for surely they were necessary for some of the fine bast weaving and, possibly, the earliest work in cotton. Perhaps the simplest of all contrivances was a mere loop of string from which warp threads were suspended for the making of the fine sandals of Basketmaker III times (Fig. 3.4a). Next in simplicity would be two small wooden rods or sticks about which the warps were strung (Fig. 3.4b); perhaps some means of securing these sticks in a taut position was devised. Several examples of short bands have been found with these rods in position. Then, of course, there were the important warp frames necessary to the production of fur and feather robes, larger pieces of bast thread, and early cotton fabrics. Two upright posts supported a cross-bar; from this were suspended the warps, often thrown over the bar and hanging free at the bottom. This may have been the type used in making some fur blankets.

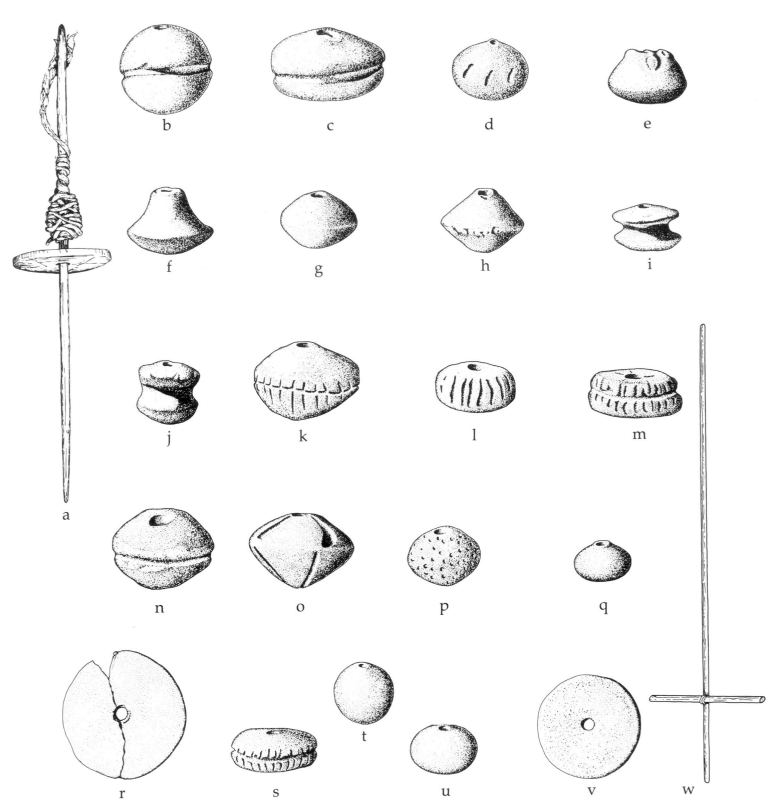

Fig. 3.3   Spindle sticks and whorls (all but *a* and *w* are from Haury 1945a, thus figure numbers only will be given). (a) A typical spindle stick and whorl, with a bit of spun fiber in position. (b,c,d) Several types of decoration on clay spindle whorls (72 a,b,c). (e,f) Both of these clay whorls show Mexican traits in their slipped and polished red surfaces; *e* reflects another trait from the south in its triple lumping near the top aperture (71 k,l). (g,h,i,j) Four more clay spindle whorls from Los Muertos. Quite regular in form are *g* and *h*. The depression in the sides of *i* and *j* are thought to be decorative features (71 g,h,i,j). (k,l,m,n) Further varieties of decoration on clay spindle whorls (72 d,e,f,g). (o,p) The decoration on *o* is more organized in the grooves above and below the widest diameter, while *p* has rather scattered holes over its entire surface (72h,i). (q) A plain, rounded whorl. (r) A thin, flattened whorl. (s) A whorl which is similar in decorative style to *m* but is better made (71 c,e,f). (t) A very round whorl. (u) A slightly flattened version of the same. (v) A thinner, disc-shaped style whorl (71 a,b,d). (w) A simple spindle used by the historic Pima Indians. It is likely that the Basketmaker spindle was of this type (Russell 1908, Fig. 73).

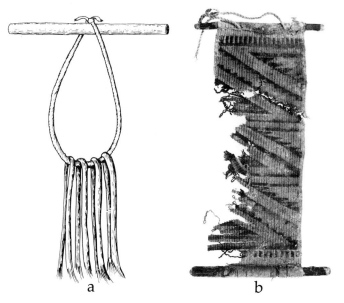

Fig. 3.4 Simple methods of weaving. (a) Suggested manner in which crescent-toed sandals may have been woven. from a loop of cordage were suspended the threads which formed the warps of the sandal; weaving started at the top. (b) Band with two sticks in ends. Warps were probably wound around the sticks, the latter secured in some manner, and the weaving was done on these warps.

In other instances, the warps were also secured at the bottom, to a second pole; this, of course, kept the warps taut and in position and made weaving somewhat easier; in the first case, the weaving started at the top, in the second, at the bottom. Apparently there was a vertical warp frame of this type used at least from early Pueblo years in the Anasazi, with a comparable fixed-warp (warps secured in a permanent position) type of horizontal nature among the Hohokams. It is possible that originally the Anasazi type was horizontal, but perhaps when they took weaving and the loom into the more restricted space of the kiva, they made it a vertical type. And it was probably to this fixed warp, vertical-type loom that the string loop heddle was attached, making it a true loom.

The previously mentioned warp frame, sometimes called the half-loom, is perhaps the simplest device of the several mentioned here. The warps were thrown over the bar or they were secured to a heavy cord, which was suspended from the bar. In some Northwest Coast looms resembling this type, the warps are suspended from a secondary bar, which is inserted in a groove along the lower edge of the stationary cross-bar; thus, the warps are held securely. In the 1970s Hopi Indians were still weaving the rabbit fur blanket on a loom that functions very much like the warp frame or simple loom. Colton says that rabbit skin robes are "made on a

rough loom frame" with bottom and top poles "attached to the floor and ceiling," respectively. "The warp is attached to the poles as on an ordinary loom. The warp cord is continuous, composed of a heavy wool yarn wrapped with strips of rabbit hide with the fur on."[7] It is noted in this reference that the warps are secured at the top and bottom alike; some say that the fur strips may hang free at the bottom in Hopi weaving. In any event, the strips are secured by twining weft cordage across the warps at regular intervals and several inches apart throughout the fabric. A double strand is attached at the edge and the two resultant wefts are carried across by twining with the fingers. It is likely that the same or a similar process was followed in prehistoric times.

Some archaeologists believe that around the year 700 the belt loom, complete with heddle, was introduced into the Southwest from Mexico (Fig. 3.5). Because of its heddles, this belt loom can be termed the first true loom. A belt loom is one in which the warps are strung continuously around two end bars; then one bar is attached to a fixed object, such as a tree, a pole jutting from a wall, or a post in the ground, while the other bar is secured around the waist of the weaver, hence the terms waist or belt loom. Or the belt loom can be strung with warps attached as in the larger loom. In this true loom, the heddle is the critical device; it is a stick which is attached to the face of the warp by looping a string to every other warp (for plain weaves), then fastening each loop string to the stick as the worker proceeds. The weaver can pull this stick forward with its attached warps, thus creating a shed or open space through which the weft or pick can be passed. Meanwhile the weaver has inserted

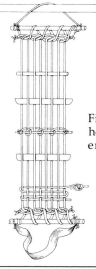

Fig. 3.5 A simple belt loom, with heddle, and with warps secured at ends (after Kent 1957, Fig. 7B).

another stick between warps in such manner as to have the warps, which are looped to the heddle, *behind* it; when this stick is brought forward, the warps left behind by heddle action are brought forward, and vice versa for alternate threads. By alternating the use of the heddle and shed rod, thus making an opening or shed each time, the weaver can quickly pass the wefts across the fabric, without the finger motion necessary for every warp-weft manipulation in all the preceding types of weaving devices. Elaborate weaves require more than one heddle, and the attachment of warp threads to them becomes very complicated; finger weaving may also be involved.

The following description of the true loom is based on contemporary Southwestern Indian procedure (Fig. 3.6). First, the warps are strung between two poles which are placed parallel to the ground and a few inches above it. This stringing is usually done in a figure-8 fashion, with the warps close together. Then the warps are secured in position by twining them on the outside position of each pole with a string heavier than the warp thread; this becomes the end selvage cord. Another pole is placed on the outside of each of these poles, and a heavy cord is looped alternately around the new pole and under the selvage cord of the older one. The first poles are removed and the second ones, with the warps attached, are placed in the loom, to become the upper and lower bars. The upper is beneath the stationary beams in

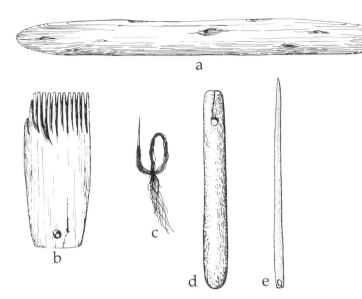

Fig. 3.7   Weaving tools. (a) Batten stick. Such sticks vary in length (8″–30″) and width (1″–3″). (b) A wooden comb used in pushing down threads in the weaving process. (c) A ready-made needle-thread combination, using a pointed yucca leaf and fraying out the fibers in the body of the leaf. (d) A bodkin made of bone, from a pit dwelling at Kiatuthlanna (Roberts 1931, Plate 28c). (e) A more slender bodkin, or, possibly, a needle.

the loom set-up, while prehistorically the lower was sometimes fastened to loops in the floor. These loops have been found in position in prehistoric floors; they are made by bending heavy withes (probably while wet) into loops, tying them together with other objects, and mudding or claying the whole mass into the floor with the loop exposed. With the exception of this last step, the lower loops, the Navajos follow this procedure; these historic Indians secure the bottom warp pole to a stationary lower pole in the loom.

In addition to the important heddles, the prehistoric weaver had several additional pieces of equipment which were used in the weaving process. A batten stick, which is from 1 to 3 inches in width and from 8 to 30 inches in length, may have been made then, as in contemporary times, of special woods and with loving care (Fig. 3.7a). Sword-shaped, with one side a bit sharper than the other—or both may have been worked down to an edge—they were rounded on the ends. In the upright face position, this stick was used in certain weaves to push or batten down the weft threads; or, inserted and turned on its face, it would hold open the shed. The other major tool is a comb (Fig. 3.7b); this is a fairly long, narrow piece of wood with teeth cut in one end and a handle formed of the opposite end.

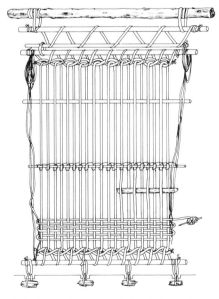

Fig. 3.6   True loom, with heddle and heald rod in position (after Kent 1957, Fig. 7A2).

It was used for pushing down wefts in smaller areas. Plain "needles" have been excavated (Fig. 3.7e); others were made of yucca leaf points, with attached fibers serving as threads (Fig. 3.7c). A variety of bodkins (Fig. 3.7d) and awls (see Fig. 2.2) have been found archaeologically; their exact uses are not known, particularly that of the bodkin.

TECHNIQUES

Prior to the introduction of the true loom the weavers in the Southwest had developed a variety of techniques for the manipulation of bast and, possibly, cotton threads. Naturally, plain weave was among these; so too was tapestry. However, with the acquisition of the true loom with its heddles, potentials became greater than ever, and the natives explored these possibilities extensively. A brief explanation of the majority

of the weaves known to and used by these people follows.

As weaving continued to develop in the Southwest, and, perhaps, as influences were felt from further Mexican contacts, many new techniques and styles of decoration appeared. The variety of weaves known to and expressed by these simple stone age Indians is astounding; some were basic and had been expressed for centuries; others were complicated in technique and productive of elaborate design. These new trends had all appeared by Pueblo IV times; some were widespread in distribution, while others were more restricted to limited areas.

Plain weave, wherein both warps and wefts show, was widespread and, in many pieces of workmanship, became more refined through the appearance and use of cotton. An over-one-under-one alternation prevailed (Fig. 3.8a), and thread counts averaged from 20 to 30, although

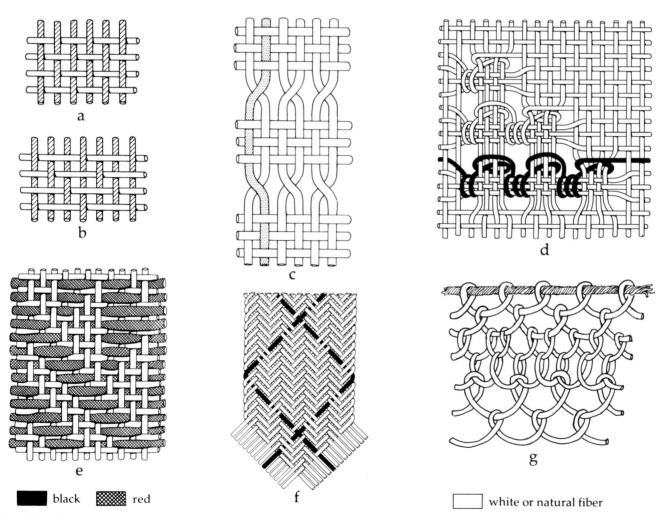

black   red   f   white or natural fiber

Fig. 3.8 Weaving techniques. (Figs. c through g after Kent 1957.) (a) Plain weave, single warps and wefts, over-one-under-one alternation. In plain and twill tapestry weaves the same (and other) alternations may be used but the weft threads are battened down, concealing the warps. (b) Twill weave, under-one-over-two. (c) Gauze weave: two warps are crossed and held in this position as one or more wefts pass through them, making an open-work effect in the fabric (after Kent, 28A). (d) Detail showing the process of weft-wrap weaving. A current weft thread is wrapped around warps and/or already inserted wefts, and pulled taut, thus making a hole (18D). (e) Detail showing method of brocading. The dark threads which carry the design are inserted along with wefts (29B). (f) An example of flat braiding, using an over-three-under three alternation (105A). (g) Detail of coil-without-foundation technique (98G).

one piece, perhaps the finest of all, counted 53 warps and 53 wefts to the inch.

With familiarity in handling this new material, cotton, finer spinning resulted in finer fabrics, both in plain or decorative weaves. One heddle and one shed rod were used in the plain technique. The simplest and the vast majority of fabrics in this weave were all white, or the color of the cotton; a few were of a single dyed color. Striped or banded plain weave fabrics resulted from the insertion of either wefts or warps of different colors; red-brown and black were the chief colors used. In plain weave, plaids or check patterns were made possible through the use of colored elements in both warps and wefts; experimentation occurred with these two styles and varied patterns were effected. Isolated solid patterns were not possible in this weave. Plain weave cotton cloth has been found definitely from the year 700 on, and is distributed from the Mogollon into widespread Anasazi and Hohokam sites.

In contrast with the simple alternation of over-one-under-one, plain weave has several other variations, such as over-two-under-two warps and the use of a rag weft, among others. The results of the first give no feeling of diagonal lines, as in twilled basketry, for a different approach is taken in the cloth; namely, the warps are used as pairs, without any skipping in successive rows. This is called by Kent a "half basket weave";[8] one piece using this technique has checks in the patterning. The second variation, rag weft, involves the use of old fragments of cloth rolled up and inserted as regular wefts, in an over-one-under-one rhythm. Sometimes bundles of cotton thread were substituted for the roll of cloth. The end result is something like a rag rug. Warps in pieces of this type may be of cotton or bast fibers, the latter usually yucca.

Both plain and twilled weaves appear in the tapestry technique (Fig. 3.8a,b). Because the warp threads are completely concealed by beating down (battening) the wefts, this tapestry weave, in both plain and varied twills, held a great potential for design; this possibility was widely explored by the prehistoric Southwesterners. Because colored threads could be introduced at any point in tapestry weaves, the potential in designing included isolated or continuous allover patterns, or designs in bands or stripes, in large or small elements, and in geometric or life forms. Despite the great variety in this weave, and despite a few life forms in coiled basketry, these people did not explore life designs in this or any other textile technique.

Gauze weave is more limited in design because of the nature of this technique (Fig. 3.8c). It is the only instance in native weaving where the warps are moved from their original loom position: two warps are crossed and held in place by a weft; thus, simple, edge-to-edge, narrow bands are created—the sole gauze weave design used in the southwestern United States. Characteristically, gauze weave bands alternate with wider plain-weave bands. The only other variation expressed in gauze weave in the ancient Southwest was a combination of gauze weave with weft-wrap. Some Peruvian fabrics reveal much more elaborate designing in the gauze technique itself.

Weft-wrap weave is productive of a greater variety of designs than is gauze weave. Basically, the principle involved in the former weave is the manipulation of wefts in relation to warps and/or other wefts. A selected weft is wrapped about warps and several wefts below, then about the next warps and pulled tightly about all of them (Fig. 3.8d). Sometimes the same weft may enclose three or four warps in this manner, and then do the same to two or three wefts below; the number of wrapped warps and wefts varies. This weave can produce edge-to-edge, end-to-end, continuous or isolated patterns. Quite varied designs were thus effected by the Southwestern weaver. Weft-wrap fabrics resemble drawnwork; the difference, basically, is that the former is done during the weaving process, and the latter after the fabric is removed from the loom. It is interesting to note that weft-wrap weave did not survive into the historic period in the Southwest.

Two additional decorative techniques are brocading, which is accomplished during the weaving process (Fig. 3.8e) and embroidery, which is done after the fabric is removed from the loom. In brocading, an extra element is inserted along with the regular weft, moving with it only so far as needed to create the design; actually, in so doing, the brocade element alternates with the regular weft. Embroidery is not a weaving process, for it is applied with a needle, usually carrying colored thread on the surface of the finished fabric. The design follows the lines of warps and wefts in prehistoric Southwestern textiles.

Perhaps the oldest of all forms of weaving are

those produced without true warps and wefts and without benefit of a loom. These include, among others, braiding, netting, and closed loop (often called coiled-without-foundation) (Fig. 3.8f,g). These involve the use of a single or of multiple threads and finger processes of manipulating them. In the first, braiding, which is a form of plaiting, threads are fastened at one end point or plane and worked over and under each other in some definitive scheme in the mind of the weaver. Twined plaiting, a related technique, also involves threads attached along a common plane; however, they are twisted together, that is, "adjoining threads make one or more twists about each other, separate to become units of new pairs, and then return to their original positions."[9] A twine-plaited shirt was excavated at the Tonto Ruins (see Fig. 3.34).

Design Layouts

In textiles, as in baskets and ceramics, definite styles of adaptation of the design to the total shape of the object are called design layout. Design layout is also referred to as area of decoration or primary layout; if there is additional division within the basic layout, this is called secondary layout. Very definite styles are found in prehistoric textiles, with a limited number being more popular than others. Compared to pottery, there are not as many layout styles in textiles.

Basically, the primary and secondary layouts in textiles include the following (Fig. 3.9). Allover primary layouts were very popular; also, this type has more secondary layouts than any of the other styles; they include banded, repeated, integrated, and off-set quartered. This allover style presents the most complicated designs on fabrics; although favored for use on large pieces such as blankets, this arrangement is also found on smaller objects such as breechcloths. Two simpler styles of design arrangement include centered and banded. Centered is a large or small pattern placed literally in the center of the fabric. The term banded is included as a layout style for there are examples of end-banded decoration that cannot be placed in the allover banded category. There might be one, two, three, or a half dozen bands and/or stripes confined to the two ends of the piece, with the central portion left undecorated. One addition to this layout class might be termed single-end or

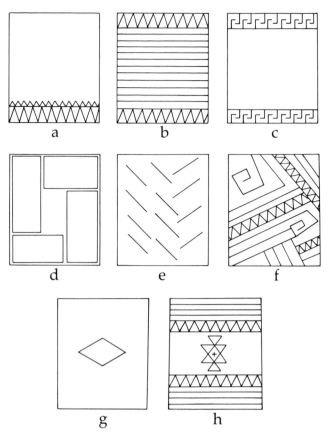

Fig. 3.9 Design layouts found in prehistoric Southwestern fabrics: (a) end half-banded; (b) allover banded; (c) end banded; (d) off-set quartered; (e) allover repeated; (f) allover integrated; (g) centered; (h) composite: centered-banded.

one-end banded; such an arrangement appears particularly on kilts. Comments relative to this last style can also be applied to a single half-band, one in which there is no straight line on one side of the band, usually on the inner side. A composite layout might combine a centered and a banded style.

Transitional Weaving

Since many fabrics are represented in small fragments only, they cannot be identified as to original form, size, design layout, and, in some instances, design elements or motifs originally used. Insofar as is possible, complete or nearly complete, or restorable examples will be discussed; details from fragments will supplement facts noted in whole or nearly whole pieces. More is known about Anasazi textiles than is known about those from the Mogollon and Hohokam areas, only because the Anasazi area enjoyed better preservation. Technique only is discernable in some of the charred pieces or in clay or other imprints of fragments from some of the sites in the other two areas; too frequently this is all there is to study. Only when design was expressed in the weave will patterning be so much as indicated.

A number of lesser pieces of weaving serve to exemplify intermediate stages in the development from basketry to true weaving. Although many of the transitional types of weaving were confined to the Basketmaker Period, some did continue into Pueblo times. If there were no drastic changes in materials, technologies, and/or forms, pieces of transitional weaving will be considered in this section; however, if significant changes did occur in one or several of these matters, they will be discussed in the next section of this chapter on loom weaving and cotton textiles. The first section will deal primarily with the Basketmaker Period and examine both small pieces—sandals, belts, and bands of bast—and larger pieces—mats, robes, and blankets of basically noncotton materials; and the following section will discuss the Pueblo Period and the large variety of fabrics—primarily cotton—produced on the true loom. Some overlapping occurs between Basketmaker and Pueblo times.

SANDALS

Hide sandals, generally simple and crude and sometimes with yucca ties, were made by the ancients, but far more important to this story are those of whole bast elements such as yucca leaves or cedar bark strips, or of twisted filaments or fibers of the same. In shape, technology, and decoration, these varied from period to period, with, of course, certain carryovers (Fig. 3.10). The earliest Basketmaker sandals were square-toed and square-heeled, while later in the same period, they became crescent- or round-toed. In Pueblo times, round-toed styles preceded a notched-toed sandal. Even pointed toes were made by these prehistoric people.

Methods of producing varied forms also reflect the general time factor involved. Square-toed sandals were made in either a plaited or wicker technique, both definitely within the basketry tradition. Plaited sandals were often woven of the whole yucca leaf in these alternations: in wider leaves, usually a simple over-one-under-one rhythm was characteristic and produced a large checkerwork; or, in narrower leaves, possibly a twill plaiting with an over-

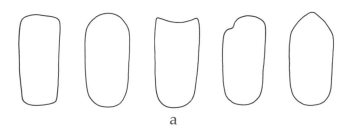

a

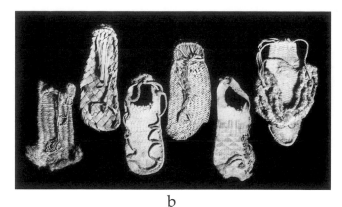

b

Fig. 3.10 Variety of shapes in sandals: (a) In the sketch, from left to right, are square-toed and square-heeled, round-toed, crescent-toed, notched-toed, and pointed-toed. (b) In the photograph from left to right are: a square-toed sandal of feather cord; an almost round-toed, yucca sandal; one round-toed, woven; a notched-toed, of yucca leaves, plaited; a beautifully designed crescent-toed cordage sandal; and a pointed-toed example, with a heavy feather cord tie.

two-under-two resulting in simple allover zigzags or chevronlike designs (Fig. 3.11a). In the Sierra Anchas, Haury found sandals woven in an over-two-under-one rhythm. Leaves were carried straight or diagonally across the sandal, bent at the edges and then woven back again to the opposite edge in the same manner. In the over-one-under-one alternation found at Tularosa Cave, one sandal had the ends of yucca merely tucked back onto the top of the piece, while another had the ends woven back into the same position.

In these plaited, whole or split-leaf sandals, there is quite a range in quality. In the plain plaited, generally there are 4 to 12 leaves, while in the twill, leaves tend to be more numerous, ranging from 8 to 16, and, rarely, up to 20 or 25. Quite naturally, the higher count of elements involved split leaves or narrow-leafed yucca, while low count sandals resulted from the use of whole, broad leaves. The use of heavy elements may account for the square-toed sandal.

The second type of crude sandal, that made of juniper bark, was produced by loosely gathering together a number of shredded pieces or heavy fibers of this material and using them as a unit. The sandal was then woven as was the crude yucca piece. Perhaps because the material is softer and more flexible, the cedar-bark sandal often had a rounded toe. Coarse yucca cord was used to make the pointed-toed sandal, which was the best piece made in the southern part of the Anasazi; it did not, of course, measure up to the standards of the crescent-toed northern Anasazi sandal.

A sandal made in the wicker technique might utilize either a single yucca leaf, double leaves, a stem or rod (or several), each bent to form a U-shape which served as an end-to-end foundation over which the yucca leaves were woven back and forth across the sandal width (Fig. 3.11b). If the leaves were longer, they might be woven back and forth several times; if shorter, they might go over twice and under once. Often in this style the wider portion of the leaf was brought out on the under or sole side and frayed, thus making a cushionlike bottom to the sandals. Some variations in this type include the following: warps might be 4 to 6 in number, and they might be of leaf strands or even of yucca cordage; wefts might be of crushed yucca leaves or of slightly twisted yucca fibers. There was no particular artistry in this sandal.

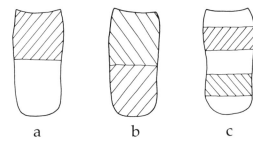

Fig. 3.12   Areas of decoration on sandals: (a) the front half of the sandal in one weave (or design) and the other plain; (b) both halves decorated but in different ways; or (c) banded decoration. There are other styles, of course.

Without question, the finest and most decorative of all sandals, along with some rounded- or notched-toed styles (Fig. 3.11c), are the crescent-toed variety, made in Basketmaker III times. Fine yucca or apocynum cordage was used for this crescent-toed sandal; weaves of which it was made include plain and tapestry, with variations on the latter. The number of warps might vary from 15 to 36; there are differences in the quality of the weftage, too, with some of it coarse and some exceedingly fine. The variety of decorative styles was expressed in either: two types of weave in a single sandal; one or two types of weave plus color, the latter usually woven in; color painted on the finished surface; the insertion of extra cords during the weaving process to produce raised designs; the tying of knots, also during weaving, and also to produce raised patterns.

When two different weaves or designs (Fig. 3.12) were employed, the front half might be in one, the back half in another. Or, as in some of the Prayer Rock sandals, the center portion is in a plain weave while the heel and toe sections are in more complicated workmanship, or the front portion alone might be decorated. Another interesting feature in many of these fine sandals is the following combination: a geometric design woven into the *upper* part of the sandal, in red, black, and yellow, in the center, the toe end, or all over, plus some kind of raised design on the *under* surface, confined to the toe or heel section or all over.

Designs on the often beautifully woven crescent-toed sandal are geometric and include lines, bands, frets, meanders, triangles, checkers, stepped and terraced figures, and a few more complex combinations of several of these (Fig. 3.13a,b). A sandal in two different weaves might combine a plain-weave front portion of about one-third or one-half the length,

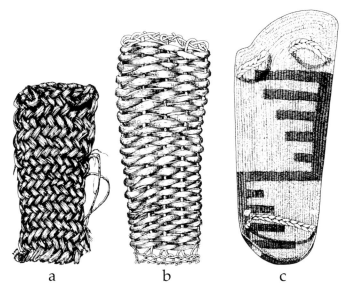

Fig. 3.11   Basic weaves in sandals. (a) Sole of yucca twill-plaited sandal, of the square-toed, square-heeled variety, from northeastern Arizona (Kidder and Guernsey 1919, Fig. C, pl. 35). (b) Example of a sandal made in the wicker-type weave, from a cave in the Upper Gila region (adapted from Cosgrove 1947, Fig. 92, Type 12). (c) A fine woven sandal of yucca cordage, from Aztec Ruin, of the notched-toed style (Earl Morris 1928a, Fig. 28).

a

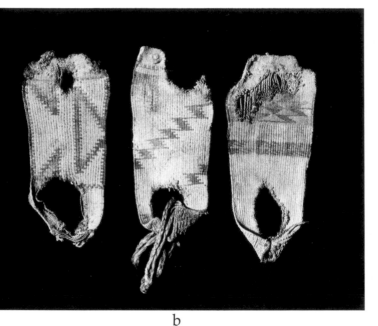

b

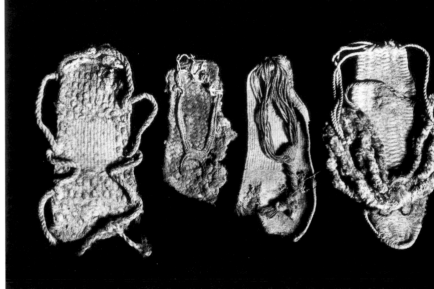

c

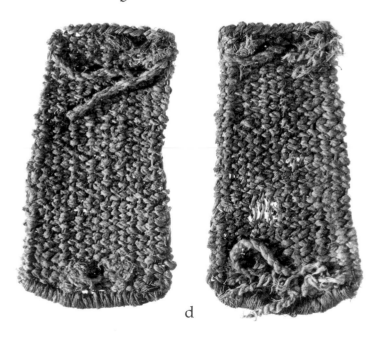

d

Fig. 3.13 Two styles of decoration were popular in the crescent-toed sandal, raised or colored designs. (a) In the first category of raised design, left to right, top row, are: end to end bands; allover almost zigzags; a plain forepart plus an elaborate stepped geometric theme; a plain front and a different stepped geometric decoration in the back half; another plain forepart, and an allover short-line decoration in the remainder of the sandal. (b) In the color decorated examples, the designs in two are in the central and frontal parts of the sandals. First are large open triangles, then fancy and diagonal zigzags. In the third sandal, the design is confined to the front half and includes a band and a group of triangle motifs. (c) Different methods of securing the sandal were practiced. Left to right are: loops at the sides through which heavy cords passed to tie the sandal to the foot; the next two show toe loops and extended cord which went around the ankle; and the fourth sandal shows a great abundance of feather cord which reached from several toe loops to cords which encircled the heel. (d) A pair of miniature sandals.

with the rest in a tapestry weave which utilizes some of the design units just mentioned. Seemingly, much attention was given to the weaving and decoration of this particular style of footwear, not only for wearing purposes (many are found with holes through the heels), but also the Basketmakers apparently thought that a new pair of these fine sandals was necessary for every burial. Methods of securing the sandal to the foot are illustrated in Figure 3.13c. Tiny sandals were also found (Fig. 3.13d).

Early in the Pueblo Period the sandal lost its previous artistry. At this later time it was rounded or pointed in the toe, and seldom decorated; sometimes the underside carried a coarse pattern. The weaving, too, was coarse. Although a bit of raised, colored design appeared in the full Pueblo Period, it was simpler by far, and the weaving continued to be coarse. Also, it was at this later time that the sandal assumed another style, the notched toe.

Some interesting variations on weave were observed in Tularosa or Cordova Cave cordage sandals.[10] For example, some had a continuous outer warp, and some had concentric warps. It is of interest to note that in the noncrescent-toed, cordage sandal, which was often round at the toe, found in earlier or later levels, the number of warp elements varies considerably, from 4 to 12 or occasionally more. However, they never reach the higher numbers of the crescent-toed style.

Through the years, archaeologists have come to some interesting conclusions regarding the making and wearing of sandals. Some believe that this foot-gear was more or less paired, and surely it would seem that at least one type, the notched-toed sandal must have been. The finding of a pair of sandals in many Basketmaker burials would support this idea also. On the other hand, Morris thinks it is quite possible that the Basketmakers did not necessarily pair their footgear, with some exceptions. "The majority of the houses contained from one to many worn sandals, often in piles on the floors or benches ... The footprints on the floor of one house would indicate that the people went barefoot when indoors, at least some of the time. The piles of characteristically unpaired sandals may be interpreted to be a common store from which a person could take two to wear when he went outside."[11] Another interesting suggestion made by Morris is that perhaps the plaited or twilled sandal of wide yucca leaves was used

more frequently in the winter, and, because of its larger size, possibly as an overshoe, to be worn over finer sandals.

TWINED-WOVEN BAGS

Another interesting item which bridged the gap between baskets and textile weaving is the twined-woven bag. It is quite possible that in the production of this piece a device was resorted to which would make it a true transitional type: some archaeologists believe that a number of warp elements were suspended from a stationary point or object, such as a stick secured in a house wall, or from a sturdy limb of a tree, thus freeing the hands for the weaving in of wefts. This, too, is an idea comparable to that mentioned in relation to the suspension of cords in making the crescent-toed sandal.

Twined bags were made of fine apocynum or yucca cordage. They are straight sided and almost flat bottomed, rather like deep but flexible pails; or they are slightly constricted at the mouth, with full bodies, and more rounded at the base, making them egg-shaped (Fig. 3.14). Characteristically, they are decorated with red and black bands; these run the gamut from simple stripes of either or both colors, to wider bands of one color bordered by the opposite color, or two narrow stripes of one color; between them are diagonal lines or other simple geometric themes such as stacked or zigzag triangles, joined tiny squares forming cogwheels, and plain zigzags (Fig. 3.14). Often the design covers all or most of the bag's surface. Guernsey and Kidder report that color was attained by rubbing the current weft with dye. They also give sizes from about 1½ inches to 2 feet or more in length in bags they excavated in northeastern Arizona.[12] There are also examples of woven bags with designs painted on them.

There were, of course, other types of bags, most of them inferior to this woven style. Some larger storage bags were made of cedar bark or whole, narrow yucca leaves; simple twining was employed with the first material, while in the second, twill plaiting was done, for example, in a 2-1-2-1 alternation. And there were bags, particularly smaller ones, made of human hair and yucca cordage in earlier days, and with cotton later, which were produced in a coil-without-foundation weave. Three such almost-complete yucca bags from the Prayer Rock District measured between 13 and 13¾ inches in length and between 7½ and 11¾ inches in diameter.[13]

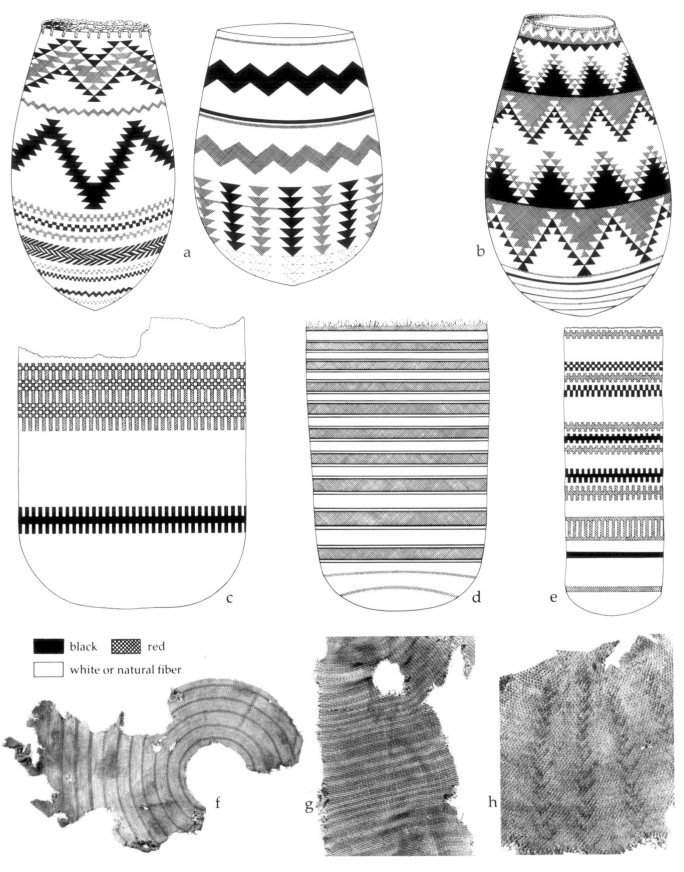

Fig. 3.14 Varieties of woven bags. (a) Two twined-woven bags of apocynum, both in black and red, northeastern Arizona (Guernsey and Kidder 1921, pl. 26A). (b) This bag was painted on both the inside and outside in red and black, from White Dog Cave (ibid., pl. 28). (c) A twined bag; the original was egg-shaped, with designs in red and black, from Prayer Rock District (Elizabeth Morris 1959a, Fig. 95). (d) Twined woven bag from White Dog Cave, decorated in red and black (Guernsey and Kidder 1921, pl. 30g). (e) A bag made by the coil-without-foundation method, with red and black designs. Prayer Rock District (Elizabeth Morris 1959a, Fig. 97). (f) In the photos are: fragment of twined-woven bag with parallel rows of small zigzags and plain, wider bands; (g) piece of another twined bag with various widths of bands; (h) Close-up of twined-woven bag fragment showing rows of nested chevrons.

Poorly preserved designs on two had what appeared to be red and black bands around the bags; a third example had alternating red and black horizontal units of short or longer cogwheellike, or line, patterns.

BANDS AND BELTS

Many and varied were the bands made of noncotton and cotton materials. These were narrow or broad, long or short, plain or decorated. They were used as hair ties, belts, tump straps, garters, cradle ties, possibly for upper arm bands, and for other purposes. All of the materials and several of the techniques so

far mentioned in this chapter were used at one time or another in making this variety of narrow pieces. For many of the Pueblo bands, cotton tended to replace the Basketmaker bast materials.

Tump straps were slightly more specialized than other bands, particularly in a finished loop at each end. Frequently they were short, measuring about 22 inches in length, and about 2 inches in width. Several examples thought to be tump straps were 18 to 20 inches in length and 2 to 3 inches in width. Some of these pieces were in plain weave, but more were in tapestry for the latter made them stronger (Fig. 3.15a). Cruder straps were made; for example, one was made

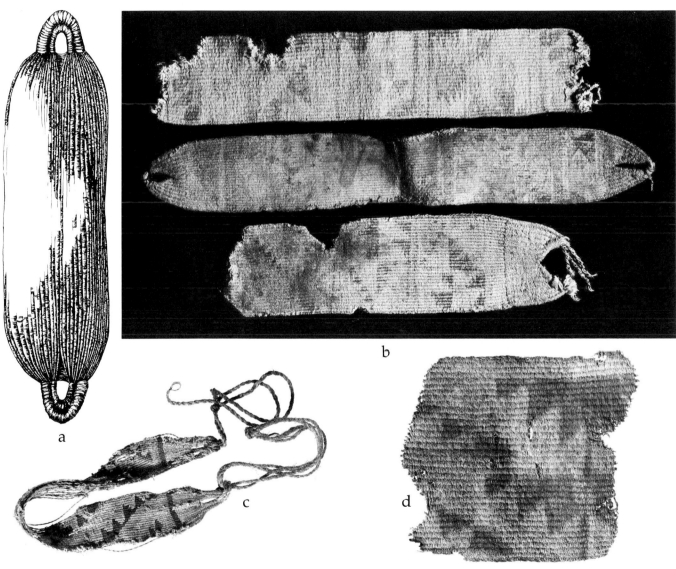

a

b

c

d

Fig. 3.15 Tump bands or straps. (a) Sketch of a plain tapestry woven tump strap showing manner of looping ends in the weaving process, the loops to receive cords for fastening to burden. (b) Three yucca tump straps, tapestry woven and designed. The patterns in all three pieces are dim but seem to have featured cross bands, diagonals, and triangles, all Anasazi. (c) A tump strap complete with looped ends, and heavy cords in position. Designs in this tapestry woven piece include cross bands and diagonal stepped triangles. (d) Fragment of a head band, perhaps of the type worn for tump straps. Made of yucca, the design is painted and consists of rows of joined triangles.

by sewing two or three yucca leaves together, fraying their ends, then twining or wrapping them in such a way as to make loops. Surely these were not as serviceable as the woven tump straps. Decoration in the woven band was in color or in the weave; yucca, or apocynum was dyed black or red, or rarely other colors, for the geometric designs (Fig. 3.15b–d). Stepped and triangle themes in black alone or in black and red were the most common; sometimes there were projections from each step. Dominant elements in these stepped or terraced themes in one piece include rectangular blocks and triangles. Another such strap from Canyon del Muerto, in the Texas Technological Museum in Lubbock, has L-shaped figures irregularly placed on either side of the strap; they are outlined in black on a red ground. An example that is interesting from the standpoint of colors comes from Duggagei Canyon, in northern Arizona; it includes black, red-orange, and blue in its design. Triangles are dominant in this painted design, and they are combined in several different ways; there are also diagonal bands with cogwheel edges.

Many fragments of other belts and bands and a few whole ones belonging to this early period have been found in the Southwest (Fig. 3.16). Bands thought to be head, arm, and leg pieces tend to be smaller in size than tump straps, but they are done in the same weaves and are decorated in the same colors; however, designs tend to be somewhat simpler. One piece is plain weave of human hair and apocynum; it has a

Fig. 3.16 Fragments of two yucca belts, which show tapestry weave and clear patterns. Many bands were made in this manner.

checker pattern in the dark hair and light apocynum. An all-apocynum band has a stepped pattern in dyed red and black elements against the natural color of the bast.

The more elaborate bands and belts of Pueblo times cannot be included in the category of transitional weaving, for many are both woven of cotton and produced on the loom and, hence, will be described later. However, a rare find is herein presented for it fits both time-wise and technically into the transitional situation. This most outstanding archaeological find in the way of belts comes from the Prayer Rock District, Obelisk Cave, and consists of six finely woven and two coarse belts, all of dog hair.[14] The six belts were found tied together in a bundle perfectly preserved. Each is braided and terminates in long tassels at both ends; they range in length from 58 to 106 inches, including the tassels. Two belts are brown, two are white, and the remaining two are white with brown decoration (Fig. 3.17). One pattern features a zigzag close to the edge and running the full length of the belt. The motif on the second decorated piece is made up of continuous, joined diamonds which also run the length of the belt on both edges (Fig. 3.17a, b,c). Other belts are also made of dog hair or yucca (Fig. 3.17d).

NETS

Nets of bast fiber cordage of varying sizes were produced in Basketmaker times (Fig. 3.18). Knotted together in an even and regular manner, they were made for a variety of objects: large and small bags; traps to be set over rodent holes; covers for gourds, clay jars, or other containers to facilitate carrying them; large ones, perhaps to help in catching birds and rabbits; and probably other nets for unknown uses. Artistry in most of these pieces is vested in the regularity and evenness with which they were made, and in producing the repetitive openings of even sizes and shapes. Early nets were not decorated.

APRONS

Aprons were made in the Basketmaker Period of various materials and in different ways. The simplest were of juniper or cedar bark strips or yucca cords thrown over a yucca waist cord, and fastened with yucca, apocynum, or human hair cordage by plain twining (Fig. 3.19a). Much more elaborate were the decorated woven belts

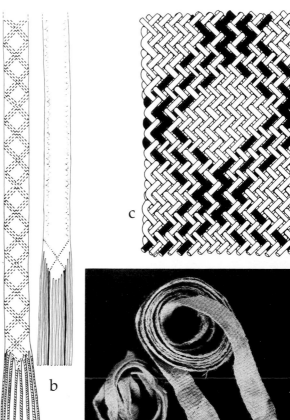

Fig. 3.17 Sashes or belts. (a) Dog hair belts from northeastern Arizona. (b) The end to end design down the edges includes in one, a simple zigzag and in the other, triple-outlined diamonds. The others are undecorated. (c) Detail of the pattern in one of the dog hair sashes of *a* (Elizabeth Morris 1959a, Fig. 76e). (d) Two other sashes or belts, the wider one (right) of yucca, from Ventana Cave, and the narrower one (left) of white dog hair.

with a hanging fringe. This style was made of yucca, other bast fiber, or of human hair, and they were about 2 to 2½ inches wide; one example from Prayer Rock combines yucca and dog hair, the latter contributing the white part of the design. Hanging from the woven belt is usually a mass of yucca cordage forming the body of the apron. Tapestry weave was the rule

Fig. 3.18 Fragment of a net. Even though it is a small piece it shows the regularity with which the knotting is done.

for these belts, with the design woven in or painted on the finished piece. Quite elaborate designs appear on several of the Prayer Rock belts. One has two horizontal, simple rows of joined geometrics in red (Fig. 3.19b); another presents a comparable theme in a more elaborate vertical arrangement in black, red, yellow, and the natural color of the yucca (Fig. 3.19c); a third features diagonal patterning, combining low, T-shaped units with zigzag bands and stepped triangles, with a play of black and red on natural (Fig. 3.19d); a fourth example, in black, red, yellow, and natural, repeats banded extensions from steps (Fig. 3.19e). As a matter of fact, there is a great deal of interplay in color, design, and form in many of these apron bands, with continuous or integrated themes the rule (Fig. 3.19f). Some of the most intricate and best designing of Basketmaker times is found in these women's apron belts.

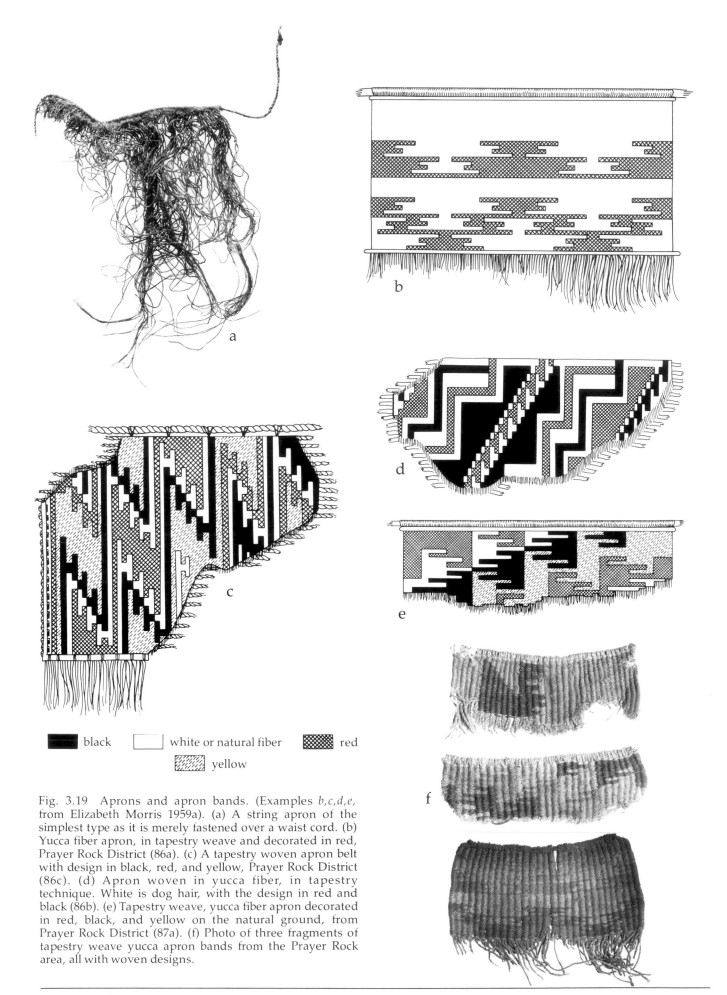

| ■ black | ☐ white or natural fiber | ▨ red |
| ▨ yellow | | |

Fig. 3.19 Aprons and apron bands. (Examples *b,c,d,e*, from Elizabeth Morris 1959a). (a) A string apron of the simplest type as it is merely fastened over a waist cord. (b) Yucca fiber apron, in tapestry weave and decorated in red, Prayer Rock District (86a). (c) A tapestry woven apron belt with design in black, red, and yellow, Prayer Rock District (86c). (d) Apron woven in yucca fiber, in tapestry technique. White is dog hair, with the design in red and black (86b). (e) Tapestry weave, yucca fiber apron decorated in red, black, and yellow on the natural ground, from Prayer Rock District (87a). (f) Photo of three fragments of tapestry weave yucca apron bands from the Prayer Rock area, all with woven designs.

FUR AND FEATHER CORD

Fur and feather cord products bear no designs. Serving utilitarian purposes as robes or blankets, they were very simply made. Continuous, soft, and heavy pieces of either material might have been suspended from the top pole of a half loom, or perhaps they were fastened at both ends of a weaving frame, or later, on a horizontal loom, and simply twined together at regular intervals of about two inches, with self material or yucca cordage. It is possible, even, that the material was not suspended at all, but rather the fur or feather cords could have been placed side-by-side on the floor or ground and twined together in this position. The latter may have been an early practice, but it seems more logical that one of the former procedures would have prevailed, particularly in later years. Certainly the weaving frame was known by Basketmaker III times, if not II, but it might not have been known to Early Man weavers. Evidently, the horizontal loom was known to Hohokams, but at an unknown date,[15] and the vertical loom may have been known to the Anasazis around 1100.[16] Kent notes that the belt loom, for narrow cloth, was in use perhaps before 700.[17] Morris suggests support for the use of the top bar weaving frame or half loom in the notation that one end of feather cord blankets is even and neat while the opposite end is not as regular.[18] Further, she notes that early fur cord pieces were made in the same way.

One fur piece among several from Ventana Cave measured about 31⅞ by 33½ inches (Fig. 3.20). Haury suggests, on a basis of these pieces, that, at best, these fur garments reached only to the waist. A few fur and feather cord robes have been found wrapped about adult males and indicate that in parts of the Anasazi, at least, these robes were large enough to cover the entire body. Fashion existed among primitives as well as civilized folk. Despite their lack of decoration, these fur and feather robes were probably most attractive to their makers in their soft grays and browns, and certainly their warmth was desirable to these people who had so little clothing. Seemingly, fur cord remained popular at Ventana to the end of prehistoric years, while feather robes began to supplant the fur types in the Anasazi in Pueblo III times and became more popular thereafter. Nonetheless, the rabbit fur robe was still made in the 1970s, though rarely, by Hopi Indians.

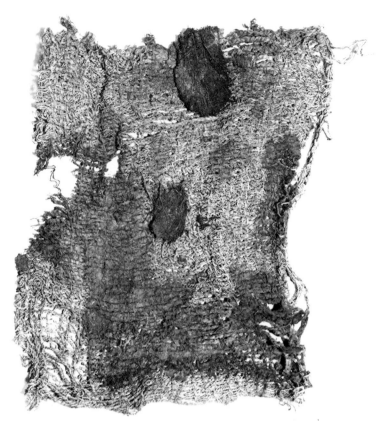

Fig. 3.20   A fur robe found on an adult burial at Ventana Cave. The fur was wrapped on a yucca cord base.

MATS

Large or small, early or late, mats were made basically with a basketry technique, either plain or twill plaiting, or by placing elements close together and twining them. The mat was made of a wide variety of locally available materials including, among others, whole yucca leaves or parts of them, tules, grasses, cornhusks, willow, reeds, rushes, or bark. Mats were made in an equally wide range of sizes, from about 8 by 14 inches to about 5 by 6 feet. Smaller pieces were probably used to set various items upon, perhaps even to serve food upon, as in the case of the modern Hopi flat (*piki*) bread tray. Large mats served many purposes, among others, sitting and sleeping pads, floor coverings, partition walls, part of roof construction, and wrapping for a body in which to be buried.

Although many of these mats were produced in a plain weave, and therefore had no artistic merit beyond good craftsmanship, others which were produced in the twill style were often decorative; borders were frequently ornamental in a fancier weave. As in baskets of twill weave, some had diagonal patterning, with zigzags, diamonds, or other simple and fairly large geometrics covering the entire piece (Fig. 3.21a,b,c). In some instances edges were plain, while in others a heavy border was attained by weaving the ends of elements back into the mat for an inch or more (Fig. 3.21d). Reeds that were twined into mats seldom carry patterning; one such piece used as a cradle back will be discussed.

One mat from the Prayer Rock District measured about 8 by 14 inches, and was woven with a 1-1-1 rhythm. It utilized the full yucca leaf, with both tips and bases of these long elements left unwoven at the two ends, thus forming a fringe. Other mats from the same area were made from juniper bark strips, corn leaves, or grass; each material was bound together with either single or double twining. A willow mat at

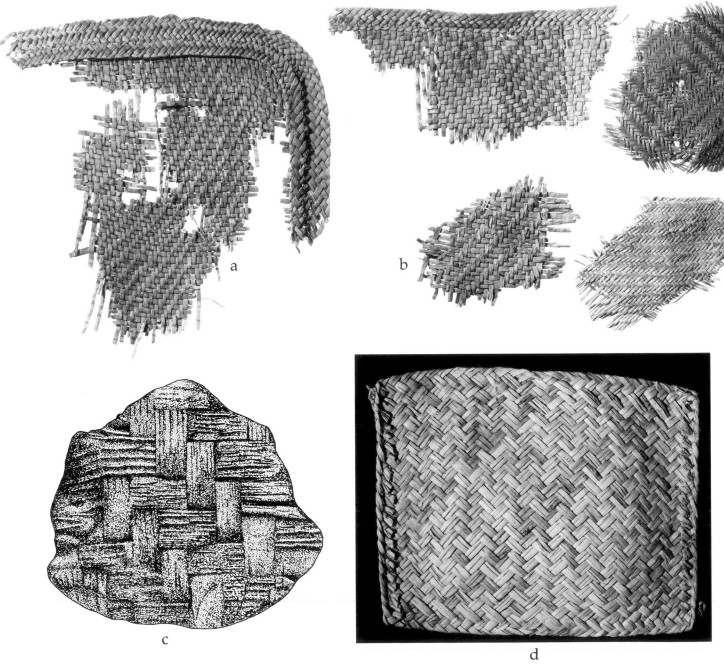

Fig. 3.21 Mats and a mat impression. (a) A large fragment which shows a carefully woven edge, and also a diagonal patterning over the entire mat. (b) Four fragments of mats, two of them showing diamond twill weave, one diagonal twill, and the fourth a twill which produced horizontal bands. (c) A cast of matting on the underside of a clay baking griddle, from Los Muertos, the original woven in a twill checker pattern (Haury 1945a, pl. 75a). (d) Complete mat showing how edges are finished off by weaving ends back into main fabric then clipping them off.

Pueblo Bonito measured 35½ inches wide by 53½ inches long. Another mat from this same site was made of carefully peeled willows, which had been bored at 3-inch intervals, and cordage was put through these holes to string the mat together; this piece served as a burial mat. A second mat like this but made of unpeeled willow and laced at wider intervals measured 5 feet 3 inches by 6 feet. Other fragments from this site show twilling of 2-2-2 and 3-3-3 alternations; in one of these mats there is an unusual variation in the form of alternate broad and narrow elements.

An interesting selvage occurs in an over-two-under-two rhythm twilled mat from Painted Cave. This 1⅝ inches wide edge utilized every other element for weaving back into the piece to form the selvage. Also, "at the inner border of the selvage a 2-element twine has been added to gain additional strength."[19] The corners of this mat are very rounded. Quite different are the selvages on several mats from Canyon Creek Ruins. Both are twilled, following a 3-3-3 rhythm. One had a two-ply yucca cord laid at the edge over which elements were carried; then they were woven back into the mat proper. In the other piece, the rushes were split down the middle: one half was cut off at the edge, and the other half joined like elements that were then braided into a sturdy edge. A floor mat recovered at this site measured 50 inches wide and 54 inches long. Generally edges are the same in a single piece, but sometimes two edges will be finished off in one style and the other two in another way.

Cradles should be mentioned in conjunction with mats for frequently the latter formed the main part of the baby carrier. (Discussion of cradle bands will follow.) In one cradle, horizontal parallel twigs were twined together to form the cradleboard backing. Interestingly, this twining was done in such a way as to create contiguous diamonds. A later example, from the pueblo ruin of Canyon Creek, has 20-inch-long side pieces of split agave stalk, with three horizontal twigs holding these two elements apart; the twigs were secured in holes of the side pieces, one brace close to each end and one in the center of the cradle. Slender rods were laid parallel to the side bars and were carried over the central brace and under the two end braces, secured to them by yucca string. To a comparable, but longer, frame (26½ inches long) was added a piece of twilled matting, with nested

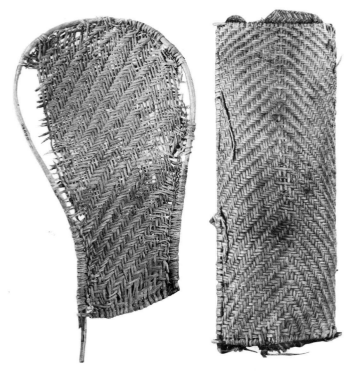

Fig. 3.22 Two cradle boards, the one on the left of twilled plaited yucca matting, with simple diagonal patterning, while the example on the right is decorated with allover chevrons woven in the yucca matting. The latter is from Canyon Creek.

chevrons running the length of this piece (Fig. 3.22). This cradle board is also unusual.[20]

Both rigid and flexible cradles were reported by Guernsey and Kidder.[21] A small, rigid example is 14 inches long and 10 inches wide; like others of this type, it has an oval frame made of a heavy withe bent into this shape. Unpeeled twigs were twined together to form the body of the cradle. Another rigid piece is 23½ inches long and 14½ inches wide; horizontal rods were placed very close together and lashed to the frame with yucca cord. Five vertical rods were lashed to the others with sinew in such a way as to create a zigzag design. Edges of the cradle were carefully padded with soft fiber and dressed skin. For the flexible cradle, comparable oval withes enclosed a backing of twined-woven rows of yucca leaves or matting.

Loom Weaving and Cotton Textiles

From the foregoing, it can be seen that the Basketmakers were active weavers throughout their history. Both cotton and the true loom were introduced into the Southwest, or at least became significant, at the end of this important period. It took years for these two significant items to spread throughout the Southwest; this statement is made in spite of the possibility of the introduction of cotton into the Mogollon area as early as the time of the opening of the Christian Era. Evidence for the earlier introduction of cotton is so slim and the known development of textiles in this southeastern section so mediocre, that one can raise this doubt.

In spite of their use of coarser fibers, in many ways the Basketmakers were most significant relative to later weaving: they were producers of a variety of objects; they developed many important weaves; and they produced a great deal of artistry. The items which they produced include: sandals; large and small bags; a great variety of belts and bands, including tump straps; string aprons which often involved beautifully woven belts; robes and blankets of fur and feather cord; mats; and cradles. A great variety of materials was employed by these weavers, including the two most important, yucca and apocynum; equal variety was expressed in the technologies they developed, most importantly, plain, twill, and tapestry. And certainly high standards of artistry were set by these early craftsmen, with simple and complex geometric patterning woven in colored elements or painted on the finished product; illustrative of these trends are the striped woven bags, patterned sandals and bands, and, particularly, the complex and sophisticated designs in apron belts.

All of these trends continued into the later Pueblo years in the Anasazi, and some woven pieces have been found in later levels of the Mogollon and Hohokam regions to tell of their survival in these areas also. Sandals continued to be made of yucca and occasional other fibers, but no later example equalled the excellent Basketmaker III styles in fineness of weave or in design. Tump straps, belts, and various bands not only lasted into subsequent years, but are frequently made of cotton and often are equally fine in weave and design. Also, the use of cotton and the loom produced new styles in belts and sashes that exceeded earlier types in all these matters. Generally, feather and fur cord blankets continued into later times, the former becoming more important in the north and the latter in the south. Cotton became far more significant as a material for both robes and blankets, perhaps in part because of the potentials

for decoration and the use of these items for ceremonial purposes. Mats persisted and were made largely of the same materials, served the same purposes, and enjoyed little, if any, changes in weave and design. New items or greatly changed old ones were produced with the loom and cotton, such as shirts, breechcloths, kilts, dresses, quivers, wide sashes, ponchos, and cotton cloth, which probably had a wide variety of uses.

Although cotton may have begun to spread over the Southwest around 700 A.D., much of the following discussion might well be placed between 1,000 and 1,400. A few comments might apply to earlier times, by two or three hundred years, and references to the kiva murals at Kuaua or in the Jeddito area would be a little later, around 1500. Areally, as wide a distribution of materials as possible will be given, with emphasis on the Pueblo Anasazi of northern Arizona, northwestern and northcentral New Mexico, southwestern Colorado, and southern Utah, because of the more abundant remains in these sections. Quite a bit of material has been found in what is called by some the southern Anasazi or the Sinagua and Salado; many examples of weaving will be drawn from ruins of these cultures. Unfortunately, there are too many open sites in the Hohokam area to provide any quantity of fabrics, but a fine selection comes from Ventana Cave and a few remains from other sites; these will be used for discussion relative to the most southerly weaving. Mogollon sites, particularly eastern ones, were not frequently protected, and some of those which were shielded are not in sections where cotton was cultivated; thus, little remains to tell of the details of weaving developments in this area.

CORDAGE

In discussing more evolved weaving of later years in the Southwest, it is well to begin with cordage (see Fig. 3.1). To be sure, cordage was equally important in Basketmaker times. Quantities of this material have been found in many sites, unbelievable quantities in some of them. Although cotton is most important, it is not always the most common material used for cordage at certain sites; at Ventana Cave, for example, very few of the 653 pieces recovered were of cotton. The majority of cords at this site were of yucca, with many of beargrass and soapweed;

human hair cord was very rare here. Two-yarn, Z-twist pieces were the rule. At two cave sites near Phoenix, cotton cordage was abundant, with very little yucca and apocynum; most of the former was single strand but there were also a few two-, four-, and six-strand cords. At Canyon Creek Ruins, cotton fibers were loosely twisted into two-, three-, and four-strand cords; some were colored black, brown, or yellow. Agave and yucca cordage were found at this same site, either loosely or tightly twisted. Cordage from caves in southwestern New Mexico presents several interesting variations. Very little hair has been found, but there was an abundance of cotton and yucca. Yucca was usually, though not always, Z-twisted; generally it was two-strand, although some was four-strand; and this cord was either dyed red, black, or yellow, or had color rubbed into it. Cotton was commonly S-spun; strands ran from two to nine-ply, with some cords made up of 14 or 15 soft strands; and it might be dyed red, black, yellow, or green, or rubbed with yellow. Interestingly, at Painted Cave, where an abundance of cotton textiles have been found, there was more cordage of yucca than of cotton. The small amount of cotton was loosely spun, two-ply, and black, white, or red. Yucca was made into two-ply, Z-twist cordage, which found many uses at Painted Cave. Human hair cordage was also abundant at this site; one piece was 12 feet long and made of light and dark brown hair. Human hair may be of Z- or S-twist.

Probably all the uses of cordage are not known, but many are. Also, there were different kinds of cordage for different purposes. Quality ran the gamut from very fine to coarse, from 1/32 to ¼ inch or more in diameter, with larger dimensions for rope; twist varied greatly also, from loose and soft to tight and hard. The more durable of available materials were generally used where there was greater strain; human hair was favored for heel-and-toe loops on sandals, for loops on burden baskets, and for some nets. Yucca also survived into this later period and was used as a sturdy supplement to cotton for nets, for fastening mats to cradles, for sandal ties, or because cotton was scarce. Other uses for the many varieties of cordage produced in the prehistoric Southwest include, among others, the following: the hanging front elements of string skirts, breechclouts, ornamental hair bindings, straps of various sorts, ties for innumerable things, fringes and balls on garments and sashes, selvages, braids, for the foundation of fur and feather cord, for mending, and sometimes for weaving in with regular threads to give greater strength to some fabrics, or because cotton was scarce.

Cotton thread was generally one-ply Z-spun, and usually tightly spun.[22] Almost all loom weaving was done with this type thread. Frequently weft elements were more loosely spun, therefore slightly larger and softer than the warps; sometimes they were of the same tightness and size. Two-ply cotton thread was used for selvages, mending, sewing, and embroidery; seldom was it used in loom weaving except for selvages. Three-ply cotton thread was also used for selvages. Four-, five-, and six-ply cotton threads are rare.

TIES, BELTS, AND BANDS

Ties, belts, and bands were numerous, and they varied in size, length, weave, and decoration (Fig. 3.23). They have been found in fragments and full length pieces all over the Southwest. The majority of these pieces are between 1

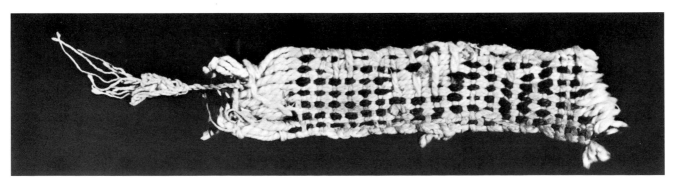

Fig. 3.23 Fragment of a small cotton belt, woven of coarse black and white yarn in such a way as to give a checkered effect.

and 2 inches in width, with some over and some under these measurements. Since so many are fragmentary, little can be said of lengths except to mention examples of complete ones that have been found; for instance a yucca belt at Ventana Cave measured 110 inches in length and 1 inch in width.

A few examples of belts, ties, and bands will reveal the general characteristics of such pieces. Probably the majority of these items were produced on the belt or true loom, although there are some exceptions to this statement. The yucca belt from Ventana previously mentioned had 23 warps and 7 wefts per inch. The main part of the belt combined plain and gauze weave, which would demand the use of the loom. From this same site are other loomed belts in floated warp and tapestry weave, and some nonloomed braided pieces of cotton. Fragments of beargrass and yucca carrying straps have been found in all periods in caves of southwestern New Mexico; braided cotton belts have also been found in this area in Pueblo times. Tapestry weave ties come from Montezuma Castle and Tonto Ruins;[23] in both instances they are designed. The Montezuma Castle piece is about 1 inch wide; the slit tapestry design is made up of parallel nested steps running the length of the tie, in white, light tan, dark tan, and orange-red. The piece from Tonto is ¾ inch wide and has rather crude black triangles along the two sides, arranged in such a manner as to leave a zigzag white line between them down the center. As both of these ties are so narrow, they might be classed as either hair ties or garters. This type is still made by the Hopis in modern times and runs about 20 inches long and 1 inch or less wide; the garter is tied just below the knee, at the top of the footless stockings still knitted by the Indians.

Loom-woven, warp-face belts, usually undecorated, have been found widely in the southern Pueblo area, the Sinagua and the Salado, and in Ventana Cave. None has been found in Pueblo III sites, according to Dixon.[24] Kent summarizes these belts as plain weave, warp face, some with weave stripes the length of the belt; their probable uses include bands for breechcloths, mummy ties, and possible hair ties and garters.[25] She claims, further, that they spread into the north during Pueblo IV times; certainly their later popularity would support this idea. A twine-plaited narrow band, 1 by 11 inches, comes from Mule Creek. Plain tapestry and tapestry twill were used for small bands from Basketmaker III through Pueblo IV times.

SASHES AND BRAIDED BELTS

Wider sashes and braided belts may be represented in pieces of cloth that are never found complete but are decorated. These fragments were produced on a regular loom in a majority of cases; the exceptions were probably belt-loom products. Apparently, since no full-length piece has been found and because often it is a decorated portion that has been preserved, these are thought to be the ends of sashes. Such styles exist today among the Hopi Indians and lend support to this idea. Also, on a figure on Mimbres pottery of southwestern New Mexico there is a representation of such a fringed sash. Figures on the Kuaua murals, a northern Rio Grande site, are represented wearing wide sashes without fringes, but with decorative ends (Fig. 3.24a). Kent is also of the opinion that some of the fragments that are both embroidered and brocaded are the end pieces of the broad sash, and well may they be; certainly the

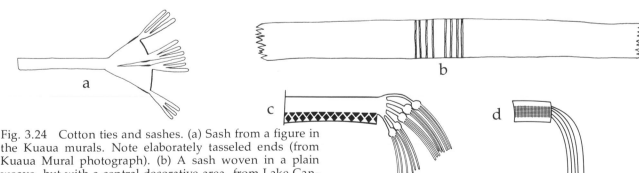

Fig. 3.24   Cotton ties and sashes. (a) Sash from a figure in the Kuaua murals. Note elaborately tasseled ends (from Kuaua Mural photograph). (b) A sash woven in a plain weave, but with a central decorative area, from Lake Canyon (after Kent 1957, Fig. 114p). (c) A sash which resembles the contemporary braided wedding belt in its ends with balls (cotton?) and long fringes. Along the sash proper are what seem to be pendant objects (conus shells?). (Smith 1952, Fig. 26k). (d) A long fringed sash represented on a pot from the Mattocks Ruin of the Mimbres area (Nesbitt 1931, pl. 23B).

heavier quality of these pieces would aid in their preservation.

A fragment from White House, which may have been a sash (or possibly a breachcloth), is of twill weave and has an interesting design made up of opposed nested chevrons. This is an unusual arrangement of chevrons, a theme which is not uncommonly used in twill weave; in this particular instance, it is in self weave, with no use of color. A plain weave example from Lake Canyon has two groupings of four vertical brown stripes on white cotton; these are placed in the center of the 7½ inch-wide sash (Fig. 3.24b). Another possible sash fragment, 10½ inches wide, is decorated in red, brown, and white zigzags; it is a twill weave, and again may be an end portion of such a piece. An example from Wupatki, which may have been a sash, is a 6-inch fragment in a reverse twill, with a chevron pattern that may have extended the length of the piece. It has a plain-weave border from which a fringe was suspended. Diamond-twill borders appear on plain-weave fabrics of widths that fit into the wide sash category. Irregular twills occur in like manner; one such piece, a possible sash, has a meandering fret pattern in the end portion. Haury reports "a band of gauze weave, six and one-half inches wide, which is bordered on each side with a strip of plain weave," which may be another sash end.[26]

The foregoing gives some of the possibilities in the variety of weaves and decorative styles that appear in wide sashes. Basically, plain weave was involved in many of these sashes, but it is quite possible that others may have been popular in this sash style at certain times; this possibility would merely follow the general trend in weaving as a whole.

Like techniques apply to small and large braided belts, although the larger belts involved greater complexity in arrangement and manipulation of the elements used. Braiding was done, in the simplest expression, with a continuous warp and small rods which serve somewhat like heddles.

Narrow braided belts, from just under ½ inch to about 1½ inches wide, were excavated at Ventana Cave; several of these exceeded 17½ inches in length, but none was complete. They were made of yucca or cotton; this is a good example of the late survival of yucca as an important material for weaving in this area. In the Anasazi, Pueblo III–IV, smaller braided belts were about 1 to 2 inches in width, and were made of white cotton in the usual flat braid. These probably served as hair ties, garters, and bands for miscellaneous purposes. From Painted Cave comes an unusual example, a brown-and-white-plaid patterned cloth that was torn into two pieces, each 1½ inches wide, and then sewed together to form a belt 3 inches wide, which is wider than usual, and 17 inches long. This braided belt is made of unidentified wool. Many narrow belts and bands are represented in kiva murals.

Another very interesting sash which appears late in the prehistoric period, is the wedding, or rain, sash (Fig. 3.24c,d). The latter name is applied to this attractive braided belt because of the long fringes at the ends which, according to the Hopis, symbolize rain. The first appearance of this style is thought to be in the Jeddito mural representations; however, there are many pieces of smaller braiding which preceded this mural by some centuries.

The late prehistoric wedding sash has survived to the present, but it is not as finely made now as some prehistoric examples. The modern piece, measuring 4 to 8 inches wide and about 10 feet long, has long fringes and decorative balls or pompoms at the ends; these additions have been found prehistorically also. As aforementioned, the fringed sash is represented in some of the kiva paintings in the Jeddito, but not in the Kuaua murals. The fringing of the rain sash is unique as compared to that on earlier braided pieces. Kent summarizes this as follows:

> Pueblo III belt fringes generally consist of square or round braids, often with a soft cotton ball, or pompom at their ends. Contemporary wedding sashes and those in the Jeddito murals are finished in a series of narrow braids an inch or so long, from which hang great lengths of braid strands which are twisted together, instead of being braided round or square. A ring of braided corn husk bound with cotton thread is tied at the point where a narrow braid gives way to twisted strands. Similar rings, appended to square fringe braids, and found by Hough in Bear Creek Cave, probably date to early Pueblo III.[27]

Kent feels that these rings were not a part of the northern Anasazi Pueblo III belt, but they are to be noted on belts of the Pueblo IV Jeddito murals.

This very old technique of braiding developed in many directions in the prehistoric Southwest. In addition to belts, a variety of articles were made by this process, for there have been found

a braided shoe-sock, an apron band, a sling, and a small bag. Then there is a multitude of square, round, and core braids (sennit), the uses of which are many (Fig. 3.25). These braids, which are widely distributed, serve as tassels on blankets, tie cords, and fringes on flat braided belts; this varied sennit probably served many more purposes than herein listed. An elaborate shirt with sleeves, found at White House ruins, was made in a combination of round, square, and flat braiding. Originally attached to the bottom of the shirt was fringe about 15 inches long, made of square braids with heavy tassels at the ends.

CRADLE BANDS

Cradle bands, measuring 3 to 5¾ inches wide and 12 to 16 inches long, were woven for the express purpose of fastening the baby over the stomach, to hold it securely on the cradleboard. Several weaves were used in the production of this piece, including plain and slit tapestry, brocading, and braiding. Examples of the last-named technique will be described.

Kent discusses nine cradleboard bands, identifying four of them as plain tapestry, one brocading, one a flat white braid, another of braided brown and white cloth, and two of plain-weave, white cotton cloth.[28] Cotton is the

Fig. 3.25   Sennit. Two upper examples are of heavy fibers (or leaves) but the lower one is made of a number of pieces of twisted cordage.

Fig. 3.26   Cradle band in twill tapestry weave, of cotton weft on a yucca warp with checked and striped patterns. From Antelope Cave, Canyon de Chelly. (Courtesy of Arizona Archaeological Center, Tucson)

predominant material in later years but several have bast fiber warps (Fig. 3.26). Generally these are woven on two sticks, or if not, the ends of the bands are attached to sticks, which then serve as toggles securing the pieces in position to the side bars of the cradle. One slit tapestry piece from Nitsie Canyon, with sticks in position, shows the use of brown and yellow on natural white cotton. There are three bands of design cutting across the width, a typical design division in Basketmaker times, with a pleasing finishing detail at the ends of the designed area, a brown line with short pendant lines on the outside. The main design themes are narrow bands and rows of sharp-pointed triangles, both oblique, another pre-Pueblo feature. Because the piece is made of cotton, it is difficult to identify it as to time.

TUMP STRAPS

One of the most interesting pieces made by the prehistoric Southwesterners was the tump strap, a narrow band with a built-in loop at each end (see Fig. 3.15). The latter detail, the bound loop, made the piece far more serviceable and longer lasting. Materials were also selected to give the straps a longer life; sometimes yucca cord warps were used with cotton wefts, or human hair was employed close to the end where the greatest strength was needed; tapestry was the common weave. As in the cradle band, tump strap warps were strung as a con-

tinuous thread between two sticks set far enough apart so as to produce the desired length for the piece. The loops were made in this fashion: warps were separated into bundles at one end and bound; the weft was then woven from this point over and under ever smaller groups of warps, from edge to edge, until finally it was moving over one warp, under one warp (Fig. 3.27). Generally, a short section of plain tapestry was woven, then the design started. Patterns, which were often combined with slits, include among others the following: a white line design of lines and steps on a brown ground; blue and brown stepped triangles ending in stepped "flags" and several meandering lines; limited and simpler triangles with plain "flags." Braided tump bands are also reported.

This brief discussion indicates that prehistoric Southwesterners produced belts, ties, bands of various sorts, and sashes, which varied greatly in size and weave; all these items were decorated in many ways. They ran the gamut from ribbon-like widths, under ½ inch, to wide sashes of 10 or more inches. Lengths are more difficult to characterize, but at least one example is 110 inches long. Uses were many and include the following: hair ties and garters; a multitude of belts and sashes worn to hold up kilts or to secure large garments at the waist; a band from which to suspend fringes for aprons or to hold breechclouts in position (these two will be discussed); protective devices to secure babies on cradles; wrappings on mummies; and probably a long list of carrying straps, many unknown. Furthermore, every known major weave developed in the prehistoric Southwest was employed in the production of belts, ties, bands, and sashes: plain weave alone or plain weave in combination with any one of several fancy weaves such as twill, brocading, embroidery, or weft-wrap; tapestry weaves, plain, patterned, or slit; weft and warp floats; braided; and gauze.

APRONS

Aprons have a long history in the Southwest for they are commonly found in the Basketmaker Period (see Fig. 3.19). Many of the traditions established then in relation to this piece were carried over into Pueblo phases. For one thing, yucca, apocynum, and other bast fibers continued to be combined frequently with cotton in the making of aprons. The basic form remained the same: a rather narrow belt which reached part way, or rarely, all the way around the wearer's waist with cordage filling out if it was short, and with hanging fringes, generally in the front only, in the style of precotton examples. Probably they were woven like tump straps, with warps between two supports; weaves involved were tapestry, which seems to have been favored, plain weave, and slit tapestry. Fringes are of two basic types: the first is an extension of weft threads, and the second type has fringe additions, which were made while the piece was being woven, in the form of threads pulled through the weft loops. In width, the apron belts are somewhere between ¼ inch (a veritable ribbon!) and 1½ inches; lengths vary generally between 8 and 15 inches. Fringes are, for the most part, about 8 or 9 inches long.

An apron band found at Painted Cave measured 1½ inches wide and 15 inches long.[29] It has yucca warps and cotton wefts, the usual Pueblo combination, and is in tapestry weave. "A piece of yucca fiber string was used as a belt to hold the apron in place"—this quote gives the probable general method for fastening the apron in position. At Canyon Creek the material in aprons is apocynum fiber made into very uniform thread. One of these aprons, which was found on a burial, reveals an interesting feature, in fact, an exception to the rule of front fringe only: "It consists of two duplicate parts, one being worn in front, the other behind."[30] Fringes along the front are about 10 inches long while those at the back are 18 inches long.

One all-cotton apron from Kietsiel has a designed band 1¼ inches wide. Of plain weave tapestry, the design is in brown and white, with the dark motifs so placed as to let the white show through as a negative pattern. Elements and units that make up the design include diagonally placed bands, heavy zigzag lines, triangles, and meanders. Another apron band from northern Arizona, one which appears to have been woven for a child, measures 1 inch in width and 11 inches in length. It is woven in slit tapestry and is decorated in brown stepped units in four pairs, which are separated by vertical lines. The background is the natural white cotton.

Not all aprons had these finely woven bands, and not all bands were decorated. Sometimes bundles of cordage were secured at one point and a string was run through at this same spot to hold the apron in place; such were some of the aprons excavated by Cosgrove in Upper Gila caves.

BREECHCLOTHS

Breechcloths were made of a fair variety of materials, cotton being most prominent but with some use of milkweed cordage and bark. Several styles of breechcloths were developed: the first, a long narrow strip of cloth; the second, a piece which is wider in front and narrower toward the back, the tapering of the cloth fashioned on the loom (Fig. 3.28a); and third, a short rectangular cloth which is doubled and fringed at the bottom. Some breechcloth fronts were doubled over and woven into position on the loom. The majority of these cloths are plain, but some are decorated on the front portion, either in twill or brocading. Breechcloths are typically narrow, measuring from around 5 inches to 9 or 10 inches in width. Length, of course, is more dependent on style; for example, one of the tapered types measured over 67 inches in length, while a rectangular cloth piece measured only 9 inches long. String breechclouts have been reported over a large part of this area; in particular, they seem abundant as reported by Bluhm in the Mogollon and by Cosgrove in the Upper Gila. Kent says of this popular style: "Breech coverings of string—worn either as clouts or with free-hanging fringe—had a wide distribution in the prehistoric Southwest."[31]

One fine example of a decorated breechcloth comes from White House Ruins; it is of plain weave with a brocaded central pattern. The main design is made up of concentric diamonds with

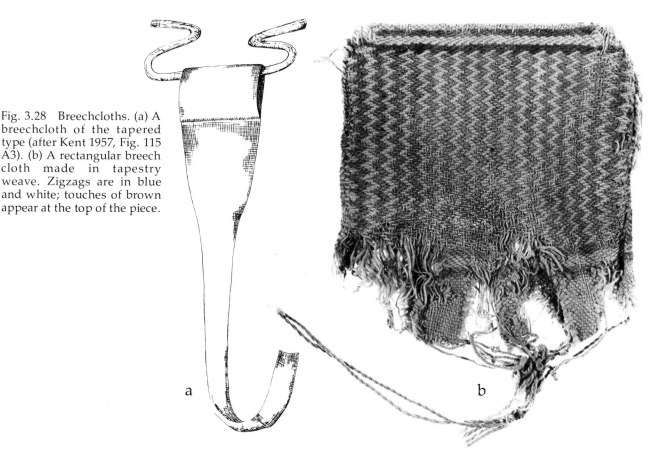

Fig. 3.28 Breechcloths. (a) A breechcloth of the tapered type (after Kent 1957, Fig. 115 A3). (b) A rectangular breech cloth made in tapestry weave. Zigzags are in blue and white; touches of brown appear at the top of the piece.

a

b

a second central theme of four balanced and opposed pairs of steps or half-terraces. Actually the pattern is black on natural cotton but it is done in such a way that it appears in the negative. A second decorated piece comes from Tonto Ruins; it is in twill weave, in brown, blue, and white. The design consists of meandering bands of brown and blue joined triangles with comparable meandering white bands between them; within the latter are repeated small squares, also in brown and blue. The resultant asymmetric pattern is effective, despite the small size of the piece.

A most decorative breechcloth was found at Gourd Cave; it is in blue and white, with a touch of brown, and woven in a double-weft twill (Fig. 3.28b). Basically this twill is accomplished with the use of two wefts, each a different color and each inserted in every shed. One weft color goes over every other warp, while the second color goes over those skipped by the first weft. In this front section of the breechcloth, there are two brown and one white horizontal stripes at the top, and over all of the rest are vertical, alternating blue-white zigzags.

Some plain weave belts appear with these breechcloths. In other cases masses of cordage served as belts, and in at least one instance a net served in the same capacity. At Ventana Cave

one breechclout was in place on a male burial while a number of them appeared on or near the burials of women. These included a belt and the cover which, according to Haury was a "mass of loosely twisted 4- to 6-yarn milkweed cordage, worn closely against the body and lodged under the belt, front and back. The cordage ends were free and dropped over the belt for a short distance. Belts were masses of cotton or milkweed cordage, smaller in diameter than the clout cords."[32]

KILTS

The presence of kilts seems to be problematic until Pueblo IV times in the Anasazi area. Dixon claims there is little evidence for such a garment prior to this last prehistoric phase, and denies that a wide rectangular cloth found at Hidden House is one, even though its dimensions fall well within the measurements of historic kilts.[33] Kent, on the other hand, contends that this interesting piece is a kilt, and thus it will be described here (Fig. 3.29a,b). The piece is 36¾ inches wide and 15¼ inches long (the latter is the warp length). It has "a design consisting of colored tapestry-weave units woven on the plain-weave warps."[34] These decorative units are parallelograms, 14 in number, and, Dixon reports, are "arranged in two alternate rows of

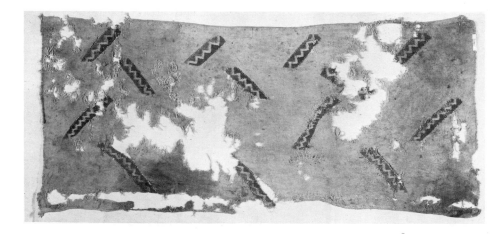

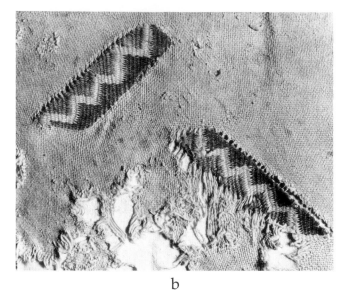

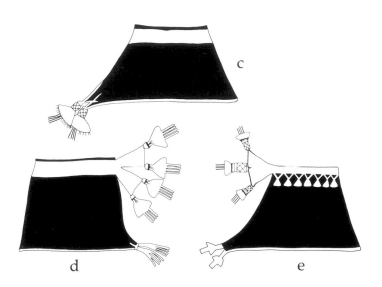

Fig. 3.29 Examples of kilts. (a) Kilt from Hidden House, Sycamore Canyon. The decorative areas are in tapestry weave and are insets in the plain weave piece. (b) Detail shows insets. (c) A black kilt from Kuaua Pueblo decorated with elaborate tassels at the kilt corners. (d) A Kuaua kilt with rather simple decoration at the corners but with an elaborate belt. (e) A black kilt from Kuaua ornamented with tassels at the bottom corners and with an ornate belt (last three adapted from photographs of Kuaua kiva murals).

a

b

c

d

e

three, slanting obliquely to the left, and two alternate rows of four slanting to the right.'' The parallelograms are made up of double rows of joined triangles, with their points alternating so that a zigzag is created down the center. In each unit one row of triangles is gray-blue, while the opposite row is dark gray-green. Wefts within the design units are heavier than those in the background fabric, and they number two to one in the plain weave.

There is no doubt about kilts in Pueblo IV times, for they are represented in great numbers on kiva walls at Awatovi, Kuaua, and Pottery Mound, and on pottery. Kent says there are no other actual remains of kilts beyond the one described in the preceding paragraph. However, there are such graphic representations of them in kiva murals that a summary of their features will be given based on illustrations of them. Too, certain additional suggestions can be based on the historic pieces.

The majority, if not all of the woven Kuaua kilts are black in color, and, with one exception,

seem to be plain (Fig. 3.29c,d,e). The one exception has several light areas on it that may represent design. On the other hand, kilts represented on the Jeddito walls are both numerous and often elaborately decorated. A summary of the illustrative material in Smith indicates the following possibilities in colors, designs, and weaves. [35]

One Jeddito kilt is apparently plain white with a fringe or, possibly, shells on the bottom edge. Another simple one is black with a light (or white) border at the bottom; this could be a plain woven band. Quite simple, too, is a plain white example with a narrow edge stripe in black, which is worn on the right side; this appears so simple that it might be suggested that it too is a woven border. Several kilts appear to be plain black with a light design on the bottom border that incorporates triangles with hooks. Diagonal geometric designs in the form of squares with dots in the center appear on several kilts; these may be representative of tie-dye decoration. Elaborate allover geometrics, including triangles, squares, and others, in at least two instances, may represent painted kilts; also, several examples of vertical bands may be painting. One kilt has edge-to-edge almost-stripes over the greater part of its surface; near the bottom is a row of triangles, and at the bottom a wide band with zigzags in it. This piece looks very much like a modern Navajo twilled saddle blanket; hence it is proposed that the example painted on the kiva wall could have been in this weave.

What might be a weft-wrap (or tie-dye?) kilt in the Jeddito area has outline diamonds with dots within them over all the fabric. Perhaps the most

popular kilt style at the Jeddito sites was a white one with a lower border in one or several colors and in what appears to be embroidery (Fig. 3.30a–g). A band or a half-band, this area of decoration characteristically features a row of triangles; these may be in a solid color (Fig. 3.30a), or each half in a different color (Fig. 3.30b,d,e), or with an internal negative pattern, usually a T-shaped device or a hook (Fig. 3.30c,d). Taking off from the top of the triangle is also a hook (Fig. 3.30a,c,g), sometimes with multiple "fingers," or, in one case, five lines which diminish in length from outside to inside.

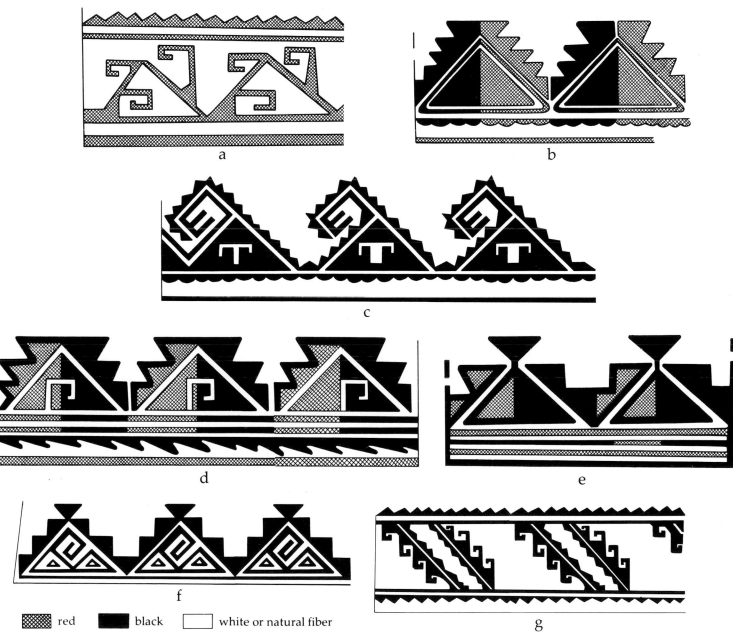

red ▓ black ■ white or natural fiber ▢

Fig. 3.30 Examples of kilt decorations. (All examples adapted from Smith 1952, Fig. 25., *a-f* from Awatovi kiva murals). (a) Kilt decoration in red and white. (b) Red and black decoration on a white kilt. (c) Black on white designs at the bottom of a kilt. (d,e) Two kilt patterns in red and black on white. (f) Black design on a white kilt. (g) Kilt decorated in black on white, from Kawaika–a mural on a kiva wall.

There are also rows of triangles outlined with stepped triangles (Fig. 3.30b,f), sometimes in multi-color arrangements. Certainly many of these kilt patterns compare favorably with the designs on contemporary pottery in the Jeddito area. It should also be mentioned that much of the feeling of this work and some of the specific designs, particularly hooked triangles, survive in the embroidered patterns on historic kilts.

PONCHOS AND SHIRTS

Two additional items of wearing apparel—ponchos and shirts—are of interest, and, at least in part, should be considered together. Generally speaking, they are different in that the poncho is a long, rectangular single cloth or two pieces put together to form this shape, with a vertical or horizontal slit in the center to allow the garment to be slipped over the head; and the shirt, on the other hand, is the same shape but

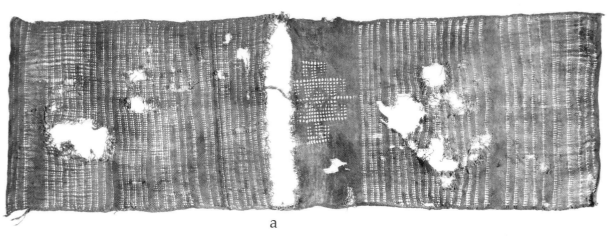

a

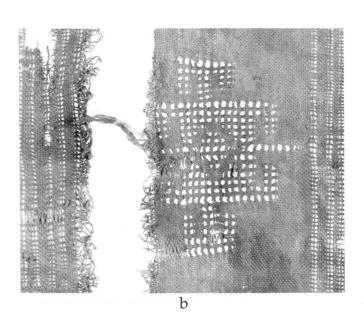

b

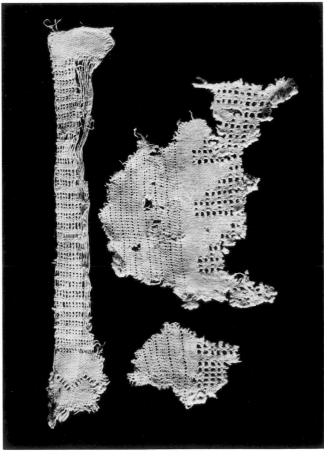

c

Fig. 3.31 Poncho of weft-wrap and gauze weaves. (a) This child's poncho is from Ventana Cave. The main body of the piece is done in gauze weave, thus creating the edge to edge open-work lines. (b) Detail of the central pattern, done in weft-wrap. (c) Comparative pieces of weft-wrap (left) and weft-wrap-gauze weave (two fragments to right) which show design variety in these weaves.

usually has sleeves added to the body garment. The pieces referred to in this discussion will be labelled according to these definitions. Of course, some confusion results when the archaeologist has the body of the shirt but not the sleeves.

There is no question regarding a poncho found with a child's burial at Ventana Cave. The single piece was elaborately woven in a combination of gauze and weft-wrap weave, the former producing an allover lacelike effect, and the latter used to produce a geometric pattern at such a point as to fall on the chest of the Indian wearer (Fig. 3.31a–c). For the neck opening, a slit was made horizontally a little toward the back of center. The dimensions, 28 inches by 8⅝ inches, would bear out the suggestion that it was woven as a child's garment.

Another poncho was found by Haury at Painted Cave, as the innermost wrapping of a burial (Fig. 3.32). The piece found measured 32½ inches by 33 inches, and is believed to be one of two similar fragments that had been sewed together over the shoulders to form the poncho; this supposition is borne out by the presence of a vertical slit in the center of one selvage, and with sewing along this edge. The slit also has its own selvage, indicating that it was probably made during the weaving process.

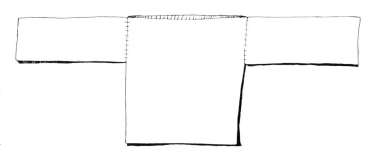

Fig. 3.33   A simple pattern of a shirt with sleeves.

Fig. 3.32   Man's poncho from Painted Cave. This is one-half of the original piece. Note neck slit in top center.

At the opposite end, and at the corners, are ornate tassels. The latter seem to be common on ponchos. A simple linear pattern in brown adorns the upper and lower parts of the poncho, while two broad black bands appear toward the center of the piece, with an open white area between them. Kent calls this garment a sleeveless shirt. A second, smaller poncho also comes from this cave; it is dark brown in color and has a slit definitely produced during the weaving.

Definite shirt types can be determined on a basis of sleeves (Fig. 3.33), and, in one instance, a sleeveless garment that has woven armholes in it. A true poncho has a straight edge and no sleeve line. Two elaborate shirts are in fancy weaves, one, from Tonto, is done in twined-plaiting, and a second, from White House, is a braided piece. These two, of course, are not true loomed pieces since they are finger woven; but they are included here because of their large size, form, and Pueblo III time, in addition to the elaborate technologies used in their production and the material, cotton. Finger weaving certainly continued into late years for the production of other pieces. The Tonto shirt is a lacy garment with woven armholes and neck line; it is designed with oblique rows of triangles and continuous and interlocked fret themes (Fig. 3.34). The example from White House is much more elaborate, being finger woven of flat, round, and square braiding. A heavy fringe originally decorated the bottom of this shirt; it is probable, too, that fringes decorated the sleeves at the wrists. Large diamond motifs formed of bands ornament the body of the shirt and the sleeves.

A plain shirt from Poncho House was painted after it had been woven. It was made of four pieces, a front, back, and two sleeves, each a rectangular cloth. It is quite likely that this and

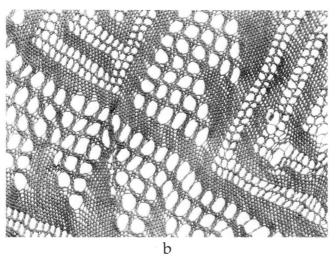

Fig. 3.34 Tonto shirt. (a) This lacelike shirt from Tonto Ruins is twine-plaited of cotton. Note the intricate design involving triangles, meanders, and interlocked frets. (b) This detail of the Tonto shirt shows how threads are often twisted together.

from the body into the sleeves, which may suggest the possibility that the sleeves were woven as part of the fabric, perhaps in a plaited weave. But there is not enough refinement in the drawings to determine whether certain other examples are one or the other. Some are represented as belted; this may help explain the previously described example from Painted Cave, a shirt (or poncho) with two broad black bands and a white undecorated area in between, which may represent a design woven in with the idea in mind of wearing the shirt with a belt over the white section. It is likely that most shirts and ponchos were decorated with lower corner pompoms and/or tassels, for many are so represented in the kiva mural paintings.

There are garments on human figures (ritual performers?) in the Jeddito murals that leave much to the imagination as far as style and use identification are concerned. Some come close to the knees... were they long shirts? Some figures are covered over one shoulder and the other shoulder is bare (or the second shoulder is not showing in the picture). Are these blanket dresses or shirts? What is the strange garment that reaches from both arm pits to the knees, with either kiltlike decoration on the lower border or simply left plain? Is it a version of a small blanket dress worn by men? These are usually belted, sometimes with a narrow, gaily tasseled belt or one of the braided rain sash types. Again, the question might be asked: What part does artistic license play in all these representations?

BLANKETS

Cotton blankets were probably woven in great abundance in the prehistoric past. Perhaps many of the small fragments of cloth, which have been found so widely, may be all that remains of the larger pieces of weaving. Plain weave is the most common for this largest textile, but there are some examples of striped twills and at least one diamond twill. Generally they have a two- or three-thread selvage, these often combined to form braids or tassels that frequently decorate the corners. Perhaps the majority of blankets were plain white, but there are examples of plain brown or red, as well as both simply and elaborately decorated pieces.

Blankets were of two basic types, a rectangular shoulder style and one which was a body cover; the latter was almost square everywhere except

other shirts, and ponchos, too, were not securely sewed under the arms; rather were they caught or tied at intervals, in the manner of the fastening of the historic shirt. This Poncho House shirt was covered with brown paint, leaving two large circles and a number of small squares in white showing through the brown. Incidentally, circles on this fabric represent the only example of curvilinear design in weaving except for the tie-dye motifs. Apparently there were tassels at the lower corners of this shirt and possibly also fringes at the wrists.

Both ponchos and shirts are represented in the Jeddito murals, although it is not possible to distinguish the two in all instances. There are several with sleeves, and surely these are shirts. At least two examples show design continuing in the Ventana pieces. The greater width of the shoulder blanket was a weft stretch, while the rectangular Ventana type had its greater length along the warps. One blanket from Painted Cave measured 54 inches along the warp and 53 inches along the weft, a typical body type. Another example from Canyon Creek had these dimensions: 39 inches for the warps and 50 inches for the wefts, which typifies what is generally called the shoulder blanket. A large blanket from Hidden House measured 58 inches by 64 inches. One of the Ventana pieces was 48 inches (warp) by 15 inches (weft).

Among the most elaborately painted blankets was the aforementioned large one from Painted Cave (Fig. 3.35). It had an elaborate allover offset quartered design with wide diagonal bands of solid red and solid green, other wide bands of

a

Fig. 3.35   Painted blanket from Painted Cave. (a) This color photo of a drawing demonstrates that even when a design is painted on a finished woven piece, it retains the angular geometricity of textile weaving (Ray Manley photo). (b) Detail showing the condition of the design in a corner of the original blanket.

b

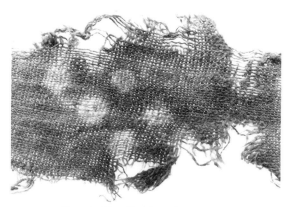

Fig. 3.36 Tie-dye fragment, the original in blue and natural.

black and white negative patterning, and red-line motifs on green bands. There were also wide, red end borders and narrow, red side borders. Tassels at each one of the four corners were made by joining the side and end selvage threads in an inch-long braid.

The only complete, large tie-dye piece is in the form of a blanket 51½ inches along the wefts and 44 inches along the warps (Fig. 3.36). Here too are found the corner braids but with the addition of a pompom or ball to each one of them. This brown blanket has 25 small diamonds, each with a tiny brown center, arranged in 5 rows of 5 each. This piece is from Lake Canyon in southeastern Utah.

The striped twill material from a probable blanket previously mentioned, comes from Canyon de Chelly (Fig. 3.37). The incomplete 20-inch fragment has what appears to be edge-to-edge bands and stripes in white, brown, and red; some bands are seemingly a solid color,

Fig. 3.37 A striped twill fragment, possibly part of a cotton blanket. Seemingly these bands ran from edge to edge; colors in the piece are white, brown, and red.

while others have dark bordered edges enclosing a lighter area, with 6 dark wavy lines of single wefts in the latter band. All of this designing is on a diagonal twill material. A diamond twill piece from Grand Gulch, in southeastern Utah, has a 24-inch incomplete width. Patterning is built up of tiny diamonds, with the following elements and units arranged diagonally on the cloth: bands, opposed and stepped half-terraces, and squares. The subtlety of the combination of colored and woven design is repeated in historic years in the Hopi man's blanket, which has one or two woven twill designs on which appears a plaid motif in black and white over the entire piece.

From Hidden House comes another elaborately designed blanket (Fig. 3.38). An offset-quartered pattern is arranged in a manner contrary to other pieces decorated in this fashion: the patterning follows lines parallel to warps and wefts rather than being diagonal to them. Basically, the motifs consist of bands of small geometrics. There are short rows of plain opposed triangles with interlocking angular hooks, or plain triangles arranged so as to create a zigzag between them, both bordered by sets of framing lines. There are also double rows of triangles on a grid background. Black on a white ground is limited to small individual areas, in contrast to the massive color areas in wide bands in the Painted Cave example. Also, the design on this blanket is very much like the patterning on pottery of the Kayenta area, which suggests the possibility that the blanket may have been a trade piece.

One interesting blanket from Ventana Cave involved the sewing together of two long, narrow strips, to produce a fabric which measured 48 by 30 inches. One strip was red, the other white.

These examples illustrate the outstanding styles of decoration on blankets in the prehistoric Southwest. It has been suggested that the larger and more ornate pieces were worn as robes and allowed to hang free down the back, thus displaying all the decoration. Some specific ways of wearing blankets are illustrated in Smith's work on the Jeddito mural paintings.[36] For instance, several shoulder blankets are draped around the shoulders and caught under the chin. A blanket dress is caught under both arms and is belted at the waist with a rain sash; another dress has a bottom border decoration, perhaps embroidery. It is possible also that the

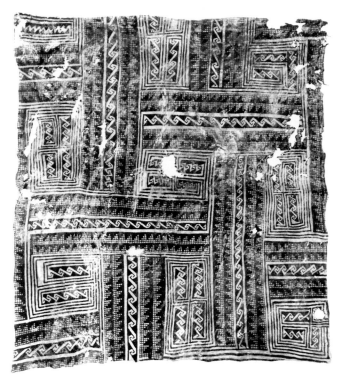

Fig. 3.38 Black and white painted blanket from Hidden House. The blanket was woven of plain natural cotton, then painted in an allover design in an off-set quartered layout. Stepped triangles on a net-like background and rows of stepped or plain triangles, some with interlocked fret ends, are the main design themes.

Regional variation is a significant factor in blanket styles. Many fragments of cloth have been found with striped patterns in them; certainly some of these were pieces of blankets. Kent makes a strong point relative to this and the relation of this style to the Anasazi: "The term *Anasazi* was chosen for these striped cloths because they are so patently the product of Basketmaker-Pueblo culture. For one thing, all were found in Anasazi sites. None has so far been reported from villages in central or southern Arizona or southwestern New Mexico. Furthermore, decorative bands on these Pueblo III loom-woven cottons are strikingly similar in nature to those on San Juan Basketmaker twined-woven bags of apocynum and yucca fiber.... It is almost as though Basketmaker twined-woven bag patterns were copied in loom-woven twill cloth by early Anasazi weavers, and the traditional red and black stripe designs handed on right through Pueblo III times by the conservative people of the north."[37] Continuity of culture traits, as passed from one craft to another, is also indicated in this design style.

women may have worn some of their blanket dresses as do their lineal descendants, the Hopis, with the piece wrapped about the body under the left arm and caught over the right shoulder. Robes or blankets were also used as shrouds. Interestingly, a piece so used may be new, apparently made specifically for the purpose of burial, as in the case of two such pieces about bodies at Vandal Cave. Or they may be old and worn, patched and repatched, as in the case of the very ragged remnant of a blanket about an old man buried in Ventana Cave. Perhaps wealth and poverty played their parts in the lives of the prehistoric Southwesterners and the development of their customs.

MISCELLANEOUS WEAVING

A variety of lesser woven pieces might be discussed at this point, including such items as quivers, cigarette sashes, leggings, a turban, and bags. Some were planned and woven as conceived, while others were made in make-shift fashion, frequently from scraps of larger pieces of cloth.

Cigarette sashes are among the most interesting of these pieces (Fig. 3.39). In spite of their small size, they were woven as individual and complete pieces. Seemingly, they are Hohokam in nature; perhaps string-wrapped pahos (prayer sticks) or cane "cigarettes" are their Anasazi area counterparts. Some of these sashes have been found in Double Butte Cave, near

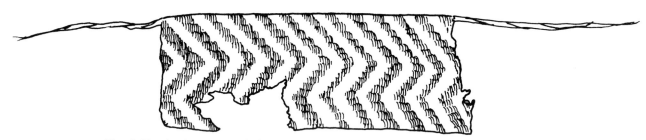

Fig. 3.39 A cigarette sash from Double Butte Cave. It is a bit larger than the average of these sashes, being 2½" by ⅞". Of blue and white cotton, it carries a zigzag pattern in its twill weave (adapted from Haury 1945a, pl. 90h).

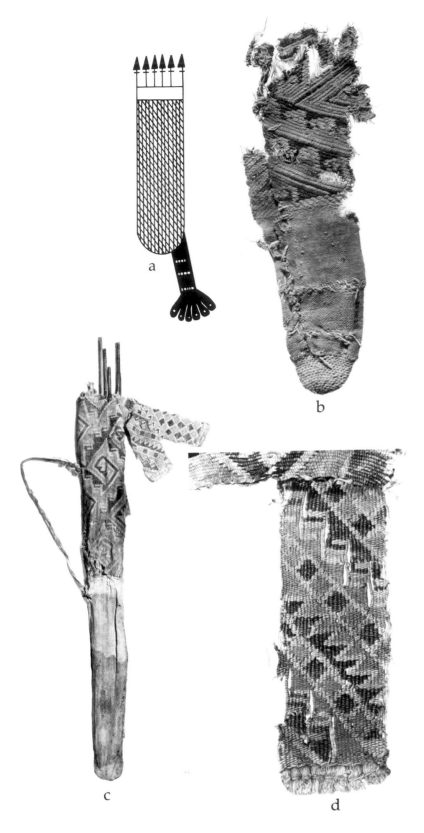

Fig. 3.40 Quivers. (a) A fine example of a quiver filled with arrows, painted on the interior of a Mimbres bowl (adapted from Cosgrove and Cosgrove 1932, pl. 227e). (b) For comparison, part of a small quiver (or bag?), from Hidden House in coil-without-foundation and plain and split-tapestry weave, and patterned in brown and natural. (c) A large cotton quiver, also from Hidden House. (d) Detail of one flap of the large quiver, showing the slit-tapestry weave and design detail. Blue (light) and brown (dark) patterns appear on a natural ground.

Phoenix, and in other cave sites where ceremonial materials were deposited. Some are characterized by the fact that both warp and weft form one continuous thread. One example is ½ to ¾ inch in warp length and 2 inches in weft width. Another is slightly larger, ⅞ inch wide and 2½ inches long, and woven with blue wefts in an over-two-under-two reversed twill. A third such piece, only 2 inches wide, is embroidered in blue and brown, with opposed design elements that seem to be steps.

Quite a few pahos are represented in the Jeddito murals. Here they are complete with string bindings and feather and other attachments. Then, as historically, both the prayer plume, or paho, of the Anasazis and the ceremonial cigarette sashes of the Hohokams must have been colorful and attractive pieces.

Another interesting object produced by the prehistoric Southwesterners is the quiver. Like so many pieces of weaving, it is quite likely that many were produced but have not been found. They are represented in kiva murals. A fine example from Awatovi shows a man in full war or hunting regalia: a bow is in hand, feathers at the back of his head, and a quiver slung from the far shoulder, oblique to the body. The quiver has a "flap" hanging down from the top of the main part of the piece, and the quiver proper is filled with feathered arrows.

Another example is illustrated on a ceramic piece in the Cosgrove Swarts Ruin report; the body of the quiver is possibly of fancy weave, and an elaborately decorated flap (?) hangs from the opposite side, showing below the main part of the quiver (Fig. 3.40a,b). Sharp tips of six arrows project from this quiver, which is held upright by the right hand of a man wearing a breastplatelike affair and holding a shieldlike device in his left hand.[38]

From Hidden House comes an excellent example of a quiver, made in three sections (Fig. 3.40c,d). The lower part, or the boot, is of plain weave and is undecorated; the midsection is the same; but the upper portion is in slit tapestry weave and bears a colored design. The first two parts appear to have been crudely woven compared to the upper decorated area. Total length of this quiver is about 32¼ inches, while the tapestry section is 17¾ inches long. The latter is well woven; there are 35 warps (17½ pairs) and 40 wefts to the inch. The design is in the form of diagonal rows of hooked triangles, and rows of triangles with frets, which terminate in two triangles on their ends, all in brown and blue, and with slits along the edges of design elements. The flap, which is sewed to the top of the quiver, is decorated in diagonal rows of plain triangles and squares, and has slits outlining parts of design elements. The carrying strap is in the form of two pieces of belting sewed together end to end, one a little wider than the other, and one in plain weave, the other in warp face.

Another piece from Hidden House might be either a bag or another quiver. In favor of the latter is the fact that it is made in three sections, as was the quiver just described from this site. The bottom part is coil-without-foundation; the middle section is plain weave, undecorated; and the top is of fine twilled tapestry weave.

Surely quivers of skin must have been made in some quantity. Haury found one at Ventana with the burial of a man; it is of simple tubular form and had cane arrows in it. Kent postulates the possibility of the woven flap, which is represented in the examples cited, as a feature surviving from the skin style in which the leg or tail of the animal was left on the quiver, to hang down as a decorative element. This would not be unlike the elaborately woven kilt with a flap worn by pharaoh of ancient Egypt, which was reminiscent of the animal skin, complete with tail, worn in earlier years as a symbol of village leadership.

Kidder and Guernsey report "a skullcap (?) of coiled-without-foundation in yucca cord..." found in hard-packed rubbish just outside a room of a cliff house.[39] From Hidden House comes a piece labelled a turban that is made of loose hanks of white, brown, and red cotton yarn built up in spiral fashion to form a rounded cap. A heavy cord was secured through the center of the turban and wrapped about a queuelike style of hair-do at the back of the head of the mummy on which the piece appeared. These are the only headpieces made of cordage found in prehistoric sites; yet there is a representation of a duncelike cap worn by a lively dancer painted on a piece of Mimbres pottery.[40] At least one example of a leather cap has been reported, from Mesa Verde.

Leggings have been reported from Anasazi sites only and these largely in northeastern Arizona and southeastern Utah, with one example from Hidden House. They are also represented in the paintings of Awatovi. Further-

more, at least two examples of designed leggings are represented on Mimbres pottery, one on the warrior (or hunter) previously mentioned and a second illustrated in Bradfield's Cameron Creek report.[41] Vertical zigzags appear on the latter two. It would seem that these two examples probably were not made in the looped technique, which will be mentioned. Perhaps these are footless stockings and not sandal uppers.

Anasazi Pueblo III leggings and socks are made from a variety of materials, generally of a cotton base with hair or wool of some sort twisted in with it for warmth. A looped technique is usually employed in the production of these leggings, which are usually uppers for sandals. One, from Two Mummy Ruin, Nitsie Canyon, has a cotton base and a brown wool addition, some of the latter still visible in this unpatterned piece. A second example, from Gourd Cave, has wide dark bands throughout the legging; again, animal hair was twisted in with a multi-ply cotton string, and the resultant heavy cordage was hand woven in a closed technique (Fig. 3.41). Other materials used include animal hair twisted in with yucca string only or yucca string wound with feathers. Occasionally cotton, sometimes in the form of rags or in feather cord, was used in combination with yucca at points in the sandal proper where there is more pressure from the foot, thus making for a softer pad.

Cotton cloth bags seem not to have been common, yet they enjoyed a wide distribution, extending even into Texas. In some, yucca or human hair was substituted for the cotton. Weaves ranged from looped styles (Fig. 3.42a,b) to crude plain weave to finer plain weave, or

Fig. 3.41 Gourd Cave legging, one of a pair, with broad dark and white bands. Light and dark animal hairs were twisted with cotton string to produce the material used in this "shoe-sock" or legging.

Fig. 3.42 Looped technique bags. (a,b) Two cotton bags from Gourd Cave, of plain white cotton made in this technique. (c) The larger piece was apparently one of a pair of leggings; later it was sewed up at the bottom to form a bag. It is made of human hair cord by a simple looping process.

braided, brocaded, weft-wrap open work, twilled weave, and others. In some instances bags were made from scraps of cloth. The non-loom weaves were generally used for small bags, about 1 inch in width and 2 or 3 inches long. Small bags seem to have had ceremonial uses, to hold a medicine man's ritual articles, special seeds, or various ceremonial items such as knives. Larger bags were undoubtedly multi-purpose in use, and probably served any need of the moment.

Usually the bag was made as a rectangle in the particular weave desired, and, with the exception of the tubular woven or looped types, the piece was folded over and sewed with running or overcast stitches down the side and across the bottom. If made from two pieces of cloth, as was one bag from Tonto, then there was sewing down both sides. Two larger bags, both from Hidden House, were, respectively, 21¼ and 23¼ inches long and 9⅜ and 11 inches in circumference (Fig. 3.42c). They seem to have been a pair, and some believe that they were originally a pair of footless stockings or leggings that later had been sewed up at the bottoms to make bags of them. They were woven of human hair cord, and they were produced by a simple looping method; it was common practice to use human hair or yucca cordage in looped bags. Several plain cloth bags, both smaller than the last example, were also found at Hidden House.

Both were made of cotton, and both seem to have been made of larger fragments of cloth which were adapted to this specific use.

One very interesting bag from Montezuma Castle was woven with double black wefts floated over single white warps in a twill, but with many irregularities. The pattern is allover and it is diagonally arranged on the bag. Basically, there are bands, wide and narrow, short and long, of the following small elements and units: both continuous and interlocked frets, lines with wavy cross-lines, and zigzags that form parts of meanders as they are combined with plain lines. This bag is 25 inches long and 5¾ inches wide.

From Grand Gulch comes a bag made from a piece of twill woven material with a brocaded weft-float pattern in the center of the 13¼ inch square cloth. Top and bottom borders are white and in plain weave; at the edges of these are two narrow stripes in black. It is thought that the central pattern, which is badly worn, was a large diamond outlined in either triangles or points. Most probably there was some additional patterning within the diamond. The cloth was gathered at the two ends, then a braid was sewed down the two remaining sides, forming the bag.

Bags were closed in a variety of ways. Some fragments of cloth were merely caught up at the four corners and gathered to the center, then merely tied. Some were woven to be smaller at the bottom and perhaps the top also, then were tied to close the opening. Drawstrings were added to some bags; it would be a simple matter, of course, to run strings or cordage through the top of the most widespread style, the looped bag.

In summary of textiles, it appears that prehistoric Southwesterners equipped themselves very well indeed to do a fine job in this craft. A wide variety of materials, techniques, objects, and decorative styles resulted from the ancients' ingenuity and perseverence, and from trade throughout most of the area. The loom helped greatly, but long before its introduction these Indians had exploited native yucca, apocynum, and many other materials to a high degree; too, they had adapted technologies in such ways as to produce a wide variety of surface finishes and decorative effects. Cotton also offered many new potentials, but surely the cruder basts served these imaginative folk in full measure until the finer fiber was introduced.

Almost every form produced in textile weaving was a square or a rectangle, the latter ranging from short to very long: rare exceptions are the sleeve and breechcloth; each might be gently tapered to one end while still in the loom. Comments in the literature relative to cutting and fitting garments can be discounted for such was rarely, if ever, done, as noted in the preceding discussions. Clothing was limited, too, more so in earlier years, less so in later times; in fact, there seem to have been more garments in Pueblo IV than in Pueblo III times. Almost all weaving was directed towards the production of clothing, except for the rare quiver, some bags, nets, and a few other objects. There seems to have been some specialization, for example, the large and beautifully decorated robes which probably served in ritual situations.

Much local variation is to be noted in all matters pertaining to textile weaving; this may be reflected in materials, forms, weaves, and decoration. At Ventana Cave and in parts of the Mogollon, there was less cotton and more yucca and other fibers, possibly as there was not enough water in these areas to cultivate cotton.

Preference for certain materials might well have been due to traditional usage in some instances; perhaps this might explain the continuation of yucca in women's aprons in the Anasazi region, for surely there was ample cot-

ton, at least in some areas. An example of local color usage, the green at Painted Cave only, may have been due to preference or simply to limited knowledge of sources. Certainly there is a greater frequency of more elaborate weaves in the south—weft-wrap and gauze—and in decorative additions—embroidery and brocading; in the north there is greater use of the wide upright loom with emphasis on weft-face cloth and twill weaves. Even in the matter of warps and wefts there are areal differences. In western Pueblo sites and in the Mogollon, warps and wefts are the same in number or there is warp predominance. In all pieces at Hidden House, warps outnumber wefts, as is true in the Hohokam. In the northern Pueblo section, as exemplified in the Kayenta in particular, wefts generally predominate over warps, yet there is fine weaving in both the south and the north, with peaks of about an 80 per inch count for both warps and wefts in a piece from Aztec Ruin and 87.5 count for both in a Tonto fragment. Characteristic throughout the Southwest was the use of Z-spun single yarns for both warps and wefts.

In form, there seems to have been a definite trend toward a more nearly square blanket in the north, and a more rectangular shape in the south, the latter well illustrated at Ventana Cave. Too, all large pieces at Hidden House show a greater weft dimension, while the opposite is true at Ventana Cave, where the warp dimension is greater.

Although there is not enough material in all parts of the Southwest to give a detailed temporal and areal comparison of design, there are still enough examples to point up certain additional trends. For one thing, the Hohokams may have been more affected by the Mexicans than the Anasazis, or both may have been influenced by Mexico, perhaps the Hohokams more directly by the West Coast of Mexico and the Anasazis by Chihuahua, through the Mogollon. Great changes occurred in the Hopi locale textiles following the Little Colorado migrations to their area after 1300; this would indicate limitations during earlier times in one part of the Anasazi not to be noted in other parts of the same culture area.

Stripe twills, as noted, became distinctive of the Anasazi. Was this inspired by the weave itself or was it a lingering pattern from twined bags of earlier years? Stripes early became popular and remain so to this day among the descendants of the Anasazi. Tapestry weave itself is productive of the half-terrace, terrace, terraced lines, and squares and rectangles. As they appeared in textiles, were these designs the product of technology, or were they borrowed from pottery and used because they were possible in this technique? Tapestry designs became more complex in all areas than they were in the Anasazi. Tie-dye gave birth to a square or diamond, both with rounded corners, with a dot in the center. One may well ask if this design, and negative patterning as a whole, may not have come from ceramic decoration rather than from tie-dye as intimated by Kent.[42] Then, many designs appeared on painted cloth, some from tie-dye, some from tapestry weave, and some not related to any other woven elements; this is to be expected when the decorator became free of technical controls in design creation and expression. Among the last designs to appear were triangles with hooks; the latter were either angled, sawtooth, or combined with the half-terrace; and in some cases, the triangular fret was painted. Again, possibly the textile decorator was influenced in the use of many of these elements or units of design by the pottery decorator. With the exception of one good example of painted textile at Hidden House—and that may have been an import—this is an Anasazi trait.

In relation to regional and temporal variations in the weaving craft, offset quartering and limitation of the field of decoration by borders are both Anasazi traits. "Weaving in the Hopi country between 1300 and 1550, as depicted in the Jeddito murals, was a blend of Anasazi Pueblo III and southern Pueblo and Hohokam *techniques*. The textile *designs* shown on kilt borders are, however, almost entirely southern in character."[43] In time, embroidery replaced various fancy weaves and became a prominent decorative technique in historic years. Some of this is demonstrated in the designs on kilts and other pieces in the Jeddito murals.

In summary of textile decoration as a whole, it can be reiterated that all design is angular geometric, and not entirely because of technique, for painted patterns follow this same tradition. There is, of course, the one exception to this, tie-dye. Basic elements include lines, triangles, squares, zigzags, chevrons, barbed lines, checkers, hooked triangles, frets, and cross-

hatching. Despite the relatively few elements and units, no two designs are alike. Weave, of course plays a part in many of the details of design. The size of warps and wefts affect design, as does their spacing. For example, broad triangles result from tightly battened tapestry weave or closely spaced warps in a plain weave, while twill tapestry will give a smooth oblique.

Design layout is a relatively simple matter in prehistoric Southwestern textile weaving. Quite commonly it is allover, following banded, repeated, or offset quartered schemes. Centered layouts appear occasionally, usually on smaller cloths. End banding is encountered infrequently, perhaps on one end only, as seen in the kilt; this style became more popular toward the close of the prehistoric period.

These textile decorators used small and large elements, although small ones seem to predominate. Design covered practically every inch of space in most of the allover styles; in some instances, the white background of the fabric was incorporated into the design. Less common is a simple spacing out of the design. Patterns were arranged end to end, edge to edge, or allover integrated, rarely without order. Except for banded patterns and a few allover styles, such as in the Hidden House blanket and several others, design was so often obliquely oriented in large pieces; this is true of small and large pieces alike. It may well be that bands, sandals, and other small pieces of the Basketmaker Period set this style and it remained popular throughout the prehistoric period.

And last, the prehistoric weaver usually finished off a piece in an attractive manner. Generally it was nothing more than the heavier cords of the selvages, occasionally it was more. For example, in decorated pieces, borders might be of solid color or of a different weave. Ends might be fringed, or have tassels and sometimes pompoms; corners of blankets frequently utilized the latter two treatments.

The prehistoric craft of textile weaving merged into the historic without a break. Much of the beauty of the past was lost in time, some to be replaced by new ideas, a new type of embroidery, new colors, and new materials. Where religious usage has prevailed, the old and traditional linger.

Chapter 4

Pottery

"In a deftly chosen single exhibit of ceramics, one might see the whole story of art laid out graphically."[1] This statement by Cheney can be applied to pottery of the prehistoric Southwest as much if not more than to any other area of the world. Further, for even the smallest broken piece, or sherd, there is little or nothing that can upset preservation—this contributes to the completeness of the record. The time of the introduction of already developed pottery into the Hohokam and Mogollon areas is thought to be well established, around 300 B.C.; crude beginning phases are to be noted in the Anasazi after the opening of the Christian Era. In all three regions there is much evidence of the growth and development of this craft, with stylistic and other changes well documented in the remaining whole or fragmentary pieces of vessels.

According to Roberts, pottery manufacture in the Southwest was "a general household industry, not a specialized craft restricted to skilled workers."[2] This in no way refutes the Cheney statement, for lack of leisure allowed no time for the development of the fine arts. It does, however, alert the reader to the great importance of the craft; it indicates that there will be a fair quantity of pottery, which will serve as a fine measuring rod of the general nature of the art accomplishments of the prehistoric Southwest Indian as a whole. It has also been contended that there is no comparable neolithic culture that has exceeded the attainments of Southwest potters. Their standards were high in both technology and artistry. To be sure, there were variations in quality of ceramic production, from

area to area and from time to time, but in the overall picture, there is no contender for greater performance.

Textile and ceramic arts are closely related, particularly in the beginning phases of the latter in the Anasazi area. The basketry craft responded to the needs of its creators, for cooking utensils, for carrying and storage baskets, for all-purpose bowls and trays. After the fulfillment of, yet not interfering with, the basic needs, basket weavers branched out in refinement of form. By the time pottery appeared, there were many and varied local forms, each a reflection of, first, need and, second, local artistic trends. Thus, pottery became functionally the offshoot of basketry and, interestingly, remained under this basic control to the end of its use by the natives. The greatest variations in these prehistoric wares are expressions of local styles of art. Obviously, the potentials for variations are greater in modelling clay, since there are not the technical controls in creating form that are so evident in basket weaving.

In general, the same broad concepts that apply to basketry can be applied to ceramic decoration and to form, particularly in the earliest pottery phases. In fact in the Anasazi area, where the first ceramic wares are reflective of fumbling beginning stages, some pieces of pottery were not only made inside tray baskets and thus carried the identical form, but also some reflect a direct influence of basket design on pieces of pottery. Basketry technique served as a strong control of design style, with geometricity and angular lines prevailing. These same qualities are to be noted in early ceramic design. However, there were not the same technical controls in pottery; in fact the smooth surface of the clay vessel was generally finished before design was applied. In a way, it is surprising that geometricity and angularity prevailed in pottery decoration for as long as they did. Then as now, however, there were individuals who would not or could not adhere completely to tradition; consequently, curved lines appeared early in some ceramic decoration. Too, one cannot . . . and should not . . . forget the ever present matter of chance, of a slip of the brush that accidently produced a curved line. Curved lines did occur early in some local wares, and did become dominant at times among certain ceramists. No other craft art was so abundantly produced as pottery. Coupled with these points, it is, therefore, not surprising that in pottery decoration these people "expressed the major part of their artistic impulse, with rhythmic, skillful, heavily conventionalized design."[3]

Actually, the ceramic art itself gives rise to few or no particular design elements, therefore it had to borrow heavily from other sources. It has been indicated that forms and designs were borrowed from basketry; it can be further suggested that other craft arts, or, even such expressions as pictographs, body painting, wall decorations, or other sources may have stimulated the pottery decorator. In like manner, other vessels or forms may have inspired the potter, such as wooden containers, a bird, an animal, or other objects of nature, or free forms. The plastic quality of clay allowed for greater freedom of choice of expression in ceramics, in form, and variety of form. By the same token, the lack of technological control in using the brush allowed the ceramic decorator the greatest diversity in design of all Southwest Indian craft artists.

Technical Background

The technical background of ceramics involves materials used, methods of manufacture, and types of decoration. Each of these aspects will be treated in a general manner in the following pages and more attention will be given to variations and detailed qualities within each of the several cultures later in this chapter. Certain basic similarities appear in the major groups of the Southwest that bind all of the pottery types together; certain basic differences are not of sufficient significance as to deny membership in the ceramic tradition of the greater Southwest culture. The differences are reflected in local and regional wares.

MATERIALS

Materials used in pottery manufacture throughout the prehistoric Southwest are essentially the same: clay, temper, and water. Clay is found abundantly in the three areas, with some variation in quality and texture. The finest, kaolin, a good white clay, is found and was used primarily in the northern or Anasazi area; although there are deposits of it in southern Arizona, the natives there had not discovered these beds. Mimbreños of the late Mogollon culture area of southwestern New Mexico, did use kaolinite for a slip. Clays with various mineral impurities in them are also found throughout the Southwest. Small quantities of iron in a paste may burn to a light gray or cream color; a large amount of iron results in a brown or almost-orange color, while a quantity of iron in between these extremes will produce a yellow or buff-colored base clay after firing. Control of fire as to amount of oxygen and temperature are further factors influencing color of the fired clay.

Temper is a material either present in or added to the finer clay to give it more body and to keep the paste from cracking when it is fired. Cedar bark was common in the Southwest in very early Anasazi years; later they used crushed pottery sherds, sand, quartz, mica, crushed rock, and other substances. Probably the clay and temper were thoroughly mixed and water added. Then as now, no doubt, the native potter measured nothing; she merely used a handful, or two, of temper to a pile of clay of a certain size, then added water until a certain "feel" resulted in the mixture. The paste was then ready to be formed into a vessel.

Materials for painting the pot or otherwise coloring it included the following. All paints were of mineral or vegetal origin. In the first category were hematite, manganese, copper, or even a thin wash of pure kaolin for white base color. Beeweed was the chief source of vegetal paint; it provided a black color, and was more limited in use than the mineral paints. Some black coloring was also derived from the smoke of a smoldering fire.

METHODS

Throughout the Southwest methods of making and decorating vessels varied only slightly. No potter's wheel was used, nor was a true kiln known. All work was done strictly by hand, with a bit of assistance from a few simple tools. First the clay was ground, probably on a metate or metate-like device, the same as used by Indian women for grinding corn. Frequently paints were ground on flat stones surfaces or in small mortars. Sometimes the clay was further refined, again possibly as in historic times, by tossing the material in the air on a windy day, thus letting the fine particles blow into a basket or onto a cloth close by. Often the temper had to be crushed; this was probably accomplished in a manner comparable to that of preparing the clay by pounding and grinding it.

After the mixing of the clay, temper, and water into a doughlike mass, it was kneaded. Again each woman was familiar with the desired consistency, which she probably learned through practice. It is likely that the woman started the bottom of the vessel from a lump of clay, moulding it by hand, or by pressing it into the inside of a fragment of a pot, or by working it over the outside of a whole or a broken pot. From this beginning, the potter of the Anasazi, Hohokam, and Mogollon areas built up the rest

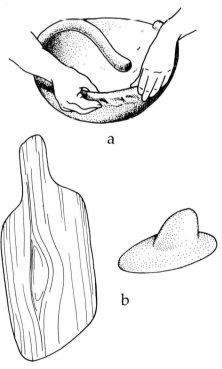

a

b

Fig. 4.1 Method of forming vessels. (a) In building the wall of a vessel large rolls of clay were added, and while wet and soft, pinched to the preceding portion of the wall (DiPeso 1956, Fig. 44). (b) A wooden paddle and stone anvil. The latter was held on the inside of the vessel and the former used to work on the outside, shaping and thinning walls in the process.

of the vessel from large round rolls of clay, one piled on top of another; this is called the coiled method (Fig. 4.1a). With her hand on the inside of the vessel and a small even-edged piece of gourd on the outside, the worker smoothed and shaped the walls, and at the same time shaped the entire vessel into the desired form. This process of scraping and forming was peculiar to the Anasazi and Mogollon people but was not practiced by the Hohokams.

In the Hohokam region, presumably, the potter used the so-called paddle-and-anvil technique of the modern Papagos, forming the base of the vessel over an inverted pot. This base is quite thick, and after a drying, then a wetting, of the clay, it is thinned down and worked into a partial wall by holding a stone anvil on the inside of the vessel and patting against it on the outside with a slightly curved wooden paddle (Fig. 4.1b). Large round coils are added, pinched together, and worked with anvil and paddle to make them smooth and of the same thickness as the rest of the vessel. Additional coils complete the neck. Thus the Hohokams often neither scraped the interiors nor polished exteriors of vessels as did other potters.

Throughout the Southwest, a water worn pebble is next used to surface the pot; sometimes this is a mere smoothing, while in other instances the process is continued to the point of giving a lighter or heavier polish to the vessel. In the Anasazi area, polishing was common from early years; the Hohokams did not polish the vessel walls or, if they did, only slightly; and the Mogollon did much more polishing than the Hohokam. The Cosgroves say that vessels (bowls) were smoothed with a polishing stone both inside and out, and sometimes, after the addition of the slip, "were given a secondary rubbing with a polishing pebble to produce an added gloss."[4]

A slip is a thin wash put over the surface of a vessel. Frequently this was watered-down clay from which the pot was made, or it might be from a different source, such as hematite. To be sure, the slip might be thick or thin, either as a general trait of the culture in question or as a matter of individual variation. The slip is smoothed and often polished; historically, slip has been put onto the vessel surface with a small cloth swab or a rabbit tail; the latter may have been used commonly in prehistoric times. This remains the finished surface or it serves as a base for decoration of the vessel. In some

Anasazi vessels, polishing brought fine particles to the surface, thus giving the appearance of a slipped finish.

It should be stressed that there are both temporal and spatial variations in many of the steps of pottery manufacture and decoration. Too, there is the ever present individual, some adhering strictly to traditional methods, others doing things a little differently at one point or another.

The basic firing process in the prehistoric past was probably accomplished by using wood, although there are some evidences for the limited use of coal in areas in north-central and northeastern Arizona. Perhaps in the past as today each group used a particular type of wood, and probably each followed this general procedure: the fire was kindled, built up to the desired point, and allowed to burn down; vessels to be fired were arranged over the embers, then the fire might receive additional wood; the burning continued for an established time, then the pots were removed and allowed to cool.

Firing of pottery was very likely done in a variety of ways in prehistoric times. It has been established that two basic techniques were used, namely, in an oxidizing or in a reducing atmosphere. The former is an open situation, one in which oxygen gets to the vessels as they are fired; the latter involves some device for cutting off of the oxygen supply. Today the oxidizing technique is represented by those tribes which do not cover the vessels during the process of burning, or they may protect the pots by merely putting a bit of tin around the collection of pieces being burned. On the other hand, in the reducing process, the vessels are completely covered over, thus reducing or almost cutting off the oxygen supply. Perhaps large pieces of broken pots or buffalo chips were used to enclose the vessels in pre-Columbian days.

FORM

Form in pottery, as in basketry, is always dictated by function. However, as soon as a form is established for a general purpose, such as a bowl for eating, mixing, or holding various items, or for a more specific use, such as a water jar for carrying and storing liquids, then the ceramist is free to move in a wide circle in further refining that form. Actually, there are but a few basic forms in Southwest Indian pottery; yet there are so many refinements of these that one gets the impression of a wider range of shapes than

actually existed. In this area as a whole, bowls and jars (or ollas) were most abundant, then, in various sections there have been found pitchers, scoops and ladles, canteens, vases, mugs, plates, and a few other miscellaneous shapes (Fig. 4.2).

Each of these forms fits, first, into one of three possible general categories of certain proportions which are significant within themselves, and, second, with emphasis on one of several possible variations within each of the three classes (Fig. 4.3). Each is important in connection with decoration. The three basic vessel shapes are: one, about equal height and width; two, tall and narrow; and three, short and wide. In the first category, if the greatest diameter is located centrally, design is apt to be well balanced above and below and often to right and left; if the widest point is above center, there will

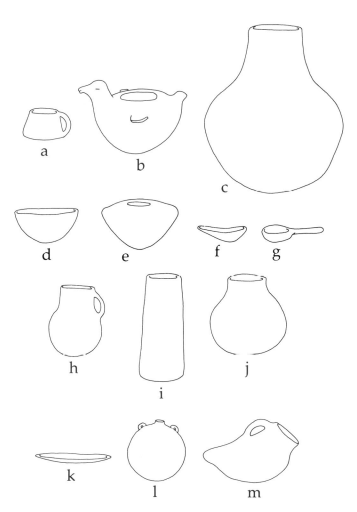

Fig. 4.2 Basic shapes in Southwestern pottery: (a) mug; (b) effigy jar; (c) jar or olla; (d) bowl; (e) seed jar; (f) scoop; (g) dipper or ladle; (h) pitcher; (i) vase; (j) jar; (k) plate; (l) canteen; (m) "boot" jar.

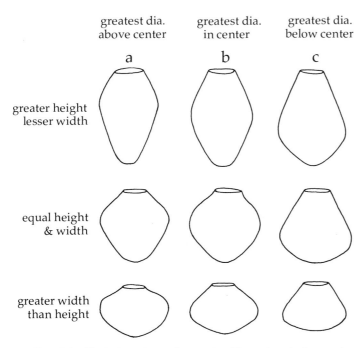

greatest dia. above center	greatest dia. in center	greatest dia. below center
a	b	c

greater height lesser width

equal height & width

greater width than height

Fig. 4.3 Variations in jar forms significant in relation to the placement of design. (a) Where the widest diameter of the vessel is high, decoration is apt to appear above this, particularly if the turn is abrupt. (b) In like manner, if the greatest width is at or near the jar midpoint, design is above and may terminate here. (c) Most abundant patterning is apt to occur on jars in this row, for frequently it is drawn down to this greatest diameter.

be more patterning about the upper part of the vessel, but frequently some or much below; and, similarly, if the greatest width is below center, then design concentrates in the upper area but often down to this lower point of widest diameter. This is emphasized in Southwest pottery by the fact that if the widest diameter is low on a vessel there is frequently an abrupt in-turn to the bottom of the vessel that naturally demands the termination of design at such a point. There is a comparable distribution of design on the other two basic forms. Within the Southwest, there were preferences for certain of these forms, with design rather naturally falling into related positions. There are, of course, exceptions which are reflective of the problems encountered by the potter. In discussing design, the arrangements which were used will be explored.

Another important aspect of decoration in relation to form is *where* design will be placed, inside or outside a vessel (Fig. 4.4). As openmouthed containers, bowls invite interior decoration; however, there are exceptions in the Southwest. For example, some bowls have

incurving rims; if slightly so, design may still appear on the interior, or on both interior and exterior; if at all exaggerated in this feature, design may be confined entirely to the exterior. Plates are decorated on the interior almost exclusively, although there are a few exceptions to this statement. Jars, because of their closed form, are decorated on the exteriors. Rarely, a bit of design slips onto the neck interior, but this is the exception and not the rule. A specialized Southwest form called a seed jar sometimes has a flat shoulder which turns abruptly into the wall; only the flat area may be decorated, or if the turn is a little more gentle, design may dribble below the turn. The same principles are followed for pitchers as for jars. Scoops (short handled) and ladles (long handled) may present two basic areas for decoration, the bowl and the handle. Too, the bowl may merge into the handle (this form will be called a scoop), or the bowl may be separate from the handle (this will be referred to as a ladle). In the scoop, design is usually continuous from the bowl into the handle and on the interior, but when the two parts are separate the pattern appears on the bowl interior and on the outside of and around the handle. Two shapes of canteens offer two decorative potentials: the first is rounded and more like a jar except for a small orifice with loops for suspension, and is decorated in the manner of jars; the second is a jarlike shape except for one side which is flattened; this offers several design potentials as either side may or

Fig. 4.4 Decoration of bowls and jars more commonly appears on bowl interiors and jar exteriors, often in bands or allover (bowls) or nearly allover (jars) or in other arrangements.

may not be decorated. Vases were tall, slender, and flat-bottomed, and frequently were painted from rim to base on the outside. Mugs were decorated on the exterior of their handles and bodies.

Decoration

Decoration of pottery involves many aspects, such as layout, or adaptation of design to a specific vessel form; types of decoration, with painting the most common; and design analysis, which involves elements, motifs, and the total decoration. Each of these reflects both general traits peculiar to the Southwest as a whole and specific qualities applicable to major culture areas or to locales within them.

DESIGN LAYOUT

Design layout means the choice of a decorative area and the manner in which the design is to be applied to that area. Again, the basic form not only has a great deal to do with this, where the design falls, inside or out, but also what part of the available surface is to be used, all or a part only, and the type of layout that is to be used thereon.

Two larger categories of layout will first be set up, namely, divided and undivided (Fig. 4.5). In divided layout, specific lines are drawn by the decorator within which the pattern will be confined. In ceramic decoration, there is less dependence than in basketry on natural features to be used as dividers, such as rims or the sharp turn on a jar, but there is some dependence. Undivided layout is one in which no prior lines are drawn, a layout in which every line that is painted on the vessel is a part of the design. In a divided layout, the pattern lines may or may not touch the basic division lines.

Included under divided layouts are two classes, sectioned and banded (Fig. 4.5-I-1 and 2), found basically in bowl interiors, although banded is common to exteriors of many forms. These are primary layouts. Sectioned types include bisected, or cutting the area in half; quartered, or drawing two lines at right angles to each other and rim to rim; sectored, or cutting smaller sections of equal "pie shapes," but not to the center; offset quartered, with lines to the rim from the corners of a small square in the center of the bowl; trisected, or creating three equal parts with three rim-to-center lines; segmented, with two parallel lines, rim-to-rim cre-

ating equal segments on either side and leaving an open banded center; lunate, with two curved rim-to-rim lines creating crescent moon shapes on either side, leaving an ovoid form in the center; and nongeometric, where lines are drawn to create irregular but specific areas that will contain the pattern. Bisected, trisected, and nongeometric are rarely found. In segmented, the design appears in the two edge segments, and with them, possibly also the center, which would create a composite layout. Obviously, if a pattern was painted in the central area alone, it would be a banded pattern. In lunate layout, pattern might appear in all three areas, but it must be used in the two moon-shaped sections to be so classed.

Banded layouts are perhaps the most common of all, for they may occur on virtually any form. They were particularly popular on bowls and jars, but equally favored for some more limited forms, such as mugs and pitchers. A band is created by drawing two parallel lines; the definition indicates further that to be a true band, the length must exceed the width. In some Anasazi bowls ornamented with very wide bands it would seem that this was not true, but upon closer analysis such is found to be the case, in spite of the fact that in these instances there may be a very small circle in the center of the bowl.

Subdivision of a band is not uncommon in ceramic decoration; lines drawn within the band create the secondary layouts (Fig. 4.5-I-2b). The nature of these lines includes the following: vertical, creating square or rectangular areas; oblique, creating parallelograms; or horizontal, which make for further, but narrower, bands. Design is placed within each of these differently shaped areas. Bands also serve the decorator without need of secondary division. Within these open bands appear two types of decorating, a continuous pattern or a repeated pattern. Included in the divided category is the half-band: this involves a single line from which a pattern is suspended and which functions partially like a band (Fig. 4.5-I-2c). It is popular for rim decoration.

Undivided layouts lend themselves to more dynamic allover patterning, for the drawing of lines within the decorative area to enclose patterns, as in divided layouts, tends to make them more discrete and, obviously, also makes them more restrictive. To be sure, this is a quality which is further influenced by the nature of the design itself, for great scrolls can be and are

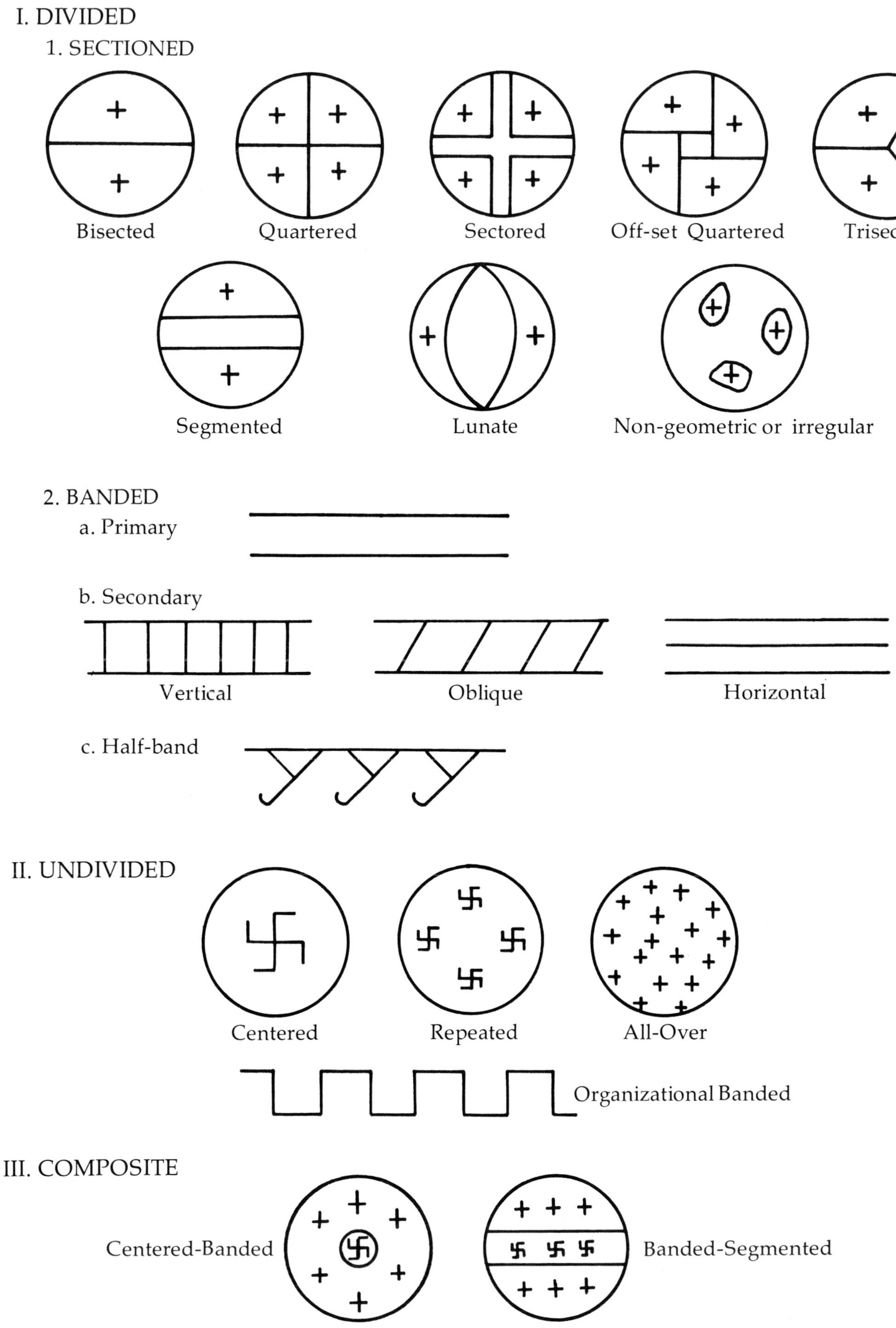

I. DIVIDED
1. SECTIONED

Bisected   Quartered   Sectored   Off-set Quartered   Trisected

Segmented   Lunate   Non-geometric or irregular

2. BANDED
a. Primary

b. Secondary

Vertical   Oblique   Horizontal

c. Half-band

II. UNDIVIDED

Centered   Repeated   All-Over

Organizational Banded

III. COMPOSITE

Centered-Banded   Banded-Segmented

Fig. 4.5 Layouts for application of pottery design, all found in the prehistoric Southwest. More formal arrangements occur under Divided Layouts, while freer styles occur in the Undivided ones.

drawn in an enclosed area as well as on a surface which has no division lines. There are fewer classes of undivided layouts (Fig. 4.5-II); they include centered, wherein a smaller or larger pattern appears in the center of a bowl or plate; repeated, with two or more motifs recurring usually in an organized or balanced manner; allover, in which large and/or small elements or motifs are regularly or irregularly repeated over the entire interior surface of bowl or plate; and organizational-banded, in which a continuous or repeated element or motif is so arranged by the decorator as to appear like a band, but without benefit of any enclosure lines.

A look at the general application of layout to all the vessel forms follows. Every layout, including all divided and undivided types, is adaptable to interior surfaces of bowls and plates and the bowl part of the ladle. Banded, half-banded, and organizational-banded are found on exteriors of some bowl and plate forms. Banded, half-banded, nongeometric or irregular, organizational-banded, and repeated layouts are used on jars, pitchers, vases, and mugs; other types of layouts are not usable on these forms. Pitcher handles usually have banded or other layouts different from the body style. The scoop is sometimes a little different in its layout from any form other than bowls for the shape itself is so different whether short or a bit longer-handled. Frequently the layout is banded or organizational-banded. The canteen may be decorated like jars or pitchers, with repeated patterning all the way around; or, in the form which is flat on one side, it may deviate somewhat in its layout. For example, the flat surface is either undecorated or it may have a layout like that of a bowl interior; so too may the rounded face of this form carry a layout of the same type.

Two other generalizations may be made regarding the problem of layout: some do not fit into any of the categories given here, and, not infrequently, two of these styles may be combined to form a composite layout (Fig. 4.5-III). A decoration which cannot be placed in one of the layout styles might be called irregular, and is unpredictable and, therefore, has not been included in this layout analysis. Probably it represents the work of a child, a beginning decorator, or one who was just doodling. Composite layout combines banded and centered, or half-banded and centered, organizational-banded and centered, or segmented-banded, and, occasionally, others.

There is a great deal of variation in the popularity of different layouts at different times in the three major cultural areas of the prehistoric Southwest. These, of course, will be treated in relation to their specific occurrences. In general, the Anasazi favored the more precise divided layouts, particularly the banded. On the other hand, even though they used the banded frequently, the Hohokams excelled in the use of the more free, undivided styles. Divided layouts were most popular among the Mogollon, although a composite style, using banded and centered together, was equally evident among the late expressions of this area, namely the Mimbres.

TYPES OF DECORATION

The decoration of pottery in the prehistoric Southwest presents a complicated, elaborate picture. Not only was painted decoration favored above all other styles but also this style alone was greatly varied, both in space and time. Too, there was tremendous variety in ways of applying designs, in design elements and motifs, in the relation of design to form, and in other matters. A general discussion of these decorative features follows, with some details pertaining to each in relation to regional styles and time sequences. By no means is every local style included herein.

Although plain wares were most common in all areas at all times, certain basic colors dominated the decorated styles in each of the three culture areas of the Southwest; there was considerable range within each of these styles as well as additional combinations in most of these territories. Color is subject to many vagaries, both within the color itself and frequently in relation to the user. One may question the color observed in the excavated pieces of pottery: Are they the same as they were originally? Are some of the variations due to use, weathering, or chemical or water action while in the earth? Furthermore, there are the variations due to the use of more or less paint; to a different shade related to different sources of a single color; to the results of longer or shorter firing, higher or lower firing temperatures; and other matters. Controls were not possible in the past as they are today with kilns and cones and scientifically prepared paints.

Throughout Hohokam time there was a dominance of red designs on a buff background, with some red-on-brown and also a limited red, buff, and yellow polychrome in very early days, and in very late times an outside-influenced use of red, black, and white. Further, there was tremendous range in the color red, running from pink through rust and into brown tones. The buff ground, also, diversified into gray shades on the one hand, and to brighter pink overtones on the other. In the southernmost part of this area appeared an interesting but limited combination of a purplish tone plus red on a buff ground.

In the Anasazi area, black pattern on a white ground was the most widespread basic style and the longest lived; the white ranged in color from a pearly gray to a dead chalky color, while the black varied from a thin gray-black to a good solid black. Later red was introduced into this northern area, to be combined with black at first, then still later with white also, to produce in the latter case one of the fine Anasazi polychrome wares. Red varied even more than the other two colors, with everything from a deep blood red to a light and bright brick red. Anasazi potters also developed other polychrome wares, including a local four-color combination of black, white, red, and an indescribable and rich, rosy tan. A black- (or brown-) on-yellow ware was also developed by the Anasazi decorator.

The earliest wares of the Mogollon area utilized simple red designs on a brown ground, the colors very much melded. A red-on-white combination followed; this in turn was replaced by a black pattern on a white ground and a negligible amount of black, white, and yellow polychrome.

In addition to color decorated wares, there were a number of other types of ceramic ornamentation. Popular in the Mogollon area were textured wares. Crudest of these was a simple scoring of the damp clay with a bundle of stiff grass (Fig. 4.6a); better control was possible in pieces scored with a tool (Fig. 4.6b). Punching a simple pattern on the soft clay was accomplished with the fingernail, a stick, or a reed (Fig. 4.6c). Sometimes the coils used in making a vessel were left unobliterated (called corrugated) (Fig. 4.6d); also they were indented (indented corrugated), often to produce a simple design (Fig. 4.6e). Cutting with a blunt pointed stick into the soft clay produced simple patterns, while a sharp implement cut into dry clay made for more distinct, incised designs.

Some of the Anasazis favored corrugated and indented corrugated types of decoration; in the latter, there was more designing than in other textured wares. Incised decoration was limited. Some appliqué was effected in this area, with ribbons or fillets of clay forming simple patterns on plain or corrugated surfaces (Fig. 4.6f).

Smudging of vessel interiors was a popular technique of Anasazi decoration that spread into other areas, particularly south into the Gila and

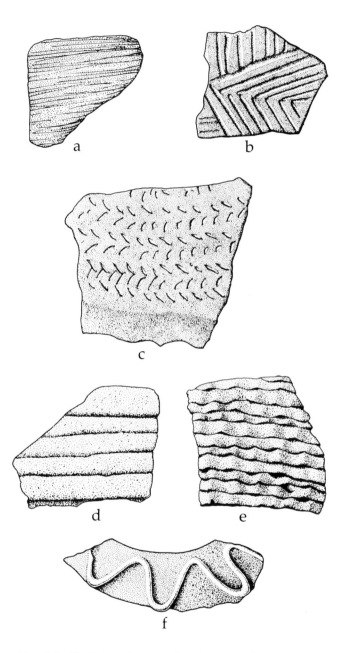

Fig. 4.6   Varieties of textured and appliqué decoration. (a) A pot sherd which shows grass marks, made when the clay was soft. Examples of tool marked pottery: (b) incised and (c) stick marked (Cosgrove and Cosgrove 1932, pl. 95 c,q). Examples of corrugated pottery: (d) plain and (e) indented (Guthe 1925, pl. 2 a,c). (f) An unusual type of decoration, with applique of clay curving around the opening of a jar which has no neck (Haury and Sayles 1947, Fig. 21a).

Fig. 4.7   Varieties of modeled decoration. (a) A full, round bowl with head and tail of a bird added at each end. The bowl carries a characteristic design of the ware from the White Mound area of east central Arizona (Gladwin 1945, pl. XIe). (b) A bird-shaped bowl with head and tail modeled and with body markings and wings painted on, Pueblo Bonito (Judd 1954, pl. 63e). (c) A Tularosa Black-on-white pitcher with a fully modeled effigy handle, from eastern Arizona (Martin and Willis 1940, pl. 81,7). (d) Fully modeled effigy jar with Mimbres decoration, and with a hole in the head to make it usable (Cosgrove and Cosgrove 1932, pl. 87f).

on into the heart of the Hohokam. This was accomplished, according to one authority, by building a small fire and smoldering it by placing a bowl upside down over the embers. This put the fire out and created an intense smoke that penetrated the interior walls of the vessel. Generally, this black interior ware had a red exterior.

One last decorative technique known throughout the Southwest was modeling. Here, again, there is much variation in the end product. Sometimes it was no more than crudely forming the head and tail of a bird on a bowl or jar (Fig. 4.7a), or, on some, painting the wings and any other details which were represented (Fig. 4.7b), or, even simpler, a suggested outline of a bird's body. Or the handle of a pitcher might be formed in the shape of the body of an animal with all details painted on except the modeled head (Fig. 4.7c). Complete shaping of the entire figure of a human, a bird, or an animal may serve as a jar or pitcher or the creature may be done as an independent piece of art (Fig. 4.7d). Thus these early modelers expressed an artistic range from low relief to full round.

DESIGN ANALYSIS

Further analysis of ceramics involves the matters of design, including elements or units, motifs, and the full or completed design or pattern (Fig. 4.8). Unfortunately, in archaeological literature these terms are so bandied about that one is left more confused than enlightened after reading some reports. Therefore, definitions of these terms will be kept on a simple level so that they may be applied to a wider survey of native ceramics.

In art, the term *element* is used with several meanings; so too is it in reference to design in archaeological materials. If employed in the dictionary sense of "irreducible simplicity," the term is greatly abused in both archaeological and artistic usage. Particularly in archaeological literature are certain privileges taken to include a few limited expressions which are so peculiar to the Southwest and so commonly used, as are the definable elements, that they are called elements. However, in this analysis a different approach is taken. A design element is the simplest irreducible part of a design, including a dot, a line, a line segment. A design unit is a combination or extension of elements, used to create forms which are employed as distinct and discrete entities within themselves, to be used alone or in combination.

Leavitt gives a number of "the common elements of Southwestern geometric design," as he

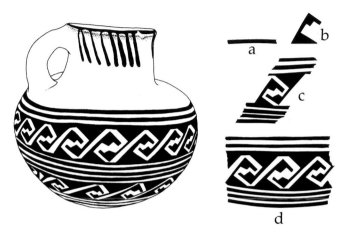

Fig. 4.8 Analysis of design: In the breakdown of design to the right, the thick line (a) is the only true element, and the triangle with the stepped "flag" (b) is a typical unit. Put together they form the motif (c); the latter is simply repeated for the decorative band which is the main theme of the vessel.

labels them;[5] most of these are herein referred to as elements or units. Later he gives "Basic Units in Southwestern Geometric Design," repeating many of the elements and really adding elaborations of these to form additional units.[6] Granted that the latter are commonly used as units, they are nonetheless developed directly out of his Figure 12 elements, or are repetition of some of his elements.[7] The following chart, therefore, includes various artistic expressions that have been labelled by different individuals as elements or units; many so named in various publications have also been omitted on the basis that it is thought that they are fundamentally elaborations of elements or units.

Elements, then, include the basic dot, line, and line segment (Fig. 4.9). Units, on the other hand, are much more numerous, and, although all are not included in Figure 4.9, the majority of them are found here. They are comprised of certain well-known, basic geometric forms such as the square, the rectangle, various triangles and diamonds, the circle, the parallelogram, the semicircle, and the parabola. Other units which

were distinctive of so much Southwestern decoration, and which are related to or evolved out of the element or simpler unit, include scrolls and frets, circular and angular hooks, triangular frets and hooks, both U- and V-shaped (chevron) figures, and the very popular step, the last in outline or as solid terraces or stepped triangles. Diminutive life forms (Fig. 4.9b) and so-called "small elements" (Fig. 4.9b,d) were also used as units of design by the Hohokams.[8]

One other very interesting development featured by the Hohokams is the so-called "bull's-eye," an artistic expression used as a unit (Fig. 4.9c). However, generally it is comprised of at least two units of design, for example, a large triangle, solid except for a circle at one point within it, and in the latter an additional element, unit, or life form. Here it is use value which makes this composite theme a design unit.

Life forms may be considered as developments of units, if they are presented in a more geometric and simple style. Otherwise, they are difficult to classify unless broken down into units or elements. Generally they are recognizable in their simplest form—man, animal, or bird; sometimes they are further identifiable in the latter two categories, as deer or dog, or as quail or duck, whatever the creature may be. In the Hohokam area, such creatures were frequently nothing more than continuous flowing solids, or bird or animal outline, in larger drawings perhaps with some geometric form appearing on them here or there. More complex geometric or more realistic forms are found among the Mimbreños: very frequently strictly geometric elements or units were added over the animal's body; these became more than units of design.

Motifs may be simple or complex; they may include design units used as the main theme in total pattern or a combination of one or more design elements and/or units to form the main theme in the allover pattern or total design. Examples of these might include in the first case, repeated single frets or interlocked simple scrolls, while the second style might be represented by a triangle with a hook attached to it worked out in a simple repetitive form (see Fig. 4.8) or in some more elaborate arrangement. In the decoration of a vessel, there may be a single motif used one time only or the motif may be repeated. There may be two motifs of equal importance; generally they would be used in an alternating, repetitive fashion. Or one motif may be elaborate and dominant, while a second one

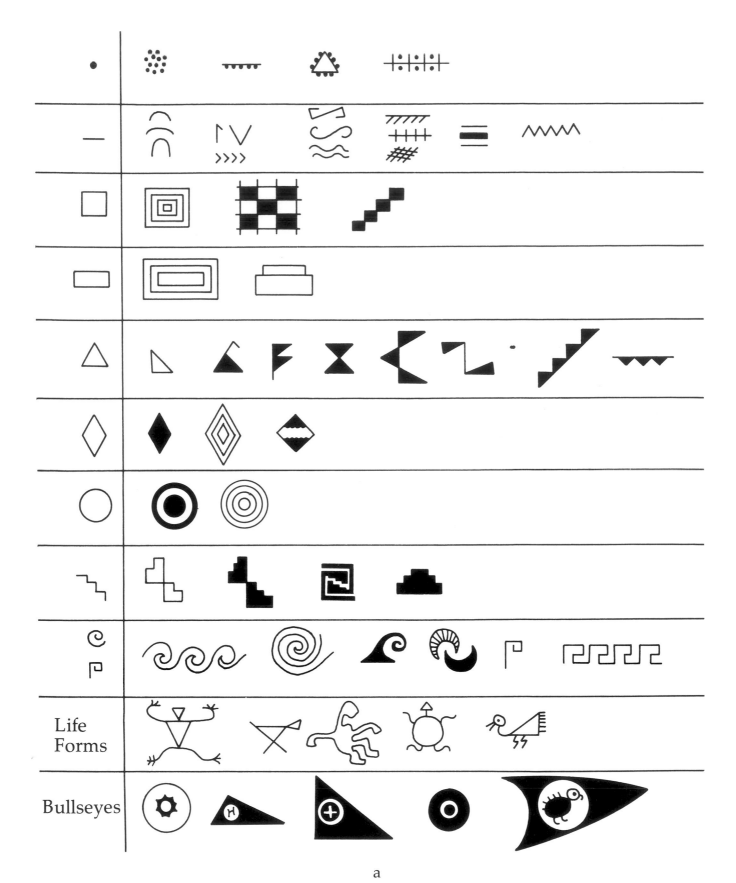

a

Fig. 4.9 Design elements and units used in pottery decoration. (a) From the basic dot, line, square, rectangle, triangle, diamond, and circle, there developed a variety of design units. In the Southwest, there were more regional elements or units, such as the step, the curved and angled line, which contributed heavily to additional units of design. (b)

Simple line or solid figures of life forms were commonly used as units, particularly among the Hohokam, as was (c) a theme highly developed by this same cultural group, the bullseye. Other Hohokam small elements (d) were suggestive of flying birds; here are a few which decorated pottery at Snaketown (Gladwin et al., miscellaneous illustrations).

b

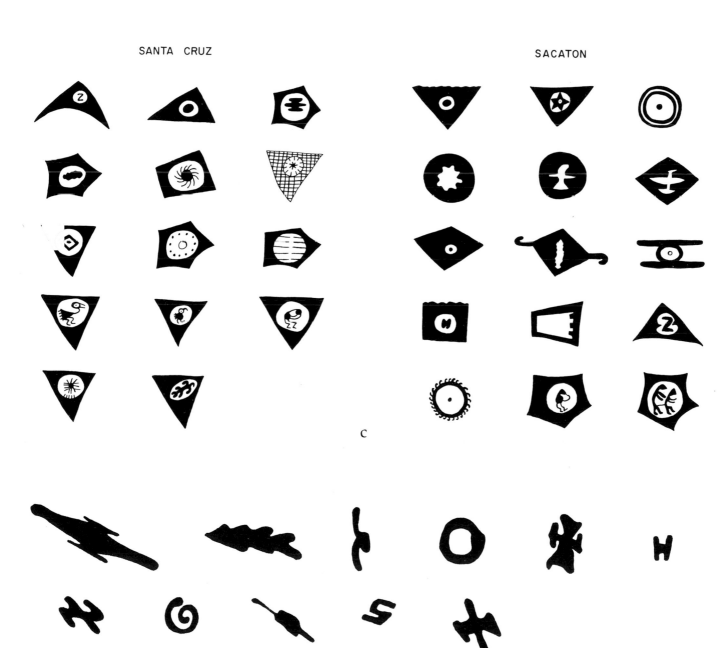

SANTA CRUZ

SACATON

c

d

is simple; these would be primary and secondary motifs, and might be represented by a band with a large and elaborate fret-triangle-line motif alternating with a single solid triangle.

One basic point should be kept in mind relative to the relationship between units, motifs, and patterns: all three could be the same, or the unit and motif might be the same but the pattern be different, or all three could be different entities. The first possibility reflects the simplest kind of artistic expression: a diamond in the center bottom of a bowl. An example of the second would be three rows of joined diamonds encircling the outside of a jar. In the third situation, the units might be scrolls and triangles, the motif large interlocked scrolls outlined with joined triangles, and the pattern a repetition of four of these motifs repeated on the walls of a jar.

Generally a given culture builds up through the years and centuries a selection of design units, and frequently some design motifs. However, creativity is expressed by the new combination of these basic units into different motifs and patterns. The Southwest is no exception in this matter; it is amazing that no out and out duplication is to be found in the thousands of vessels which have been excavated. There is, to be sure, much repetition of simple units or simple motifs, but even here the individual quality appears for it is not copying, it is simply a matter of using in various ways the themes from the common design-unit pool of one's culture. A few of these variations that contributed to diversity include the following: one, there is much variety in sheer size of units or sizes of juxtaposed units; and two, single, multiple, or alternating repetitions offer variety, as do the use of one, several, or many units to form a motif.

It has been noted by several that the Southwestern potter spends quite a bit of time just gazing at her pot before she touches her yucca leaf brush to the surface. If she is a conscientious worker, this is understandable, for she has to evaluate many points: the overall shape of the vessel and where the design should go; what kind of layout to use, single or multiple, and, if the latter, what type of division; what type of design is best suited to the chosen area or areas; and, finally, which design units, how they should interact, and which motifs should be developed and what should be their interrelationships. Slight wonder, then, that when all these problems are well established in the painter's mind, and once she puts her brush to work, there is no hesitancy, there is no delay. The imagination and creativity as well as technical ability of the potter will greatly influence the end product.

Regional Styles of Decoration

Classification of pottery is one of the most important duties of the archaeologist and art historian, yet one of the most hazardous of their tasks. Not infrequently, the classification runs away with the classifier, resulting in an overabundance of styles of decoration for a given area or site. Variations in certain features may account for this, and, of course, opportunities for individuality in expression and variation were many.

Not all women of a given village gather clay from the same pit, nor do all of them prepare clay and temper to the same degree of perfection. Burning offers variations in temperature and in the amount of time the vessel is in the fire. Specific forms tend to be culture-wide, but the individual expresses a range in both directions from the normal type. Even the choice of where to put the design and the choice of layout affect the end product: one has a better eye for balance than another. Then down to the final choice of design units, motifs, the allover pattern, and the colors to be used—again, much individual difference prevails. One is a conservative and adheres more to tradition; another is a free soul and a slave to nothing, yet there is a modicum of control in the available design units and motifs, and in the subconscious control of the tribal values. After all, the woman has been looking at the wares of her tribe since she was a baby on a cradleboard, and seldom has seen much else in the way of decoration.

Not only are all of these wheels of chance put into motion when the vessel is produced but also the classifier of some hundreds of years later has to face another series of problems in the pursuit of his classification. Is any piece of pottery ever "mint pure" in terms of clay surface and colors? Was the vessel placed in a grave as soon as it was made, was it used a short while and carefully, or did it have long and hard usage? Was it handled with greasy fingers, or was it frequently too close to the fire? And then, after the piece was left and buried in the earth for a few or more centuries, was the spot dry or wet? What minerals were in the soil?

Certainly the job of classifying pottery is not simple. In the following pages, larger categories of pottery styles will be discussed. Neither time nor space would permit a full pursuit of the many classes of wares which have been identified within the archaeological Southwest. The general trends in the artistic manifestations of the Southwestern ceramist can be demonstrated in a brief temporal and spatial analysis of a variety of representative wares. The larger cultural area will be cited first, with the major trends as a whole, then some local wares will be cited to demonstrate and support the artistic attainments of these pre-Columbian cultures.

Although pottery appeared later in the Anasazi than in the other two major cultural areas, it will be discussed here first. Some of the reasons for this include the fact that more archaeological work has been done in the Anasazi, a more extensive analysis of the wares from this area has been made, and, in general, there is more knowledge pertaining to the habits and customs of the people of this region as evidenced not only in archaeological materials but also among their lineal descendants, the contemporary Pueblo Indians. The fine preservation of materials in the cliff dwellings in which some of the Anasazis lived contributed to the more complete record of their ways of life.

Anasazi

Pottery appeared shortly after the opening of the Christian Era in the Anasazi area. It is quite generally accepted that this was several centuries after it was known in both the Hohokam and Mogollon Cultures. Inasmuch as it is thought that pottery came to the Southwest from Mexico as an already developed craft, it would have taken a while for it to have reached the more northern, and also at that time, more removed peoples who were developing Anasazi culture in the limited Four Corners area. Haury found pieces of thin-walled, well-made pottery in the lowest levels at Snaketown, apparently placing these first wares about 300 B.C.[9] A comparable date has been posited for Mogollon ceramic beginnings. It is not until 200 or 300 A.D. that the first pottery appears in the Anasazi; some of the very earliest pieces were comparable to a brown ware which is found in pre-Christian times in Hohokam and Mogollon sites.

The sequence of events in the Anasazi will follow the Pecos classification of Basketmaker I, II, III-Pueblo I, II, III, IV chronology. As noted in Chapter 1 (see Fig. 1.6), Basketmaker I was a period during which the Indians of this area were still somewhat nomadic, hunting game within a rather limited area. Although it is thought that they settled in caves for longer or shorter periods of time, the probabilities are that they did not settle long enough to have made pottery a practical accompaniment of their way of life.[10] Neither had these early northern people made contact with the southern Arizona and New Mexico people who had acquired this craft. It was not until late in Basketmaker II times that the first evidences of crudely made wares appeared.

BASKETMAKER III-PUEBLO I

In these first wares of Basketmaker II times, some fairly heavy-walled brown ware appears about the same time as a crude gray ware. Both are undecorated. The brown pottery was better made and smoother than the light ware; the latter was, in some instances, merely modeled inside an open basket bowl (Fig. 4.10). It has been suggested that perhaps the idea of pottery making came to this northern area through trade pieces from the south (brown wares). Or, possibly, the idea of pottery making might have reached these people by word of mouth and they experimented a bit (gray wares), with the resultant crude efforts of basket molding. The earliest gray ware was sometimes tempered with organic material such as grasses, and was undecorated.

By the beginning of Basketmaker III times the Anasazis had learned more about pottery and were producing larger quantities of it. It was still relatively crude compared to later wares, but some of it was decorated. Many of the trends of Basketmaker III times extend into Pueblo I, therefore the two periods will be discussed together. To be sure, there are improvements as

Fig. 4.10 An early Basketmaker III vessel, the lower portion of which retains the impression of the basket in which the clay was formed.

Fig. 4.11 A typical black-interior bowl, with a touch of indented decoration on the light colored exterior.

the years go by, and there are style trends of significance to the whole tradition of Anasazi Culture.

Basically, the Basketmaker III-Pueblo I pottery was coiled and smoothed. There was either no slipping or the slip was poor; sometimes there was a slipped appearance to the surface which was due to polishing the vessel to the extent that finer particles of clay were brought to the surface. There was some local variation in these matters; for example, slipping appeared later at one site than at another. Some of this early ware was decorated; a black decoration on a white (or gray) ground or a black design on a red base were the two main color schemes. It was on these decorated wares that slip appeared most commonly. In addition, there was a little crude punched ware; this gave the appearance of having been done with a stick while the clay was still damp.

Two unique types of decoration, if the term may be so applied for it was merely an alteration of the normal surface, were black-interior (Fig. 4.11) and neck band wares (Fig. 4.12). The former has been explained by some archaeolo-

Fig. 4.12 A clay pot with neck banding, from a pithouse at Kiatuthlanna (Roberts 1931, pl. 11d).

gists as having been accomplished in this way: bowl interiors were, as described before, smoke blackened over a smothered fire. This type of decoration became ever better and more popular through the years, and spread over the Anasazi and into adjoining areas.

The second ware, neck banded, seems to have started late in this period, perhaps even well into Pueblo I. To be sure, it too was earlier at some sites than at others. As the vessel was smoothed, some neck coils were left unsmoothed. In time two things happened: more of this banding appeared and a finger nail or a stick was used to indent these coils. In Pueblo III times, the entire vessel or the greater part of it might be covered with these so-called corrugations; this type of decoration dwindled in Pueblo IV times.

Roberts says of the Basketmaker III-Pueblo I Phase, "At no other period in the prehistoric Southwest was there such a diversity of form in ceramic objects. The variety of shapes is so numerous, the lack of rigid convention so marked, that it makes classification of form even more difficult than of the ceramics of the later periods...."[11] This statement is pertinent to early Anasazi forms for several reasons. First, irregularities of form indicate that here one sees manifestations of the true beginnings of ceramic effort; these irregularities consist not only of a large number of a given form, such as a jar, but also variation within any one of these deviations, for example, variety in an egg-shaped jar. Second, the craftsmanship in so much of this early pottery is poor, sometimes with lopsided vessels and often with bumpy surfaces; this poor workmanship contributed to diversity of form.

The two basic forms of all Southwestern pottery, the bowl and the jar or olla, were well established early in the Basketmaker III-Pueblo I Period. Other forms in the Anasazi include seed jars, pitchers, and ladles, with a few of these additional types: plates, cylindrical vessels, double-lobed styles, and animal and bird forms. All of these will be considered individually, with attention to form variation, types of decoration, layout, designs, and artistry. Some indication of relative time and distribution will also be noted.

The following is a brief analysis of Basketmaker III-Pueblo I vessel forms and layout based on the sites of Kiatuthlanna, Shabikeshchee, the villages of the Piedra District, and several other early sites.

Jars were varied, some of them reflective of basket or gourd forms, and some unrelated to

Anasazi

a

b

Fig. 4.13 Gourds and pots—related forms? Jars of the Basketmaker III–Pueblo I period were varied in form. (a) The double-lobed gourd to the left above (partially covered with skin) may well have been the inspiration for this same shape in ceramic vessels which have been found in prehistoric sites. The red jar on the right is mindful of the more rounded gourd in the center. (b) The pitcher form (lower left) is like coexisting jar forms, and they, in turn, were like the gourd to the right, even to the bulge in the neck in some.

any known local shapes in other materials (Fig. 4.13). Perhaps the latter were introduced from the outside. Types that were probably used for storage of water and foods include full-bodied forms that had either a long, small, slender neck, a shorter and slightly wider neck, or a shorter and very wide neck, and a spherical or egg-shaped form without a neck. The vessels with necks show definition between neck and body. One other jar has a very wide mouth and a rather continuous line from the rim to the body; its use was probably for cooking.

Many of these vessels were not decorated; certainly cooking pots were not. The relatively few jars which were decorated had a limited number of layouts, with banded most common. These might involve single or double bands, half-bands, or some combination of these two. Occasionally, and probably very early, are crude repeated layouts. Decoration appeared high on the shoulder of the jar, on the neck, or neck and shoulder, or, infrequently, on or near the widest diameter of the piece.

Bowls were of several shapes including hemispherical, straight-sided and round-bottomed, and shallow, the latter not unlike the tray basket. Bowls were more frequently decorated than were jars, or any other form for that matter, and they were also the most elaborately decorated. Decoration appears on bowl interiors most persistently, with rare exterior ornamentation in these early years.

Many design layouts appear on Basketmaker III-Pueblo I bowls. Banded was the most common; it appears around the rim, a little below the rim, or closer to the center. Quite popular was a band or a semi-band which cut across the center of the bowl, from rim to rim. Quartered patterns were fairly numerous, with repeated identical patterns within each quarter (a-a-a-a) or alternating designs (a-b-a-b) or, less often, completely different designs in each quarter (a-b-c-d). The latter would seem to be a bit of experimentation on the part of the decorator, with not too satisfying results, for this style did not gain popularity in later years. Tripartite arrangements are rarely found, with an a-a-a design repetition when this style was used, but it never became popular. Centered and allover layouts appeared during these years, although they too never gained great popularity with the Anasazi potters. Radiating allover disposition of pattern is mindful of basket arrangements. As on the jar, there are few repeated arrangements. Infrequently, bands or half-bands appear on bowl exteriors; almost never was any other style used on the outside of a bowl.

The general shape of the seed jar is globular with a depressed or flattened top and a small orifice; one common form in this early period is more rounded, while a second one has a sharper turn at the shoulder. Decoration involved a lighter band near the orifice, or a heavier band down to the shoulder, or, on the more rounded form, a band that extended down to or below the widest diameter.

Pitcher forms repeat several of the jar types. One is rather formless with a smaller neck which blends into the rounded body. Another has a short squat body and long wide neck, and a third shows a more rounded body; each of the latter two shows a more definite break between body and neck. All have handles, usually of the flat, oval, or rounded type. Decoration was fairly common on pitchers in these early years; when it appeared, it may have been a mere wavy line or simple theme, or more complicated geometrics carelessly repeated in half-bands or bands, or a combination of the latter two styles, or in organizational or double bands. Handle decoration was frequently no more than simple lines. Ladles were of two styles, the scoop type and the true ladle; decoration responded to the shape of this piece. The scoop usually had an allover arrangement if decorated, while the ladle was ornamented like the bowl, with banding or half-banding the most common layout.

Of the miscellaneous forms, plates were rare and not usually decorated; several had simple indentations on the underside, near the rim. Canteens, if ornamented, used a single or double banding, or repeated layout. Double-lobed, or hour-glass styled, jars were not decorated. Modeled life forms had a simple delineation of body features.

The extent to which design as a whole on all these forms had certain common characteristics will now be discussed. In the first place, painting tended to be sloppy and showed a marked lack of skill on all vessels, although some better work did appear on bowls; this may well have been the result of applying decoration to this form most frequently. There is poor line juncture, lines are uneven in width, and irregulari-

tics are common (Fig. 4.14). Much of the painted design was borrowed from basketry; thus there was continuity in decorative styles. Roberts says that in the Piedra area this is particularly true.[12] A geometric style of drawing prevailed, this in part due, no doubt, to the basket examples from which many design elements and units were borrowed, but also because textile patterns as a whole influenced pottery painting. Roberts also claims that curvilinear and life forms appeared at the same time as did angular patterns and that "one did not grow out of the other or result from it in the early development of southwestern [Anasazi] pottery designs."[13]

Curvilinear and life designs may well have been suggested by other types of painting. On the other hand, curved lines may have "just happened" as the pottery decorator's brush slipped, intentionally or accidently, when drawing an angular pattern on the finished vessel, of course, with none of the technological controls peculiar to both basketry and textile arts to keep her design straight lined.

Whether angular or curvilinear, all Pueblo designs remained basically geometric throughout the prehistoric period. Some are of the opinion that the development of certain types of social organization that centered about the tightly ordered pueblo may be reflected in the always-popular, but conservative and ordered, divided layout and geometricity in most patterns used by these people. Living in such compact villages, cheek by jowl, a more restrained and more ordered society was necessary for the puebloans. Art reflects the society it represents. The pueblo, then, may well be an outstanding example of the frequently expressed idea that society molds the art style.

During Basketmaker III–Pueblo I times, the main design elements and units of all Anasazi pottery were introduced: straight and wavy lines, dots, stepped and zigzag themes, triangles, some with "flags," squares and rectangles, checkers, diamonds, volutes and frets, and several odd-shaped geometrics (see Fig. 4.9a). Life forms are rare, and when they do appear, they are very angular. Two examples are a triangular-bodied human and an angular corn (?) plant (Fig. 4.15a,b). There is an elaboration of design in Pueblo I times, although some of the Basketmaker III patterns are by no means simple. Again, the strong basket influence might account for this. There is also a certain boldness of conception in much of the patterning of both

Fig. 4.14 Basketmaker III–Pueblo I pottery featured bowls, jars, and pitchers. Decoration was often crude, even sloppy, as in the two upper bowls, but some better work was also done, as illustrated in the pitcher and lower bowl.

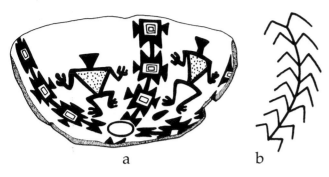

a   b

Fig. 4.15 Life figures on early Anasazi pottery. (a) Interior of one-half of a bowl with triangular bodied figures similar to those found painted on cave walls and identified as Basketmaker. This specimen was found across the wash from Pueblo Bonito (Roberts 1929, Fig. 32). (b) A centipedelike figure which appeared on a bowl from Shabikeschchee Village, nine miles from Pueblo Bonito (Ibid, pl. 16d).

phases of this earliest Anasazi pottery. It would seem to suggest that, freed of technological controls of basketry and textiles, the potter expressed a feeling of abandon, despite the fact that there was poorer draftsmanship than later.

PUEBLO II, III, AND IV

In the Anasazi area, Pueblo II, III, and IV may well be considered at the same time. Drastic changes occurred in Pueblo II, at least in some locales, which set the stage for the culmination of ceramic decoration in the two following periods, Pueblo III and IV. In Pueblo II, forms become more stabilized, and design, although greatly simplified, is more precise and better drawn. These changes occurred slowly but surely.

In the matter of forms, during Pueblo II times there was a tendency, first, for overall simplification; second, for a more limited number of forms; and, third, for greater refinement of shape. Late in this period a trend started which was to culminate in Pueblo III and IV, namely, the development of definitive forms and the further localization of these forms. Following are some of these trends with emphasis on the distinctive forms of each area mentioned.

Some bowls from the Chaco Canyon area are almost cone-shaped, others are more hemispherical. In the Mesa Verde, they are rounded and shallow and flat edged. In the Kayenta, they are fuller bottomed and more generous in the lower portions as a whole; some have a slight incurve in the upper walls and then an out-curved lip; and some have a single, strap handle just below the rim. The latter is a diagnostic of Kayenta bowls. In similar ways, many areas

worked out forms that became diagnostic to a degree of their respective cultures, with some more distinctive than others.

Comparative jar shapes are exemplified in the following styles. In the Chaco, the major form is a full-bodied, wide-mouthed, long-necked jar. A Kayenta wide-mouthed, short-necked, full-bodied jar shares favor with a jar that has a smaller mouth and a short straight line from the rim to an even fuller body. The latter may have inspired a late prehistoric Pueblo form that is very squat, with an incurved shoulder from about the midpoint of the jar to the base of the neck; this late form also has a smaller neck. Mesa Verde jars are either rounded in lower body, with a straighter, but sloping, upper body line merging into a short neck and wide mouth with slightly outflaring rim, or a full round body meeting a straight and smaller neck. Sometimes the latter form has two strap lugs placed low on the jar, often at a down-raking angle.

Pitchers varied somewhat, although in some areas they were not unlike jars in their general forms. In the Mesa Verde this was true as seen in a form like the first jar of this area just described, with the exception that the more sloping upper body or neck line becomes a little more perpendicular, and of course, a handle was added. A comparable form was produced in the Chaco; in addition, there was a pitcher distinctive of this area: a long neck with straight or nearly straight sides merged into a short or very short, squat body. Either a longer or shorter handle was placed on the neck of the jar. Kayenta pitchers were muglike in shape or were round-bodied with gently sloping necks.

Ladles were found quite generally in these developed Pueblo phases. Most areas, as represented in the Chaco, Mesa Verde, and Kayenta, made bowl-handle ladles with long, round handles; frequently at Mesa Verde they had an abrupt upturn at the end of the handle. In some Chaco types, the bowl continued into a long handle; this piece would not be considered a scoop in the sense of Hohokam varieties of this form, for in the southern type the handle was very short.

Small canteens are not uncommon throughout most of the Anasazi area. Generally they are the same shape as the local jar, or comparable thereto, but have two handles or lugs with holes in them, one on each side. The large jar found in the Mesa Verde, with low lugs, may be classed as a canteen. Some smaller ones have flat backs and rounded faces.

There are several forms that are much more limited in distribution; these include mugs, vases, and the colander. The last piece has been found exclusively in the Kayenta area; it is a more shallow bowl with holes produced in the bottom during the process of manufacture. Mugs have been found in the Mesa Verde only, their sides sloping from the rim straight down to a wider base; also they have a single large flat handle. Straight-sided, or almost straight-sided, vases are peculiar to the Chaco Canyon; they are tall, slender, and flat-bottomed.

The techniques of decoration in Pueblo II, III, and IV were numerous and varied. They included painting (the most abundant and most varied), corrugated, smudged, relief, and full modeling.

Corrugated decoration ran the gamut from simple neck banding to allover corrugations (Fig. 4.16). Neck banding was similar to that of Pueblo I times (see Fig. 4.12); it was most common in

Pueblo II. Allover corrugation reached a peak in Pueblo III times and subsided in Pueblo IV; it disappeared before the arrival of the Spaniards.

During Pueblo II, there were better smudged wares than before, the black was deeper and there was a slight luster. Late in this period, there was a good, highly polished red exterior, and the black interior often has a soft, velvety finish. This fine type continues into later periods.

In relief and modeling, there is considerable variety. The simplest type is in the form of fillets of clay added to vessels, particularly to corrugated surfaces, in strips or bands, as volutes, or occasionally in other patterns. These techniques were widespread in Pueblo III times. Modeling is found in conjunction with life forms, and may appear as the simplest "pinching up" of clay for a head and tail to the fashioning of the complete or nearly complete life form as a bowl or jar.

In Pueblo II times, the most popular color combination was black-on-white (Fig. 4.17), while black-on-red was the only other color-

a

Fig. 4.16 Varieties of corrugated wares. (a) From neckbanding (lower left) to decorative combinations of plain and indented styles (upper left), and a variety of indented styles (upper right and two lower right). Occasional other types of surface marking occurred (lower, second from left). (b) Two styles of corrugated ware, Reserve Patterned corrugated on the left and McDonald Painted corrugated on the right. Both types have glossy black interiors.

b

Anasazi

Fig. 4.17 A Pueblo II black-on-white vessel. Featured in this period were solids and broad lines; combined with the latter are stepped triangles on a bowl interior. Precise painting is outstanding.

decorated ware. Both of these wares continued on into Pueblo III and IV; in fact, black-on-white was the most popular combination of the entire Mesa Verde and Chaco Canyon prehistoric development (although a little black-on-red was produced), and also was popular in all other areas of the Anasazi during these years. Three-color decoration became more popular in Pueblo III in all parts of the Anasazi except the Chaco and the Mesa Verde. Black, white, and red ware seems to have been the most common and widespread; it is found in the Kayenta, in fact, throughout the Little Colorado drainage, and on south into the upper reaches of the Gila River as a puebloid manifestation. In some locales, other colors appeared, such as yellow or yellow-tan in the Hopi area and a rosy shade in the Kayenta that defies definition. Other combinations of color, which tend to be more limited in distribution, will be treated in their respective locales.

The application of decoration is most varied on the black-on-white pottery, and black-on-red wares reflect some of these styles. On ollas and pitchers, there is usually separate neck and body decoration. Interior decoration prevailed on bowls, and, generally, ladles carried out some of the same schemes. As most kiva jars had a shoulder, the ornamentation was spread from orifice to the turn of the shoulder or sometimes below the turn. Generally mugs were painted with two panels or bands that covered all but the bottom of this specialized form.

Black-on-white pottery of the Pueblo II Period reflects more of what happened at this time than do other decorative styles. Basically the white is better than it was in the previous periods for it is more white than gray; so too with the black, for it is less washed out than it was in previous times. Banded layouts were most popular, although there were quite a few half-banded types. Whereas angular patterns had dominated the Basketmaker III-Pueblo I pottery, in Pueblo II there was a fair amount of curvilinear work. Broad lines were common and were done with much greater regularity than in previous years. Triangles are often long raking affairs and solid; they are either plain or with dots on one side. Simple scrolls, some of them just barely interlocking, are of heavy lines; they appeared late in Pueblo II. In fact, practically all line work is heavy as are the dots. Despite the wide lines (in many instances, they average one quarter of an inch) and solid triangles, and despite the limited number of design elements, the drawing in much of this Pueblo II pottery is more meticulous than it had been in prior years. The design style might be characterized as simplified, particularly as contrasted with the rather uncontrolled drawing of earlier years.

Quite a change occurred in corrugated pottery during Pueblo II. First, frequently it was corrugated over the entire surface of the neck of the vessel, often on small cooking ollas. Second, it was far better executed than before; the corrugations were even and fine, and often indented; however, designs were not made in this earlier ware.

Pueblo II stands as a period during which there were rather drastic changes in ceramics, particularly in more carefully drawn patterns. Was the more restricted and better executed design reflective of the development of more formal patterns in the social organization of the Pueblo-type society? Does it tell of the necessity for stricter rules when all in the village lived in a single house, in the tightly knit single apartment? Was less personal freedom a part of this social trend? Or did the pottery makers become a bit discouraged with the sloppy work of Basketmaker III-Pueblo I times and turn to new artistic efforts? Or was the more meticulous work of Pueblo II decorators the natural result of evolution of design, with early work merely representing freedom of expression due to no technical controls, such as geometricity in technique-controlled basket-textile crafts? It would almost seem that the latter was true of the earlier decorators and that the brush led them astray, perhaps willingly and happily on the painters' part, rather than the ceramist directing the brush. But then came a day of reckoning: and Pueblo II seems to represent that day. All in all, it would appear that several factors served together to bring about slow change. It spread gradually, and perhaps it was not felt at all in some areas until later times.

Whatever the reasons, Pueblo II served as a substantial stepping stone for potters to progress into peak attainment in either, or both, Pueblo III and IV. Both periods, and particularly Pueblo III, saw some further refinement of form, a great growth of painted design, many new local styles of decoration, and, probably, the spark of individual genius at various points. As is true of so much design growth in the craft arts around the world, there was little that was new in the way of elements and units among these later Puebloans: rather was it a matter of recombinations of the old. In many instances the old basic geometric forms are hardly recognizable in their new garb; change and growth are manifested largely in more complex and intricate patterns. Even corrugated wares, modeling, and several other types of decoration changed during these later years of full Pueblo development.

Corrugated wares reached a peak in Pueblo III times, then began to degenerate in Pueblo IV, and had disappeared by the time of the arrival of the Spaniards. Certain regional styles of corrugation are of interest because they reflect the strong trend of localization of art at this time (see Fig. 4.16).

In the Mesa Verde, shapes whereon corrugation is found include large jars and small pitchers. The former have wide mouths, some more flaring than others, and egg-shaped bodies; the latter are like jugs with single handles. The thin-walled, graceful jar has regular, small, fine, and evenly spaced indentations.[14] They were designed with alternating bands of plain and indented coils, or with indented triangles against a plain-coil background.[15] Further, there was some relief on the corrugated background, for example, double spirals made with fillets of clay, with perhaps two of these on a jar. Pitchers carried comparable but less varied decoration.

Fat, round-bodied pots with large apertures from the Kayenta were decorated with less regular and not so well-executed corrugations, with some unevenness in size of coils. There was added decoration here also, including scrolls and "turkey tracks" (three spread-out, short pieces of clay meeting at one end). Earlier Kayenta work of this type was better, later work was degenerate.

Large jars with wide mouths were the prevailing form for this corrugated style of workmanship in the Chaco area. Corrugations were well made, and usually were sharp and clear-edged. A variety of pleasing textures was produced by varying the depth and arrangement of the indentations; for example, an allover swirl effect resulted from placing indentations in a definite pattern.

The large olla was also popular and fairly well corrugated in the upper Gila, but large, deep, and flat-bottomed bowl forms were far better made. The latter have the finest corrugations of any vessels in the Southwest: some count as many as 12 coils to the inch. A great variety of indented patterning occurs on these bowls, and some have a fugitive white paint over the exterior surface following the lines of pattern. These bowls have black interiors and red or red-brown exteriors. A small band just below the rim or over the entire exposed exterior surface might be corrugated, with smaller or larger indented triangles, nested triangles, bands, or parallel zigzags. One of the most distinctive of these indented wares is McDonald Corrugated.

Considerable improvement is to be noted in the modeling ability of the Pueblo III-IV potter, although there are many representations which are comparable to earlier, simple expressions (Fig. 4.18; also see Fig. 4.7). In many areas there

Fig. 4.18 A pleasingly modeled figure of a mammal forming the handle of a "boot" bowl. The little rascal (could it be a fox?) appears to be drinking out of the bowl.

was limited head-tail modeling on opposite ends of a bowl, with the rest of the vessel painted in a conventional, geometric style or with an adaptation of this painting to suggest feathers of a bird or other features of the creature represented. From these simpler types, there was advancement into such details as the hands, feet, and face of effigy vessels, for example, in the Chaco Canyon. Proportions of such details may be fair or completely unrealistic. The shape of the vessel varies also; for instance, the full form of bowl, pitcher, or ladle may be retained, with the head and tail merely additions on these three forms; on the second, the handle may be in the vague shape of an animal; or a baby might be modeled in the handle of the third form. In all these cases there is no deformation of the vessel shape. On the other hand, the bowl or pitcher may be tapered at the end that represents the bird's tail; or the full form of the animal may be modeled and a hole made in the top so that it can serve as a pitcher or jar. Several of these shapes are well represented at Pueblo Bonito, as illustrated in Judd.[16] At Pueblo Bonito there are fine fragmentary examples of modeling, including hands with fingers, feet with toes, and faces with eyes and nose in relief. A bear paw shows the claws, and animal snouts have eyes in relief. A great deal of modeling appears in the Upper Gila, with less in the Little Colorado. In both areas the head of the animal or bird may be modeled in full round and serve as the handle; in other instances, the full figure of the animal is crudely modeled to form the handle, with the head at the top and often in full round.

Painted decoration presents such an overwhelming picture for Pueblo III and IV that one can but touch the surface of this subject. So many local wares developed that only a few of the more important ones will be discussed. Black-on-white types are prominent in every Anasazi area; they remain so into the historic period. The same is true, on a smaller scale, for black-on-red pottery. Polychrome wares (three or more colors, including the base color) are more restricted in distribution; basically, the combination of black, white, and red, and sometimes several other combinations are often diagnostic of their respective locales.

In the San Juan area, black-on-white was important early and late, in Pueblo III-IV times, particularly in the Mesa Verde and the Chaco. In the Mesa Verde, the basic forms decorated in

this manner (in these later periods) include short-necked, round-bodied, lugged ollas, both large and small; bowls with a fairly even rim-to-rim curve; bowl-and-handle type ladles; mugs; life forms, particularly birds; and kiva or seed jars with lids (Fig. 4.19). Surfaces of vessels were carefully polished, were of a creamy, or more frequently, a pearly gray color and were decorated with a sharp black paint. Much of this black-on-white pottery had flat rims that were characteristically decorated with short lines or "ticks" as they are commonly called. In general, Mesa Verde designs are bold and free, despite the fact that they are typically confined to bands framed by multiple lines on both edges. Although geometric patterns prevailed, there were some life forms, such as birds and mountain

a

b

Fig. 4.19 Mesa Verde styles of pottery: (a) Above are typical black and white pieces, a bowl and a jar, with a banded design on each. Characteristic, too, are the multiple bordering lines on either side of the black designs, and the "ticking" on the flat rim of the bowl. (b) Most distinctive of the Mesa Verde wares is the mug. The above three show some slight variations in form, flat strap handles, and several styles of decoration. On the central mug, repeated parallel lines enclose the checkered and hatched design; the examples to the left and right show heavier bordering lines and feature bold plain or stepped triangles in the main designs.

sheep. Single units or paired and opposed units are repeated or continuous within the bands, or they may be large and all over a bowl interior. The drawing may be in solids or in hatching. Triangles, keys, checkerboard, some volutes, dots, and varied lines and bands, which are usually parallel, are included in the design motifs.

Rare but typical of the Chaco Canyon area are vessels modeled in human forms; many bird effigy pots were also produced here. Other forms include both bowl and handle and bowl merging into handle ladles; pitchers, both with fuller bodies gently sloping into short necks and, more characteristically and mindful of earlier years, one with a long neck sharply turning into a squat body; bowls with a smooth and continuous curve from rim to rim; tall slender vases; and occasional canteens (Fig. 4.20).

Chaco layouts are basically banded, yet also popular are organizational-banded, allover, and occasional other arrangements. Two layouts reflective of the close relationship between this problem and form are to be noted in Chaco pitchers: the style with the elongate upper and squat lower parts features two separate bands,

while the pitcher with the shorter neck blending into the body usually displays a single-band design. The first style also has more discrete and ordered patterning; often the second is composed of a meandering design. Single bands from rim to base (or almost to the base) are featured on the tall vases, and vertically stacked geometric patterns are favored.

Perhaps two of the most characteristic features of Chaco decoration are the chalky white slip and fine diagonal hatching enclosed by slightly broader lines. The latter feature contrasts with the coarse Mesa Verde hatching enclosed by lines of the same width. Too, the commonly solid black painting of the Chaco rim is quite different from the light ticking of the Mesa Verde rim. Another contrast is found in the single upper and lower lines for enclosing zonal patterns as opposed to the multiple enclosure lines found in the Mesa Verde. Fine-line and solid patterns are both found in the Chaco, with triangles and other geometric elements, stepped figures, checkers, and meanders prominent in the designs. So-called wing patterns of angular type are prominent; in fact, most of the Chaco designing is on the angular side, with curved lines rather uncommon. Several forms with scroll designs found at Pueblo Bonito are probable imports from Mesa Verde. Designs tend to be open in the Chaco area, despite some interlocked scrolls and frets, opposed triangles, and other more closed styles.

In the Kayenta area to the west, there seems to be greater variety and originality in forms and design and more change through time than in the Mesa Verde and Chaco areas. For example, there are variations in bowl forms not found elsewhere, there are two distinctive black and white decorative styles, and there is the addition of abundant polychrome wares. Another distinctive local feature is a clear white slip in the black-on-white wares.

Some Kayenta shape variables include the following. In bowls, there are deep, straight-sided forms, sometimes with a single horizontal strap handle; or some have a slightly outcurved lip; or others are completely incurved and either rounded or flat shouldered, which are called kiva bowls (or jars); or the simple, rounded, small type made into colanders. Many ollas have very rounded bodies and very small necks (Fig. 4.21).

The styles of black-on-white decoration evidenced in the Kayenta region include a positive

Fig. 4.20 Typical Chaco Canyon pottery: pitchers with long or fairly long necks and squat bodies, varied life forms, and ladles, many of continuous bowl-handle shapes. Painting in this area featured fine hatching within broader enclosing lines, best illustrated in the decoration of the pitcher, with rather coarser lines on the strange little animal with the olla neck on his head. The ladle features solid triangles with pendant dots.

Fig. 4.21 Fine example of Kayenta jar. A large round-bodied Kayenta style. Its black and white opposed triangles and bands are suggestive of a stage between positive and negative painting.

and a negative (Figs. 4.21 and 4.22). In positive decoration the design is carried by the black paint, which is added after the surface of the vessel is finished in white, whether it is slipped or not. Negative decoration on the other hand, is a style in which the black paint is used in large quantity but does not carry design; rather the design is evident in the background color, which is a white slip in the Kayenta negative wares. Thus it *looks* like a white design on a black background.

Positive black-on-white Kayenta pottery seems to be both earlier in time and contem-poraneous with the negative wares. Also it survived into a later period. It features a greater variety of designing; however, in general it is not as distinctive as the negative. Positive decoration is found on all vessel forms, while the negative style is restricted largely to jar and bowl forms of shapes peculiar to the Kayenta. Layouts are about the same for both styles, with banded and half-banded used for both jars and bowls, although there are more multiple banded styles in the positive ware. Offset quartered is popular for bowl and dipper interiors. In a broad sense, lines and small solids appear more frequently in the positive style, while larger solids are not uncommon in the negative ware. Greater complexity is apparent in the negative style, whether real or suggested by the background of lines or netlike effects against which the main themes of the pattern are painted. Positive-ware design elements and motifs are actually more varied and include a wide variety of shapes and uses of triangles, interlocking scrolls, continuous or interlocking frets, wing patterns, and so-called octopus designs (a meandering free form with irregular enclosure lines containing parallel zigzags or lines). Although scrolls are found on the negative wares, step patterns are more frequent, particularly with the netlike background where the steps follow the checkering or crosshatching.

Great ability is reflected in the negative style, which frequently follows the outlines of crosshatching; perhaps *because* of the use of these very devices, the painter's work was superior for surely she was often guided by the previously drawn lines or network. Nonetheless,

a

b

c

Fig. 4.22 Kayenta pottery. (a) A bowl (or dipper) with distinctive handle; (b) a jar; (c) a seed jar or bowl, all with negative designing. Large black areas allow patterning to show through in the white slip. Even in the jar the white really carries the burden of the pattern. The most unusual extended and upturned handle on the bowl is also a Kayenta trait.

Fig. 4.23 Little Colorado area ware. A Reserve Black-on-white pot. Painting in the band is very well executed, with quite a play of solid and hatched design. The two "footprints" in the center are more carelessly painted.

lines not controlled by this network are drawn with great skill. Kidder and Guernsey believe that this network was significant in relation to design "in locating and measuring its units by means of the underlying lines. In this way they attained great accuracy of spacing and regularity of repetition, and those parts of the preliminary

hatching or cross-hatching that cross the narrow white spaces between the black figures give to the whole decoration an almost textile appearance."[17]

There are many other black-on-white wares found in the Anasazi, with the majority of them following the general trends so far mentioned, except for the negative type, and with certain local styles and characteristics. A few of these additional wares and some of their diagnostic traits follow.

In the Little Colorado area, there were several types of black-on-white wares. One, Reserve Black-on-white (Fig. 4.23), is well represented by pitchers and bowls. The former feature fairly wide necks, globular to squat bodies, and usually neck and body decoration, bands or half-bands on the former, and bands characteristically on the latter. Bowls are fairly deep and sloping-sided and typically have interior decoration. In Reserve decoration there is solid line and mass black treatment, but there is also much balanced solid-hatched decoration, or some play between these two. Angular geometric styles prevail, but there are some curvilinear motifs, such as interlocked scrolls. Related styles include Tularosa Black-on-white (Fig. 4.24) from the Upper Gila and some of the Roosevelt wares (Fig. 4.25). There is more variation in pitcher and bowl shapes; some of the former feature charming

Fig. 4.24 Tularosa Black-on-white vessels. The two pitchers have life form handles which are so typical of this area, the upper one with a head alone, and the left example with an animal with winglike additions. Both of these vessels are decorated with characteristic balanced solid-hatched decoration. The dipper is of the bowl and separate handle style.

Fig. 4.25 Roosevelt Black-on-white vessels which reflect some of the Little Colorado styles of decoration, although they came from farther south. Note the balanced solid-hatched themes in the ladle and bowl. The pitcher has an almost negative decoration, and the head on the bird pot is well formed.

animal handles. In this ware there are quite a few miniatures and much balanced solid-hatched painting.

In some, though by no means all, of the Reserve wares, drawing reflects lack of skill, yet there is much vigor in the use of large sweeping scrolls. Interest is created in varied subject matter, opposed solid and hatched themes such as steps, scrolls, and triangles. Animal heads of full modeled forms, although crude in their craftsmanship, enliven pitchers. Similar to the Reserve wares in design and its treatment are the Tularosa wares. However, in the latter, there is much superior skill exhibited in the drawing of large interlocked scrolls and other units; solid areas are smaller and the opposed hatched parts reveal finer line work. Because of these qualities, Tularosa painting seems more complex, yet an out and out comparison would reveal identical motifs. Handles on pitchers are not any better in the Tularosa wares. Pitchers of this area have more squat, fuller bodies and a sharper line of juncture between neck and body; this may explain a lack of continuous neck-body decoration plus a wider undecorated section between the neck and body bands in the Tularosa pottery.

Although Judd reports no black-on-red pottery at Pueblo Bonito,[18] there was a little made in the Chaco area and in adjoining territory. Typical Chaco bowl and pitcher shapes were so decorated. As a whole, the designs are simpler than in black-on-white wares, perhaps for the reason that the red style was much more limited in production. Simple bands prevail, although two bands usually appear on jars. Parallel-line or narrow-band patterns are frequent, and some hatching appears.

In the Mesa Verde area, there is relatively little black-on-red pottery; rather is there a mixture of wares, some with a red base and some with an orange base. Much of this ware is Pueblo II in time, some possibly a bit earlier, some a little later. Some of the orange-base ware, with red decoration, seems unrelated to other Mesa Verde types; in fact, much of its decoration is so simple (broad-lined steps and zigzags, heavy triangles attached to scrolls, and meaningless geometrics), and so crudely drawn as seemingly not to be related to Pueblo II black-on-white styles at all. Black designs on the red wares are more frequently better executed and more like the Pueblo II black-on-white styles. There is the probability that some of the so-called black-on-orange pieces are color variants of the black-onreds, revealing an affinity with earlier or contemporary black-on-white ware. Thus, black-on-red and black-on-orange in the Mesa Verde may be related (or the same ware with differing base colors) and more local in development, while the red-on-orange seems unrelated in design and color to this immediate area.

Red wares were popular in the early Kayenta; later there were black-on-orange and still later black-on-yellow wares. Design analysis has led some to believe that there are transitional stages through several black-on-white styles with later ones merging into or influencing the black-on-orange. Black-on-yellow, which overlaps the late prehistoric and early historic years, shows many influences from the highly developed (and the last) black-on-white series and from polychrome wares which were contemporaneous.

Although some of the black-on-red pieces of the Kayenta are simple, others reflect direct black-on-white influence (Fig. 4.26). A good example is a Tusayan seed bowl with a curvilinear wing pattern extending from the orifice onto the body proper, which is mindful of a squat black-on-white jar with the theme adapted to the area from the base of the neck well onto the rounded body. The pattern in both cases has heavy diagonal hatching within a heavy outline of the wing. Characteristic of Jeddito black-on-orange, themes are both curvilinear and rectilinear wing patterns, plain and interlocked scrolls, frets, and steps, all frequently large in size, plus lesser and smaller geometric motifs. All of these are reflective of the decoration of the highly developed and contemporary black-on-white styles, not only in the themes themselves but also in the manner of painting, the boldness and freedom of expression.

The third and last of these Kayenta two-color wares, Jeddito black-on-yellow, reflects some of the lingering high developments of the last black-on-white styles and further reflects some of the artistry of contemporary polychromes. Although the variety of design is great, scrolls, frets, and wing motifs are prominent, but much subdued in size and vigor. On jar exteriors, heavy broad bands contain the more discrete and simpler geometric patterns. Some of these earlier black-on-yellow pieces demonstrate fine drawing, or, at least, smaller and well-executed geometrics. In some of the later pieces of this ware shapes changed, that is, bowls may have outcurved rims and there are many poorly or more simply executed geometric designs and

Fig. 4.26   Tusayan (Kayenta) Black-on-red pieces. Both of these colanders (or sieves) are shaped more like the seed jar, the one on the left having a very flat shoulder. The left example also is decorated in the style of Kayenta negative Black-on-white.

quite a few life motifs, such as humans (including masked figures), rabbits, birds, and others. Some of the last of the prehistoric black-on-yellow ware drawing was very degenerate.

Throughout the Little Colorado area, and extending southward into the upper Gila, there are several black-on-red styles of ceramic decoration. As in connection with other areas and other types of color decoration, by no means can all Little Colorado wares be mentioned; however, one of the characteristic styles will be discussed from the standpoint of artistry.

Although the base red of the Little Colorado varies, it is usually of a clear shade, and the strong intense black used with it makes for a pleasing contrast. Wingate Black-on-red will serve to illustrate this style. Jars and bowls predominate, although a few other forms are found. Jars are medium- to short-necked or have no necks, as in seed jars, and have full to almost-squat bodies; the division between the two parts is generally abrupt and makes for a separate neck and body design. Bowls are semicircular and almost always decorated on the interior. Single bands or half-bands prevail on jar bodies while necks of this form utilize organizational bands most frequently. Bands prevail for bowl decoration, although allover styles of layout are not infrequent. Large balanced, or almost balanced, solid-hatched scrolls, and less often frets, are common decorative motifs on both jars and bowls; sometimes other geometrics are used in like manner. Triangles and stepped themes are also handled in the solid-hatched fashion. Thus Little Colorado Black-on-red wares may be more dynamic in decorative style, in the use of large and moving elements or units, or they may be more staid and stable in appearance since they employ static geometrics of smaller sizes.

Jars and bowls are the common forms of the Upper Gila area, and they are not unlike the black-on-red wares of the Little Colorado. Sometimes jars have shorter necks on which the decoration is reduced to a mere repetition of paired lines or other small themes. Body decoration is frequently simplified to a single theme, such as diagonal stacked triangles in alternate and balanced solid-hatched fashion.

Polychrome ceramic decoration was abundant and widespread in the prehistoric Anasazi; it represents, in its many local manifestations, peaks of artistic attainment in this craft endeavor. Although it is absent or found in limited quantity in the extreme northeast, polychrome tends to be the most popular of decorative styles in the last days of ceramic expression in all other parts of this area. Most of the polychromes are three-color wares; however, a few styles employed four colors. Some of the polychrome styles are but reflections of contemporary two-color varieties, while others branch out in completely new directions, some undoubtedly reflecting far distant styles which came to be known through trade, and others, perhaps, expressing the work and influence of a local genius.

So limited are sherds from the Mesa Verde which represent polychromes of this area that little can be said on the subject. Swannack illustrates two pieces from Wetherill Mesa and calls them local polychromes;[19] he further identifies them as polychrome variations of two local black and white wares; one has a cream slip with a simple broad line in red outlined in black, while the second has a white slip decorated in red-brown on a tan filler. Admittedly, the latter is probably an experiment and nothing more.

Polychrome wares, except for obvious imports, are conspicuous for their absence in the Chaco Canyon area. To be sure, the major, true Chaco culture was early; this time factor alone would tend to eliminate three-color wares.

Quite the contrary is true of the Kayenta, for here the use of more than two colors on a single vessel seems to have been a delight to these potters, whether they added a slip part way down the vessel wall to add to color effects or otherwise manipulated paint. Too, the Kayenta culture is the only Anasazi, in fact, the only Southwest group of prehistoric times, which ventured into four-color decoration of pottery. Whether the polychrome idea came from the outside or was developed locally has not been proved, but there is so much continuity in design from one style to another in the Kayenta that one is tempted to suggest a local growth for the three-color wares. Also, some of the early addition of color in the form of a slip part way down the vessel exterior, plus the use of typical Kayenta layouts and design elements in the earliest polychromes, would seem to support a local development. In the first instance, a red slip was applied to a part of the buff vessel, then a black design was painted on the red. Certainly this could be noted as transitional with full polychromes developing very quickly, including both black, white, and red, and these three colors plus buff. Even though broad lines in red outlined in black have been looked upon as possibly from the south, they are too readily associated with the Kayenta wing and other elements of pattern to consider them not of local origin. The lunate layout, which is also local, is found in some of the very early Kayenta Polychrome; this too should support a probable local origin for this multicolor ware.

Vessel forms in Kayenta Polychromes are often similar to those of the various two-color wares, with some additions, of course. For example, the simple-line bowl, even to the single handle on some pieces, is apparent in polychrome wares. Round-bodied jars and pitchers with wide and medium or short necks prevail. Major changes are to be seen in Kayenta Polychrome types: in squat bowls with incurved or incurved-outcurved rims, and in two jar forms, one with a wider neck and outflaring mouth on a more rounded body, and a second more squat form with a gentle curve from neck into bulging body, the latter sometimes with a most abrupt inturn to a rounded base.

Fig. 4.27 Kayenta polychrome vessels. The bowl on the right is an excellent example of this style, with black and red decoration outlined in white on an orange ground. A small strap handle appears on one side. Another Kayenta type (Tusayan) is represented in the piece to the left; its polychrome decoration is confined to the bowl portion of this ladle.

There are several different types of polychrome in the Kayenta that are reflective of the artistic trends of these people. First is Kayenta (or Kietsiel) Polychrome, then Bidahochi, and last Sikyatki, which continues into early historic times.

A ware called Kayenta (or Kietsiel) Polychrome has a red base with black decoration outlined in narrow white lines. Other Kayenta styles differ (Figs. 4.27 and 4.28). It is dated from about 1270 to about 1300. There are areas of black hatching or cross-hatching, such as a triangle with a white enclosing outline. Occasionally a white line design is painted against a broad black panel. Both bowls and jars were so decorated.

Bidahochi Polychrome (ca. 1320–1400) has a yellow base color with black decoration outlined in white. The simple bowls are decorated on interior and exterior alike. Interior design may be banded, offset-quartered, or allover, while exterior design is frequently repeated, simple geometrics. Broad black lines outlined by relatively narrow white lines dominate interior design, with much small geometric patterning and hatched areas playing secondary roles. Rather plain pitchers, except for an occasional outflaring neck, are decorated in a comparable manner, with perhaps more emphasis on large solid black triangles.

Bidahochi Polychrome is thought to be a development out of Jeddito Black-on-yellow with which it is contemporaneous in part. There are similarities in the two styles, for example, the use of the wide broken band almost in the center of the bowl. Frequently the black-on-yellow designs have a heavier quality about

Fig. 4.28 Kayenta polychrome styles. The upper pitcher is Jeddito, decorated with black and white designs on a red base. Kietsiel in type are the fairly large olla to the right and the canteen to the left, both decorated in the same colors as the pitcher but in a rather different design style. The small pitcher is decorated in a very simple manner in the same colors as the other vessels.

Fig. 4.29 Late (largely Pueblo IV) styles of Kayenta two color and polychrome wares. The upper bowl and the ladle are painted with black parrots (?) on a yellow base color. The effigy pot, another parrot, seemingly, is decorated in brown (almost black) and orange on yellow, as is the bowl to the left, the latter with an irregular four-part pattern.

them while the polychrome patterns seem lighter, perhaps in part because of more delicate hatching on the latter ware.

In much of the drawing in this ware there is superior craftsmanship; precise geometric themes, rather well balanced in size throughout the decoration, are featured. In one example, there are large triangles outlined in black, which appear smaller as they are filled with either horizontal hatching or cross-hatching; diagonal black bands outlined in white contain black diagonal fretlike opposed small steps; and comparable bands enclose white-outlined black bands made lighter in feeling by continuous white-line scrolls. This Kietsiel style is complex but quiet and reserved.

About the time when these styles ended several additional types of pottery appeared that are of interest (Fig. 4.29). One in particular, the Sikyatki, is especially important as it is the ware that inspired a revival of better ceramics by an Indian woman in the late nineteenth century. When the site of Sikyatki was excavated by Fewkes in the 1890s, a Hopi-Tewa woman named Nampeyo saw some of the fine work from this site and was inspired to improve the

then-degenerate Hopi style of ceramic decoration.

Sikyatki pottery appeared about the time of the end of Bidahochi Polychrome, around 1400, and continued for almost a century after the historic period opened, to about 1625. Some believe that Sikyatki Polychrome also is a derivative of Jeddito Black-on-yellow with the addition of red. There are some similarities; there are many differences.

To begin with, Sikyatki forms show definite changes through the years. Jars reveal an exaggeration of certain features, such as more squat forms and lower and wider necks, with more emphasis on the greatest diameter (this sometimes was accomplished by making an abrupt in-turn to the base). Some vessels have almost a hump at the greatest diameter, and some have a long unbroken line above the greatest diameter. All of these features affected design, inviting more shoulder pattern, or stressing design at or above and below the greatest diameter, or even below alone. Bowls became more shallow during the popularity of Jeddito Black-on-yellow wares and remained so throughout the Sikyatki period.

Design, of course, responded to these changes in bowls and jars as well as to some outside influence, and, in time, to the usual advancement or retrogression that is reflective of the normal processes of any art. Perhaps the shallower bowl was more suitable to show off the growing popularity of asymmetric design and life forms. Abrupt turns in the jar from a high greatest diameter encouraged shoulder designs, while the more rounded turn invited design to drop below the widest diameters. Shorter necks decreased the importance of heavier design in this area. There is a decrease in quality of design drawing in some ways: poorer drawing accompanies expanding interest in subject matter, but in time the draftsmanship became more proficient. Whether some of the poor work on earlier Sikyatki pottery can be attributed to changing forms or to just plain inefficiency cannot be determined, but there is no doubt that drawing improved in later years.

In some of the poorer Sikyatki pottery, drawing is sloppy and design is poorly coordinated. Irregularities appear in repeated motifs; for example, one eye in a mask may be slimmer than the opposite eye (and not meant to be a different eye as is sometimes true in masks); or repeated bands show great differences in width and length. Too, the paint is often poorly applied, with the result that there are darker and lighter areas, or even a more brownish than black coloring. The latter may also be caused by poor firing. There are free forms, or very abstract-appearing designs, many of them quite modern in style, either better executed or not so well painted.

To be sure, there is much fine painting in Sikyatki pottery. Some of the best work features wing motifs with a great variety of them on both jars and bowls. On the former, wings are usually repetitive, balanced, and beautifully drawn, while in the latter they are frequently asymmetric and often not too well executed. From the standpoint of design, both presentations are superb. On jars in particular there is fine rhythm, flow of line, and great dynamism. Solid and hatched or cross-hatched line work is well balanced, to become most effective in the total pattern.

Possibly derived from the Little Colorado Black-on-red wares is St. Johns Polychrome, which occurred roughly 1100–1200 (Fig. 4.30 right). Undoubtedly there is a relationship here, but it would seem to be more than a mere addition of white decoration on the outside of vessels with a black-on-red interior design of Wingate style. Bowls are the only form. Banded layouts prevail, with organizational-banded common on the exterior of the bowl; some are decorated in allover style; and a few are in the composite manner, using a band and a centered arrangement. With some exceptions, the interior design is in black-on-red (red to red-orange base); the exception shows a touch of white added to the interior design, usually as a white outline around solid motifs. The exterior decoration is in all-white and is a clear, permanent paint.

In most instances, the true band in this ware is made by drawing a circle in the center of the vessel and tying the design to this. In other cases, however, there is a rectangular or square termination of the otherwise banded pattern, and frequently in this style, a broad banded solid or hatched square beyond this. Double bands are sometimes used. Infrequently, the interior edge of the design terminates in a star.

The St. Johns Polychrome band (Fig. 4.30 right) is generally used in a continuous manner; a drawn division within bands is rare, and usually when used is part of the design itself. Continuous, repeated, and often integrated patterns are used. Although the same motif is commonly repeated, it is a solid-hatched repetition that keeps the pattern from becoming monotonous. Sometimes a second theme is placed between the repeated one that adds further design interest.

Actually, there is not a great deal of diversity in elements and motifs in this St. Johns ware. Triangles, stepped patterns, and broad lines predominate; scrolls, squares, diamonds, and zigzags are sometimes used. It is in the variety of ways in which these are combined and recombined that the decorator gave diversity. Opposition is favored; usually it is expressed in the use of like motifs, solid and hatched. Sometimes the solid motif is narrow, the hatched one broad. Occasionally the opposed motifs are different, for example, a diagonal line of solid triangles and a wide and hatched zigzag.

In general, there seems to be more large drawing in St. Johns Polychrome than in Wingate Black-on-white, and there seems to be less cluttering in the pattern in St. Johns. Many of the same motifs are used in these wares.

Picking up about where St. Johns leaves off are several other wares, for example, Querino

Fig. 4.30 Little Colorado polychrome bowls, with exterior view (above) and interior view (below). To the right is a type similar to Pinedale with spaced-out black and white exterior designing while the interior is a later style with black patterns outlined in white. The central vessel is a Four Mile polychrome with a continuous exterior decoration and with a single motif pattern. St. John's ware is represented on the right, with an all-white exterior band and a black on red interior band design.

(ca. 1250–1300) and Houck Polychromes (1200–1250). They are similar to the St. Johns style, particularly in interior decoration, but the exterior design is exaggerated in size and much more carelessly drawn. About the same time another style developed, Pinedale Polychrome (ca. 1250–1325), which is more important and will be discussed at greater length.

Pinedale Polychrome shows certain traits that would relate it to St. Johns, especially in the exterior single motifs and in the predominant black-on-red interior design (Fig. 4.30 left). Changes did occur, of course, to make this a distinctive ware. Exterior designs varied somewhat, but typical was a relatively simple white one outlined in black in spaced-out arrangement; plain white, usually in panels, also occurred. Interior design was, at first, comparable to that of St. Johns, but in time there was more outlining of the black with white; the large interlocked, solid-hatched scroll became more popular; there were more wide black bands and more smaller geometric elements added to the total pattern; and large asymmetric patterns grew in favor.

Four Mile Polychrome (Fig. 4.30 center), dated about 1350–1400, followed the Pinedale style. Characteristic pieces show the use of black and white on red on both the interiors and exteriors of bowls or on jar exteriors. Bowls tend to have flatter bottoms that may well have affected some of the patterning. Other bowls were comparable to preceding types in both shape and design.

Exterior design in this short-lived Four Mile Polychrome is a band with a continuous pattern, generally a black design outlined in white and enclosed in black; these bands above and below may form part of the design. Much of this patterning, because of the shape and size of elements in proportion to the red background, has a negative feeling. The main decoration on Four Mile jars resembles the bowl exterior style except that it is larger in size, has larger motifs, and usually is more complex. Whereas a bowl exterior may involve no more than a simple or complex fret theme or repeated small zigzags (a-a-a-a), the jar exterior has the same but alternating with a second motif (a-b-a-b); bowl interior patterns are much more complex. Generally more red is left blank between motifs than in the two preceding wares, St. Johns and Pinedale. Asymmetric patterns are common in the Four Mile, but less well organized than design in Pinedale Polychrome, with three or four motifs involved, and with scrolls and/or frets most important. Spacing is not as well handled, but there is a greater feeling of freedom in design. Solid and hatched motifs are both used, but frequently they are not balanced and opposed. Necks of jars are interestingly painted: frequently they have a white base on which are black repeated elements such as crosses, stepped figures, or perhaps merely a broad line.

In the area of historic Zuñi, there developed prehistorically several crude types of glazed pottery; because of location, they are called Zuñi Glazed Wares. One is a red slipped ware with a simple white St. Johns-like decoration on the exterior; on its interior are designs which inspired its name, for they are done in a black or greenish paint which has a low glaze quality. Some variants of the glazes appear on white slipped wares, with either black or green glaze designs. Banded patterns prevail, though occasional quartered, sectored, or other layouts appear. Familiar opposed themes occur, although they are generally solid; most of the geometrics are small in size. Sometimes the limited motifs are sparsely spaced in a band. Often the painting is sloppy; sometimes it is better executed. Bowls and small jars appear in the glazed wares.

Located southward from the Little Colorado area are the Gila and the Salt, or Salado, rivers, the Salt the main tributary of the Gila. Here lived many prehistoric peoples who reflected their cultural contacts with the more northerly areas in ceramic expressions, although colors differed and distinctly local styles were developed. The Upper Gila and part of the Salado river areas were more directly related to the Anasazi, and the cultures here are generally referred to as the Salado. The middle Gila and lower Salado were penetrated by this Salado Culture and became mixed with the Hohokam, the latter native to the area. Pottery was one of the most important manifestations of this culture, and the wandering of the Saladoans can be traced through this trait.

One of the many later wares of this area is Pinto Polychrome. As in all of the Salado multicolor pottery, it is black, white, and red. Bowls are hemispherical; they have several different layouts, including banded, offset quartered, and allover. Some scroll designs are quite like those on St. Johns Polychrome, save for the duller red; also the bowl form of the Pinto style is more open. In other designs, there is much hatching and solid patterning, often in opposed fashion.

Fig. 4.31   Two later Gila-Salado polychrome vessels, Pinto (left) and Gila (right), both in black, white, and a deep red. Discreet interior painting is featured in the left vessel, often with large scrolls mindful of some Little Colorado pattern- ing. To the right is a more carelessly painted vessel, with interior and exterior decoration, all features of Late Gila polychrome wares.

Later there developed the so-called Gila Polychrome, which also had the deeper, darker red slip (Fig. 4.31). Slip was added to the surface in several ways; sometimes it was put over the entire interior of a bowl, or three-fourths of the way down a jar, or, later, just a band of it was applied only where the potter wished to add design. Forms include simple hemispherical bowls, or large and small ones with recurved rims; and jars have short and wide mouths and squat, full bodies, or full rounded bodies with even shorter necks and medium-sized orifices, or long necks that were decorated with slowly curving lines flowing onto rounded bodies.

There were two significant Gila Polychromes, an Early and a Late style. The Early Gila Polychrome was by far the better of the two wares. It had a creamy white interior with black decoration, which was frequently allover in layout, sometimes asymmetrical in arrangement. Although designs were made up of conservative geometric motifs, they were well proportioned, beautifully executed, and neatly arranged. Fine parallel hatching is common and often is combined with small solids; too, there are many balanced solid and hatched motifs. In some

bowls, the allover design is further unified by a broad and carefully drawn meandering band, giving a feeling of both control and freedom. There are also zonal patterns devoid of framing lines or bands. Again, there may be an open band just below the rim but not tied to the pattern; this is commonly called the "life line" and is found in areas other than the Gila. Design units include triangles, lines and bands, a very popular triangle with a curved hook, stepped triangles, and a few other geometrics. Curvilinear elements are not common, although as arranged on bowl interiors, some designs lose their angularity.

Late Gila Polychrome represents a great change, in craftsmanship in particular. Bowls may be decorated on the exterior; for example, one has a simple white band limited to the area needed for the black fret-type interlocked stepped triangles; its interior is plain red. Or some may have allover interior design: in one instance, the yellowed white slip was put over the entire interior and over the flat rim, and a casually drawn, reversing wing pattern and a complementing motif fill the large center, while a broad life line occurs just below the rim. Many bowls are decorated on the interior with limited white bands for the design, or with the full allover white slip and then with most carelessly drawn motifs such as mirrored wings, steps, interlocking scrolls, and some other geometrics. There is much curvilinear designing on many of these bowls, and although most sloppily executed, the designs are dynamic. Pitchers are similar to bowls. One example will suffice: vessel lines are gently curving from the rim into the body. Then the lazy decorator (or was this their happy "mod" style?) applied a painted band of white slip as background for a half-band decoration suspended from a black band at the rim, then a meandering zigzag band below the middle of the body and connected to a white band low on the vessel, which rises to peaks at four points. On the zigzag are painted black squares; these alternate with white squares in the center of which is painted a black dot (the so-called corn motif). The bottom band is painted black except for white edging, and a triangle fills the top of the peak, with a simple interlocked scroll below it. Sounds horrible, doesn't it? It is. Sometimes effigy birds are decorated in this same manner. One has black lines outlined in white to represent wing and tail feathers; it looks as if the white was put on first and the black painted over it.

Thus it can be seen that the Anasazis were widespread and active producers of ceramics. Many different local styles developed, and many of these influenced other peoples and their pottery efforts. Some of the styles of decoration were artistic; many of the forms were esthetic. And yet no potter ever lost sight of the prime requisite in her effort: utility. No variation in form despoiled its basic use value, yet within that potential great accomplishment was attained. And, of course, pottery, because it was abundant and because it had to be produced, offered the prehistoric artist many opportunities to experiment. And that the Anasazi potters did, to their lasting credit.

Hohokam

Although not as widely excavated as the Anasazi area, the Hohokam has been intensively investigated in one large and long-lived site,
Snaketown. Not only was it excavated in 1934, but also again in 1964. The reinvestigation of this vitally important site, which spanned the time from the inception of this culture to the end of the true Hohokam, plus more knowledge collected from other excavations in the interim, gives a very complete picture of the artistic development of ceramics as well as other crafts at Snaketown. Further, it is probably typical of the River Hohokam Culture.

In this survey of Hohokam pottery, the major periods of development as outlined in the first chapter will be followed (see Fig. 1.6): Pioneer, Colonial, Sedentary, and Classic. Also, comments made relative to pottery forms, layout, and design analysis in the Anasazi section will serve to guide general remarks about Hohokam pottery.

As the Hohokam potter developed forms, she was guided always by the practical. Throughout the Hohokam there were few or no handles or other projections of any kind; it was not until the Salado people invaded their territory that they began to use pitchers with handles and long-necked jars. Further, the basic Hohokam form was kept so simple that there is generally only one area that invites decoration. This does not mean that their vessel forms were dull; quite the contrary is true in such typically Hohokam jars as the one with the abrupt inturning Gila shoulder, a form that offered one suitable area for decoration between the neck-less or very short-necked mouth and the turn in the wall of the vessel.

The basic forms in the Hohokam are the same as for the Anasazi: jars, bowls, scoops and ladles, plates, and effigy vessels, plus an additional one, a legged vessel. However, these shapes differ in details of outlines.

In the Hohokam area, vessels started as rather small pieces. In the Pioneer Period they were particularly small, and remained small to medium during the Colonial; many became much larger in the Sedentary; and some few remained large in the Salado-influenced Classic while the majority of forms returned to medium or small sizes. This sequence, particularly the turn to very large sizes, affected design. A less artistically equipped people might have been completely defeated by this turn of events, but not the Hohokam. Several devices were used by these imaginative Indians to accommodate to such changes. Large drawing took care of part of the problem and an increased complexity of design rid the decorators of some of their "headaches," while some painters thought of widening bands and putting hatching or plaiting within them, or of using larger and more solids in place of small elements. With the development or introduction of new areas of decoration, such as neck and handle in the Salado-introduced pitcher, the Hohokam potter again responded to new needs, this time learning to use this second decorative area probably as did the Saladoans. Thus it can be demonstrated that Hohokam ceramic decorators adjusted to modifications in their own vessels or in newly introduced pieces equally readily, whether in size or shape, or whether their own ideas or the schemes of others.

Layouts found in Hohokam pottery are primarily of four types: banded, quartered, sectored, and allover (see Fig. 4.5); there are a few others, such as half-banded, but they are quite limited in number; significant ones relative to the artistry of different periods will be mentioned.

Inasmuch as the Hohokam decorated wares were earlier than those of the Anasazi, the problem of origin of design is of interest. The earliest pottery at Snaketown was undecorated, but it was thin walled and well made; certainly it does not represent a beginning stage of ceramics. Then there appeared a gray ware with decoration in red. Lines were broad and crude, and there was an unusual roughness to their edges which was produced by polishing, apparently while the paint was still slightly wet, quite like the first Mogollon decoration except in color. All of this was entirely different from the earliest Anasazi ware. Also designs on the pottery of the latter seem to have been derived from textiles, either baskets, early bands, or other small pieces of weaving. The broad lines of the Hohokam decoration were anything but textile in origin. It is possible that other Hohokam painting (body?) may have influenced these first designs, or that the pottery of the Mogollon may have inspired Hohokam efforts; or it is also possible that both cultures borrowed their early ceramic designs from or were inspired by another culture, perhaps from Mexico. Many other Mexican influences are found in early years at Snaketown.

The basic Hohokam color combination is far simpler than in other areas: red-on-buff pre-dominated from early times to late. There was a very limited amount of red-on-gray in the beginning of decorated styles, but this did not survive; nor was the red-on-buff replaced by other colors in later years in the true Hohokam culture. To be sure, when the Salado people came into the Hohokam area and settled down, they brought with them their multi-colored style of pottery decoration. Foremost among these were the Gila Polychromes, red, black, and white. There were a few short-lived and local efforts away from the red-on-buff during the Classic Period; one particular type called Tucson Polychrome adapted the Gila Polychrome colors in a slightly different manner.

Types of decoration other than color are conspicuous by their rarity. There was a little incising early in the Pioneer Period, and there is modeling from the Estrella Phase on to the end of the Hohokam and into the Salado (see Fig. 4.36). But there is little else.

Design in Hohokam pottery evolved from the simple to the complex (Fig. 4.32a–c), culminating in the Colonial and Sedentary periods in fine examples of a free style of painting. Outside influences may have affected the growth of pattern along the way, but, generally speaking, there is so much in the way of comparable design and artistic concept with the other crafts, that, borrowed or not, these folk made all of it unmistakably Hohokam; in essence, they put their own stamp on all of their art expressions.

A number of artistic qualities apply to Hohokam design or parts of design. It was mentioned previously that much of their design style is free; contributing to that freedom is a rhythmic repetition of the same pattern, an a-a-a-a repetition. Broken rhythm such as a-b-a-b is used but not as frequently as the unbroken; rarely is an a-b-c type expressed. Small elements are generally employed for this repetition, either in geometrics or tiny life figures; the latter may be more realistic or more abstract. Whether in a single row or over the entire vessel, this repetition adds greatly to the dynamism so typical of Hohokam pottery decoration.

A lightness pervades much Hohokam design; two reasons for this are the extensive use of line and the avoidance of large mass. This is particularly true of early drawing, for later expressions do employ some solid painting. Even in the use of mass paint frequently the end result is negative design, which in these red-on-buff wares, and because of the closeness in value of their colors, has a lighter quality than the black-on-white negative style of the Kayenta region.

Some variety is expressed by Hohokam pottery decorators in the use of line. Fringed lines were very common in the Colonial Period; many of these were fine in contrast to some of the heavy fringes of the Sedentary Period. Broad, straight lines are the earliest decorative element, often expressed in chevrons; they become narrower through the years and then become wavy in still later times, and eventually turn into meanders. Lines in the form of hatching are outstanding in Hohokam ceramic decoration. Frequently the hatching is carelessly done; generally it has a diagonal trend. It started out in a straight style, then became wavy. Quite early both straight and wavy hatching occurred within a common motif. Cross-hatching appeared but was by no means as popular as the other two styles of drawing. The main use of hatching was to fill quarters or quarter segments of the interiors of open bowls; however, it was also used to fill other areas, such as bands or odd-shaped segments of a decorative area.

Scrolls were popular from the beginning of Hohokam painting; then they were heavy and solid and simple; later they were hatched and some were interlocked; and still later they were finer and usually interlocked. They are represented in quarter sections or are pendant from lines. In the Colonial and Sedentary Periods, they are emergent from or combined with solid triangles, or, occasionally, with other geometric forms.

One of the most fascinating of all the units or motifs developed by the Hohokam pottery decorators was the "bull's-eye," (see Fig. 4.9c). Broadly defined, these are geometric forms with a solid or hatched ground on which is an open space, and within this is a simple or complex unit of design. The internal design may be anything from a dot to a full life form.

A last basic theme, used as either a unit or motif, is the small element. Amsden says that here the Hohokam potter "is a master of the extemporaneous stroke, using her brush in truly creative delineation," and, in comparison with the Anasazi, "the Pueblo decorator used hers as a methodical generator of prim lines in formal geometric figures. The latter is a well-schooled draughtsman, the former an unschooled artist."[20] Amsden continues to describe the small elements: "Flying birds are evoked with a Z and a horizontal dash, or two down strokes to form a curving V. Two squiggles make a swastika—a dog's ear is cocked with a single cunning blob, his tail set for wagging by a touch of the brush. A bird's leg posed nervously for a forward step, a human arm caught in the rhythm of the dance, a lizard's pointed head—all are rendered with one simple stroke. Best of all are the birds; lanky roadrunners or fat little quail, they have individuality and life. The drawing is too free and joyous to be conventional, too simple to be realistic. Perhaps simplified realism best characterizes it." Herein is described the quintessence of Hohokam painting applicable not only to the small element but to other motifs as well.

The major periods of Hohokam ceramic development will now be presented, with emphasis on attainments within subdivisions as warranted. There will be evident, in this analysis of decoration, a steady growth through the Pioneer phases, with peaks reached throughout the Colonial and further expression of high attainment throughout the Sedentary. The Classic Period is not a true Hohokam period, for there was a heavy measure of Salado culture that greatly changed the ceramic picture, yet many Hohokam ceramic trends continued. There was much pottery manufactured by this peaceful invading culture, and there were influences from the same on the red-on-buff tradition of the Hohokam.

In the Pioneer Period pottery forms are basically simple (Fig. 4.32a). Bowls are of two types, a shallow and a deeper form. The shallow style changed little from earlier times to the end of this period, having a more gently curved side wall first and becoming a straighter side later. There is also a flat-bottomed, deep, and gently outflaring-sided bowl. The deeper form is expressed in two styles, one a wide and open-mouthed form, while the second has a more incurving rim. Both are rounded in form. A simple short-handled ladle appeared in the Sweetwater Phase. Jars are wider mouthed and open, or incurved and smaller at the orifice; both of these have no necks. Another more common olla or jar form is a little larger in size and has a short, straight neck or an incurving neck line and an outflaring lip; the latter becomes wider at the orifice in the last phase of this period. All three types have short necks which tend to become still shorter in the Colonial and to disappear in the Sedentary Period.

a

Fig. 4.32 Hohokam pottery of the Pioneer, Colonial, Sedentary, and Classic periods. Characteristics of Hohokam pottery can be briefly summarized as to shapes and designs in the four groupings of these illustrations.

(a) Pioneer Period. In this arrangement of six pieces of pottery are presented the simpler lines of early forms and the heavy and irregular painting of the beginning decorator. Scoring on bowl exteriors (upper left) was not uncommon; effigy forms began to appear, and the barest promise of a flare in the rim is to be noted in the bowl center right. Jars (upper right) and bowls (two in lower row) were simple in form. (b) Colonial Period. Early in their years of ceramic development the Hohokams achieved distinction in both form and design. Now they made outflaring rimmed bowls (upper left) and took advantage of the spacious form with allover "flying bird" and other dynamic designs. Expand-

ing form is also reflected in a jar (upper right) with the lines of a rounded, squat body carrying into a generous neck with an outward spreading rim. A large scoop (lower left) encourages curvilinear patterning in its four divisions. Mass paint in the interlocked scrolls suggests a negative effect. Angular forms (lower center) are not common in prehistoric Southwest ceramics but the Hohokams devised rectangular bowls and decorated them effectively, here with a procession of horned toads. Red mass and line were pleasingly combined on the buff surface of this plate (right upper). Thick walled vessels were also distinctive of the Hohokams (lower right).

b

Although there is some bowl exterior design, most of it is interior. On the simpler forms the layout was allover at first, then half-banded, and then segmented layouts became prevalent. In the last phase of the Pioneer, all three layouts plus full banding are popular. The exterior design is chiefly half-banded, except for the flat-bottomed bowl where it is banded. Jars are banded in layout.

Despite the presence of pottery in the Vahki Phase of the Pioneer Period, there are no paint-decorated pieces. Artistry is reflected in some of the graceful forms. By Estrella times, however, there are crude designs in red on a more gray than buff surface. Although there was a well-polished, undecorated red preceding this red-on-gray, there was no surface polishing or slipping on this first color-decorated ware. Throughout the history of the majority of Hohokam pottery, paint was applied directly to the unslipped surface, thus, this technique has become a diagnostic of Hohokam wares. Thin washes do occur, of course.

Red wares of the Vahki should also be kept in mind, for one is a possible link between Hohokam and Mogollon cultures; also this type continues into later periods, showing continuity from early to late years. In the Estrella Phase the red ware is frequently grooved on the exterior. In the Sweetwater some vessel exteriors have either simple geometric red line work on a plain or grooved gray surface, or grooving alone. Interiors of both Estrella and Sweetwater vessels are often decorated on the unpolished but smooth surfaces. Sometimes there is polishing over the broad designs. The earlier designs were broad-lined and included much parallel-line work, open or tight and nested chevrons, short and fat curved elements that sometimes become immature scrolls, and, rarely, a fret. These same elements plus other small designs carry over into the Sweetwater Phase, becoming slightly less heavy-lined and, in a few instances, more complex. An example of the latter would be a crudely interlocked scroll made of heavy, broad, hatched bands. A surprising variety of designs was produced in the Sweetwater Phase. One other ware in the Sweetwater should be mentioned for its rare nature, the only polychrome that can honestly be called Hohokam. Red and yellow designs appear on the gray surface of a scoop and on several sherds. Alternating and fairly broad red and yellow lines appear in a band across the center and longer axis of the scoop, with parallel and irregular arrangement of the same on either side. Seemingly, this style of decoration did not appeal to the Hohokam people and it "died on the vine" during this period.

Red-on-buff wares predominate in the Snaketown Phase, although in some pieces where burning was not too well done, there are gray areas. Whereas design organization was rather haphazard in previous wares, now there is better planning, with pleasing symmetry and arrangement of motifs. Patterns are often painted in such a way as to have the buff ground show through as the design; this negative style was to remain popular for years to come. Smoothing surfaces with a tool and a rare thin wash on some decorated pieces would imply better craftsmanship. New elements added during the Snaketown Phase include bull's-eyes, more small elements, and life forms; scrolls and keys are greatly improved; and hatching is much finer and is commonly used as a background as well as a filler. Exterior bowl incising was still popular. Simple effigy forms appear.

Many changes are to be noted in the transition from Snaketown to Gila Butte Phase (Colonial Period) pottery (Fig. 4.32b). Haury notes, however, that they are changes more of degree than kind, in spite of his further comments: "Gila Butte Red-on-buff occupies an interesting position in the scale of Hohokam pottery because it stands between two decorative styles—the tradition-bound hatching of Snaketown Red-on-buff on the one hand and the freer, more cursive, painting of Santa Cruz Red-on-buff on the other."[21] It is obvious where this in-between style has carried on the tradition of hatching; how it developed life themes, small elements, and bull's-eyes; and how it elaborated already established motifs. Further, it does reflect the important shift from highly conventionalized Snaketown to more realistic Santa Cruz portrayals of life forms.

In line work, the Gila Butte pottery painter executed medium to fairly broad delineations, all better executed than in earlier years. Hatching is continued and becomes very popular; it is used as filler for both geometric and life forms and as background for life themes. A few solids appear, and it is obvious that they are new because of their poor execution. Keys and scrolls are more

c

Fig. 4.32 (cont.)

(c) Sedentary Period. More dramatic forms and stronger patterning characterize pottery of this period. The interior of the graceful and deep bell-shaped bowl (upper left) is ornamented dominantly with a line pattern, basically of large interlocked frets. Vertical arrangements of tiny frets and short lines serve as a grid against which appear wandering and large masses of curving design on a jar (upper right). One plate (lower left) has cross bands of angular, paired zigzags and frets while a second one on legs (lower right) features curvilinear design in its scrolls and wavy hatching. Bird and scoop (center and lower center) are both covered with simpler and basically line patterning. (d) Classic Period. Simplicity is again dominant in Hohokam pottery, but now it is an interesting combination of remnants of the past plus influences from newcomers into this area. Declining ability in painting—still in red on buff but not with the vigor, abundance, and variety of the past—and the featuring of handles and necks makes this a different ware. Bowls (upper left) lose their flair, jars (upper right) are more stolid, and the pronounced Gila shoulder of earlier years is greatly diminished (lower left). Necks are common; jars and pitchers become fairly common.

d

elaborate and better executed. Repetition and allover or nearly allover arrangements add to the verve of the painting of this period. Dynamism is suggested in many ways, from simple curving lines to flying birds and groups of ceremonial dancers. There is great variety too, as expressed in the following. Small elements, which may appear in positive or negative painting (Fig. 4.33), include dots, large and small circles, checkers, bull's-eyes, and a great variety of conventional drawing classed under the one term "flying bird" elements, which include many forms from the letter H to highly conventional and recognizable birds. More realistic are some readily identifiable birds, such as little quail with their top knots or cranes with their great beaks wide open. Reptiles are represented by snakes, lizards, and horned toads; scorpions are the most prominent recognizable insects; and dogs and deer sometimes can be identified among the mammals. The famous bird-snake motif, which probably came out of Mexico, appears on pottery of this period for the first time. Humans are in evidence usually in lines or rows, some represented with a cane and a pack basket suspended from the forehead by a tump strap, this the so-called hump-backed flute player. All of these creatures may be marching or flying or dancing from left to right or from right to left; they may be repetitiously crowded together; they may be presented against a plain ground or a hatched ground; or they may be individually enclosed within an oval area. In their simplified realism, they tell much of the life of the times of the Gila Butte people.

Few if any changes were made in this great array of life designs as the Hohokams developed from the Gila Butte into the Santa Cruz Phase, and they left a record of the same in their ceramic decoration (Fig. 4.34). If possible, the lines and rows of figures became more crowded; occasionally they are so close together as to give a feeling of merging. Frequently, the rows of life forms are enclosed between bands of fringelike lines; or there is nothing to contain them and they are piled row upon row. The hump-backed flute player is more recognizable as such. There is greater variety than before in the lines of hand-holding dancers; human figures are more varied in their costumes and headgear and in their positioning. More imagination is expressed in these lines of performers, as they dance up one side of a hill and down the other, or appear as paired dancers. Other life forms, such as quail and other birds and dogs, are postured in numerous ways. More varied and also more crowded are the flying bird elements. Larger and better painted solid areas appear.

In geometric styles there are changes during the Santa Cruz Phase. A straight line may break into a zigzag at regular intervals, or become completely zigzag or curvilinear; scrolls and keys are perhaps a bit more complicated through their combination with a wider variety of other elements. And, whether geometric or life forms, the total arrangement of motifs on the vessel often adds to the dynamism of painting; one of the favored dispositions of small elements was in circling fashion, from the center to the edge of an open bowl. Negative painting continues in popularity during the Santa Cruz Phase.

Large bowls and tremendous jars, which developed during the Sacaton Phase of the Sedentary Period (see Fig. 4.32c), were a challenge to the ceramic decorator. Perhaps many of these were ceremonial vessels, a fact which would further spur the artist into different channels of decoration. There was the greatest variety in each of the major forms of vessels known at any time. Add to these thoughts the fact that the prehistoric Southwestern artist was not a copyist; herein is one explanation for the high level of artistic attainment of the Hohokam pottery painter of the Sacaton Period, the peak of ceramic decoration for all Hohokam history.

Jars and bowls were the most important forms of this period. They reflect not only the greatest variety and refinement in form but also the pinnacle in the adaptation of design to form, in

Fig. 4.33 Gila Butte open, flare-rimmed bowl, with the entire inner surface covered with negative (buff) squares with a red dot in each.

Fig. 4.34   Vessels of the Santa Cruz and Sacaton Phases. *Top, left,* is a ladle, or more properly, a scoop with a sectored layout and a pert little quail in each division; *second from the left* is a legged vessel with a platelike surface, with red-on-buff painting showing two large birds feasting on a snake (rattler?). Right is a Santa Cruz "cauldron" or deep bowl with outflaring lip, with great scrolls, one of the important developments of this period, which cover the wall of this piece, combined with some straight-line work. *Center, left:* Simplicity marks the form of this Santa Cruz jar, and conventionalized figures dance around its circumference.

Dramatic is the shape of the Santa Cruz jar, *right,* and the design is no less so, with its three rows of dynamic dancers, moving in unison about the jar, separated by precise rows of fringed lines. *Bottom row,* three red-on-buff jars. Two of Santa Cruz times reflect details of this period: the deep, wide-mouthed form (center), and the gently rounded jar (right). The interlocked scroll pattern on the latter is reflective of high development in this period, and it carries over into the Sedentary Period, as is to be noted in the Sacaton jar (left). This last jar has another characteristic of the later period, namely, the low and sharp Gila shoulder.

painting ability, and in composition. The percentage of decorated wares in the total ceramic output also reached its highest level. In many ways one feels the Hohokam artist's delight in painting, and her response to the challenges. Many decorated vessels of this period show more controlled abandon than is true of earlier work, and they reflect more planning in the adaptation of design to space.

Geometric design prevails on the large Sacaton jars, but this placed no limitations on the artistic ardor of these decorators. Also, there is great variety in secondary layout; primary layout

Fig. 4.35 Additional examples of Sacaton Red-on-buff pottery styles. All of these vessels were found in cremations. *Upper row:* two plates show the popular off-set quartered (left) and sectored, almost quartered, layouts (right), with practically all space filled with design in both. The large continuous scroll remains popular. *Lower;* two shouldered Red-on-buff pieces: the jar on the left has the characteristic Sacaton sharp Gila shoulder and is decorated with large bullseyes. The second pot features still larger bullseyes with simple dots in them.

is banded almost without exception, for the nature of the vessel allowed little else. The lack of a neck other than a shallow one at the jar aperture, plus the abrupt turn of the Gila shoulder, usually low on the body, created a large area adapted to a band almost exclusively. Generally there was a gentle outcurving from neck to turn, but in some instances there was an outcurve and a very gentle incurve within this same space. Such variations seem to have disturbed the decorator not at all. Within this primary band area the Hohokam artist might use any one of the following secondary layout schemes on the large jars: multiple horizontal banding; organizational banding arranged in either horizontal or diagonal style; vertical multiple banding; or a single-band decorative area. Many different ways of adapting the design might occur in the latter usage of the band, with elaborately integrated horizontal or diagonal arrangements prevailing. Seldom is a single motif used in any of these large jar decorations; usually there are two basic themes that are alternately repeated in a single row or in alternate rows or panels.

On the very large jars with wide mouths, some with low, in-curved sides and low, sharp shoulders, the Sacaton decorator often favored vertical arrangements, usually panelling in bands. Within these areas, further decoration was like that of the previously described large jars. Miscellaneous forms utilized a variety of layouts, with banding favored (Fig. 4.35). However, on wide and open plates or bowls, more variety occurred, including allover, sectored, centered, composite, or occasionally other layouts (Fig. 4.35 top left).

During the Sacaton Phase, there is more solid painting than prior to this time (Fig. 4.35 top row). Perhaps this was not only due to the increased area on the large forms but also was related in some measure to artistic intent, for frequently masses of red paint are combined with negative painting. Large geometrics or individual life forms stood out all the more dramatically when related to darker mass areas. To be sure, there were other occasions when the negative aspect was of no concern and large painted areas became a part of a regular design as well as filling space.

Many other points of interest relative to Sacaton pottery should be brought into focus as they were culminant expressions in Hohokam decorative painting. Some of the Santa Cruz Phase work equals some of the Sacaton, but in

Fig. 4.36   Sacaton jars and a bowl. *Left,* a sharply turned shoulder is featured on this jar. The wide band created between this low turn and the neck is decorated with organizational bands of alternating fringed lines and tadpolelike designs. *Center,* a beautifully decorated straight-sided bowl,

and *right,* a fine specimen of a Sacaton jar, with an almost invisible portion below the Gila shoulder. The wide band decoration features integrated and opposed but unlike solid and hatched frets, with other geometrics added.

the overall picture, the latter artist faced more difficult problems and dealt with them successfully. Toward the end of the Sacaton Phase there are evidences of a growing conventionalization and of a lessening of the characteristic vitality of the Hohokam artist; also there are indications of this long-lived art wearing itself out after its great florescence earlier in this same period. Before it started on the downgrade, however, this art style left its imprint over a wide portion of southern Arizona and in some measure in both the Mogollon area of southwestern New Mexico and the Flagstaff area of northern Arizona.

Geometric and life forms both painted and modeled were used in the Sacaton Phase (Figs. 4.32c, 4.35, 4.36, and 4.37). No new elements were introduced, but old ones received different treatment. Scrolls were prominent; as neck banding, pendant from triangles, they became

rather dull but as intricately interwoven with elaborate designs on large jars or smaller bowl or platter interiors they lost none of their former vigor. Wide bands of textilelike nature, made up of lines, zigzags, frets, and sometimes squiggles, were comparably interwoven with other themes on large jar surfaces; some of the finest combinations of rectilinear and curvilinear motifs are found in these scroll-textile motifs. Frets became more popular in later Sacaton years. Fringed lines and hatching were less popular than in earlier years, and both were finer than the lines from which they were pendant or which enclosed them. Small elements remained popular and were most varied during the Sacaton Phase; many of them were used to fill interiors of smaller shallow bowls or plates. Bull's-eyes are both large and small, both simple and complex; they may be filled with anything from dots to birds.

Fig. 4.37   Hohokam effigy vessels were also popular in the last full Hohokam period as well as earlier. *To the left* is the suggestion of a human face on a Snaketown phase jar; *in the center* is a female, both arms resting on her knees, and the

entire vessel painted in addition to the almost full round modeling; and *to the right* a bowl on the back of a mountain sheep, this also painted. The latter two vessels belong to the Sacaton phase.

Snakes and more angular birds and quadrupeds lost some of their vigor of former years. Even though the hourglass form was dominant for the human figure, it still reflected dynamism with its legs bent in dance, moving arms, and varied dress and headgear. Some humans were little more than "blobs" and heavy lines, but they too remained active and frequently told a story in their posturing bodies or in the rattles in their hands. Crowding of human figures, so common in the Santa Cruz Period, was less in evidence in the Sacaton Phase. In size, life figures ranged from tiny ones in bull's-eyes to massive ones covering the greater area of an open bowl. It would seem that angularity was taking over in life forms just as the rectilinear was superseding the curvilinear in geometric design.

Sacaton painting represents the end of what might be called pure Hohokam art of this type. Painting of pottery was continued into the next period, the Classic (see Fig. 4.32d), by the descendants of the developers of Hohokam cultures, but there was a strong outside influence to be noted in both ceramic forms and in the styles of their decoration. Jars with long necks and rounded bodies, simple half-spherical bowls, and other simpler shapes prevailed over the more exotic forms that were so outstanding in the Sacaton Period. A few large jars were still produced in the early years of the later period, but they quickly disappeared. Designs also quickly became simplified and less well executed. The "Classic" Period, then, is much more a time of degeneracy of native Hohokam culture, probably representing the natural decline of a long-lived and once high culture, a decline hastened by the intrusion of an outside culture, the Salado.

Specifically, in the Classic Period there are the ceramic efforts of the Hohokams, the so-called Casa Grande Red-on-buff peoples, and the new folk who came in and lived peacefully with the Hohokams, producing their Gila and Tonto Polychromes. The former are represented by the jar and bowl styles previously mentioned. These were painted in red on a pale buff ground, and feature line patterns, triangles, and rectilinear keys. Gila and Tonto Polychromes, as described in the section on Anasazi pottery, show no great differences as made and decorated by their relatives in the Hohokam area. There were a few new types of pottery that represent local variations of wares, some showing the Salado influ-

ence on Hohokam potters. One of the latter is the so-called Tucson Polychrome, a ware that imitated the Salado form, such as a tall-necked jar, and employed their colors but varied the use of them. Generally they painted simple designs, such as broad black lines or bands outlined in white on a red ground. Salado pottery was never thus!

Mogollon

In the Mogollon area (see Fig. 1.6), a different ceramic story is to be told. Some claim the greatest antiquity for this area, while others would place the earliest wares of the Hohokams and the Mogollones about the same time, somewhere around 300 B.C. Again let it be repeated, there seems to be no doubt about the Anasazi being later than these other two cultures. A basic brown ware has been found in both areas, prominent in the Hohokam plain wares and surely the base color for the first decorated Mogollon pieces. Although a few red-on-brown pieces found in the Anasazi are very early in time, but later than in either the Mogollon or Hohokam regions, they seem to have had slight artistic influence on the Anasazis. As a matter of fact, they were probably derived from the Mogollon.

Broad line decoration and chevrons are found on the earliest pieces of Mogollon pottery, as they were in the Hohokam, but neither of these designs is to be noted in the Anasazi area. In the Hohokam, these two trends in color and design are not as significant as they are in the Mogollon. It could be, then, that there was a broad base of common origin for the two more southerly cultures, then quickly each began to go its own way. Perhaps that same base influence was not felt in the Anasazi beyond the few trade pieces found there, and this may explain why they had little or no artistic influence in the northern area.

Texturing is another artistic quality that has some significance when comparing the pottery of the three areas. It was of great importance to the Mogollones, of some significance to the Hohokams, but of no import to the Anasazi decorators until the developments of corrugated wares in the Pueblo Period. Among the Hohokam, incising persisted through the Gila Butte Phase. In the Mogollon there were incised, scored, finger dented, and other styles of surface treatment on vessel exteriors.

From the beginning, vessel forms are more varied in both the Anasazi and in the Hohokam areas than in the Mogollon. The latter people made basically a hemispherical bowl and a simple round-bodied jar with a short neck from the beginning of their ceramic production, and there was little variation in the two forms through years of development. Occasional other forms appeared such as a few beakerlike pieces, seed jars, and pitchers. The greatest amount and best of their ceramic decoration was concentrated on bowl interiors; pitchers were decorated in rather pedestrian fashion early and late, but jar designs sometimes resembled bowl decoration. The best known of all ceramic expressions in the Mogollon area is the so-called late or classic Mimbres ware; many archaeologists believe this to be a fusion of ideas from all three areas, the Anasazi, Hohokam, and the Mogollon. Whatever it was, surely it represents one of the finest ceramic expressions in the entire Southwest.

From the first years pottery in the Mogollon was basically a dark ware; this is true of both decorated and plain styles. The earliest painted ware is San Lorenzo Red-on-brown (Georgetown-San Francisco Phase); its surface was rough and a thin dark brown slip was added and polished. Over this the red paint was applied in simple broad lines and triangles, the only elements used in this period. The design was then polished, apparently while the paint was still wet, with the result that all of this patterning was blurred; this coupled with the dark colors makes it very difficult to see any design at all. The rectilinear designing was poorly applied; in particular, line junctures were badly executed, often not meeting or, contrarily, overlapping. Usually triangles were pendant from the rim, serving as a nucleus for sets of framing lines. Sometimes the lines served as the total decoration, set into a quartered layout in the form of chevrons. There is a slight variation in width of lines, some are wide, some medium in width. There are no very narrow lines such as were common in the earliest Anasazi pottery decoration. Bowls only were decorated.

A second ware, Mogollon Red-on-brown, also belongs to this same earliest phase, the Georgetown-San Francisco. That it may have been derived from San Lorenzo is indicated in the following: it is a dark ware; the layout is usually quartered, and the design is blurred by polishing. There are several differences, too:

pitchers as well as bowls are decorated; lines and triangles become more diversified and a few new elements are introduced; and, despite the fact that the design arrangement is similar, the design itself becomes a little more complicated. Generally, bowl interiors have quartered layouts, with the pattern filling all the space. Jars are ornamented over all the exterior surface except the very bottom, within a banded layout. Decoration appears on the unslipped surface or a thin slip is first added. Lines become narrower and there are some fringed lines; new elements include a little checkerboard and cross-hatching and rare curvilinear themes, the latter sometimes interlocked. Exteriors of vessels are frequently finger dented.

The Three Circle Phase of the Mogollon culture saw several very interesting developments in the direction of greater contrast between background and design color. This is effected first, in a shift to red-on-white and later to black-on-white; second, in a distinct narrowing of lines; and third, in the use of less paint, thus letting more of the background show. Actually, there is little or no change in layout and in design elements. Bowl interiors are slipped but not polished, while jar exteriors are scraped and slightly polished; too, there is less polishing over the design with the result that edges are less blurred and the design sharper and more clearcut. In general, there is better brushwork.

It is possible that Pueblo influences which came in about this time affected the base color, thus, perhaps, the shift to red-on-white. It is possible, too, that the same influences were responsible for the greater contrast effected through the use of less design, letting more background show through. It is likely, further, that the Anasazis were responsible for the next great change in decorating Mogollon pottery, the shift to black paint on a white ground. Thus, the second Three Circle ware appeared and has been named Mimbres Bold-Face Black-on-white.

A few additional forms had appeared by this time, seed jars and pitchers in particular; bowls were still the most frequently decorated (Fig. 4.38). As a style developed primarily in relation to bowl interiors, it is quite possible that this had a great deal to do with stabilization of its form, and there is little or no change in the bowl shape to the end of the Mimbres Phase. The form was open enough to accommodate rim emphasis in pattern, leaving the center interior free of paint.

Fig. 4.38 Four Mimbres bowls. *Top left* is a typical all-geometric style with a narrow band below the rim lines combining continuous frets and scrolls. *Top right,* a mammal with a beaked head. *Lower left* is a checker-bodied three-headed turkey and *to the right* a bat with body and wings covered with geometric designs. This group of vessels shows variety in size, the characteristic plain banded or composite (centered-banded) styles, and the "kill" hole in the center bottom of the vessel.

After these artists had adjusted to a desirable balance of background and design, reflected in banded or half-banded layouts in the Mimbres Bold-Face style, then they were able to do further experimentation. This eventuated in the Classic Mimbres composite layout, namely, combined centered and rim emphasis, usually banded. This trend, of course, started in the Bold-Face wares, but was secondary until the second Mimbres Phase. Occasional other layouts are to be noted in the Bold-Face wares, including allover bisected, quartered, and irregularly segmented. This variety of layouts represents a great change over the limited styles of preceding periods.[22]

Mimbres Bold-Face bowls were well smoothed on the interiors, then a heavy, chalky white slip was added and polished; the same treatment was given to jar exteriors. Bowl exteriors were ignored. Too, in the Bold-Face wares, there was no polishing over the painted design. Brushwork improved in this period, as did composition (Fig. 4.39a–e). Further change was expressed in the addition of new design elements, particularly in a few life forms toward the end of the period (Fig. 4.39e); some of these were composed of geometric elements, some were more naturalistic. But additional geometrics also changed the appearance of this pottery. A noninterlocking scroll appears abruptly (probably coming from the outside), and in time it becomes interlocking (Fig. 4.39b), adding

much dynamism to this ceramic decoration. Wavy and fine cross-hatching are also added; fine lines are used to fill bands, triangles, and other areas (Fig. 4.39c); solids are used to pleasingly balance fine line painting (Fig. 4.39c,d,e); and frequently heavy lines meticulously outline or balance the fine line work.

The appearance of life forms in Mimbres Bold-Face pottery and their continuation into the Classic times has long intrigued archaeologists. There is, of course, the possibility that the Mimbres artist followed the same path as did the Anasazi in creating a life form, first adding a small triangle for a head and lines for feet to a larger triangle which served as a body, then moving from this form into more realistic portrayals. The survival of the geometric style into the Classic Period might support this idea. Amsden suggested that life forms came from the Hohokam. Kidder was of the opinion that they were the creation of a single artist and that, once expressed, they "took fire" and spread throughout the typical Classic Mimbres area.[23] Whatever their origin, they appealed to these artists and became one of the most aesthetically pleasing expressions in all Southwestern ceramic decoration.

Classic Mimbres Black-on-white pottery apparently continued out of the Bold-Face style.[24] There are, for a time, some of the same layouts, such as quartered, allover, and segmented, but favor was quickly diverted to the banded style with centered themes added to make for the dominant Classic plan, the composite. This latter style remained popular to the end, with emphasis on a geometric band or half-band at or close to the rim and a life form or forms in the center. There is some variation within this basic scheme, of course; further, a strictly geometric style continued.

In decoration of this pottery, brushwork executed by the Classic Mimbreño was perfected; no other group in the Southwest compares in this attainment. Variety of subject matter, particularly in the life forms and the imaginary conceptions related to them, is unequalled by any other group. Boldness in concept and painting and the creativity of these artists stand alone, too. The rich record of the life about them is indeed a treasure; although many creatures are represented in a generalized fashion, many others can be identified, even down to tiny insects.

The Classic Mimbres potters continued the use of a flat white, or, sometimes, a dead cream slip, and the same black of previous years. The decorative paint is often a reddish tone, or partly so, perhaps due to poor firing. Seemingly, these potters were not too careful when they fired their wares, for many dark firing clouds appear and frequently the bowls are misshapen. This carelessness may indicate that the vessels were not made for utility purposes but rather, were explicitly and perhaps hurriedly produced for burials. Supporting the latter idea are the facts that the vessels were also "killed," that is, a hole was made intentionally in the bottom of each bowl and the bowls are always found in burials, frequently inverted over the head. Why they put so much effort into perfecting the painting and in expressing such breadth of creativity, then carelessly fired the vessels, is something of a mystery, except, of course, for the world wide, primitive concept that one needed these things in the world beyond.

As a whole, geometric decoration of the Classic Mimbres Phase was not as interesting an attainment as was the life expression, yet it was extremely commendable (Fig. 4.40a–v). Mention was made of the continuation of some of the Bold-Face layouts; it may be added that there was a considerable retention of many of

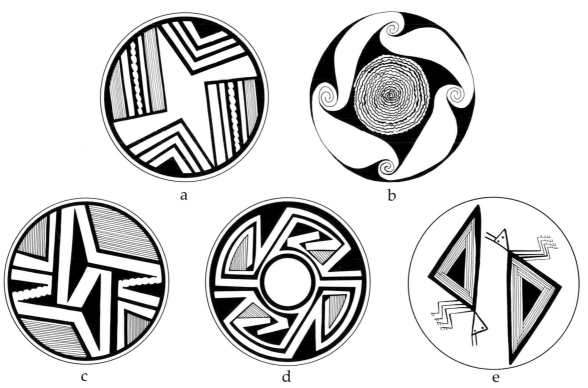

Fig. 4.39 Five Mimbres Bold-face Black-on-white bowls (all from Cosgrove and Cosgrove 1932. Plate numbers only will be given). (a) A typical layout, with opposed equal designs (115f). (b) An allover layout style with emphasis on a centered theme (109c). (c) Another allover geometric decoration, repeating in part the layout style of a (113d). (d) A banded style of decoration, with the rim serving as outer boundary and a broad band for the inner limitation (114e). (e) Some life forms appeared in this earlier style of bowl decoration; these two are stiffly geometric (120b).

a

b

c

d

e

f

g

h

i

j

k

l

m

n

o

Fig. 4.40 Classic Mimbres bowls (all from Cosgrove and Cosgrove 1932; plate numbers only will be given). All examples are black-on-white except *a*. (a) An example of the rare polychrome pottery involving black, white, and yellow. Two bugs with intertwined antennae (192e). (b) A simple geometric band, with beautiful fine line craftsmanship (130f). (c) Frequently a somewhat elaborate geometric border is combined with a life form, here an unlikely creature (199b). (d) The life theme in this bowl decoration is so intricately drawn into the geometric band that it is not obvious at first glance (224f). (e) Although the band is beautifully simple in its six fine lines and two broader bands, the total pattern is made more complex by the addition of a dynamic center geometric theme (136b). (f) An extremely wide band with the characteristic two opposed and balanced themes is a bit unusual in this later Mimbres ware. Also note the negative effect (172e). (g) Another bit of band decoration which is classic in its simplicity (175d). (h) Again, classic simplicity dominates this decoration (125e).

The following life theme decorations are so unusual in Southwest Indian pottery of prehistoric times that they are herein featured. The majority of the life subjects are centered, with a dominantly simple geometric band fairly close to the rim. (i) A highly conventionalized bird theme presented in a characteristic pose, outspread wings and head in profile (210d). (j) A different pose for a quail which expresses a little more life in more natural drawing (215c). (k) A break in the simple banded rim gives a little more motion to this design but the static figures of the geometric-decorated antelope slow this action down. Note the profile

of body and head but full front of eye and horns, typical primitive treatment of such details (224e). (l) A delightful creature of the imagination which needed nothing more than the simple line-band rim decoration to set it off (197e). (m) Ghosts of the past! Simple but effective and sufficient unto themselves—no band appears, which is rare in bowl decoration of the Mimbreños (194d). (n) Another conventional figure quite like *k* but, as always, with different geometric decoration on the body (223b). (o) Life is added to this mountain sheep figure in its full front face, a position which conventionally accommodates the baby on its mother's head (221e). (p) Although many of these insects or insectlike creatures have been identified by entomologists, others remain enigmatic (198b). (q) A grasshopper, no doubt. This simpler drawing contrasts with the more elaborate rim band (199e). (r) This could be nothing but a frog even though his "warts" have become great circles (202b). (s) A storytelling creation, showing a fish-eating bird. Or is it representative of a myth? (209b). (t) Just a plain, rounded fish, devoid of the usual geometric body decoration. There is great variety in the shapes and details of fishes drawn by the Mimbreños (204e). (u) Rabbits were favored subjects of the Mimbres artists and they vary tremendously in body shape, legs, and particularly in the size of their ears (217b). (v) Another storytelling decoration—but what? Is this a proboscis ending in a human hand? And why a partially skeletalized human? If one only knew! As suggested in the text, Fred Kabotie has interpreted some of these Mimbres storytelling decorations in terms of contemporary Hopi myths and legends (229d).

the design elements and of some of the design styles. For example, there is a continuation of much of the fine parallel line work combined with solid geometric forms (Fig. 4.40b); scrolls remain popular, with some of them expressed in repeated bands, often in the manner of earlier years; and often the application of black design on the white ground is of such nature as to suggest negative patterning (Fig. 4.40f). Dynamism continues as a prominent feature of Classic decoration; and four-fold division in design remains the dominant style (Fig. 4.40c,d,e). In this geometric work, painting is meticulous, spacing is very good, and line work is often exquisite (Fig. 4.40f,g). Composition is varied and pleasing, despite the fact that most of it is confined to bands.

Life subjects are varied and wondrous. Included are many birds, insects, reptiles, fish, mammals, humans, and creatures of the imagination (Fig. 4.40a,c,d,i–v). Some of these are so conventional that at best one can say "bird" only (Fig. 4.40i), but in other instances they are so well defined that one can be equally sure that this is a turkey or a quail (Fig. 4.40j). Humans may be pencil-thin or balloon-fat. If not in black silhouette or in white against a black ground, almost all life forms are decorated with geometric designs on their bodies, and infrequently on their heads for normally just the eye is represented (Fig. 4.40k).

Further discussion of the life decoration reveals more of the whimsy, ability, imagination (Fig. 4.40l), and other qualities of these artists.

Although geometric decoration predominates, there is a very high percentage of life forms in Classic Mimbres pottery. And the fine draftsmanship is outstanding in both life design and in the geometric. According to the Cosgroves, in life forms, "naturalism is somewhat conventional. It was brought to a high degree of perfection, both in positive and negative drawing, for the depiction of animal and insect life. Representations of the human form and features are less well drawn, though they show action and record events with accuracy. Naturalistic figures are usually framed by bands or combinations of geometric units which form panels for the objects illustrated."[25] The band of framing runs the gamut from simple to complex. Included among the simpler ones are one or more broader lines alone or these plus one or more sets of fine lines, or a group of fine lines alone. Or the band

may be more complex, composed of the fine and/or broad lines alternating with some other geometric theme; or with the life subject integrated into the band lines; or with much more in the way of geometrics incorporated into the band of lines; or as a half-band within or separate from the plain band. Sometimes the life design is not centered but alternates with an inner geometric motif.

Not only were animals, birds, insects, reptiles, and such broad categories of living creatures portrayed in this art as previously mentioned, but also specific species could be identified and then double checked in the bones of the same found at the Swarts Ruin. A good cross section of the life of the times was established in this painting. Further, it is likely that certain myths and tales of these people were represented in some of the bowl decoration; at least the Hopi artist, Fred Kabotie, was convinced of this and wrote about such matters in a book titled *Designs From the Ancient Mimbreños*.[26] Surely many of the composite creatures which reflect such delightful imagination might well be representative of the mythological. What could these be—a lizard with the tail of a fish? A bird with deerlike head and teeth? Two birdlike figures joined at midpoint, and with heads of goats? An antelope body with the tail of a turkey and the head of a mountain goat? Half human, half fish? Human head and limbs and a snake's body?

Many activities of the Mimbres people are portrayed in their decorated bowls. There are hunting scenes, including one showing a man carrying home a deer and a picture of a man fighting with a bear (or is the latter a legendary scene?). Dancing figures are presented; one of them has a "shield" in his left hand, a quiver full of arrows in the right hand, and is wearing a fancy "breastplate" (or sleeveless poncho)—is this a religious performer or a warrior? And is the following a religious scene, perhaps a circumcision or a child-naming rite: two men are sitting on the ground, a tiny figure on the lap (almost) of one of them, and both men are gesticulating with their arms. A mobilelike affair is held by a man, with a fish dangling from one string, a mammal with a very long tail from another. Cultivation of the fields was a matter of first concern to the prehistoric Southwesterner —slight wonder that the planting stick appears several times in what may be ritual scenes. There is a simple presentation of the birth of a baby, its little head and one arm already out. Another painting shows two men (priests?) holding tubular devices (pipes?) in their hands. Concern for their crops is depicted in a scene where four men are removing bugs from corn stalks. Masked dancers are portrayed also.

Details of dress and costume are to be noted in Mimbres ceramic decoration. There are elaborate hairdos, with maidens wearing the whorl style (also worn by pueblo girls historically). Men wear fringed breechcloths, elaborately designed footless stockings, kilts, fancy headgear, flowing bands, feathers and ornamented headbands, and a great tasseled cap. Jewelry is well represented: earrings which appear to be mosaic with a large central piece; multiple strand necklaces, and one close-fitting necklace with a huge pendant in the form of an arrowhead.

The depiction of life forms varies greatly. Humans may be realistically portrayed, with rounded arms and calves of legs or they may be veritable stick figures (Fig. 4.40m). Full front or profiles appear, although the profile view is favored in more realistic presentations. Even if the head is in profile the eye is full front. Human eyes may be round, oval, or diamond-shaped.

Animal forms vary tremendously with a tendency for the artist to make certain ones more geometric and others realistic. Highly conventionalized were the turtle, deer, and certain birds (Fig. 4.40i,n). Some birds have triangular bodies and wings and tails (or suggestions thereof), while quail and turkeys may be realistically portrayed. There is some variation in the manner of presenting birds also: more realistic styles are almost always in profile, while the highly conventionalized forms are painted with outstretched wings and tail, and head only in profile. Absolute left-right balance and symmetry is sometimes attained in bird forms as the head is straight up! Some mountain sheep and goats and wildcats are frequently more naturalistic but have geometric patterns on their bodies. One charming presentation of a mother sheep shows her body in profile, her head turned full front, and her baby standing on the top of her head (Fig. 4.40o).

Insects often have a variety of geometric themes on their bodies—bands, diamonds, and checkers (Fig. 4.40p,q). Plain and stepped diamonds, circles, checkers, or wavy bands appear on frogs (Fig. 4.40r). Turtles have a fair variety of geometrics with the checkerboard

prominent, to suggest the natural patterning of their backs. Fish are ornamented with a wide variety of simple or complex geometric designs; they are always represented in profile (Fig. 4.40s,t).

Rabbits are presented in a semirealistic style, but their ears, both large and small, tend to be geometric (Fig. 4.40u). The bodies of most of these creatures are plain, although a few have a little geometric patterning on them. Diamonds are featured on the bodies of deer and antelope, and a few other geometric designs appear on them.

In summary of Mimbres life painting it can be reiterated that much imagination and ability were displayed in this expression and much of the life and legends of the people (Fig. 4.40v); and the life in nature about them was revealed in this art form. Capability in the age-old conventional styles and in less known naturalistic portrayals were displayed in this unique ceramic painting.

Pottery was one of the most diversified of all the prehistoric Southwest craft arts. There were endless forms; there were large and small sizes; and design, which was generally painted, knew no limits of expression. In fact, painted decoration ran the gamut from a simple line band to the most complex of geometric or life forms.

Perhaps one of the reasons for such diversity in ceramics was because it was the chief vessel-producing craft. And, as noted previously, there were many adaptations to use, not alone in form but in type of decoration as well. Color would have been lost completely on a cooking pot with its first blackening use; it may well be that all-over corrugation among the Anasazi was for decoration as well as for the practical purposes of greater ease and security in handling the hot vessel. Whatever the reason, surely it enjoyed a widespread distribution and much artistry. Other textured wares, particularly among the Mogollones, are further reflective of variety in this technique.

Painted wares enjoyed distinction not only in terms of the larger cultural areas but also in more limited regional expressions. Examples in some of the discussions stressed a few of these, but by no means were all of them covered; the few described will testify to high artistic attainment.

Colors were effectively handled; designs were always different although expressed within and directed by the traditions of the group. Although utility value was never forsaken, pottery forms were numerous as well as local in style.

It may be said that prehistoric pottery design had exhausted its potential of expression within the framework of its native growth and development, and that new impetus and inspiration would be necessary to call forth further artistry. Perhaps this has been supplied in the totality of European and Anglo-American contact and influences, to find fruition in the growing sim-plicity, yet sophistication, in the finer ceramic products of some of the pueblo people in the mid- and later-twentieth century.

Surface finish and some changes in decoration have preoccupied these later ceramic decorators, as exemplified in polished-matte styles of San Ildefonso and other pueblos, in the addition of turquoise and other nonclay materials to surfaces, and in exploration into new sources for paints and new colors. Combinations of several of these types of decoration on single pieces is the most recent trend.

Chapter 5

 Ornaments

QUITE GENERALLY it is maintained that basketry is the oldest of man's developments in the way of artificial production of items which he then used. However, one may posit the question, is not jewelry older? Certainly body painting could have preceded every other decorative art, and it is a short step from painting the body to wearing an ornament on it.

Although they have been found sparingly on Early Man levels, certainly throughout the sedentary phases of man's development there were many evidences of paints, for example, balls of yellow ochre, which might have been used for body decoration. Then there were palettes found so abundantly among the Hohokams that the question might well be asked: What else could they have been used for except to grind paints on to be used for body decoration? Pictographs and kiva wall murals further support this expression, for example, at Awatovi, in two instances: a body and face are painted, black in one figure while the adjoining one has yellow body and face coloring.[1] In another case, at the same site, a nude body of a man has what appears to be an ear of corn painted on his side. Three large stars are painted on a human body pictograph from San Cristobal, New Mexico (Fig. 5.1). A Basketmaker pictograph from Chaco Canyon shows a triangular-bodied man with dots painted all over his torso. Then, to further support this idea, there is the superabundance of body painting among all known historic Southwest Indian groups.

It is quite probable that at an early date some fellow twisted or braided together several fibers to wrap about his wrist, or took a stone and altered it slightly, to hang about his neck. Shells, of course, are found in the Old World as early as Mousterian (Middle Paleolithic) times under circumstances that indicate their probable use as objects of adornment. In the New World, there is no evidence of man quite this early, but there are some indications that the first Americans did adorn themselves with shell.

In the Southwest, there are, of course, evidences that people were interested in articles with which to adorn themselves in archaeological times comparable to late Paleolithic of the Old World. Shells came to light in early levels at Danger Cave in northern Utah; they had been imported from the West Coast of the United States. As in the case of the finds of the same in the European area in Mousterian sites, it is possible that some religious attachment was involved in this use of shell. Even so, it is difficult to say just where the religious began and ended and where the sheer pleasure of wearing something about the neck took over—and even if religious, it is still jewelry. So far, no humans have ever been known, no matter how primitive, who did not adorn themselves in some manner, be it ever so crudely. Some Tierra del Fuego natives did no more than twine a bit of fiber about their wrists. Others simply cut off some branchlets and tucked them behind the ear or through a hole in the same, or perhaps, through the septum of the nose. Man everywhere and at all times has been greatly imbued with the idea of wearing a bit of personal adornment.

In addition to the example of shell, other finds have been made of Early Man's efforts in this direction. A small piece of soapstone or talc was roughly shaped by a Folsom man, to serve as a

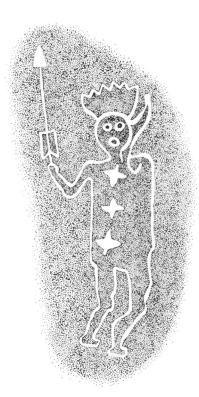

Fig. 5.1 Petroglyph from San Cristobal in the Galisteo Basin, northern New Mexico, showing three stars, probably painted on the body (Sims 1950, pl. VII, lower right).

served in the burial situation. Nonetheless many beads and fragments of other objects have been found among the ashes of the dead.

Before discussing the actual types of jewelry produced by the three major cultures of the Southwest, it is important to have in mind something of the materials used, methods of manufacture and of decorating, and objects made by these folk.

Materials

Although a variety of materials was used in the manufacture of jewelry in the sedentary prehistoric Southwest, unquestionably the two most important were turquoise and shell. Both were employed from very early times in all three areas. Other stones were fairly popular, particularly any colorful ones the Indian came upon. A red stone, argillite, was widely used in the Anasazi area; other stones that were occasionally or more abundantly worked in various parts of the Southwest would include, among others, sandstone, limestone, travertine, serpentine, soapstone, shale, slate, malachite, azurite, hematite, fluorite, galena, schist, steatite, fine grained argillites, and jet. Judd reports a limited use of calcite and selenite, and even a bit of mica for jewelry.[2] Stone might have come from the immediate vicinity where the maker lived or it might have been traded in from a closer or more distant source.

Shell is found all over the Southwest. Most of it came from the Gulf of California or the West Coast; relatively little came from the Gulf of Mexico. Depending upon the size and nature of the shell, it was traded into the Southwest as whole shell, or it was worked into blanks at its

pendant. It was indented around the edges and then was polished. Another example would be fragments of what appear to be three bone discs from the Lindenmeier site in Colorado (Fig. 5.2). Small incised lines occur around the edges of the pieces. Some contend that as there were no perforations, these may have been used as counters, perhaps for some game. One, however, has a chunk out of it which might well have been the result of attempting to perforate the piece for use as a pendant.

It is possible that other examples of the uses of jewelry by Early Man have been lost to posterity. The very nature of the way of life of these hunters and food gatherers would seldom allow for the preservation of those limited small objects which formed their store of jewelry. Too, it is quite likely that what little they had went to their graves with them, except for the occasional piece which was lost in the normal pursuits of their daily lives. But their graves have never been found. When the Indians began to settle down to an agricultural life, the picture changed. Whatever they had in the way of material culture was likely to survive in larger quantities than in the previous hunting state of their existence, sometimes in and about the village itself, and frequently within the grave. Those who practiced cremation frustrate the archaeologist, for these people destroyed far more than they pre-

Fig. 5.2 Early Man Jewelry. A carved bone disc, fragmentary, recovered from the Lindenmeier Site, eastern Colorado (Wormington 1957, Fig. 11, lower right).

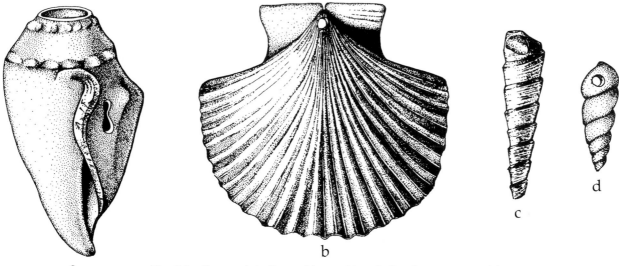

Fig. 5.3 Types of shells used by prehistoric Southwesterners: (a) a Strombus type; (b) Pecten; (c) Turritella; and (d) Cerithidea (?).

source, and these were traded into the area to be used as desired by the natives. From the Gulf of California, much shell, whole or in the form of blanks, was brought up the Gila River and into the heart of the Hohokam area; from there it might have been traded to the north in the same forms, or made into specific pieces of jewelry and then these were traded. It is quite likely that West Coast shell followed several routes into the Southwest, reaching directly both the northern and southern parts of this area. From the Gulf of Mexico, the route traveled is not clearly known; certainly more shell from this area was used in the eastern parts of the Southwest, particularly in the Mogollon, than in other sections.

The varieties of shell used were many and varied. There was also diversity in the distribution of specific varieties. Rather common and widely distributed were Oliva, Olivella, Glycymeris, and Conus; and, although less abundant in some instances, the following were fairly widely reported: Haliotis, Turitella, Abalone, Vermetus, Spondylus, and Nassarius (Fig. 5.3).

In addition to shell and stone, there was a wide range of "odds and ends" in the way of materials used for jewelry by the prehistoric Southwesterners. Some of the earliest beads in the Anasazi were made of Ephedra seeds; walnuts were found at Pueblo Bonito. Clay was widely used in the making of beads; potsherds were not infrequently formed into vari-shaped pendants. Bone served for several forms of jewelry and pieces made of this material were of various shapes. Wood, basketry, shell, and

occasional other materials were used as a base for mosaics. Copper bells were imported; as a result of the detailed analyses of this metal, it has been concluded that the bells were definitely not native, but were made in and imported from Mexico. Too, the method of producing these bells, the lost wax technique, was too advanced for a people without any further knowledge of metallurgy to have made them.

Technology

Methods of working this great variety of materials were, of necessity quite varied. Simple cutting was applied to softer substances, such as shell, nuts, and to a large number of stones. After all, it was a matter of the use of stone implements only, for these prehistoric people had no knowledge of metals. Some incising and carving were done on the same wide range of stones and on shell. Incising was usually a simple cutting into the surface of the material at hand. Carving was either simple bas or flat relief, true relief, or full round; it may have been executed in a simple, generalized style or in a style with considerable detail. Abrading, or a simple wearing away by rubbing or friction, was also applied to some materials, particularly shell and stone. Stones with narrow, long grooves in them have been found by archaeologists who label them abraders (Fig. 5.4a); this grooved type was used in beadwork. Drilling was one of the most interesting accomplishments of the jeweler, for he seemed to have been familiar with several

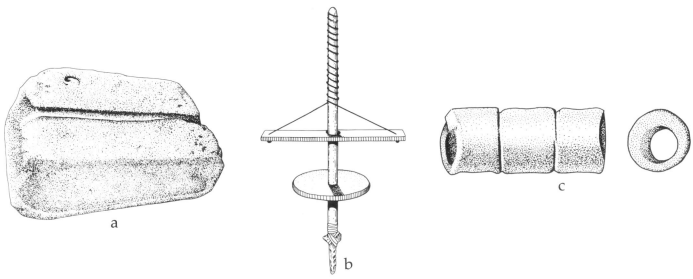

Fig. 5.4 How beads were made. (a) Stone with a groove for shaping beads, made of tuff, from Los Muertos (Haury 1945a, Fig. 86). (b) A hand pump; probably this type was used for drilling holes in making beads (Knoblock 1939, pl. 21, No. 1). (c) Some beads were made by wrapping clay about a stem of grass, incising all the way around at regular intervals where the beads would then be broken away after baking, from Los Muertos (Haury 1945a, Fig. 75).

methods of doing this type of work. In thicker and cylindrical beads, the driller worked from first one side, then the other, ending up with an hour-glass hole or one constricted toward the middle. In thinner, flatter beads, a hole was drilled straight through. The drill was a stone-tipped, hand-pumped device (Fig. 5.4b); it is still used by several pueblo groups in the Southwest today. Clay beads were made by rolling this material on a grass stem, marking it, burning it (this destroys the grass), and breaking off the beads where the clay was marked (Fig. 5.4c). Mosaic and inlay were fairly highly developed by these prehistoric people. Sometimes for the latter they drilled holes completely through the recipient material and set the stone so as to show equally on both faces, as can be seen in one pair of earrings; or they drilled a hole or cut an area part way into the material, such as shell, and set a contrasting substance such as turquoise or red stone, into the hole or area, cementing the piece or pieces in position. Or mosaic fragments were glued onto the flat surface of the desired piece, the small fragments made permanent in mesquite gum, possibly, in the Hohokam area, or in piñon pitch or lac, the latter substance made from a resinous deposit of a tiny insect that lives on the creosote bush. Lac was traded into the Anasazi from the south. Much of this mosaic might better be called overlay, particularly that which was set onto the surface of the base piece, as was often the case.

Still another technology that developed in the Hohokam area should be discussed for its rare nature. Etching was discovered and practiced on shell in this area centuries before the technique was known in the Old World. Too, it is concluded that this process was actually developed here without benefit of any influence from Mexico or anywhere else.

It is thought that etching was done in the following manner. A brew was made from the fruit of the sahuaro cactus and allowed to set. Historic Papagos of southern Arizona have done this same thing, allowing the liquid to set for four days, then ceremonially drinking it; at this point, the "tiswin," as they call it, has a very low alcoholic content. If allowed to set for a while longer, the liquid develops an acetic acid content of about six percent strength; this is sufficiently strong to eat into shell. Probably the prehistoric people of the area were equally familiar with the brew and with its potentials for working shell. At any rate, Haury found in the re-excavation of Snaketown a piece of shell with a coating of pitch forming the shape of a horned toad, the remainder of the shell left uncovered.[3] It is presumed that the worker would have dipped the shell into a solution of the sahuaro juice-turned-acid, and that the liquid would have eaten slowly into the uncovered portion. Years before the discovery of the piece covered with pitch, Haury had postulated this very procedure, basing his assumption on several facts: a slight undercutting around the edges of the designs and the fact that the natural ripples in the shell remained in the etched areas. Neither of these results would have been possible in the mere carving of such a piece. Sometimes the piece was left in this simple, but sophisticated, etched style, while in other instances, the worker added paint. Several examples show the use of a combination of pink and blue, using one color for the raised area and the other for the etched or depressed sections. Incidentally, painting of other than etched shell should be mentioned as another interesting technique of decorating articles of personal adornment. Painting on fragments of material or whole pieces has been found at various widespread sites.

A last technology, pseudo-cloisonné, will be described, even though it was used in the making of articles called mirrors, which were worn or used, seemingly, for ceremonial purposes. The latter, of course, cannot be said unequivocally; further, objects worn by priests are jewelry as much as a piece worn by the layman, as inferred before in connection with other rather special items of personal adornment.

These mirrors were made in the following manner. A piece of stone, often sandstone, was cut and ground into a circle, frequently a perfect one, with plain edges or with a bevelled edge on one side of some of them. Two holes (or sometimes more) were cut through at each edge for suspension, or two at each edge in such a manner as to accommodate a suspension cord on that one side only. Other holes sometimes appeared on other pieces. Some of these plaques were then ornamented in the following manner. On one side, small fragments of iron pyrites were set into an adhesive; the pieces were very thin sections and they were so used as to fit closely together, then they were polished, thus making for the so-called "mirror" surface. The bevelled edge of the mirror (and sometimes the reverse side) was covered with the pseudo-cloisonné produced by the following process as described by Haury.[4] First a layer of gray material was placed on the stone surface, with a thick black layer on top of it. The latter was smoothed, then incised with the desired design. The incisions were first half-filled with a white substance, then on top of the white were added the various colored paints necessary to carry out the design. The colored materials might be flush with or slightly above the black layer. Designs were worked out in various combinations of red, yellow, white, and light blue. Mirrors with some combination of bevelled edges, pyrites mosaic, and this pseudo-cloisonné represent a peak of artistic attainment in the later years of Hohokam cultural development.

Forms of Jewelry

Forms in jewelry are many and varied; too, it must be kept in mind that some of them were possibly for wear by any member of the community, while other pieces were meant to be worn by "specialists," such as priests, as mentioned in connection with mirrors, and probably on ceremonial occasions only. Mention will be made relative to this dichotomy in several instances, thus attempting to throw a bit of light on an interesting aspect of these peoples' lives. Probably then, as now, few natives wore jewelry except for special gatherings. In the main, all forms appear to have been worn by members of both groups; sometimes the pieces belonging to the specialist were larger and frequently more elaborate. Some few pieces are not jewelry in the proper sense of something to wear. Rather, they may have been carried by the priest, or placed at an altar, or used in some other manner in connection with rituals. Nevertheless even these pieces are manufactured like other pieces of jewelry; they are of the same forms, and are made of the same materials—and, of course, some were worn—hence, some of them will be described under this topic.

Basically, the major forms of jewelry would include necklaces of beads and pendants, earrings, bracelets and anklets, rings, buttons, and other objects to attach to clothing, hair ornaments, and nose and lip plugs (Fig. 5.5). Each of these forms will be discussed relative to their respective variations, materials used in their manufacture, and how they were ornamented. Specific examples of each will be given.

Bracelets were, perhaps, the most popular item throughout the Southwest. Generally they were cut from Glycymeris; at Snaketown, no other species of shell were used in the making of bracelets. The basic form and shape of the bracelets varied: they were narrow and thin, medium width, wide and heavy, or wide and thin (Fig. 5.6a). Many were plain circlets; some were more carefully carved as well-defined smooth-edged circles, while others had rough or unfinished edges; still others were carved in a zigzag or wavy form, to resemble a snake's body. Middle-width and wide bracelets might retain the umbo of the shell, the craftsman leaving it in its natural shape or carving it, usually into a frog or other life form (Fig. 5.6b).

In addition to these decorative features in the forming of bracelets or in the use of the umbo,

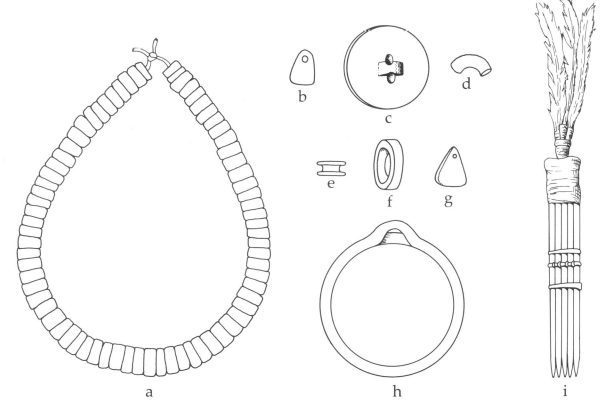

Fig. 5.5   Forms of jewelry made by prehistoric Southwesterners: (a) necklace of beads; (b) earring; (c) button; (d) nose plug; (e) lip plug; (f) ring; (g) pendant; (h) bracelet; (i) hair ornament.

there were many ways in which native tribes decorated their shell bracelets. Some were incised with either geometric designs or life motifs. Geometric elements were simply or more elaborately used; lines, dots, chevrons, zigzags, or other geometrics were employed alone or in various combinations. One or several snakes' bodies might be carved around

the bracelet, sometimes with a bird holding the head of the reptile in its mouth. These life themes might be represented in bas-relief or in full-modeled style. Occasionally pieces of turquoise, jet, or red stone would be set at intervals into the white shell.

In addition to the shell bracelet, there are a few rare examples of basketry bracelets or

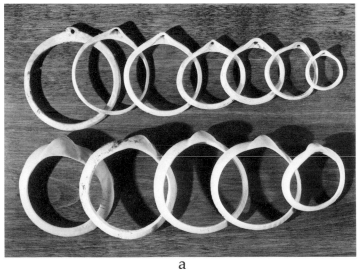

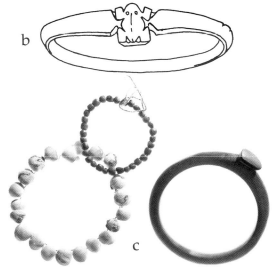

Fig. 5.6   Bracelets. (a) A great variety of sizes is to be noted in plain shell bracelets from the tiny child's style in the upper and lower right to the large—and probably anklet—example in the lower left. Almost all of the bracelets preserve the umbo of the shell, and certainly a vast majority

are plain. (b) A popular form of bracelet among the Hohokams with the umbo carved into some life form, here a frog. (c) A short string of seed beads and one of clam shells, plus a stone object, probably all bracelets.

wristlets. Several of these were covered with turquoise mosaic, one with no design, another with an elaborate geometric pattern. Two additional forms should be mentioned in connection with bracelets, namely, upper arm bands and anklets. Both are found in position on burials, so there can be no doubt about their use. Both tend to be broader and heavier than bracelets; they are usually wider in diameter, and the majority of them are undecorated. Also, it is evident that short strings of beads were worn as bracelets (Fig. 5.6c).

Necklaces were the next most popular jewelry item. They consisted of one or more long or short strands of beads or of a pendant suspended from a string twisted of native vegetal fiber, such as yucca or cotton. Beads were made of shell, turquoise, red stone, or any other available stone, of clay, of occasional other materials, or of combinations of any of these. One favored combination, apparently, was an alternation of several disc beads, usually of shell, with a single pendant, often of turquoise. This is a still-popular necklace, frequently worn by long-haired (older) Indian men and often for ceremonial occasions. Beads ran the gamut from rough-cut and irregular forms to beautifully shaped and graduated styles. Although the majority were made in the form of a flat, thin or thicker disc, many other shapes were used, such as cylindrical, bi-lobed or figure-8, whole small shells, barrel-shaped, spool-shaped, cuboid, and wedge-shaped, (more rounded, more angular), or irregular (Fig. 5.7). Seeds and nuts were used in their natural forms, although on rare occasions some nuts were altered in shape or finish. A few necklaces were made of potsherds, which were both decorated and undecorated and either square or round in shape.

Pendants used in the prehistoric Southwest were too varied in shape, size, and workmanship to be listed completely; however, a broad representative selection can be discussed briefly (Fig. 5.8). They were made of whole shells, large or small; or of bracelets or parts of them, carved or plain, and usually drilled for suspension in the center (in the umbo if there is one present), or at one end of a fragment of a bracelet. Pendants of geometric shapes, and made of stone, shell, bone, or rarely other materials, were most popular; these shapes included keystone, square, rectangular, oval, round, cogwheel, sunburst with sharp rays, and other geometrics. Life form pendants were presented in highly stylized, to fully realistic, figures of birds, humans, frogs, tadpoles, horned toads, and a few additional subjects. They were carved in flat presentations or full-round forms. Birds were represented with outspread wings and with the head in profile, or the entire figure was in full profile; the former were frequently in flat, thin forms, while the latter tended to be in full round. Craftsmanship on these birds often represents a peak of attainment. Mosaic pendants were also varied and some of them were highly artistic. In general, variety is expressed in the base form, from simple circles to birds with outspread wings. They varied, too, in combinations and methods of arranging materials, from allover turquoise placed on the foundation without plan, to careful disposition of turquoise and shell, to stress tail and wing feathers. Perhaps no other form of jewelry utilized so great a variety of materials; this, combined with variations in form and technical treatment, made for one of the most interesting and artistic expressions of the prehistoric Southwesterners. Inasmuch as there was no large sculpture to speak of among these natives, carved pendants are important as they express certain potentials which were not fully explored by these people.

Rings were of bone, stone (with jet favored in some areas), and shell. They were narrow or broad, this quality varying with time and distribution (Fig. 5.9). In turn, decoration was in some degree related to form, wider rings usually being decorated. One exception to this is in the Hohokam where narrow rings were beautifully and delicately engraved or carved; both geometric and life themes (serpents in particular) were used. Broad rings might bear this same type of decoration, or they might be ornamented with inlay, or in some instances the umbo might be cut in a plain fashion or with a carved life form. Shell rings were more frequently decorated than any other type; they were usually made from Glycymeris, particularly in the Hohokam area, although some of the broad and plain rings in the Anasazi were cut from Conus. In rare cases, both carving and inlay were combined in the decorating of rings.

Earrings are something of a problem in the prehistoric period. Nothing is lost more readily than an earring, even when tied to a string which in turn is suspended from a hole in the ear lobe. When not worn or when buried with the dead, they are readily separated; when found by the archaeologist, they are thus usually labeled

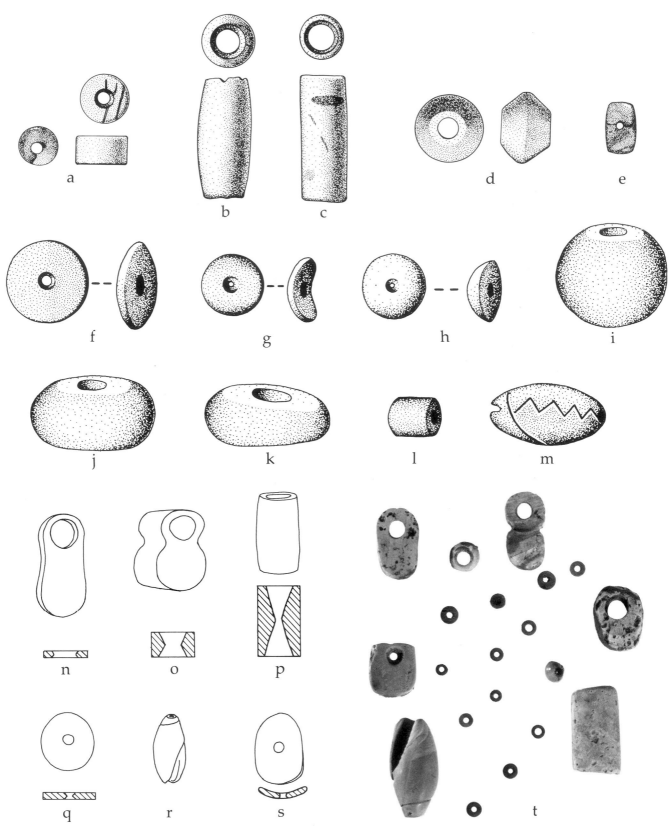

Fig. 5.7 Examples of stone, bone, and shell beads to show some of the great variety of this form of adornment. (a) Disc bead of a hard crystalline rock; (b) argellite and (c) steatite, the latter two elongate forms, all with cross-sections (McGregor 1941, Fig. 67 l,i,j). (d) A ridged form, rather unusual in these beads, and (e) a rectangular bead of stone (Elizabeth Morris 1959a, Fig. 62h). (f) Disc shell bead, (g) bead of Olivella shell slightly cupped, (h) a bone bead rounded on one face (Guernsey and Kidder 1921, Fig.10 f,g,h). (i-m) Several stone beads of various shapes (Guernsey and Kidder 1921, Fig. 10 a,b,c,e,i). (n-s) A variety of beads including figure 8, tubular, disc, whole shell, and irregular. (t) This photograph repeats the general shapes of beads given in *n-s*. Note the variation in size.

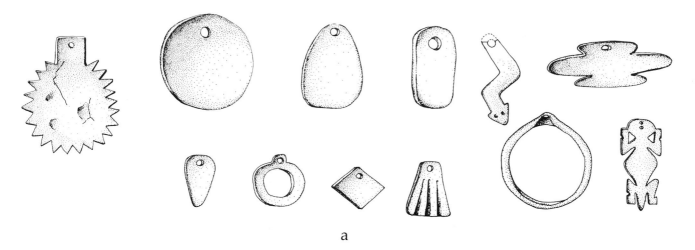

a

b

c

Fig. 5.8 A variety of pendants. (a) That these were used as pendants is indicated in the hole at the top of each piece (Judd 1954, Gladwin et al., 1937, and others). (b) Both geometric and life forms were popular pendant shapes. These were made of a variety of stones and of shell. (c) Figure of a frog often used as a pendant.

Fig. 5.9   Rings were made of stone (especially jet), bone, and shell. They varied in width and finish. Most rings were plain, but a few in this photo show how the umbo was sometimes left on the shell as a bit of decoration.

"pendant," particularly when only one is recovered. Some archaeologists are keen enough to be wary of these hazards and will recognize as earrings two like pieces which are found at different points in a burial, in trash, or elsewhere. On the other hand, two drops found together, or both found at ear position in a burial, or a pair found with a necklace, or representations of such in the ears on a figurine or in a wall painting would all point to the wide practice of the wearing of earrings. It is also possible that a pair of like or nearly like pieces of this nature might well serve as both earring and pendant, or perhaps, as pieces for necklaces.

Earrings were made of shell, stone, and possibly other materials still unknown for lack of identification of these articles of personal adornment. They were plain, incised, carved, and, in rare cases, they combined two materials. One such instance was mentioned previously, wherein the turquoise was cut with a small projection for the drilled hole for suspension; then a large hole was cut in the main part of the earring into which a piece of pink shell was placed, showing on both sides. Most earrings were simpler than this, one of the most popular being a

plain keystone style (Fig. 5.10). Round, teardrop, square or rectangular—these are other shapes of pieces which were probably earrings. Sometimes life forms were carved to serve as earrings.

In addition to earrings, some of the prehistoric Southwesterners made and wore ear plugs. These, too, are represented in the ears of figurines in the Hohokam area, so there can be no doubt about their use. Although such plugs appear on figurines as early as Estrella in this area, the actual pieces are not found until Sacaton times. This, of course, does not mean that they were not worn at an earlier date, for, like earrings, such small items would be difficult to find in archaeological sites. The ear plugs that have been recovered are of ring form,

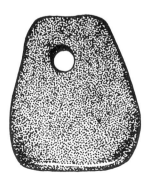

Fig. 5.10   A generalized keystone shape which was widely popular for earrings as well as pendants; often it was made of turquoise but other stones were used.

with fairly large, open centers and with a front and back flange. One, made of schist and deeply grooved, had an incised decoration on a flange, probably meant to be the front one.

Nose plugs or nose buttons were also made prehistorically (Fig. 5.11a); in some Hohokam burials they were of late Colonial and early Sedentary times. The use of wood for these pieces has been determined; there are also stone

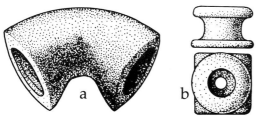

Fig. 5.11 Nose and lip plugs. (a) Fifteen nose plugs of red argillite came from the Winona and Ridge Ruin area. This is one of six different shapes of plugs (McGregor 1941, Fig. 71f). (b) Lip or cheek plug (Ibid, Fig. 71l). Eight of these were excavated in the Winona area and all were made of argillite.

pieces from the Hohokam area that are probably nose plugs. In the Anasazi, there is no question about stone nose plugs: several have been so identified beyond question in the Flagstaff area. Nose plugs are more abundant in the Anasazi area. The stone plugs were ground into shape; usually one material was used in these nose ornaments, but two materials might be combined in a single plug in some examples. These plugs are more or less cylindrical in shape, with a slight bend or crescentlike form. Although the Hohokam figurines do not show these plugs, a mummy burial was uncovered at Ventana Cave which had one in position in the nose septum.

Another unusual bit of personal adornment was a plug that was apparently inserted in the lip, often at the lower corner of the mouth (Fig. 5.11b). Like some of the nose plugs, they were made of stone; in certain respects, they were like the Northwest Coast labret. They are represented in Snaketown figurines; these, as worn in the corner of the mouth, resemble the Mexican style labret.

The foregoing constitutes the major forms in jewelry, but there are some others which will be thrown into a miscellaneous category; some of these are abundant in quantity while others are rare specimens. Too, some may have had a restricted ceremonial usage, while others may have been worn by anyone, but perhaps on limited occasions.

Buttons were fairly common (see Fig. 5.5). They were of various sizes, and jet or lignite was a common material used for their manufacture. Some were plain; how they were attached is still a question. Others had holes drilled in their backs in such a manner as to allow the passage of a string through the hole and then the button was tied to a garment. As is true in primitive groups in general, some of these so-called buttons may also have been used as pendants.

A varied group of objects might be added to a category labeled "garment ornaments." This would include beads, which were sparingly or abundantly used to ornament skirts, or pendants, which also served this second duty. Also, there were Conus "tinklers" which not only were worn as bracelets and necklets but also were fastened to garments for an additional decorative note (Fig. 5.12. Also see Fig. 3.29e). Further, in a burial to be described, these Conus pieces were used in loops about the knees perhaps for rattles, and in strings down the sides of the legs, possibly as kilt ornaments. It may be that this same Conus shell was used at the lower border of belts for decoration; one such example is to be noted in a kiva mural.

Most limited (sometimes to "one of its kind") are such items as a beaded headpiece, or bracelet ornaments. Several examples of the latter involve elaborate pieces of mosaic which added greatly to the shell bracelet; too, this may have been more common than is indicated in archaeological specimens.

Another important type of adornment was facial and body painting. These were undoubtedly "high style" at one time or another, if not all along during the prehistoric period. There are, of course, lumps of color materials, although they were probably used for purposes in addition to body and face decoration. Paint palettes, so popular in the Hohokam culture, were most likely used to grind paints for body and face usage. Designs on bodies in pictographs and petroglyphs probably represent body and face painting, like the three "stars" on the body of a figure from San Cristobal[5] (see Fig. 5.1). Perhaps the most conclusive evidence for this practice is to be noted in discolored flesh or color on bones, where, in the latter case, the original facial paint finally penetrated to the bone. At Hidden House there is a "yellowish pigment" in evidence on one burial. On the faces of eight burials at Tuzigoot were blue and green pigments. King's

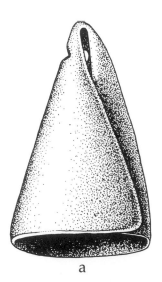

a

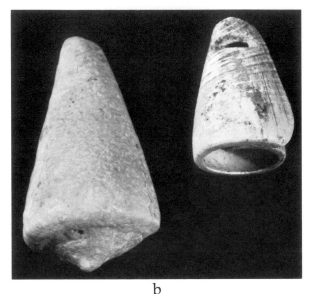

b

Fig. 5.12 Conus shells. (a) A Conus shell pendant, with a hole drilled for suspension. Often these pieces were strung as necklaces or were worn about the wrist. It is possible that sometimes they were worn on the lower edge of a belt (Earl Morris 1919, Fig. 68. Also see Smith 1952, Fig. 61b. The bangles on the bottom of the kilt could be Conus shells). (b) The photograph shows a complete Conus shell and a worked one, with the tip cut away from the latter and drilled.

Ruin also revealed green paint on eight skeletons, while facial bones at Chavez Pass had green and black on them. Dixon concludes, from these evidences, that skin painting "may be an occasional western Pueblo trait."[6] However, all the other evidences mentioned previously would indicate much more than a portion of the Pueblo area.

The following procedure will be used in connection with the description of various pieces of jewelry. First, several general examples will be spotted both in time and space, to illustrate the various forms, materials, and technologies. Then, secondly, several sites which have produced rather spectacular examples of jewelry will be brought into focus and examples of outstanding pieces from them will be described.

Examples of Ornaments

Ornamentation and examples of jewelry, may well be discussed together for it is difficult to speak of one without the other. Certain types of jewelry tend to be regional, but some pieces and even styles of decoration are found throughout the Southwest. On the other hand, there are distinct regional differences; therefore the approach to these last two topics will be in terms of their appearance in the three major cultural areas. Obviously, there will be some overlapping.

ANASAZI

Turquoise was apparently used as early as Basketmaker II times; a few beads have been recovered from sites of this period. There is no question relative to the presence of turquoise and other materials in considerable abundance by Basketmaker III. Rectangular and oval pendants were found at Shabikeshchee village, as well as small fragments of turquoise that were encountered under such circumstances as to suggest that they were used in mosaics, perhaps on perishable material such as wood or basketry.

From White Dog Cave come special types of necklaces, full strings of beads or limited numbers of beads or pendants attached to the center of cords.[7] Beads from this site are strung in various ways. In one example, 71 thick discoidal and graduated lignite and white limestone beads were alternated to produce a most attractive necklace. A clever device was resorted to in this string to make it hang more perfectly as wedge-shaped beads were inserted here and there throughout the necklace. Strings of plain Olivella shells were found here also, some of them long enough to go around the neck several times. Guernsey and Kidder also describe another necklace, a "string which was recovered in order, is made of one hundred little saucer-shaped shell beads; seventy-five thin, roughly discoidal shell beads; and eighteen olivella shells, one of which bears an incised zigzag decoration. These different kinds of beads are grouped together."[8] An interesting necklace of shells and mountain lion claws illustrates another variation (Fig. 5.13a).

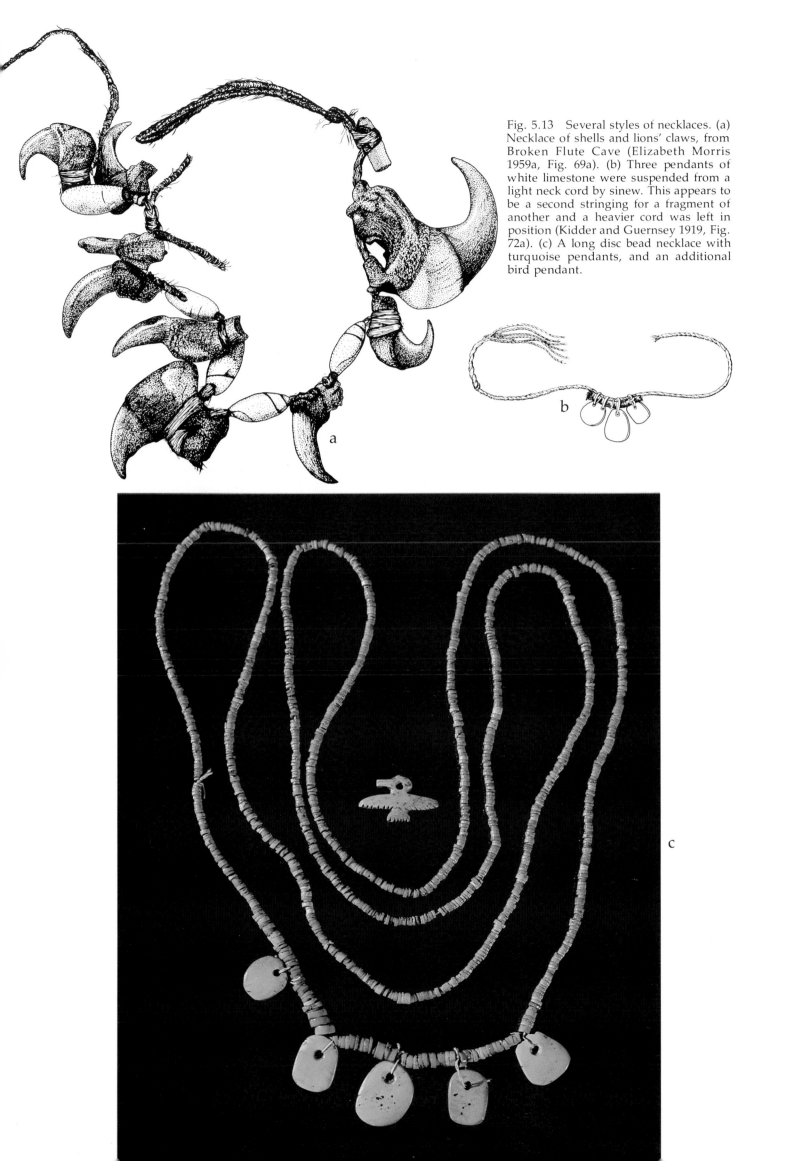

Fig. 5.13 Several styles of necklaces. (a) Necklace of shells and lions' claws, from Broken Flute Cave (Elizabeth Morris 1959a, Fig. 69a). (b) Three pendants of white limestone were suspended from a light neck cord by sinew. This appears to be a second stringing for a fragment of another and a heavier cord was left in position (Kidder and Guernsey 1919, Fig. 72a). (c) A long disc bead necklace with turquoise pendants, and an additional bird pendant.

A great variety of beads was found in Basketmaker sites. Guernsey and Kidder reported the following in their 1921 publication for the northeastern Arizona area.[9] Several kinds of seeds were used, including one which they compare to a seed pearl in size and appearance. Then there were quite a few varieties of stone employed in the manufacture of these ornaments, including hematite, alabaster, fine grained white limestone, serpentine, quartz, and lignite (Fig. 5.13b). In shape there is equal variety, from cylindrical forms with square-cut or rounded ends, to flat spherical, and wedge shaped. In shell there is a range from whole Olivella with the spire removed, to thin saucer-shaped types made from large Olivella shells, to thicker disc-shaped shell beads (Fig. 5.13c), or very thin ones, perhaps made from fresh water clam. In a Basketmaker III site in La Plata more than 100 beads made of juniper berries (both beads and cord on which they were strung were charred) were found, and in a second jar there were some more of the same. Juniper berry beads were characteristic of Basketmaker II elsewhere; a long strand of them was found on a child's burial in a cave west of Navajo Mountain.

On one occasion when working in Basketmaker caves in northeastern Arizona, Kidder and Guernsey found jewelry in quantity.[10] Although the sites were better protected than those of La Plata, many burials had been ransacked. On undisturbed burials, however, every skeleton had on at least one necklace. One of these was of rounded, heavy stone beads, with short pendants of the same. Another was a string of Olivella which went about the neck once or twice. A third was a double strand of Olivella shells with a pendant of white limestone, the latter with a band of red down the center. Quite different was a fourth necklace which was made of a piece of heavy cord with three limestone pendants suspended in the center. Comparable to the latter was a 16-inch-long rawhide string with a loop at one end and a knot to serve as a toggle at the other, demonstrating how some of the necklaces were fastened in position. Four loops appear in the center of this last piece, but the pendants they supported are missing. A last example to be mentioned from this group is a twisted cord with small snail shells tightly fastened into it.

Basketmaker pendants from these same sites include rather roughly shaped ones of schist, red jasper, and satin spar. No turquoise pendants

Fig. 5.14 Buttons, face and back views. Dark ones are of jet, light ones of pink shell. (a) The faces of all buttons are polished; (b) the backs are drilled from two points so that they might be sewed or tied onto garments.

were reported. From the later Pueblo periods of this area came turquoise pendants, either square-cut or rounded in form. One stone pendant of this later period is like an abstract bird with outspread wings. Shell pendants were common from early years on.

Several additional interesting pieces were found at these sites, including lignite buttons which were 3 inches in diameter and ¼ of an inch thick. They had a highly polished face, while on the back two holes were drilled at a slant and met, thus forming a means for tying the button to a garment (Fig. 5.14). A pair of lignite earrings were pointed at the ends; they were found at the two sides of the skull of an infant.

Morris illustrates a few pieces from La Plata area (Plates 173–177). Included are red shale, slate, calcite, and other stone pendants of several shapes, including keystone, rectangular, round, oval, and irregular.[11] Of lignite are the following: a bead, two rectangular and plain pendants, and a large rectangular pendant with 3 rows of 4 turquoises each, all fairly evenly distributed on the black material. There are also a half dozen shell pendants which look as though they had been made from broken bracelets.

From this area also came some beads, including a more than 5½ foot long strand of very fine black and red slate or shale disc types; they varied from .9 mm to 2.0 mm in diameter. These were the exception and not the rule. Some believe that these tiny beads were not made in the northern part of the Anasazi but, rather, were made in the south of this culture area and traded into other sections. This reasoning is based on the fact that the tiny holes for stringing, which were only .45 mm in diameter, may have been drilled only with a cactus needle, and this particular cactus grows only in the southern Anasazi.

A Mesa Verde burial reveals a cross section of jewelry in this southwest Colorado region. Varicolored stone and some shell beads ranged in shapes from thin disc styles to short tubular forms. Two of the latter, made of hematite, were inlaid with turquoise. There were also some of the minute disc beads of black shale. Pendants were simple and made of shell, turquoise, and other stones, including lignite and a soft white stone; their forms included the usual rectangle, with elongate versions of the same, and the keystone.

Of interest from Kiatuthlanna are bracelets and armlets of Glycymeris shell. There were never less than two on an arm and in some instances there were as many as twenty. The majority of the bracelets were plain and thin, with but one elaborately carved with a frog on the umbo (Fig. 5.15); this is probably an armlet for it is wider, larger, and a bit heavier than the bracelets. Tubular bone heads were found in limited quantities at this site in association with the pit houses, while they were quite abundant from Pueblo levels. Beads of Olivella shell were very important in the Basketmaker

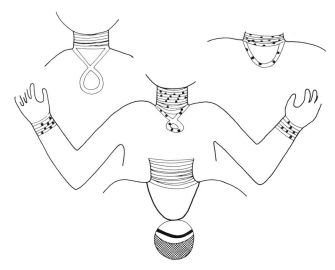

Fig. 5.16 Varieties of necklaces, showing varicolored beads and different ways of wearing them. Note alternations of the different colored beads, and a pendant which is probably mosaic-set (taken from photographs of Kuaua kiva murals).

Period, but were scarce in the Pueblo Phase. Figure-8 beads made of Glycymeris seem to be of late Pueblo III times; they are not associated with Basketmaker or early Pueblo times. Frequently beads are found in distinct arrangements in the ground as they were originally; thus they were at Kiatuthlanna (and elsewhere), indicating much variety in definite order relative to materials, colors, and sizes. Here, for example, shell beads were alternated with dark stone beads, with one large turquoise bead and two turquoise pendants at the center bottom. Methods of wearing such combinations are well illustrated in kiva murals (Fig. 5.16).

Bone was the material for finger rings in Pueblo times. One of the most interesting ornamental pieces from Kiatuthlanna was a girdlelike garment over a burial made of 300 Olivella shell beads. Pendants were made of shell, turquoise, alabaster, and shale; they were of tear-drop and other simple forms.

In excavating ruins south of the Hopi country, Fewkes found several unusual objects of adornment.[12] One was a rectangular lignite earring with a small round turquoise set in each of the four corners and in the center. Quite exciting is the turquoise encrusted frog found here. A Pectunculus giganteus formed the base on which were embedded tightly joined and evenly cut turquoises, with a piece of red jasper set in the center. The legs of the frog are just barely suggested. One shell bracelet from this area was

Fig. 5.15 A carved shell armlet as indicated in its larger size. Found in a pithouse at Kiatuthlanna (Roberts 1931, Fig. 31).

decorated with an incised, simple interlocking fret; another had a few turquoise settings near the umbo. Conus tinklers were abundant; they were made by simply grinding away the spire. Copper bells, which are widely spread over the Southwest, were found at both Chavez Pass and Four Mile Ruin of this Fewkes report.

There is considerable development in jewelry during the Pueblo Period, particularly in Pueblo III and IV. This is to be noted in increased numbers and varieties of objects and in general elaboration of them. More shell was traded into the Anasazi during these later years, and more turquoise, frequently a better quality of this stone, was used. Mosaic became popular in some villages, with beautifully crafted pieces produced at this time. Further, there seems to have been a considerable exploitation of varied stones, with color holding a strong appeal for these prehistoric people. And it may be reiterated that there were regional trends within parts of larger cultural areas; for example, a great abundance of turquoise is to be noted at Pueblo Bonito, and mosaic, using varied materials, was significant in the Flagstaff region.

Turquoise beads and pendants were more abundant at Pueblo Bonito than at any other Southwestern site.[13] Several graves or other locations for these objects might be described, in part to support this statement. On one burial alone were found the following flat disc beads of turquoise: 2,297 over the legs, perhaps originally sewed onto the lower part of a skirt or kiltlike garment; 698 over the right ankle, 1,628 around the upper right arm, and 567 more scattered around the burial. There were also more than 9 turquoise pendants in this burial. A second burial is equally impressive: about the neck were 1,980 disc beads and 1 large and 8 smaller pendants, all of turquoise; of the same material and about the waist were 2,642 disc beads, 168 small pendants plus 4 odd shaped pendants, 2 in the shape of rabbits, 1 in shoelike form, and 1 unfinished; a wristlet on the right arm made of 616 flat disc beads, 147 small pendants, plus a bird effigy and other odd pieces; on the left arm 2,384 disc beads, 194 pendants, and nearby 5 pendants; on the right ankle 322 disc beads, 5 pendants, 2 cylindrical beads; and on the left ankle 432 disc beads, and 8 pendants. Again, all of these objects are of turquoise!

In another room at Pueblo Bonito were a four-strand, turquoise bead necklace and two pairs of almost rectangular earrings (Fig. 5.17).

This necklace, which is made of graduated disc beads, is the finest and most beautiful from the entire prehistoric Southwest. Many other pairs of turquoise earrings were found at this site.

Many lovely pendants were excavated at Pueblo Bonito. Shell examples run the gamut from simple whole shell or circular, square and rectangular forms to cogwheels, zigzags (some with more rounded edges), tooth-shaped, and life forms. The latter would include, among others, birds, lizards, and humans in either shell or stone. Much lignite was used for a variety of pendants—one in particular, is a square set with turquoise in its counter-sunk border. The contrast between the black of the jet and the turquoise is appealing. There is not much variety in pendants made of turquoise as compared with those of shell at Pueblo Bonito. Despite this fact, the best of turquoise was used for pendants, with pieces of lesser quality employed in the making of beads. Both geometric and life forms were fairly abundant at Pueblo Bonito. There were also several clay pendants from this site, as elsewhere, of potsherds either in plain or decorated ware.

Mosaic seems to have been a popular expression at Pueblo Bonito. Although many of the pieces can never be reconstructed, some have been, including the previously mentioned pendant and a ring. Fragments of inlay found with burials may well be all that is left of some objects of personal adornment. Shell, jet, turquoise and red stone were utilized for this type of work.

Pepper reported a piece of mosaic in the form of a bird carved of hematite about 2¼ inches from bill to tail and just under ⅞ inch across the wing area.[14] The back was divided into two parts by bands of turquoise set in grooves level with the stone. Wings were a bit higher and were also inlaid with the blue stone. Shell was inset into the tail, with three pieces of turquoise at the very tips. Eyes were of small rounds of turquoise and about the neck was a circlet of the same stone, all set in drilled holes. In another room Pepper excavated a frog of jet inlaid with turquoise, and several turquoise birds.

At Pueblo Bonito, shell beads occur as whole shells or in varied forms including cylindrical, thick discs, figure-8, oval-and saucer-shaped. The figure-8 bead was very popular at Pueblo Bonito and apparently all of this form were made of shell. Judd writes, "Although many of our figure-8 beads resemble either bone or stone those actually tested proved to be shell."[15] In

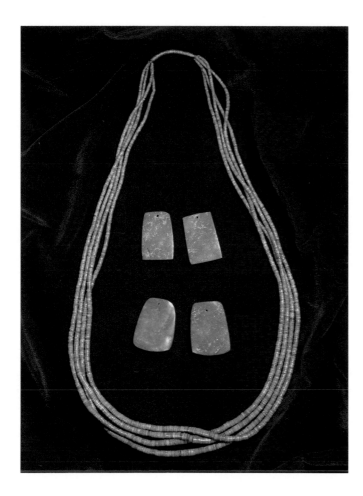

Fig. 5.17 Graduated four-strand turquoise necklace and two pairs of earrings, Pueblo Bonito (Judd 1954, pl. 19. Photograph, courtesy of National Geographic Society).

one burial, shell beads were found all about the skull. Could this have been a cap? Or was it a string (22 feet, 8 inches long when restrung by archaeologists), which was wrapped about the head?

Pendants just described may well have served as earrings. However, a great many pairs were found, either two pieces together or one at each ear of a burial. Variety of shapes seems to have characterized shell earrings, while those of turquoise were simpler in form, adhering basically to the keystone shape. It would seem that perhaps the Bonitians were sophisticated to the point of appreciating color alone for its esthetic value.

Rings were fairly numerous at Pueblo Bonito. Although some were made of bone, shell, onyx, red shale, or limestone, the most outstanding ones were carved of jet. "When one recalls how fragile jet really is and how crude the tools available for carving it, and then notes the uniform thinness and symmetry of these four rings, one's admiration for the skill of Pueblo Bonito artisans is measurably increased."[16] Three of these rings

are plain, wide bands, while the fourth has a little bird carved on top, with its wings inset with five turquoises (Fig. 5.18).

Shell bracelets were not too abundant at Pueblo Bonito. They were made of Glycymeris shell and were plain. It is to be noted that all of these bracelets were perforated at the umbo, perhaps so that they could double for pendants.

Twenty-one whole or fragmentary copper bells came from this important site. They are of

Fig. 5.18 A jet ring, thin, evenly formed, and inset with turquoises on the side of the delicately carved bird, from Pueblo Bonito (Judd 1954, Fig. 25a).

the typical small sleigh-bell type found throughout the prehistoric Southwest. Whether worn for ceremonies or strictly for adornment cannot be determined; however, only six were found in kivas.

Considerable attention has been given to Pueblo Bonito and its jewelry, for not only in quantity but also in quality was it outstanding. Here were craftsmen who seemingly had the ability, the materials, and the time to ply their trade. This situation causes one to wonder what would have transpired had these people been undisturbed during ensuing years to pursue their artistic abilities. Certainly among their descendants there may well be latent potential for high attainment. Seemingly man and nature combined to destroy the abundant forests of the Chaco area, and then the ground cover disappeared. The inevitable cycle proceeded: swollen washes increased in size and speed, with the result that no longer could the Indians of the area control the waters necessary for the irrigation of crops abundant and rich enough to support and sustain their fine and high culture. Thus, the Bonitians left their splendid pueblo. Thus, Chacoan culture withered and died. Perhaps there are reflections of the once brilliant abilities of these Indians in the finest of modern "heshi" (shell or turquoise bead necklaces) made in Santo Domingo today. Perhaps their artistry survives in the splendid ceramics of María and Tony Da of San Ildefonso, and of Lonewolf of Santa Clara, in the splendid jewelry craft at Zuñi pueblo.

Bright spots in the jewelry of the prehistoric Anasazi are to be noted in additional pieces from other sites of this area. Mosaic work, of course, extended into Pueblo IV times, and for that matter, on into the historic period. A few additional examples of this technique and others will illustrate the widespread artistry in jewelry of the native Southwesterners of pre-Columbian times.

In a burial at Aztec ruin, north of the Chaco, were found two fragmentary circular mosaic pendants. One has two circling rows of inlay in the form of touching triangles, while the second follows the same general scheme but with rectangular pieces of inlay.

From Betatakin came a pair of earrings made of squares of wood set with tiny squares of turquoise. Pale blue turquoise was cut into circles, and inset with red shell to make another pair of earrings from Nitsie Canyon. At Kinishba was excavated a fine piece of turquoise overlay: over a shell base were set 367 pieces of carefully cut and polished turquoise, with a rectangular piece of red shell positioned in the center. From King's Ruin, near Prescott, came a turquoise-encrusted stone cut in the form of a frog. At Tuzigoot Ruin much use was made of various combinations of shell, turquoise, and occasionally other materials, although the workmanship was not up to the finest accomplishments of the more northerly Puebloans. Rounded mosaics, which simulated frogs in shape, were covered with turquoise except for a small piece of red stone in the very center. A rectangular pendant was decorated in the same manner; this plan was repeated in a piece from Limestone Ruin, also in the Verde Valley. From nearby Montezuma's Castle came a shell piece suggesting a bird outline with a partial covering of turquoise mosaic repeating the bird form. Although not too regular in shape, the blue stone pieces are closely fitted. Excavation at Hawikuh disclosed a fine pair of decorative hair combs and a pair of earrings, all with wooden bases and set with turquoise. From Poncho House came an elaborate mosaic piece combining a turquoise base on which appear white and red shell zigzags, a jet end, and small jet insets at the opposite wider end.

A remarkable discovery was made about 20 miles east of Flagstaff at Ridge Ruin. Because 613 objects were found with the burial of one man, it was called "The Burial of an Early American Magician."[17] There were many exquisite pieces of inlay in this collection, and whereas certain ones were unquestionably ceremonial in nature, others surely were articles of personal adornment. Still others may well have been worn for both ceremonial and simple dress occasions. Several of these will be described and are illustrated in Figure 5.19.

Two very splendid examples of refined craftsmanship from Ridge Ruin are pendants, one a bird and the other a circular form. The bird is in high conventional form, with outstretched wings and squared-off tail and head. Four rows of turquoise mosaic outline the lower and curved portions of the wings, while two rows of the same define the remaining contour of the bird. The mosaic encloses a large piece of shell of the same form. A perfect circle of about 2 inches diameter, the second piece has the following bands of turquoise mosaic from outside to inside, with rows of shell mosaic between: triple turquoise, single shell, double turquoise, single

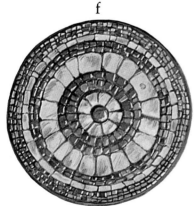

Fig. 5.19 Pieces of mosaic from "The Burial of an Early American Magician." (a) Apparently a pendant in the form of a bird. (b) A pair of turquoise and shell earrings. (c) Red argillite and turquoise nose plugs. (d) Fine turquoise and shell work on a bracelet, an unusual style of decoration for this piece (a-d courtesy of the Museum of Northern Arizona). (e) Other examples of mosaic. In particular note the crude bracelet (lower right), which is turquoise encrusted on basketry. (f) Turquoise and shell encrusted piece.

a

b

c

d

e

f

large shell, double turquoise, single shell, and a small round fragment in the very center. McGregor says of this ornament "all mosaic pieces were cut to fit accurately so that almost none of the plastic could be visible on the surface. All of the individual turquoise mosaic pieces are quite small; some are absolutely microscopic. It is a remarkably well made ornament...."[18]

A second mosaic bird from this burial was found attached to a bracelet. Its outstretched wings followed to some degree the curved line of the bracelet. Most of the mosaic is in tiny turquoise fragments, with a few larger shell pieces in right angle designs on the back and wings, and with the eyes made of circular pieces of iron pyrite inset into the rather large head of the bird.

A pair of simple but attractive earrings was made of plain circles of turquoise set with simple rounds of shell in the center. Quite unusual is the manner of combining red argillite with turquoise attached at each end, the former gently curved to make for a nose plug. That this piece was so used is indicated in its position just beneath the nose of the buried man.

Lac was used as an adhesive in all of these pieces. Seemingly in the first bird, lac was formed over a wooden base while in the second circular piece it was on shell. Both bases had disappeared. Lac was also used to attach the turquoise buttons to the ends of the argillite to form the nose plug.

A great variety of shell was found in the Winona and Ridge Ruins area, and a greater variety of objects was made of this material. Disc, figure-8, and whole shell (Olivella) beads were abundant. Oval beads and the tubular types were rare. Pendants of Conus shell are quite commonly found, while those of Pecten, Turitella, and Glycymeris are rare.

Grasshopper Ruin, in central Arizona, is a fourteenth century pueblo, dating approximately from 1275 to 1350 or 1400.[19] Here were uncovered more than 200 burials in 7 clusters. Each of 6 of the clusters had at least 6 but not more than 27 burials, while Cluster V had 120 burials. Each of the clusters with fewer burials had limited ornaments placed on or with the dead, but in Cluster V there were many rich burials.

One skeleton was ornamented with the following: on the left humerus was a bracelet made of 13 bone rings; on the right wrist were 6,850 stone beads; 7,660 stone beads decorated the left wrist, and a bone ring was on the third finger. Associated with a second burial were 2 turquoise earrings, 2 bone rings, 5 shell bracelets, and 2 bead necklaces. On a third skeleton were one bead anklet, a bracelet made of stone beads, and a turquoise earring. Both red stone beads and Olivella shell beads were on the right wrist of another skeleton, while over the left wrist were gray stone beads, and a turquoise bead and pendant. Found with another burial were a turquoise mosaic of 101 pieces, a bone "wand" or staff, 8 Glycymeris shell bracelets, 222 shell beads, 2 shell discs, and 7 earbobs. Eighteen Conus shell tinklers were found on another skeleton. A mosaic-covered shell frog was found among other items on one body. The remaining objects on the other burials of Cluster V would make up a long list of shell and other bracelets, necklaces of a variety of beads and pendants, and an assortment of earrings.

In the Canyon Creek Ruins there were not many articles of shell. The major items included a single fragment of a Glycymeris bracelet, a tinkler of Conus, a 16-inch string of disc beads, and an 8-inch strand of Nassarius shells. Several turquoise items were found here also, including two pendants and many rectangular pieces which were originally placed in a mosaic. A few turquoise and other stone beads were also found at Canyon Creek.

Pueblo III is the time given to a short string of beads from Painted Cave. They are small disc beads with interspersed black seed beads. This arrangement suggests Basketmaker times but the beads were strung on cotton thread, and were with an infant burial! A few barrel-shaped beads of stone were found here, of pink, gray, and pale green; these may be much earlier in time, perhaps Basketmaker II.

Apparently feathers were an important item of personal adornment early and late in the Anasazi. They were quite significant in Basketaker II times, perhaps because of a dearth of other materials. Many examples of sticks with or without feathers attached, found in this early period, are thought to have been tucked into the hair for decorative effect. Other types of hair ornaments were also made (Fig. 5.20). Feathers as hair ornaments persisted until Pueblo IV times; many examples are well illustrated in the Awatovi kiva murals of this later period.

In summary of personal adornment in the

a

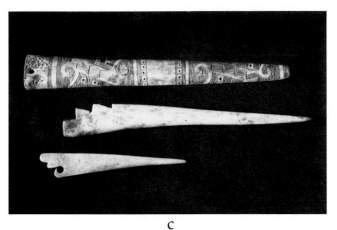

b

c

Fig. 5.20 Hair ornaments. (a) Hair ornament made of wood, Prayer Rock District (Elizabeth Morris 1959a, Fig. 111a). (b) A hair ornament made from the radius of a mule deer. The piece is highly polished; it looks like a large and slightly glorified hairpin. (c) Three bone objects which might be hair ornaments, two rather plain ones with stepped upper sections, and a third rather elaborately incised piece.

Anasazi area, it can be said that there was a widespread distribution of practically all forms, and that they were produced in all materials known to the prehistoric Southwest. In general, there seems to have been an important center for the development of this industry in the Chaco Canyon area, with pockets of higher expressions to the west. Vandalism has undoubtedly resulted in a distorted picture, but enough remains to support this general statement.

Perhaps the most common piece of Anasazi jewelry was the bead, generally made into necklaces but sometimes used as bracelets (as was one lovely string from Pueblo Bonito), or sewed onto garments (also demonstrated at Bonito). Bone beads in both disc and tubular form were widespread. Stone beads were perhaps most abundant, and color played a significant part in the choice of this material (Fig. 5.21). Shell was not as abundantly used as stone. Forms ran the gamut from very thin discs

through round and cylindrical ones into figure-8 styles.

Pendants were found abundantly at many Anasazi sites (Figs. 5.22 and 5.23). Most of the materials used in bead making, plus a few additional ones, were used in the production of pendants (Figs. 5.21, 5.22a–g, and 5.23), and their forms were equally varied. Geometric shapes are numerous and of varied workmanship, and squares, rectangles, and keystones may be sharp edged or rounded; there are also four-pointed "stars"; and cogwheels seem to have been fairly popular. One of the most remarkable finds of

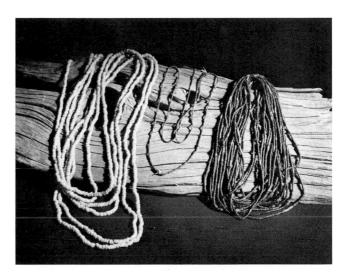

Fig. 5.21 A variety of bead necklaces: In *upper photo* are, *from left*: a long string of shell beads, a red stone and turquoise necklace, and a heavy multiple strand of dark gray (or black), red, and white stone beads. *Lower photo, from left*: an interesting necklace with an Olivella shell pendant set with turquoise, a turquoise disc bead necklace with five turquoise pendants, and a shell disc bead necklace.

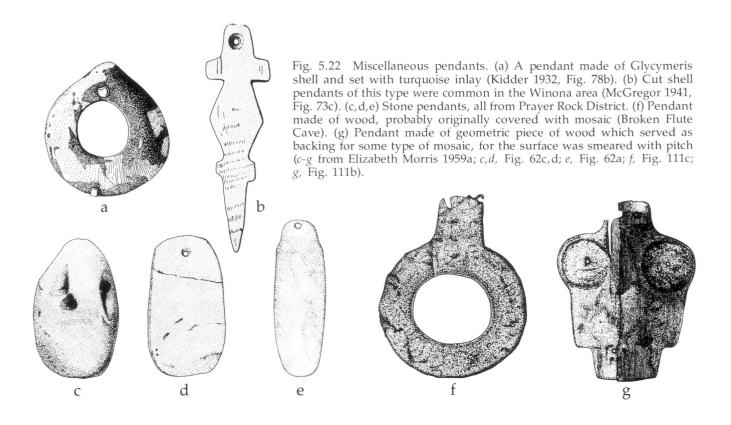

Fig. 5.22 Miscellaneous pendants. (a) A pendant made of Glycymeris shell and set with turquoise inlay (Kidder 1932, Fig. 78b). (b) Cut shell pendants of this type were common in the Winona area (McGregor 1941, Fig. 73c). (c,d,e) Stone pendants, all from Prayer Rock District. (f) Pendant made of wood, probably originally covered with mosaic (Broken Flute Cave). (g) Pendant made of geometric piece of wood which served as backing for some type of mosaic, for the surface was smeared with pitch (c-g from Elizabeth Morris 1959a; c,d, Fig. 62c,d; e, Fig. 62a; f, Fig. 111c; g, Fig. 111b).

Fig. 5.23 Photograph of a variety of pendants of stone, bone, and shell, running the gamut from rectangular and keystone shapes to highly conventionalized or more realistic birds and other creatures.

pendants was that at Kinishba: a cache of 1,141 gypsum pieces largely in keystone shapes. According to Cummings, they measure from ½ inch to 2½ inches in length, and in width from ¼ inch to 2 inches, and their average thickness is 1/16 inch.[20] A fragment of cloth was near the cache; the pendants may have been sewed onto a garment. Or they may have been intended for necklaces. Birds were in flat or full round carving; they were either so conventionalized as to be barely recognizable as such or so realistic they might almost be identified. Generally frogs were very simply carved but with suggested features; some, however are so well done as to present each individual toe. There are also lizards; in some areas, such as Flagstaff, they are fairly common. Occasional human or human-like figures appear in pendants; perhaps the bone pendant from the Village of the Great Kivas was an attempt at a smiling human face. Or is it a full figure? The features are made to stand out more distinctly as a dark substance was used to fill the incised lines.[21]

Bracelets were fairly common in the Anasazi, particularly in some areas such as the Chaco. The majority are of shell, though some were made of bone or occasional other materials. Single shell bracelets generally were carved of Glycymeris in plain style, although there were some decorated pieces, such as an incised example from Chevlon Ruins, or some with the umbo carved into a frog. Conus shells were sometimes used for bracelets as well as necklaces.

Buttons were probably sewed or tied onto garments. Jet seems to have been popular for this piece, but other materials were also used. Where two holes were drilled all the way through or a concealed perforation was made on the back, it may be suggested that these were buttons—this would add shell and a variety of stones used for their production, for such holes are found in round pieces of these materials. Nose plugs, though rare, were also made of stone, and sometimes, as at Ridge Ruin, were decorative.

Earrings were many and varied among the Anasazi, both in styles and in use of material in their manufacture. Then as now it can be suspected that a short string of beads frequently may have served the native in this capacity. Pendantlike pieces were popular (in a variety of materials and shapes), with the keystone shaped or tear-drop types of turquoise perhaps the most common of all. Materials were combined for this

Fig. 5.24 Earrings. (a) Turquoise mosaic on a piece of slate. This is probably one of a pair of earrings, from Pecos (Kidder 1932, Fig. 78a). Other earring types were varied. (b) In this photograph are two pairs, one of elongate form, and made of abalone, and a second pair suggestive of a long, thin, almost lizard form, these also made of shell.

a

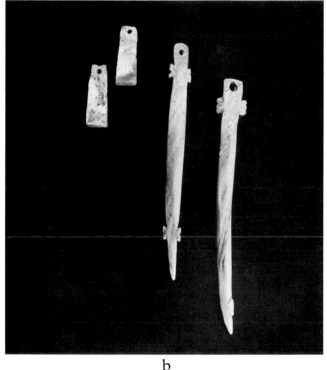

b

ornament as for others, with mosaics popular, or just a single piece of shell set into a turquoise earring. Mosaic was also used for earrings; one such piece was found at Pecos (Fig. 5.24).

MOGOLLON

Inasmuch as many combinations of all the major forms, materials, and styles of decoration have been given for the Anasazi, less emphasis will be placed on these subjects for the Mogollon and Hohokam. Rather, specific examples will be cited to illustrate either similarities or differences within these two areas.

Jewelry and other personal adornment were present in the Mogollon in early years, with a tendency toward a considerable increase in later times. A chart in Wheat shows some type of jewelry present in almost every period and area of distribution.[22] Quite abundant or present in most periods or areas were shell and stone pendants and thin shell bracelets. Slightly less significant were Olivella beads, shell disc beads and, less abundant, stone disc beads. Present but not too plentiful were bone disc beads, figure-8 beads, zoomorphic pendants, broad shell bracelets, shell and bone rings, and bone discs. The majority of the pendants were of simple geometric shapes such as circles, ovals, cones, and teardrops, with most of them on the irregular side. Compared to the other two areas, there is not a great deal of carving, and it is far simpler. Too, although mosaic is present, it is less abundant and not as elaborate as in the other contemporary Southwestern cultures.

All of the objects mentioned were present in Mogollon I times except figure-8 beads, broad shell bracelets, and shell and bone rings. During this earliest phase the pieces were also widely scattered from the southern San Simon to the northern Pine Lawn and Black River areas. Period 2 saw a more restricted geographic distribution of slightly more limited pieces, but Period 3 saw an increase in quantity of some items as did Period 4, particularly shell disc beads and thin shell bracelets. Figure-8 beads were found in the Mimbres, introduced in Period 4 times. Shell and bone rings were also exclusive to this last period; it is possible that these, along with the figure-8 bead, may have come from the Hohokam, for there these ornaments were early in time. However, all are relatively simple in form and may well have developed locally. On the other hand more elaborately carved shell pendants in the Hohokam tradition could well have come to the Mogollon from these neighbors to the west.

Quite generally in the Mogollon, turquoise was not commonly used. In earlier years there were, basically, flat disc beads and pear shaped and oval pendants of this material. Later, in the Mimbres Phase the same continued to be made, with some irregularly shaped pendants and a little mosaic added.

There seems to have been little or no shell work in earliest years, but by the San Francisco Phase there were some Olivella and Vermetus beads and a few Glycymeris bracelets. By the Three Circle Phase shell was abundant, and the bi-lobed bead was characteristic. After this period there was an increase in shell work per-haps because of greater contact with other cultures and perhaps, too, because of accelerated trade. Certainly there were more shell species from the Gulf of California and from the West Coast, although in general the Mogollones used more Gulf of Mexico shell than the other two areas. There were more varieties of shell and more diversified work in this material during the Mimbres Period. Broad bracelets and carved life forms were much in evidence.

Specifically, the following examples of jewelry will indicate Mogollon levels of accomplishment in this craft. From the site of Mogollon, on the San Francisco River near the Arizona-New Mexico border, came the following shell artifacts.[23] Beads include those of Olivella, made of the whole shell, with the spire removed for stringing, plus saucer-shaped discoidal beads. Bracelets are thin to very thin, fragile, and undecorated. Pendants include a large rectangular one, with a central hole for suspension, and a broken irregular and large piece of shell. Comparable shell materials were also found in the Harris Village on the Mimbres River in western New Mexico.[24] The main additions were the bi-lobed, or figure-8, bead, with one lobe perforated, and some beads made of hackberries. There seems to have been an increase in shell bracelets, but they remain plain: one burial had 21 on its body, 12 on one arm.

Cosgrove found a great many items of interest in the Upper Gila and Hueco regions. First among these was an unusual type of object from the Upper Gila, namely, pieces of wood with bark removed, from 1¾ to 2⅜ inches long, with heads, and the end opposite the head worked to a sharp point.[25] These have been labeled pins, perhaps used to fasten garments. Possibly other pieces of like nature, such as the longer but slender and pointed bone pin from a small ruin near Point of Pines, may have been used in like manner.[26] This latter piece was decorated with incised triangles on one face. A second item from the Upper Gila and Hueco areas is more widespread, this a hair ornament. This piece is represented by 66 specimens, 50 of them single-pronged, and the remainder with 2, 3, or 4 prongs. In length, the scraped and sometimes polished pieces ranged from 4¾ to 12 inches. As in Basketmaker hair ornaments of comparable nature these twigs were wrapped with cordage, apparently to fasten feathers on the tops, and, in the case of the use of multiple sticks, to hold them together.

A variety of materials was used in beads from this area, including, among others, seeds, Olivella and other shell, stone (some turquoise), and bone. Bone beads were tubular, shell and stone beads were discoidal, and a few were of whole Olivella shells. Seemingly there was much variation in stringing beads, from plain shell discs or seeds of a single type forming necklaces to alternations of black and white stone beads. Some beads, perhaps of Hueco Basketmakers, are exceptionally large and of white stone. Pendants from these two areas are made from circular rings of shell, pieces of shell bracelets, fluted pieces of shell (which may have been a bird shape originally), an oval piece of pink shell (3 inches long), abalone shell, and a few of turquoise. Very few bracelets were found; the one complete piece is like others of this area in general. In the Mimbres proper, Bradfield and the Cosgroves found fragments of bracelets incised with geometric designs, some with a bit of carving on the umbo.[27]

Haury reported some shell work at Mogollon Village dated as of the San Francisco Phase.[28] This includes Olivella shells which had the spires broken off so as to serve as beads. Vermetus (tubular marine worm casings) was broken into segments to serve as slightly curved beads. Circular beads were produced from the spire of the Conus, showing the markings of this part of the shell. Saucer-shaped beads were also made from shell. Although no complete ones were found, parts of thin bracelets were recovered, supporting the early date of this village. Cylinderlike tubes of both bird and animal bones are probably beads.

In Tularosa and Cordova Caves, near the Arizona-New Mexico border, Martin found cut, or sawed, Glycymeris bracelets and beads.[29] The latter were of small whole shells (Conus) with the spire removed. Pendants include a bone piece with notches on one side, the other smooth; keystone-shaped shell pieces; and another of two deer incisors.

In the northern part of the Mogollon extension, Bluff Ruin reveals a dearth of ornaments. There are almost no stone pieces, there is no turquoise whatsoever, and no shell. Later, and in the same area, there is little more at Bear Ruin, with a limited appearance of shell in the form of disc and whole shell beads and a few Glycymeris bracelets.

Of the Jornado Branch of the Mogollon, located both north and south of El Paso and east and west of the Rio Grande, and of several sites of this culture, the following can be said in general.[30] Bone rings and pendants, both usually plain, are found. Shell is fairly abundant with bracelets, beads, and pendants typical; both disc and whole Olivella shell beads are found. Shell pendants are interesting in that in addition to the usual cone tinklers and simple geometrics, there are more or less conventional fish forms. Turquoise pendants and earbobs are present, usually in simple keystone forms.

Point of Pines in east central Arizona, combines so many features of the three major cultural areas of the Southwest that it is impossible to restrict it to one or the other of these. Therefore some of the jewelry of this area will be mentioned at this point of discussion of the Mogollon.

Some of the burials at Point of Pines proper reveal typical Southwest customs regarding grave furnishings.[31] Pottery, primarily utility wares, was commonly placed in burials; frequently with infants and children were found miniature vessels. It is fortunate for the story of jewelry that personal adornment was not uncommonly an accompaniment of the burial of older people. Very few tools or "useful objects" were found in these burials.

In general, burial furnishings at Point of Pines included beads of stone (a few of turquoise), shell, and clay; rings and pendants, some of the latter of turquoise; and hair ornaments. One copper bell was recovered.

Some cremations here were accompanied by artifacts, but many were not. Of 144 pot cremations, only 38 had objects buried with them. Among other items were bone hair ornaments, rings, and shell beads. As the jewelry was charred it was probably worn at the time of cremation; miniature vessels were common with these cremations.

Two burials from this site will reflect the individual type of grave. One, an adult male, was accompanied by ten Glycymeris shell bracelets on the left arm, and a bracelet of white and pink shell and turquoise on the right wrist. A second adult male burial had in it a necklace of clay and turquoise beads with a carved shell pendant, plus one Glycymeris bracelet with incised design on the left wrist.

In summary of the Mogollon it is evident that there is not the wide variety nor the abundance of production encountered in the Anasazi. Most of the materials, techniques, and products of other areas were found here, but generally all are more limited. Turquoise was scarce, as were objects of other colorful stones. There is very little carving and mosaic. Comparatively, shell received little attention from these Indians.

HOHOKAM

Despite the fact that there is a rich story to be told relative to the Hohokam, it is a most unfortunate circumstance in connection with their jewelry that they cremated their dead for thereby much was lost. As among the Anasazi, many ornaments went to the grave, worn by or placed close to the deceased, and thus were consumed or partially burned by the crematory fire. Added to this was the custom of gathering up what one could and placing it in a small jar or a relatively small hole or trench in the ground for the actual burial. All of this adds up to partial or total destruction of certain items, and loss of many others. What has been excavated of part of what was left will be discussed in the following paragraphs.

In the broad view turquoise and shell were found in the Hohokam from the Vahki Phase on through the entire prehistoric period. It reached a peak in Sedentary times in practically all expressions and certainly in variety of forms and perfection of shell workmanship. Some peak work was attained in shell carving and turquoise mosaic during the Colonial Period and certainly fine bracelets were made into the late Pioneer Period. Both shell carving and turquoise mosaic also persisted into the Classic.

More specifically disc beads and mosaic on shell appeared in the Pioneer. So too were fragile bracelets and pendants of shell made at this early time. The Colonial saw the addition, among other things, of discoidal beads and more varied pendants, including effigy birds of turquoise mosaic on wood, a greater variety of shell rings, pendants, beads (including bi-lobed and cylindrical), new shapes for mosaics, and heavier bracelets. Great heights in shell carving were reached during the Colonial Period. Then further peaks were attained in the Sedentary in such expressions as carving, painting, and etching of shell, while much of the earlier work in turquoise continued along with important incised turquoise pieces.

In the Classic, mosaics were often on shell and frequently took the form of birds, turtles, or frogs; they employed hundreds of pieces of turquoise combined with one or a few pieces of shell, often pink, in this attractive work. Too, Haury believes that inlay very likely belongs to this last period in the Hohokam area, the Classic, for, he says, "The exceptionally full collection of shell artifacts from Snaketown, dating no later than the Sedentary Period, contains no examples of inlay.[32]

Shell, of course, was of first importance in the Hohokam area, for these Indians lived along the routes of import and trade, the Gila and Salt rivers. It is thought by some archaeologists that these people were responsible for the shell trade into the north and east, and that therefore they were also responsible for the spread of distinct styles of working this material. It may be, too, that traffic in shell stimulated other trade as well, say, for example, design styles of the Hohokams in ceramics.

It may not sound like too much was lost in the crematory when such as the following is mentioned: a string of disc-type beads that measured nearly 38 feet in length and a second strand in wedge-shapes with a length of over 11 feet; both strings were buried in the same cremation. But this is the exception and not the rule; nonetheless, many beads have been found; stone beads were more varied but less abundant than those of shell. The former included flat disc, cylindrical, cuboid, bi-convex, hemispherical, figure-8, and wedge-shaped beads, while shell types were largely disc, cylindrical, and figure-8 in shape. Stone beads were more colorful as they were made of turquoise, argillite, and steatite. Sometimes whole shells were used; their form and natural color added a bit of variety to this category of beads.

Some of the whole shells used, either with the tip cut away or a hole drilled at some point for stringing, include Oliva, Olivella, Vermetus, Turbo, Conus, Columbella, and Nassa. All of these were relatively small in size. It is likely that some colored shell was used also in cut beads. Disc beads of both stone and shell were the most common through the entire Hohokam sequence.

Stone pendants seem to be larger and heavier than those of shell; the latter are frequently small and delicate (Fig. 5.25). Simple oval or round stone pendants occur late at Snaketown; so too do the bird, lizard, and frog forms. Rather flat birds with outspread wings and profile heads seem to belong exclusively to the Santa Cruz Phase. In general the same late time is to be assigned to the simple geometric (oval, keystone, square, circular) shell pendants. On the

Examples of Ornaments

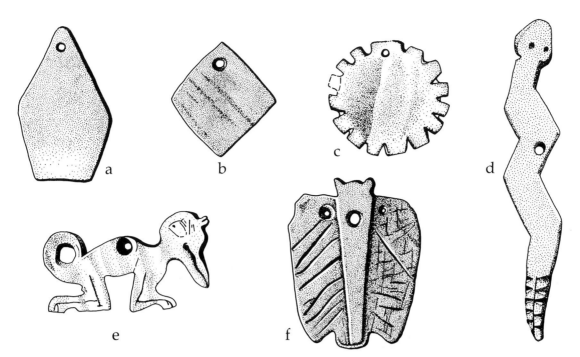

Fig. 5.25 Hohokam geometric and life form pendants of stone and shell (all from Haury 1945a, figure numbers only given). (a,b,c) Three geometric pendants cut out of shell, from Los Muertos (92 f,j,k). (d) Carved shell rattlesnake, from Los Hornos (119d). (e) Carved shell pendant from Los Guanacos (114b). (f) Small pendant resembling a bat (?) carved of stone (123j).

other hand, a conventional flying bird style runs from Sweetwater to Sacaton times, skipping the Gila Butte Phase. Some mammal forms also appear in the Sweetwater Phase but not again until the Santa Cruz Phase. Shell bird forms are more individualized, for ducks and a cranelike creature can be suggested; they too are late, appearing in Santa Cruz and Sacaton times. Shell lizards are more generalized than some in stone; frogs have fair detail in both materials; and snakes were an addition to the shell category. Rattlesnakes, fully equipped with rattles, were favored. All in all, the life form in pendants was elaborated more than were geometric themes.

Human form pendants appear late (Sacaton) and bear some resemblance to both Mogollon and Pueblo III styles. It is possible that more realistic bird forms evolved out of more conventional expressions of the same. At Los Muertos, cogwheel, scalloped-edged ovals, and elongate forms would be added to the Snaketown list. In life forms, too, there were other types at this

more northerly Hohokam village, such as a rabbit, a foxlike creature, and an elongate-snouted animal with rather vicious teeth. Incising or carving on many of the life pendants brings out their respective identifications. Inlay was also known; from Los Muertos comes a beautiful Conus tinkler pendant inset with turquoise and red shell and painted in those ever-popular geometric themes, frets and triangles. "Key patterns are used to separate the paired shell and turquoise triangles. The keys of the upper tier are painted black, the lower ones red. In addition, the mucilaginous substance with which the inlay is held in place adds a black border to the red and blue material";[33] probably this pendant was of the Classic Period (Fig. 5.26).

Although objects made of etched shell may not have been jewelry in the proper sense of the word certainly some of these pieces must have been worn as pendants or carried, perhaps on special occasions only. Generally a whole Cardium shell was used, with a design produced on

| ■ black | ☐ white or natural | ▨ red | ▨ turquoise | ▤ red shell |

Fig. 5.26 Decorated Conus shell pendant; the geometric design is carved, inlaid with red shell and turquoise, and painted (Haury 1945a, Fig. 98e).

the interior or exterior. In some instances this may have been all that was done by way of decoration, but in others, paints were then added to certain parts of the design. Horned toads were done on the exteriors of the shell; geometric designs are common on the interior. An example of the former, from Snaketown, has the tip of the rather large head of the animal fitted into the umbo, with tail and hind legs at the broad end of the shell. From the north end of the Tucson Mountains (west side of Tucson) came a nest of etched shells, found in a field. One of these will exemplify the group: it has a beautifully etched geometric allover design on the interior which involves sharp-edged bands that terminate in smooth-edged interlocked frets Opposed units of design were then painted, one side pink, one side pale turquoise-blue.

Bracelets were quite common in the Hohokam area. They first appear in the Vahki Phase and are present in every level at Snaketown. One which appears in this sequence, except for the Santa Cruz Phase, is a narrow, thin bracelet, with the umbo small and unperforated. Most abundant in quantity is a medium sized bracelet, which shows up first in Sweetwater times and occurs in all but the Gila Butte Phase. Its umbo is larger, more varied in shape, and perforated. The third style is thick, wide, and heavy, with an unaltered umbo.

The sequence of earlier thin styles, intermediate bracelets in middle times, and heavy bracelets late in time, follows the general scheme of the other two major cultural areas, except that the very fragile style is limited to the Hohokam.

Plain bracelets were more abundant than decorated ones; in fact, they represent "the most abundant shell ornaments produced at Snaketown."[34] As elsewhere, Glycymeris is the shell

from which these bracelets were made. Although carving appears on only about ten percent of all bracelets, it is extremely important as an artistic expression. This decoration occurred first in late Pioneer times and was most significant in the Sedentary Period. It includes incising, flat or bas relief, and full round or almost full round. Subject matter for this decoration includes geometric design such as dots, chevrons, rectangles, lines straight and wavy, zigzags, triangles, frets, and keys (Fig. 5.27a). Life themes include frogs, snakes, and birds (Fig. 5.27b). Sometimes a bird was represented with a snake in its mouth, or two birds back to back, each with a snake in its mouth. This theme is found on bracelets from the Grewe site. Woodward also reported human figures and horned toads carved on bracelets from the same site.[35] A frog carved on the umbo of the shell was a very common bracelet decoration in the Hohokam area as a whole.

A beautiful example of the bird-snake motif was excavated at Snaketown. The undulating body of the reptile forms the encircling part of the bracelet; the umbo was then carved into the head of a long-beaked bird with the snake's pointed head in its mouth. A bit of artistic license was taken with the rattles: they are to the right of the bird's upright head, with deep crenulations along the lower side and a heavy unrealistic section above.

In addition to carving, some bracelets were painted and/or inlaid (Fig. 5.27c). Sometimes the incised lines were filled with a black pigment or stained red, as in the instance of the above Conus pendant. Or turquoise and shell were set into the bracelet band. (Here too, as in the Conus pendant, the time for this type of workmanship would be the Classic Period.) Simple rounds or simply patterned themes such as tri-

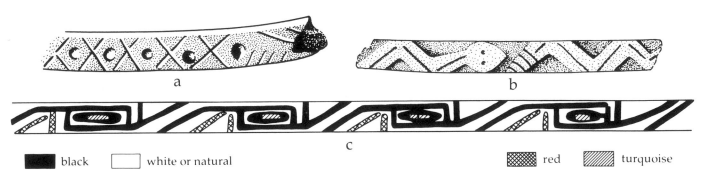

a

b

c

| black | white or natural | | red | turquoise |

Fig. 5.27 Decorated shell bracelets (all Haury 1945a). (a) Incised and drilled fragment of a shell bracelet from Los Guanacos (114d). (b) Fragment of a shell bracelet decorated with the rattlesnake motif (119e). (c) In this bracelet from Los Muertos incised lines were filled with black or red paint and gouged areas were set with turquoise (98c).

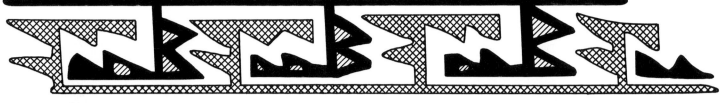

| ■ black | ☐ white or natural | ▨ red |

▨ turquoise

Fig. 5.28 Fragment of carved, inlaid, and painted shell ring decorated in black and red paint, and with turquoise insets (Haury 1945a, Fig. 98d and Frontispiece c).

angles would form the insets. The turquoise alone (or with red shell) was often outlined by the black adhesive which held the decorative pieces in place. Rings were also worked in this same style (Fig. 5.28).

In one bracelet from Los Muertos there is a single hole in the umbo where such a setting was placed. Another bracelet from the same site had three small inset turquoises, one directly opposite the umbo and one each to the right and left of the central piece. A third example shows a combination of inlay with engraving and painting on a narrow bracelet; the decorative field is but 3/16 of an inch. "The pattern consists of small incised rectangles connected with diagonals. In the centers of the rectangles small troughs were gouged out for the inlaying of small bits of turquoise. These vary in number in each space from one to three. The incised lines were filled with black pigment excepting two short lines forming an angle to the right of each turquoise-filled area which are stained red. Only the umbonal part of the bracelet is without this decoration."[36]

Rings were not uncommon, although they were far less common than bracelets. First appearing in the Santa Cruz Phase, they were narrow to medium to the end of the true Hohokam, then in the Classic they became broad bands. Most of them were plain, some retaining the umbo of the small Glycymeris shell of which they were made, while others were carved or painted and inlaid. Natural markings of the shell were left on one example. Conus was sometimes used; one broad ring was elaborately carved, painted, and set with turquoise. The pattern on this example is contained within banding lines, each grooved; the line on one side is filled with black paint, while the other bordering line is filled with red. L-shaped, triangle-bordered frets take off alternately from one then the other

framing line, then simply interlock. In each interlocking motif, one L-shaped part is set with turquoise while the opposite is carved and painted red. Both color and design are pleasing. Woodward reported two finger rings of fine workmanship from the Grewe site.[37] They were identical in decorative motifs: the main part of each was of entwined rattlesnake bodies, while the umbo was carved with two bird figures, back to back, swallowing the snake's heads and holding the snake's tails with their claws.

The story of mosaic among the Hohokams is very incomplete. Certainly a great many pieces of material used in this manner for both geometric and life forms were preserved, but a great many more, probably, were destroyed in the crematories. It is likely that mosaic goes back to Pioneer times; it is quite abundant by the Sacaton. Mosaic is earlier in this southern region than in the Anasazi; in the latter area it belongs to Basketmaker III and later times. Hohokam mosaic is more elaborate than that of the other two areas; further, it features animal life more frequently, particularly birds and reptiles.

Before leaving the Hohokam area, mention should be made of a cache of objects belonging to the Classic Period, from the Casa Grande Ruins east of Snaketown. Perhaps it was a medicine man's or ceremonialist's possessions, perhaps it was some individual's treasure trove. At any rate, it consists of a long string of heavy shell beads and three pieces of mosaic, a turtle, and two birds. The turtle is rather generalized in form but there is excellent craftsmanship in the well-fitted pieces of turquoise on shell over the entire back of the creature, plus a central piece of shell. One bird is large, the other much smaller. Both are conventional in form with outstretched wings; both have a large pink shell center with a narrow turquoise mosaic border. In the larger piece the mosaic is so well done that there are pointed tail feathers in the bottom row of this part of the bird. Pieces of the mosaic are well cut squares or rectangles, closely fitted together.

On the eastern edge of the Hohokam region is a site, Roosevelt: 9:6, of Colonial times, located on Roosevelt Lake. Ornaments were scarce at this site in contrast to Snaketown. Very few bracelets were found; they were in fragmentary form and undecorated. The most decorative and imaginative piece from this site is a shell pendant in the form of a pelican. Two pieces only of turquoise were recovered, one carved in the form of a bird's head. One unfinished steatite bead was found—the only bead located at this site.

Thus the heart of the River Hohokam area, represented by Snaketown, Los Muertos, and other nearby sites, produced an abundance of objects of personal adornment. And, in spite of cremating the dead and burning many pieces of jewelry, enough remains to indicate a high level development. Quite the contrary is true of the Desert Hohokam to the south, for very little is found in the latter area.

No shell disc beads are reported at Ventana Cave nor at Jackrabbit Ruin;[38] only three such beads were located at Valshni Village.[39] Relatively late in time are the whole shell beads at Ventana; but five of them were found. Seven whole shell pendants were recovered at this site. Ground and cut shell are also very limited, with three pendants of irregular form in the first technique, and only two of the latter, which seem to have been discoidal earrings with a large central opening. No complete bracelets were found at this site; of 30 fragments only 8 represent finished pieces. No bracelets were carved.

Stone jewelry items are next to absent, with one lone schist pendant and one stone bead from Ventana. Wooden nose plugs are found here; they are late prehistoric, and they are unique in this material—there may have been some nose plugs of stone. It is possible that these people made a few bone beads and pendants.

Thus it would seem that the Desert Hohokam had little time for the luxuries of life. But what little shell work they had was of the Hohokam tradition, certainly on a very simple level. The beautiful carving and etching of Hohokam shell mosaic work, and other high-level objects of personal adornment, are reflections of the advanced order of their society, which had suffi-

cient leisure to perpetuate such works of art. Perhaps full if not bulging larders which resulted from irrigation agriculture, would account for this, while the Desert Hohokam but eked out an existence in their dry and riverless land.

Personal adornment was of considerable interest to the prehistoric Southwesterners. In Basketmaker times, in the Anasazi area, more jewelry was worn than clothing. It can be guessed that the same was true in both the Hohokam and Mogollon areas, although the latter may have had little of either clothing or jewelry. And, of course, there were many local differences within each of these areas; seemingly at no time did the Desert Hohokams have much of anything, certainly nothing comparable to the River Hohokam, in the way of personal adornment.

One is better able to visualize the ways in which personal adornment was utilized in the Anasazi because of the kiva murals there, plus pictographs and petroglyphs that reveal something of the same. At Awatovi the most common jewelry worn by humans represented in the murals were necklaces—perhaps hands were too busy with bows and arrows, quivers, and staffs to show bracelets—besides, it was difficult enough to represent the hand alone. There are some upper arm bands, but it is difficult to determine the nature of the material of which they were made. Surely they do not look like shell armlets.

Pictured in these murals are 1 to 8 strands of beads wrapped tightly about the necks of ritual performers. In one instance there are 2 additional strands which hang rather loosely below the others. One example shows an elaborate affair at the bottom of 5 tight strands, either more beads and/or pendants. Another wears a double crescent-shaped object without benefit of any beads, or, at least, no beads show in the drawing.[40] Still another wears a round pendant, which has a white upper half and a red lower half. A companion figure to the last one wears large and long triangular-shaped, black ear pendants.[41] A figure-8 arrangement of the beads below the neck strands is most common; in one example the lower part of the 8 is much larger than the upper portion. Usually this feature rests on the chest, but on humans represented in profile, the figure-8 neckla e is placed on the shoulder! Beads are represented in different colors, white and red, gray with red dots, and white alone. Perhaps these were shell, red stone, and either clay or gray stone.

In parts of the Anasazi the custom of burying personal effects with the dead reflects how and where objects were worn. Earrings are found at both ears of old and young. Necklaces are sometimes preserved about necks and on chests, on strings or in the earth in the order of their original arrangement—a few red and many black beads alternating, or an equal number of black and white beads, or an occasional pendant or two at the bottom of a string. Smaller bracelets are found at wrists, larger ones on upper arms and ankles. Conus shells are found about necks, at wrists, or at the waist or above the knees—the latter two positions as garment decoration, corroborated by kiva mural painting. Rings appear on fingers.

It may be reiterated that the native Southwesterners exploited their environment for materials with which to make jewelry. Little went unrecognized locally, and frequently raw materials were imported such as shell or turquoise, or the finished products such as the thin Hohokam bracelet. Shell was featured for brace-

lets, although occasional stone or other materials might be so used. For beads a great variety of materials was used—seeds, shells whole or worked, many kinds of stone, clay, cane sections, sinew or cordage, sometimes with a pendant or two. Rings were made of bone, shell, and stone. Variety of stone was perhaps greatest for the working of pendants—turquoise, argillite, gypsum, shale, whatever was colorful, whatever appealed to the individual.

Form and decoration in all jewelry varied— bracelets are narrow, medium, wide; they are plain, carved, incised, inset, painted. Great variety in both geometric and life forms characterize pendants, and they are flat and plain, or incised, in relief or full round, have inset eyes alone or are covered with mosaic. Even beads are large or small discs, thicker or thinner, saucer-shaped or barrel-shaped, tubular (short or long), spheroid, or even irregular.

To their lasting credit, and to the delight of the archaeologist, these native tribes combined great skill and imagination in the creation of objects with which to embellish their persons. Objects of personal adornment present some of the finest artistry created by the prehistoric Southwesterners.

Chapter 6

Other Domestic and Ritual Items

THIS LAST CHAPTER on the crafts presents several more items of artistic expression of the prehistoric Southwesterners. Nonetheless, other expressions will be ignored entirely or only mentioned briefly, for there are many utility crafts that simply cannot be dealt with in depth in this book. Those expressions that are more reflective of the artistry of the natives will be given some attention, limited though it may be in some instances.

Figurines and effigies, palettes, musical instruments, stone bowls, and utility crafts will be examined in the following pages. It is difficult to know where to draw the line between certain effigies and figurines; both are small, both can be and usually are carved or molded; the same subject matter and materials may be used in both. Frequently, the term effigy implies a little more in the way of the ceremonial, while the figurine is simply a carved figure. However, in the Southwest, certainly there is religious significance relative to the latter as well as the former, and both may be made for other purposes; thus, because no definitive line is drawn between the two, they will be treated together.

Palettes run the gamut from undecorated and rather crude pieces of stone to elaborately ornamented forms; and they present another area of high artistic expression. Musical instruments reflect less in the way of artistic attainment, but many of these established definite forms and some were decorated. Like palettes, stone bowls present a wide variation from plain, ill-formed pieces to highly decorated examples. Too, there are some regional variations in each of these, just as there are instances of trade influence and other examples of one culture influencing another artistically.

Everyday Objects

As indicated in the introductory chapter, the strictly utilitarian stone crafts are significant not alone for their products—the major household, hunting, agricultural, and other necessity items developed by these Indians—but also because these native men and women kept their fingers busy and derived experience through such production. Many of the tools, weapons, implements, and other such pieces were beautifully

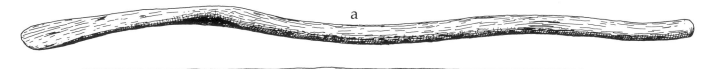

Fig. 6.1 Agricultural tools—planting sticks. (a) Planting stick from Cave 9, northeastern Arizona. It is 42½" in length (Guernsey and Kidder 1921, pl. 37f). (b) Planting stick from White Dog Cave; it is 32" in length and made from greasewood. This shows a fine, polished point (ibid., pl. 37d).

formed, many were expressive of certain basic artistic principles such as symmetry, rhythm, balance. Many of them gave the makers control and experience in working varied materials. But in the same breath it may be said that as the production of the absolute essentials of life gave little opportunity for artistic expression beyond these basic principles, this production offered

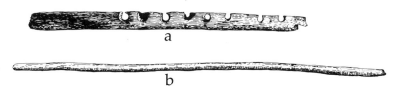

Fig. 6.3 Fire-making apparatus from the Upper Gila. The large piece with holes in it (a) is called the hearth; the long slender stick (b) is twirled between the hands on the hearth, thus generating sparks (Cosgrove 1947, Fig. 140 a,i).

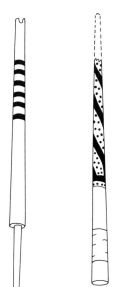

Fig. 6.2 Arrow foreshafts with painted decoration, Steamboat Cave, in a branch canyon of the Upper Gila (Cosgrove 1947, Fig. 20-7 and 9).

little or no opportunity for self-expression or originality. There is not much one can add in the way of decoration to a heavy metate, a corn grinding device, a chipped and flaked flint point, or a ground and polished axe, beyond their form and craftsmanship. Thus, the greater artistry among these early Southwesterners was expressed in the crafts discussed in the foregoing pages and the remaining ones of this chapter.

However, because of their service to native peoples and the inherent qualities expressed in them, a few words will be said about axes, points, metates, and other such utility items of the prehistoric Southwest. An effort will be made to avoid repetition of the tools and implements used in the production of the previously described crafts.

In wood, these early Indians made digging and planting sticks, sometimes with curved handles but not decorated (Fig. 6.1). Bows and arrow shafts were usually plain, although some were ornamented with incised lines or with encircling bands painted in red and black (Fig. 6.2); this is particularly true of smaller arrow shafts, which probably had religious significance. Plain indeed were firemaking equipment (Fig.

6.3), axe handles, hooked sticks, and paddles (some of the latter certainly used in pottery making), and clubs. There are plain knob-ended sticks, plain bowls, and spatulalike pieces all made from wood. In working this material every technique, from simply cutting and putting into service to carefully polishing to a high sheen, was practiced in the prehistoric Southwest. Both hard and soft woods were used.

Bone, horn, and antler served for a great variety of objects. Many of the same processes were used in the production of objects in these materials as in wood working, using flint knives for cutting, perhaps a stone hammer for breaking, and sandstone for polishing. Quite a variety of creatures provided the raw materials—birds, deer, rabbits, elk, bobcats, mountain sheep, and others. The proper material from the appropriate part of the body was chosen for the desired shape and size of the object to be made, then the essential work was applied. Foremost among these tools were awls (Fig. 6.4. Also see Fig. 2.2); there were many sizes and shapes of them, long

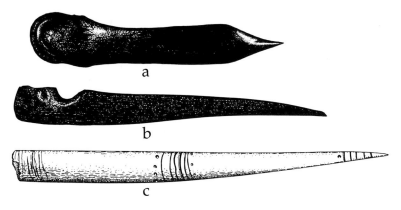

Fig. 6.4 Several types of awls. (a) Shouldered type bone awl, with a short point. Broken Flute Cave (Elizabeth Morris 1959a, Fig. 63a). (b) Slender, tapered bone awl, Prayer Rock District (ibid., Fig. 63 1); (c) Made from a bird bone, this awl was decorated with lines and dots cut in two areas (Kidder 1932, Fig. 185).

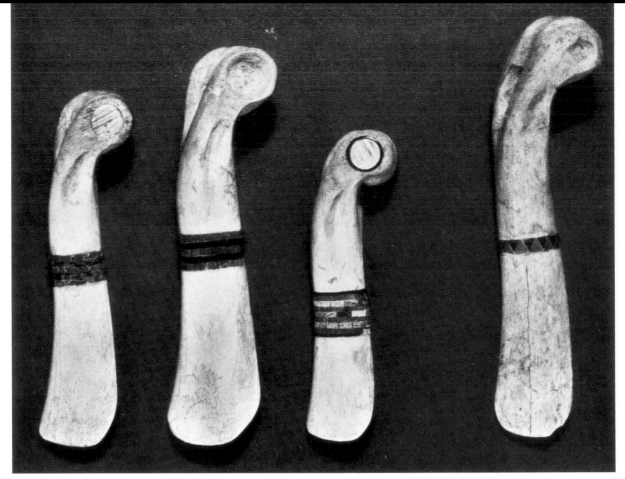

Fig. 6.5   Turquoise, jet, and shell inlay on deer humeri, Pueblo Bonito (Judd 1954, pl. 36. Photograph courtesy of Smithsonian Institution).

and short, stubby and thin. The majority of awls were undecorated, but some few were ornamented at the end of the piece opposite the point, with wrapping (some first covered with pitch) or carving of this larger end. Scrapers, fleshing tools, and flakers were made of these materials; bone tubes were quite common over much of the Southwest. Awl handles were made of horn, and some hammers, wrenches and chisels were often of bone. Cups, ladles, and spoons were of bone or antler. Wedges were probably made of antler or horn.

Most of the tools of bone, antler, and horn were not symmetrical, although some awls were more or less so. Decoration is conspicuous by its scarcity, yet it is not absent. Occasionally the large end was carved to represent a head, but this was not common practice. Also rare is the example of decorated bone scrapers from Pueblo Bonito.[1] Made of deer humeri, they are ornamented about midway with turquoise and jet inlay, plus shell in two examples (Fig. 6.5). One example has alternating and touching triangles of jet and turquoise; another has alternating turquoise and jet bands made up of squares of the two materials. The two others feature turquoise

and shell, one having three rows of the former and two of the latter, the second adding one row of each plus a narrow outlining band of jet on either edge. Opposite the scraper end is additional decoration on the distal portion: one piece is set with a round of shell, a second has the same plus an outlining in jet, and the other two were seemingly decorated in the same manner but whatever material was used is missing. Pepper also found one whole scraper and fragments of two other similarly decorated pieces; these elaborate examples of end scrapers seem to have been limited to Pueblo Bonito. There is, of course, rare use of lesser decoration on these pieces, particularly in the form of incised geometrics or life forms.

As in the case of other tools, there is regional variation in bone and related materials. One of the most significant points to mention is the fact that there were so few tools of bone at Snaketown—little more than a double-handful, says Haury of the first excavation results. The only utilitarian object of bone was the awl, he continues, but there were not enough of these to provide a basis for their needs. Probably this important tool was made of wood. Contrary to

Fig. 6.6 An example of early representation of a life form at Snaketown. Bone tubes were incised in this manner or in geometric patterns (Gladwin et al. 1937, pl. CXXVIIj).

the Hohokam situation, bone was used abundantly in the Anasazi area, and a wide variety of objects was made of this material.

Of interest in connection with the use of bone at Snaketown is the production of tubes. Although they are not utility objects in the same sense as the awl, they are, nonetheless, quite widely distributed throughout the Southwest, though not abundantly. They are the most prominent bone item in the Hohokam, appearing early and lasting until Sedentary times. Most of the decorated tubes are early and disappear by the end of the Gila Butte Phase. Incised patterns on these tubes are geometric, largely diagonal lines and cross-hatching, but with a few scroll patterns and life forms (Fig. 6.6).

It would be impossible to give with any brevity all the varieties of stone and all the objects made from them; therefore only the most important will be presented. Some variation in material reflects locale, and some specific stone objects tell of the lives of these people. All practiced agriculture to some degree; therefore, metates and manos, the tools for grinding corn, were widespread. All built houses; thus axes were equally widely distributed, although there is considerable variation in quantity of such tools between peoples who used much timber in house construction and those who had no more than a few support posts and a minimum of roof beams. Even this last observation does not apply in all areas. Where agriculture was highly developed and less hunting was indulged in, there were fewer projectile points.

Two basic methods of working stone for the production of these utility objects were practiced in the Southwest: one, pecked and ground, and, two, chipped. Materials used in the pecked and

ground technique include the following, among others: those of fine to coarse quality: sandstone, basalt, felsite, tuff, diabase, quartzite, diorite, lava, quartz, limestone, granite, steatite, andesite, and schist. The second technique, chipped, usually employed a very different type of stone, although a few of the foregoing, such as quartzite, andesite, felsite, and porphyritic basalt, served for the second method as well. These additional materials were chipped: rhyolite, obsidian, chert, chalcedony, and jasper, among others. Chipping and flaking were accomplished by one of two methods, percussion, or striking a blow against the worked material with another stone, and pressure, wherein a bone or horn tool or one of other material was placed against the stone surface and pressure applied. The former is an older technique, the latter a later one, but both were known and used in the Southwest. In pecked and ground, literally just this is done to the stone being worked, pecking by hitting one stone against another and grinding by rubbing. The form of the object is usually roughed out by pecking away at the base material with another stone, while grinding is done with one stone rubbed against another until the desired shape and finish are acquired.

Foremost among the pecked and ground tools are the metate and mano (Fig. 6.7). Several different types were made in the prehistoric Southwest, a slab type, a basin form, and a trough style. Flat metates have no ridges at the sides; trough metates have side ridges alone, thus are open at both ends, or side ridges plus one end completely surrounded by a rim. Basin types have a central depression that is often irregular. Block metates were sometimes made from almost any available piece of thick stone, some with a rounded hole or basin approximately in the center, some with a full trough, or from a

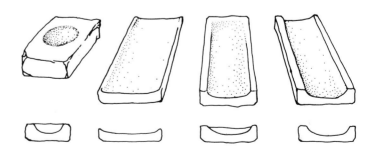

Fig. 6.7 Metates, showing variations in shapes and side ridges of these grinding stones.

shaped, but thick, piece of stone; slab metates were also shaped or unshaped but usually were made on thinner pieces of stone, and they were frequently flat-surfaced. In the more shaped metates, some were rounded ovals, some almost perfect rectangles. Workmanship varies a great deal. Manos, or the hand stones with which the grinding of corn is done, vary in size and shape: some are small and almost round; some are more or less rectangular, with parallel sides and rounded or square-cut ends, and with a gently rounded, flat, or wedge-shaped back; some are quite long and narrow. Some are unifaced, some bifaced. There are one-handed and two-handed manos, the former short, the latter long.

Mortars and pestles are also found widely for they served many purposes, from grinding paint to seeds. An unshaped piece of very thick stone was often used for the mortar; a cuplike thick-walled piece is pecked into shape; or the Indian pecked out a hole in the surface of some large living or bed rock. Sometimes there are many of these holes scattered over a large area of such rock. The pestle is sometimes cylindrical or conical in shape, with a rounded or flat end for pounding, or double conical-shaped, that is, smaller at the lower end and where the hands hold the piece, but a bit thickened toward the center. Some may be rounded at the working end only. These are more crudely or better formed. Mortars and pestles are neither as widely nor as intensively distributed as metates and manos; for example, they are rare at Pueblo Bonito. On the other hand, 114 were found at Ventana Cave.

Fine and medium-grained stones were used for the making of axes (Fig. 6.8). At Snaketown there are different types of this tool, which are characteristic of the southern area. All are three-quarter grooved; earlier they had sharp and well-defined projections above and below the groove, while later this feature diminishes and disappears. Some of the early examples are flat on the head and have long and narrow bits. The bit shortens in time and some heads become very rounded. Relative to Los Tules, an eastern Mogollon site, Lehmer says, "Hammerstones are numerous, and are simply battered nodules of igneous or metamorphic rock," but he does not even mention axes.[2] From Cameron Creek and the Alamogordo sites of the same general area came both three-quarter and full-grooved axes; some were cruder, some better finished. At a ruin in the Point of Pines area there are three-quarter and full-grooved axes; some are of a shouldered type, and some few are double-bitted. At Pueblo Bonito, axes "are not only rare but comparatively rude. In this they agree with stone axes from other sections of the San Juan basin. They were made from water-worn cobbles of igneous rock...."[3] These axes were full-grooved. Both full-and three-quarter grooved axes were found in the Flagstaff area; some had flattened heads and long bits, others varied.

Adzes were found in limited distribution; they were usually long and slender. Picks look like axes except that they have a point rather than a blade. Rasps are made of such material as an abrasive schist; some are well formed, some are rough. Elliptical in cross section, they are elongate, and they have no indentations for hafting as they were apparently held in the hand when used. Sometimes knives started as flakes and were then ground to a sharp edge. Essentially the same process was applied to the making of certain scrapers. Hammerstones and mauls may be made-over axes or produced originally from a pebble without much modification. Hammers

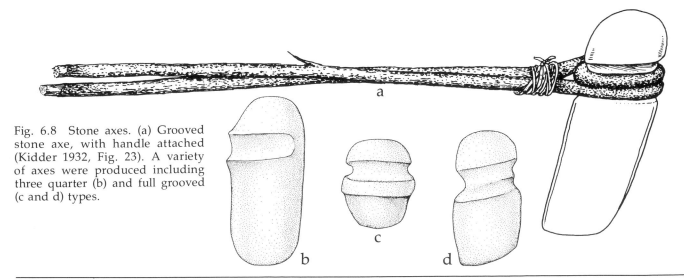

Fig. 6.8 Stone axes. (a) Grooved stone axe, with handle attached (Kidder 1932, Fig. 23). A variety of axes were produced including three quarter (b) and full grooved (c and d) types.

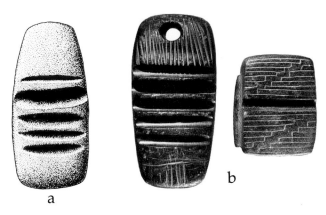

Fig. 6.9 Arrow shaft straighteners. (a) A well-shaped arrow shaft straightener made of sandstone (Haury 1945a, pl. 60d). (b) Two decorated arrow shaft smoothers, of stone.

may be rounded or angular boulders or pebbles; they may have pits for the purpose of grasping. An oval stone might bear a bit of notching on two sides of the pebble for the purpose of hafting; ends may be slightly flattened or rounded for mauls. Arrowshaft straighteners or smoothers were made from original pebbles or sometimes from broken manos (Fig. 6.9). Grooves on the top of the stone were single, or there were two of them, or they were multiple; they were transverse or longitudinal across the face of the stone or but a partial distance across it. These stones were often carefully shaped and may or may not have been polished.

Some tools may or may not have been shaped by pecking and grinding. Abraders were devices for sharpening axes or other tools; they might be in live rock, or on an unshaped slab, or on a shaped stone. Anvils were unworked or worked pebbles; other stones were broken on them. Rubbing or polishing stones were natural, smooth pebbles used for polishing surfaces of pottery or other objects. Bead rasps were pieces of abrasive stone of natural or but slightly altered form, with a groove over the face through which a string of beads would be run back and forth for shaping and sizing. Pottery anvils of the Hohokam area were round on their bases and had a second rounded surface on the top for holding the tool in the hand.

Chipped stone was productive of a number of essentials to the natives of the Southwest. Most important were projectile points (Fig. 6.10a), for hunting provided many of these people with food, with materials for a number of necessities as well as luxuries, and with skins for garments, most likely, as well as for other purposes. Points

ran the gamut from very poorly chipped and equally badly shaped to perfectly chipped and beautifully shaped pieces; they included tiny bird points or much larger ones for big game; they had straight unnotched bases or deeply notched ones; they were long and slender or short and broad. Most points were made from fine cherts, obsidian, or like materials, while some were produced in a coarse-grade stone. Some edges are so refined in workmanship that they are almost unbelievable while others are deeply but regularly notched, and still others are carelessly and irregularly worked. In west-central Arizona, some arrowheads are straight-and concave-based and have no notches. "The majority of the Alamogordo points are small, elongate-triangular, un-notched, with either flat or, more often, concave bases."[4] At Canyon Creek, the arrow points are "uniformly of a long and slender type," stemless and with concave bases, and with beautiful secondary chipping. In contrast to the elongate triangular form of these are smaller, shorter, and stemmed points that are straight or concave based. From the Upper Gila come delicate obsidian points that have fine retouching. In the Mogollon in general, points tend to be small, are stemmed or stemless, and have concave, convex, or almost straight bases. Very elongate, thin points prevailed at Snaketown; they may be more delicately or more

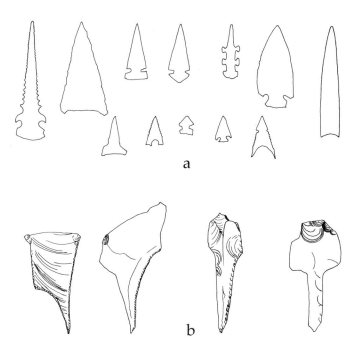

Fig. 6.10 Arrow points and scrapers. (a) The variety in shapes and sizes of chipped and flaked arrow points is great; a few only are represented here. (b) Examples of chipped scrapers.

deeply notched along the edges. There are also shorter styles, some of which have very delicate secondary chipping. Both straight and concave bases are found, the latter sometimes very deep. Few chipped points were found at Snaketown, for, seemingly, little hunting was done. Also, the projectile points changed little through the centuries, again perhaps because they were not particularly important to these people.

The chipped stone knife might be made from a flake that was not retouched, as found at Snaketown, or it may be retouched, as is common in many other sites. In addition to the point and knife, there are few other chipped stone tools at Snaketown. Drills, which are sharp-pointed, chipped tools, are usually retouched at the point alone; they are quite widely distributed for they were necessary in making many of the stone beads found so widely in the Southwest. Scrapers, another chipped tool of importance, varied from thumbnail size to several inches in length, and from very thin flakes to quite heavy ones (Fig. 6.10b).

The stone hoe was generally made by chipping but sometimes combined this technique with grinding. Its distribution is largely in the Hohokam, but it is also found in both the Mogollon and the Anasazi. It may be made on a large spall, or on a thin stone blade, or, as in an example from the Flagstaff area, from a piece of fine-grained basalt. Forms vary greatly, from an elongate, almost-pick-shape, to irregular ovals, rectangles, and the like, to a more shapely piece with the lower part and sides curved, the upper part straight, and with notches on the upper sides. The blade or working end may be irregular, straight, or evenly curved. These pieces were either held in the hand, or, presumably the notched examples may have been hafted.

Although the preceding does not cover all stone tools, it does give some of the more important ones, along with variety in materials, shapes, and a bit about the methods of working these items. No excavation report is complete without at least a few words pertaining to stone tools.

Figurines

Over a period of several years, three pieces of carving defined as heads were found in Texas. All were associated with Pleistocene fauna. One, a large sandstone concretion, was about 16 inches long and about 14 inches wide. Depressions formed eyes, nose, mouth, and ears. About 1,000 feet away, a second piece was found; it is smaller in size, but has the same markings for facial features. The third piece is not quite so readily identifiable as a human head, but it has similar markings; it is larger in size.

With these very ancient pieces in mind, figurines among the prehistoric sedentary cultures will be surveyed. First, it may be noted that no

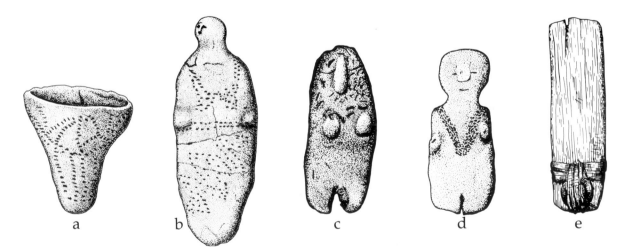

Fig. 6.11 Effigies and human figurine types (all figures from Elizabeth Morris 1959a). (a) Clay miniature carrying basket effigy, with design suggested in holes punched in the clay (120g). (b) Human effigy of clay with punched dots representing a necklace and a geometric design on the body (120m). (c,d) Crude human figurines formed of clay. Nose and breasts are suggested in c, while all facial features and breasts are indicated in d as is a multiple strand necklace (120 n,o). (e) Human figure of wood, showing a loin cloth made from corn husk. Neither facial nor body features nor limbs are so much as suggested (120a).

large sculpture developed among the later pre-historic peoples. Second, the question may be asked: What is a figurine? It is difficult to limit the term, for figurines of one sort or another are a part of many other craft arts, for example, jewelry, palettes, and stone vases, among others. One dictionary definition is, "A small carved or molded figure or statuette," and it is in this sense of a small independent object that the term will be used herein. All other carving or molding attached to any other form will not be a part of this discussion.

Figurines are widely distributed in the South-west, and they are found from earliest times to the end of the prehistoric period. They were produced in both baked and unbaked clay; a wide variety of stone, including, among others, sandstone, limestone, basalt, tuff, lava; and sometimes of perishable materials, such as wood. Techniques of manufacture include the modeling of clay, and cutting, incising, carving, inlay, mosaic, and several other techniques in wood and stone. Most prevalent of all true figurine forms are human females, plus some males (Fig. 6.11), and a great many animals and birds. In the production of these forms, everything from very generalized styles to what are thought to be portraits are included.

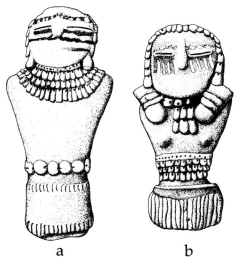

a   b

Fig. 6.12 Pillings figurines. (a) A Pillings, Utah, male figurine of clay which is much "bedecked" with facial paint, earrings, a multiple strand necklace, and an elaborate belt. Markings on the kilt may indicate some type of decoration on the original (Morss 1954, Fig. 2). (b) A female figurine from Pillings. Basket impression appears on the back, but the front perspective gives detail of hairdo, jewelry about the neck, an elaborate belt, and an apron. Black paint appears in the eye slits, with a brown base decorated with red and buff on the rest of the figurine, 5⅜" tall (Morss 1954, Fig. 7).

ANASAZI

Figurines are very widespread in the Anasazi, both in time and space. They vary in style from simple cornucopialike forms to pieces with all physical and dress details well represented. One of the most interesting finds was that known as the Pillings figurines, probably Basketmaker III in time.[5] From northeast Utah, they were found as a cache of 11 anthropomorphic pieces, all of unbaked clay (Fig. 6.12a,b). They are about 6 inches high. All but one seem to have been formed as a single piece, yet separate neck and body are well defined. The fronts of the figures are well smoothed, and the backs rather rough. Eyes were formed by making a transverse ridge of the face clay, then cutting a slit in the ridge; there is a long nasal ridge, but little indication of the mouth. Other features of face and body were added, but they were not too well bonded; too, both face and body were painted, to add to or emphasize details. Elaborate hairdos were represented for both sexes, with longer, hanging hair on the women. Facial designs were featured about the eyes, and were usually lines. Earrings were present on some; necklaces were also represented, and some believe that the chins of the figures may have been added after the necklaces were put on. Sex was distinguished in details of anatomy and dress. Women are readily identified by breasts and wide hips and they wear aprons. All of the men wear breechclouts except one and he seems to have on a kilt. Belts were sometimes added, separate from the apron supports.

A few individual features will emphasize those mentioned in the general comments. On one female, there are vertical stripes above the eyes and diagonal stripes on the cheeks, all in red. On a male figure there are a line of red paint dotted with buff on the forehead and three horizontal stripes separated by two buff stripes under the eyes. The torso of the latter figure has a V-shaped buff area reaching to the waist, with buff stripes along the edges. Some decoration is in black paint.

During Basketmaker II times, there were human figurines made over a limited part of the Anasazi. From the Segie comes a wooden doll painted red, with sketchily carved face and arms. At Cave du Pont was found an unbaked sherd with the edge cut into rough human features. Into the Basketmaker III phase, the situation changed and there are many areas where figurines are found. Among others are the Prayer Rock District, the Lukachukais, the Segie, Canyons del Muerto and de Chelly, Mesa Verde, Monument Valley, Keams Canyon, and into Utah and the Fremont River area. Most of the figurines throughout this territory are more primitive than the fine Pillings examples, yet they are identifiable. The basic modeling is more rudimentary, and many of the added elements of the Pillings examples are lacking. Facial and other features are more often the result of punctations and incisions, but there are occasional aprons of vegetal fibers. Along the Fremont, the figurines reveal several features of interest: the body may terminate in a straight bar or in stump legs, or in a skirt or apron flaring at the lower edge. When eyes are present, they may be added rounds of clay with a hole in the center. As in the Pillings figures, some of these may have fillets or blobs of clay added to suggest the hair or ornaments, yet they are not as tall, the average being about 4 to 5 inches.

From other parts of the Anasazi, and from early to late times, there was a variety of figurines, although from some other parts of this area there seems to be a dearth of them (Fig. 6.13). Kidder did not find much in the way of prehistoric carvings and no molded figurines of prehistoric age at Pecos. Several stone figurines from Pecos, a bird and a frog, have considerable appeal (Fig. 6.14a and b). Four carved human figures he calls idols are squat, squared, crude carvings that seem but slightly related to Southwest work of this nature. Of the very large number of clay effigies found at Pecos he has this to say: "Their stratigraphic position is pretty clearly established in Glaze V, for they are apparently absent from earlier strata and the very few which came to light in later rubbish may well have been accidental inclusions. The Glaze V period seems to have opened about the middle of the 16th century...."[6]

In Mug House, Mesa Verde National Park, were found several effigies. One looks like a very modern piece of sculpture.[7] On a smoothed, oval-topped and flat-bottomed piece of red siltstone are two round holes and a groove that appear to be eyes and nose of some animal. Rohn also reports that "Six small, complete or fragmentary figurines of unfired clay bear faint markings suggesting human representations."[8] Poorly modeled, they have the faintest scratches suggestive of eyes and slight ridges for noses. These vaguely resemble Basketmaker III fig-

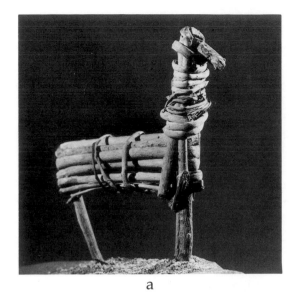

a

b

Fig. 6.13 A variety of Southwest figurines. (a) From a cave in the Grand Canyon comes this strange split twig figure. Radio carbon dates this at about 2000 B.C. (b) In the group are typical Anasazi figurines, the two to the right marked to suggest hair or necklaces. Right, upper, is a "Baby in a cradle" from Kinishba, east central Arizona.

urines from other areas. Although there is a fair number of Basketmaker III figurines from the Four Corners region, they are very rare after this time except for babes-in-cradles types. In this piece, the top side of a handle of a ladle serves as the cradle into or onto which is placed a human figurine.

A fairly good representation of animal and human figurines is to be noted at Pueblo Bonito. Among them is, first, a lion's head which "is carved from friable sandstone. A straight incised line forms the mouth; eyes are not indicated; ears are rounded knobs."[9] Two other heads like this one were also found at Bonito; they are more generalized and rather cone-shaped with a concave "face" that lacked any features except the knoblike ears. A turquoise bird effigy, which has been drilled, is thought to have been too heavy and of such shape as not to have been an ornament (Fig. 6.14c); it is very modern in its smooth surfaces, lack of detail, and abstract form. A most interesting rattlesnake effigy was also found at this site. Formed from a piece of cottonwood root which grew in such shape as to suggest a snake, it was carved a bit at the head and tail, then painted, first with black, then over this with white to simulate the markings of a rattler. Another flat, long, rectangular piece of wood was carved very slightly to simulate a human head-body division. Could this doll-like piece have been a forerunner of the puebloan cradle kachina? Perhaps this prehistoric piece had facial and body features painted on it, like a modern doll. Another human figurine at Pueblo Bonito is crudely formed of clay. It is roughly rectangular, slightly wider at the "shoulders,"

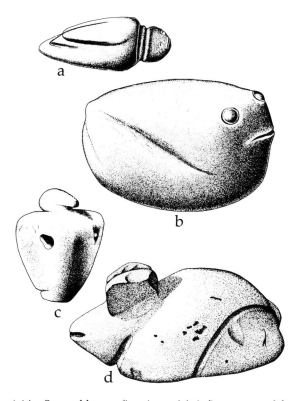

Fig. 6.14 Several larger figurines. (a) A figure carved from limestone, a bird or perhaps an insect—or a creature of the imagination? (Kidder 1932, Fig. 66a). (b) A most appealing creature, probably a frog, made from a green stone, from Pecos (ibid., Fig. 66b). (c) Although its use is unknown, this carved and proud bird of turquoise has a distinct charm in its simplicity. From Pueblo Bonito (Judd 1954, Fig. 92). (d) A delightful figure of a little pack rat, carved from sandstone. From Winona-Ridge Ruin area (McGregor 1941, Fig. 61A).

and has the slightest concavity at the base to suggest legs. Round scooped-out areas serve as eyes, an elongate one for a mouth; nose and breasts are merely pinched-up clay. Apparently there were two clay figurines comparable to the last described one found by Pepper in his earlier work at Bonito. All of these belong to Pueblo III times.

Excavated at Pueblo del Arroyo were three human figurines of clay. One has a body, which is straight-sided, rounded-bottomed, and out-curving from the body is a rounded head. Simple perforations serve for some of the facial features, smaller for eyes, larger for the mouth, plus a large pinched-up nose. A second is like this but not so symmetrical; it had charcoal fitted into squares for the eyes and a bulge on the lower right side. A third is an oval of clay, slightly wider at the head; it too has charcoal in its square eyes and a square mouth.

At the Village of the Great Kivas were found several very interesting carved stone heads. At least two seem to have been attached to perishable materials originally. Heads are well formed, with quite well-delineated features, but they terminate in cylinderlike necks, and have no remnants of bodies present. One seems to be the sacred serpent found among the Zuñi today, a second Morris identified as a frog, a third is a deer or antelope with the mouth area missing and the fourth is not identifiable.[10] An interesting pair of stones from this ruin is of the type that has been found over a fairly widespread area within the Anasazi, from the Little Colorado River to Mesa Verde. It is a simply carved stone, rounded over the top and increasing in diameter but slightly from top to base. Contemporary Zuñi identify it as the symbol of the corn goddess, in essence, a true effigy. Its smooth surface is not interrupted by any facial or body features; in terms of modern art it certainly could be labeled a figurine.

From the Winona and Ridge Ruins area come 3 stone carvings and 11 clay figurines. One of the former is a pack rat carved in full round of limestone and about life size; he is quite realistic, even to his mousey grin and large ears (Fig. 6.14d). Two smaller figures in basalt are not identifiable as their features are more generalized; all that can be said of them is that they are mammals. The clay figurines include humans and animals; the latter can be identified only as mammals, some with heads and some without. Two types of the human head were represented, one with a rather more elongate outline and coffee bean eyes, a beak of a nose, and a tiny mouth. The second type has a round face and a large nose, plus a very large round mouth. This head is on the body of a pregnant woman; the body is formless and has very slight nubbin projections for legs.

An appealing and fairly large (7⅞ inches long) bear was found at a small ruin near Point of Pines. It is made of tuff, pecked and rubbed into shape. It is a "quadruped with a thick, round, barrel-shaped body, no tail, short legs, thick heavy neck, short ears and a long snout."[11] Animal effigies of baked clay from this same site are crudely made; they are almost formless in body with short and stubby tail and legs, and a pinched up nose and ears on the head. Both head and tail are held high in all of these carelessly made pieces. An equally crude bird of the same material is made with head and tail held upright; wings are crescent-shaped and were added after the body was modeled.

Haury found an equally generalized clay figure of an animal at the Canyon Creek Ruin. "It consists of a plump pear-shaped body 3¼ inches long, the snout being somewhat drawn out and curved down. Four splints of cane, three of which have been broken off, were stuck into the body for legs. Eyes were made by pressing two small lumps of charcoal into the soft clay, and,

from between the eyes to the top of the head, there was painted a black line."[12]

Human effigies at Tuzigoot are highly conventionalized lengths of clay.[13] They have no legs and no arms, but do have two large breasts added as lumps of clay low on the body. Heads are slightly broader than the body. Facial features are lacking or they are simply done: in one, the chin is prominent; noses are pinched up clay; one head shows slits for eyes, and the mouth is a hole punched in the clay. The animal effigies from this site are extremely crude and badly proportioned, but really better made than the human figurines. They had round bodies with heads; upright tails were modeled first, then legs and ears were formed separately and added to the bodies. Incisions for eyes, and for the mouth on one example only, were made after the pieces were fired. Two bird figures were found, one with outspread wings that were well made, the second with folded wings that were extremely crudely formed. Originally feathers were imbedded in the clay forming the outspread wings, which must have made the first a most realistic figure.

MOGOLLON

Seemingly, few figures came from the Mogollon; however, they are widespread in distribution, appearing at Forestdale in the

Fig. 6.15   A variety of small figurines, largely from Forestdale, central eastern Arizona, and a few other scattered locations. Included are birds and mammals, so generalized in outline that they cannot be specifically identified.

north and in the San Simon area to the south. Both animal and human figures were found at the former site, made of fired clay (Fig. 6.15). A fragmentary and unidentifiable animal reveals little in the way of modeling in another piece. Three human figures are represented in one whole example and two pieces; modeling in these is very poor, with long and straight-sided bodies, mere suggestions of legs, and no arms, yet one has a great beak of a nose. A single stone fragment of a piece of a figure and three whole figurines appeared in a late level of a San Simon village.[14] The three whole figurines were roughed out on natural pebbles, with a slight indentation to show the body-head separation, and with a very slight concavity at the bottom to indicate legs. Arms are but the slightest projections. There are no facial or body features.

In an eastern Mogollon site of the Alamogordo area, four figurines were found. Three are thought to be bears; they are very simplified, and with practically no features. The fourth piece is "a well-executed caricature of a mountain sheep. The body was cylindrical and little modified except for an incised arm, with distinct scratches indicating fingers, which was held across the torso."[15] Two raised areas on the lower body might be legs. The horns of the animal head are quite well done. Could this represent a human wearing a mask? Two interesting heads and a leg came from the Bluff Site. The leg, which is probably that of an animal, has incisions on it to represent the toes; otherwise it is a thick, formless piece. The two heads are mindful of Hohokam types in their slit coffee-bean eyes; the slits are rather long, extending through the little round pellets, which form the eye, and continue on to the edge of the head. Backs of heads are flat. One has a suggestion of shoulders, the other is broken off at the neck. Noses are pinched-up ridges of the clay, one much longer and seemingly sharper than the other.

A wooden bird effigy was found in a cave on the Upper Gila, made of yucca stalk. It is 4½ inches in length, and is decorated in black, green, red, white, and yellow. The form of the bird is pleasingly simple and rounded, and the painting identifies parts of the bird, albeit with geometrics, and at the same time decorates it. A hole, which runs diagonally from the top of the head to the beak, may have accommodated a feather that in turn may have made the figurine look like a quail and at the same time have given it a beak.

HOHOKAM

Over 500 figurines were recovered from the first excavation of Snaketown,[16] with many more added in the second excavation. Needless to say, this is the richest site in the Southwest for a study of such pieces. A few hints on period styles occur in the Anasazi, less in the Mogollon, but here in the Hohokam not only can there be demonstrated a period by period development with distinct styles, but also it can be shown that there was a harmonious trend from early to late times. Herein are implications that figurine development took place locally and was not greatly influenced from the outside, granted that there are some evidences of Mexican contact; too, the developments so beautifully displayed at Snaketown may indicate that from this area came significant traits that affected other parts of the Southwest.

Snaketown figurines were made of a finer clay than that in pottery vessels, for the tempering material was left out. This clay otherwise resembled that in pottery as a whole, that is, it was predominantly gray in earlier years and buff later on. Earlier figurines were made of two pieces of clay put together, with small pieces sometimes added for details, while later on the figurines were produced from a single piece of clay, again with small fragments used for facial and body detail. Some painting was done on figurines, although many were not so decorated. Incising, or gouging, was done to create detailed features; sometimes fillets or other fragments of clay were added for dress or other minutiae. In general, Hohokam figurines are comparable to those of the northern periphery in size, frontal orientation, the predominance of females with breasts present, the emphasis on eyes and heavy nose ridges and no mouth, and in the mere stumps of arms or none at all. The major differences between the figurines of Snaketown and the northern periphery are: the former are fired, the latter are not, and the former have longer legs than those of the latter area.

Beginning with the Pioneer Period, Snaketown figurines appear in the earliest or Vahki Phase (Fig. 6.16). Some early heads are flat on top, or nearly so, and concave at the back; some are funnel-shaped; facial details were made by pinching up the nose and making eyes of slits or dots. Bodies were seated and heavy or standing, with legs either welded together or separated. The majority of the figures are female, and certainly all of them are conventional in style. Ears

Fig. 6.16   General Hohokam human figurine types. From the Pioneer Period are modeled heads and bodies (left, and three on bottom row) with enormous noses, dots or slits for eyes, and a mere round hole for the mouth. From the Colonial is a style with a band about the head (top, third from left), and coffee bean eyes (second from right, top). In the Sedentary Period were more portraitlike faces (top right); figures of this last type were usually modeled as clay heads alone, then placed on perishable bodies.

are represented on some of these early pieces, with ear spools or other decorations in them.

In the early Colonial Period, heads were flat on top and back, this giving them an angular caste. Slit eyes with heavily incised eyebrows are common, the nose is still pinched up, and the mouth is an insignificant dot or it is non-existent. In the later Colonial, the Santa Cruz Phase, faces are more carelessly done. The nose is often greatly exaggerated over the earlier size, and is high on an up-tilted face, thus a rather haughty bearing characterizes the general attitude of these faces. The mouth is a strange little hole or an almost rectangular slit, eyes are of the coffee-bean type, a pellet of clay with a slit, and eyebrows are gone (Fig. 6.16). Odd chin ornaments are made of bits of clay and have dots and incisions in them. Thus, the facial features are unrealistic. Bodies are made of a single piece of clay usually; they are sometimes better done than the faces, although careless workmanship characterizes them also. Bits of clothing appear

on several of the figurines of this period; for example, rather fancy leg and ankle bands and an equally elaborate piece on the body.

Quite a change was made in some figurines into the Sacaton Phase, even though there is continuity into this last Hohokam period in other ways. The greatest difference was in heads alone, seemingly modeled in clay on bodies made of perishable materials (Fig. 6.16). Continuity is expressed in other pieces where head-body modeling is still important; these are usually in a seated position not unlike that in effigy pottery vessels. The figures have a little more heaviness to them, perhaps suggested in the posture which is further characterized by the hands resting on the knees. Facial features are about as gross as those of the preceding phase. On the contrary, the independent heads are beautifully modeled, so well done, in fact, that some are thought to be portraits. Seemingly, these heads were modeled about a bundle of bound fibers, for impressions of the wood remain on the backs of the clay heads. It is presumed that the rest of the figure was of fiber or wood also, but little, if any, of this remains. Facial features are more realistic than they are in any previous styles: noses are still quite large but some have the nostril indicated, and the nasal depression is realistically portrayed. "Eyes were made by attaching small pellets of clay to the face and incising these elevations with biconvex lines, dotted in the center. Eyebrows are usually indicated by a line."[17] One very interesting feature is the projecting lips, this accomplished by adding a strip of clay, then cutting a slit through it. Ears may or may not be added; when they are, the results are not too good, but rather, no more than projecting bits of clay with a hole in the middle. Nonetheless, these fine heads are thought to be, in some instances at least, attempts at portraits of some of the Hohokams of the Sedentary Period.

In the re-excavation of Snaketown, many additional figurines were found. Among them and in a pit cache, were 19 animal figurines.[18] They are made of clay, are 5 inches tall, and look as pert as their model, a deer. Short tails are upright and all but wagging; heads are erect. Although the bodies are rather heavily modeled, and particularly heavy-legged, they are better than the majority of mammals from various parts of the Southwest. Eyes are large holes, and the muzzle is more realistic in some figures than others.

Very few human and animal figurines of clay were found at Los Muertos and other ruins of this area (Fig. 6.17a,b). At the nearby site of Los Guanacos were found 15 figurines that the excavator likened to the guanaco, a llamalike creature, and hence the name of the site (Fig. 6.17c). The little clay figures are about 5 inches long. They are thin-bodied, fairly heavy-legged, have short down-turned tails, and their heads are upright; most of the heads are looking forward but one is turned to the animal's left. Eyes are incised rings, while the mouth is cut in a straight line, and the nostrils are formed of a hole. Ears are short and lumpy. The animal represented in these figures was probably the deer, although they are presented in a style different from that of the Snaketown figurines. Before the second excavation and the discovery of the deer, few of these had been found at Snaketown. Ventana revealed very few figurines and these largely of unbaked clay. One is so generalized as to hardly be recognized as a

human; on the head and body are rows of punctate decoration; a second example is recognizable as a torso with lower limbs, and is decorated with black and white lines and a curved theme. Another figurine from Ventana seems to be a bird's head, which terminates in a tubelike piece of unfired clay. Stone figurines were almost nonexistent at Los Muertos.

In summary of figurine development in the Southwest, it may first be reiterated that there is a widespread distribution of this craft, but any intensity of occurrence is very limited.

Several areas of concentration did exist: the Snaketown and Fremont River areas have been mentioned and figurines described; two others are Prescott, where there was a concentration of humans (the most important), birds, and animals, which demonstrate rather crude types of

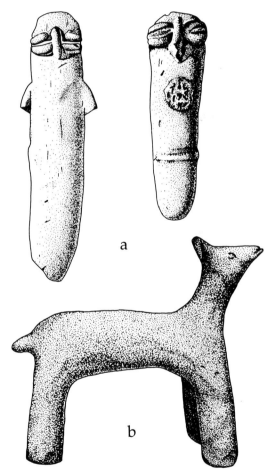

Fig. 6.17 Two styles of Hohokam figurines, human and animal. (a) Two Hohokam figurines, both extremely simple, which is characteristic of late styles. Both have "coffee bean" eyes; a nose was added to the figure on the left and pinched up on the right one. Left, Los Hornos, right, Los Muertos (Haury 1945a, Figs. 118d and 69b). (b) Clay animal figurine, about 5" long, one of a group found at Los Guanacos which suggested this name to the excavators (ibid, pl. 82e).

figurines; and Pecos, which was not mentioned previously as the figurine complex here was of historic times.

Humans, animals, and birds were the subject matter of this expression, and this rather generally over the entire area; in the Mogollon there were fewer animals and apparently no birds. Materials used included clay, both baked and unbaked, wood and other plant substances, bone rarely, and a wide variety of stone. Artistry varied both temporally and spatially. In the Hohokam, there was a definite early crudity with a culmination in the fine heads of the Sedentary Period, which may have been portraits in some instances. Basketmaker figurines were basically female, were of flat pieces of clay with one end modified into a head with rather poor facial features, and with breasts on a limbless body. The fine Fremont River pieces, with excellent details of face, body, clothing, and jewelry, exemplify the best in early times, although much of the later work remained simple.

As to the meaning of figurines, many educated guesses have been put forth. Some believe that they are toys, or at least that some of them may have served in this capacity. Perhaps there would have been more variety if they had been meant to be toys. It is possible that they may have been cult objects; the presence of some of them on or near altars might support this idea, but certainly all of them were not produced for such purposes. If they were made as representations of gods or divinities, one would expect a development of certain characteristics, which would have been considered peculiar to each deity. The chief example of such a possibility would be the figure of the snake head from the Village of the Great Kivas, a head which might have been the forerunner of the great serpent revered by several of the Southwest's puebloan groups. And of course, it may again be noted that the vast majority of figurines are of females, with breasts so frequently stressed. Such figurines are found the world over, most of them symbolizing the procreative aspects of the female or mother nature. Historic Indians have been known to offer such female figurines in their corrals for purposes of increase of the herds, or these figurines may be buried in the fields with the same concept in mind relative to planted foods. Some figurines are found in cremations or burials and might have been votive offerings.

It is not beyond the realm of possibility that they served different purposes in different areas, or, perhaps, even in a single region. Of course, it is also possible that the sheer joy of artistic creation might explain the making of many of the figurines of the prehistoric Southwest.

Musical Instruments

Many musical instruments have been found archaeologically in the Southwest; they are distributed widely throughout this area. This is to be expected, for there were many instruments still in use when the Spaniards came into this territory. A large number of these survive to this day among some of the contemporary tribes, but with other groups they have been lost completely and are neither made nor used. Interestingly, in a few instances, native Southwesterners have adapted European ideas in the making of their musical instruments and have produced such pieces as fiddles.

There are many evidences in the prehistoric past of both making and using musical instruments. First, there are the actual instruments themselves; although all types are not found throughout the area, some are found in Anasazi, Hohokam, and Mogollon sites. Second, there are evidences of the use of specific instruments in the paintings of kiva walls and on pottery, and in pictographs or petroglyphs, all of these often depicting individuals playing or otherwise involved with musical instruments. And, of course, there is the important evidence previously mentioned—the survival of the musical devices among living natives and their greatly integrated part in the ceremonial life of the Indian. The last point is particularly important among the puebloans, where native ritual remains so little changed that their presence among the living Indians might confirm their prehistoric usage.

It is most difficult to give a complete picture of the development of musical instruments, for many of them were made of perishable materials and have not survived. In the first place, there were not a great many such pieces produced, and secondly, if such materials as wood, skins, or gut should have been used, chances of preservation would have been limited. There are evidences for the manufacture and the use of wind instruments (aerophones), and vibrator types, (idiophones), but no indications that either true percussion (membranophones) or strings (chordophones) were known to these people. The latter two types of instruments are frequently made of perishable materials; sometimes, too, they are more complicated than the first two categories. Inasmuch as the foot drum was known and is found archaeologically and the hand drum is relatively simple it would seem that the latter might have been known prehistorically. However, there is no evidence of its presence in pre-Columbian times. It is quite probable that a basket was turned upside down and beaten with the hand, much as it was, and is, historically by several native tribes, such as the Papago Indians of southern Arizona. Some believe that there is the possibility that there was a pot drum made prehistorically, such as the Navajos and others use today. Perhaps there was. Perhaps some of the vessels with a fillet of clay about the neck may have been used for such purposes, the ribbon of clay serving to tie the head beneath it so that the skin would stay in position.

Among the idiophones that can be established definitely in the prehistoric Southwest are foot drums, stone and other bells, rasps, and rattles. All of these have survived to the present among native Southwesterners; even the stone bell is still used in some instances. Not only are these devices actually found prehistorically but also rattles are represented in various styles and uses in paintings of diverse sorts.

Among the aerophones were bull-roarers, flutes, trumpets, and whistles. All of these survive, including a native type of the trumpet, a conch shell device. Like the idiophones, they are widely distributed, and are found in the three major culture areas. Actual examples of all four types of wind instruments have also been recovered, and there are many artistic representations of flute playing. In fact, there is a widespread distribution of paintings on rocks and pottery of a fellow who has been labeled the hunch-backed fluteplayer; he is represented in styles from extreme conventionalization to quite realistic, either alone or with a close attendant. In some instances, there is a definite hump on the back while in other examples there is little or no indication of such. The survival of this character in myth and in portrayed personalities, for example, in sandpaintings and dancers, to the present moment, would indicate his longevity and importance.

Among the most important evidences of the presence of the foot drum would be the subfloor vaults in the Great Kivas of the Chaco Canyon. Foot drums also occur in the Mesa Verde; and in eastern Arizona not only vaults but also shelves at the room sides, which held the planks themselves, are found in late prehistoric kivas. Vaults are also found in prehistoric sites in the Rio Grande where they are likewise later in time. Foot drums are also evidenced in grooves in the floors of ceremonial chambers of the Mogollon area. As to the time of this musical device, Brown has the following to say.

> It appears that foot drums developed in the mountainous area along the southern border between Arizona and New Mexico before AD 400. By AD 1000, foot drums had spread north and become an integral part of the Great Kiva Tradition. About three hundred years later, foot drums begin to appear in the Rio Grande region.[19]

On the basis of his work in the Village of the Great Kivas, Roberts explains that with greater knowledge of the use of certain devices at contemporary Acoma a better understanding of the subfloor vaults and shelves at the room sides has come to the fore.[20] The features in the prehistoric kivas were sufficiently like those used by the present day puebloans to postulate a foot drum for the former as it serves this purpose today. A very small and an outdoor version of a foot drum is the piece of wood over a hole in the ground to be noted in the Hopi Snake Dance; the deep resonance resulting from stomping on the wood as the dancers pass by makes possible contact with spirits of the other world.

Relatively thin and rectangular stones, about a foot in length, have been identified by archaeologists as stone bells. Archaeologically, most of the stone bells that have been recovered have been from the Rio Grande; as in that area in recent years, it is thought that the ancient bell was suspended and struck with a second stone. There is little or no work on these bells; the stone seems to have been chosen for its sound qualities and for its natural general shape and size. However, Lambert indicates varying degrees of workmanship in the "kiva ringing bells," as these pieces are called, from the site of Paa-ko.[21] Bells from Pajaritan kivas are larger and better worked than the Paa-ko pieces; too they are made of basalt, while the Paa-ko bell is black argillaceous limestone. Several bells from

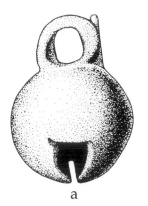
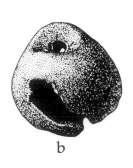

Fig. 6.18 Copper bells and copies of them. (a) A copper bell of the type traded into the Southwest from Mexico. The small projection at the upper right represents the vent necessary for pouring the liquid copper into the form to make the bell by the lost wax method (Haury and Gifford 1959, Fig. 3b). (b) A bell made of clay which resembles copper bells traded into the Southwest from Mexico (Kidder 1932, Fig. 118a). (c) Three copper bells. The right and lower left examples were found in a jar cache in the Catalina Mountains, southern Arizona.

Pecos were made of phyllite. Three of these Paako bells measured 1 foot in length, 2 inches in width, and were 1 inch in thickness.

Other bells were found over a wide area of the Southwest, particularly the copper bell (Fig. 6.18a,c). These have been excavated in a number of Hohokam sites, which is to be expected, for it is thought that they were traded in from Mexico, possibly from the west central coast. Fewer sites of the Mogollon area have revealed copper bells, perhaps even fewer in the Anasazi, with large numbers of bells in a limited number of the latter sites. They are found as far north as southwestern Colorado. The copper bell was small, measuring about ½ to 1 inch in diameter. It was made by the lost wax, or *cire perdue*, technique, a method too advanced for a people who did no other work in this material to have used it for making such bells. In 28 bells from Snaketown, the resonators were pear-shaped, with a slit at the bottom, and each had a clapper of stone or copper. A small loop of copper appeared at the top. At this site, the bells have been dated 900–1100, whereas some from Chaco Canyon and Cameron Creek (Mogollon) are dated not later than 1125. There are examples of still later bells, which tend to be larger and more numerous, and they date from 1300–1400.

Several additional sites where copper bells were found will be noted in order to indicate more relative to their distribution. They were found at Chaves Pass, Four Mile Ruin, and at several of the Sinagua sites in the Flagstaff area. At Pueblo del Arroyo, a copper bell was found in a residence room, a fragment of a large one came from a kiva, and one other complete bell

and fragments of two others were found. At Pueblo Bonito, 21 bells or fragments of them were excavated. Judd expresses the thought that bells did not reach Pueblo Bonito until after 1050. Copper bells are also found at Cameron Creek Village.

Clay bells were made in the Southwest, and apparently they were copies of those produced in copper (Fig. 6.18b). At least they were so shaped. Their distribution is rather widespread in area but limited in quantity. Some have been found in southern and southwestern Arizona, at Awatovi in northeastern Arizona, and in upper Rio Grande sites in the vicinity of Santa Fe and Albuquerque. Fewkes found a clay bell with clay pellets inside it at Awatovi.

Rasps of various sorts have remained popular in the Southwest; many of these are of perishable materials, such as a bone or wooden notched rasp used over a basket or gourd, with another stick that is run up and down the notched one (Fig. 6.19a–c). Again, it would seem probable that if the same materials had been used in the past that not too much would have survived; hence, a scarcity of this instrument is not surprising. Nonetheless, some few have endured, particularly bone rasps. They have a distribution in all three areas, having been recovered in Hohokam sites in southeastern and southern Arizona, in the Mogollon at Swarts Ruin, and for the Anasazi at least at Hawikuh and in the Rio Grande.

How these rasps were used is not known, except as may be postulated in their surviving styles and methods of playing. The rasps themselves are notched sticks or bones. The former material is rare; among others are the two wooden rasps found at Pecos and Pueblo del Arroyo. More rasps of bone and antler have been excavated, including those made of scapulae (still used by Hopis), ribs, antlers, and long bones. A deer jawbone was found that was notched and probably used as a rasp.

One of the most beautiful pieces of wood crafting is thought to be a rasp or resonator—the one mentioned from Pueblo del Arroyo. It is described by Judd as made "of mountain mahogony, dark and heavy, with a glossy sheen that could be the result of friction from another stick."[22] It has 11 skirtlike cuts between the top and bottom. Judd also reports another example comparable to this one but with only 4 notches cut into it. The latter came from a cave site south of Silver City, New Mexico. Wendorf reports two rib sections which were made into rasps; one has notches on one side only, while the other is notched on both sides. Notches are abraded from use.[23] A complete rasp from Pecos is a slightly curved, long stick with broad shallow notches on one side. It is exactly like one from San Juan Pueblo. Kidder also found what he calls "sounding rasps." These are bone, or more specifically, irregular pieces of deer scapulae and rib, which have close-set notches across them. When another bone or a stick is

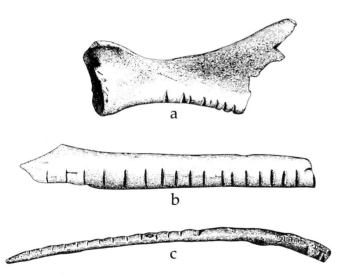

Fig. 6.19 A variety of rasping sticks. (All from Kidder 1932). (a) A sounding rasp made of a piece of deer scapula (212a). (b) A piece of deer rib was used in making this sounding rasp (212f). (c) A modern rasping stick from San Juan Pueblo. A bone was rubbed up and down the stick to make sounds. Presumably, the same was done with these prehistoric examples, using a stick or another bone (213e).

rubbed across them they produce a rattling sound.

Rattles of various and sundry sorts were one of the most common musical instruments produced in the prehistoric Southwest. Their continued popularity would seem to support this statement. Brown divides rattles or "shaken idiophones," as he calls them, into strung, pendant, and vessel forms.[24] In the first category are the rattles or tinklers made of shell, deer hooves (Fig. 6.20a), wood, and bone. Short lengths of small bones were perforated and probably strung together so that they would produce a sound as do comparable wind bells today. In like manner, short lengths of wood were fastened together at one end and served in the same capacity. Because of the wide distribution of fragments of drilled bones and pieces of wood, not necessarily in direct association, there is no way to tell how many and where these were used. From Big Juniper House came perforated mammal tibia measuring almost 5¼ inches long and with a perforation not quite in the center. There was a knotted piece of yucca cord in the hole and up through one end which had been reamed out; this, plus the common association of this type of object with kivas, might support its suggested use as a tinkler.

Conus shell was a most popular material out of which tinklers were made (see Fig. 5.12). The spire was cut away and a hole drilled close to the end for suspension. They were then strung close together, alone or with beads. These have been found in burials but in some instances it is not clear whether they were articles of personal adornment or were used intentionally as rattles. On the other hand, in the Kuaua kiva murals there is an excellent example of what appear to be conus tinklers hanging from the bottom of a white sash around the waist; Smith illustrates a comparative example of a belt decorated with cone-shaped objects from the Awatovi murals.[25] Again in the Kuaua murals other and comparable ones (see Fig. 3.29e) are represented as pendant from belts.[26] In excavations the tinklers are also found over the knees and down the legs, suggesting this additional attachment to garments. Another example is in the form of pendant objects hanging from a short kilt worn by a man painted in another Awatovi mural.[27] Smith suggests the possibility that they may be rattles of antelope hooves. As it is common for modern and recent puebloans to ornament both costumes and paraphernalia with these antelope rattles or other tinklers, it is quite likely that something served the same purpose in prehistoric times. May it be suggested that the Conus shell, which is found in such abundance, might have been one of the materials of the past so used.

The distribution of the actual Conus shells, which were seemingly used as tinklers, is greater in the Hohokam area than in the other two regions. However, they are found in enough sites to support their popularity in all three areas. Two Conus shells were found at a small Pueblo village near Point of Pines. Each had the tip removed; each also had a perforation near the tip, probably for suspension. Guernsey and Kidder report deer hoof rattles from Basketmaker caves in northeastern Arizona: "One of them consists of the horny outer coverings of two large hoofs, attached to the ends of a buckskin thong. The other is made of much smaller hoofs; these are fastened to the ends of thongs which themselves are looped over a slim pliable twig and held to it by a twining of fine cord."[28] Both are arranged so that they would rattle with any movement. Conus shells are found early and late in the Hohokam area but not too abundantly until Classic times.

The pendant rattles, or "rattling frames" as Brown calls them, are represented by two examples only, again according to him. Both were found many years ago, in Canyon de Chelly, with other ceremonial materials.

The third rattle type, the vessel, is well represented in both the prehistoric and historic Southwest. Included here would be the gourd rattle (Fig. 6.20b), perhaps the most common then as now, turtle shells (Fig. 6.20c), and rattles of clay or hide. Not only are actual rattles found, or their handles or pieces of them, but also there are representations of them as held in the hand of figures painted on pottery of all three areas, or on kiva wall murals in the Anasazi, and in pictographs. Most of these look like the gourd rattle, but of course, some are too generalized in shape to draw any final conclusions. Judd reports finding two pieces of painted gourd; both may have belonged originally to dance gourds, he suggests. "The painted design is light green with a brown border on a red (light vertical hatching) base."[29] Cosgrove reports finding fragments of gourd in nearly every cave investigated in the Upper Gila and Hueco areas; and one partially complete gourd rattle, 2 turtle

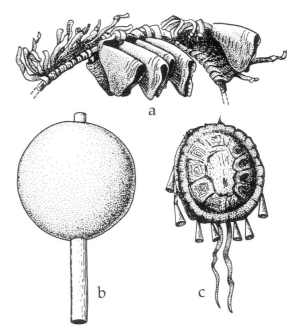

Fig. 6.20 Several types of rattles. (a) Whatever their use—as ornaments or for ceremony—these hoof rattles are secured to a wrapped stick by thongs. Shaking them resulted in a pleasing sound. From White Dog Cave (Guernsey and Kidder 1921, Plate 17j). (b) Historic gourd rattle; prehistoric examples were probably similar if not the same (Densmore 1957, pl. 4a left). (c) Turtle shell rattle, Hopi. Presumably this type of rattle was also used prehistorically (Bourke 1884, pl. XXII–11).

shells, 73 gourd rattle handles. Cosgrove further describes these pieces:

> Holes for handles were bored through the gourds at the stem and flowering ends. The holes in the turtle shell were bored vertically through the shell. The handles were cut to the desired length and smoothed by scraping or sanding, some slightly tapered, others with the part of the handle that passed through the gourd reduced in size, leaving a shoulder against which the gourd rests. Scoring on the handles shows that the gourds were held in place by whippings of cord; pitch was also used for this purpose.[30]

One handle is green, and one has spiral scoring on it, but the main parts of the rattles show no decoration except some holes drilled into several fragments—and they are not repair holes.

According to Brown the hide rattle is represented by a single example, drom Canyon Creek Ruin, and a clay rattle, also one only, from Pecos. The former was a fragment of hide about a circular frame with a bit of painted decoration remaining;[31] the rattle part of the latter is hollow and has a number of perforations in it. There are, of course, large and miniature bowls or other clay forms with hollow bottoms or handles that had small pellets put in them when they were formed; whether they were mere novelties, playthings, or rattles is a question. Turtle-shell rattles have been found widely, but sparingly, at individual sites in prehistoric times—at Vandal Cave, Upper Gila-Hueco, and Pecos, among other sites.

Bull-roarers (whirling aerophones) are fairly common today as used by native Southwesterners (Fig. 6.21a,b); they have not been found abundantly in prehistoric sites. Like some other musical instruments, they were made of a highly perishable material, wood, so their chances of survival were limited. They did exist, and some examples have been discovered in the central and eastern Anasazi. They have been reported from Pecos, the Verde Valley, and Chetro Ketl. Usually this instrument is about 6 to 12 inches in length and 1 or more inches in width. A hole is drilled in one end for the heavy cord with which to whirl the roarer. Such a simple device could well be overlooked for its real use, particularly if the end with the hole in it should be missing; this adds to the problem of so few identified bull-roarers. Kidder pictures the one from Pecos; it is a plain flat stave, one end squared off, the other tapered, and with a hole close to the end. "It may possibly have been a bull-roarer," he says.[32]

Flutes were certainly one of the most important of the wind instruments; they have been found largely in the Anasazi area, particularly in

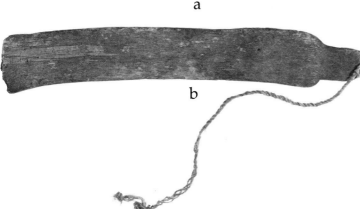

Fig. 6.21 Bull-roarers. (a) A formed and drilled piece of wood from Pecos which may have been a bull roarer (Kidder 1932, Fig. 241g). (b) Another likely bullroarer, with a string attached for swinging it.

northeastern Arizona and northwestern New Mexico. Very few flutes have been recovered within the Mogollon area; and although many representations of the flute player appear in the Hohokam, no actual flutes have been discovered there, except a cane piece from Ventana. Actually this instrument is more properly a flageolet; however, as it is constantly referred to in the literature as a flute, so too will it be labeled in most of the following discussion. A true flute is played by blowing at the side; particularly do the paintings of flute players demonstrate end blowing.

Flutes of wood seem to be more common in the Anasazi; some reed flutes have been reported in the Mogollon. Some of these have been dated by Martin as early as 150 B.C.,[33] while they seem to be no earlier than 400 A.D. in the Anasazi area. Wheat notes the presence of reed flutes in the early and late phases of Mogollon 1, but seemingly they are absent in Mogollon 3.[34]

From the Canyon Creek Ruin comes a probable reed flute, apparently unfinished. It is 7½ inches long, and has two roughly cut holes on the cane. The flutes from Pecos are made from bird bones, one from a tibia of a turkey, three from ulnae of the golden eagle, and another from the ulna of a hawk. All of the six complete flageolets have three holes toward one end and a larger hole toward the opposite end (Fig. 6.22a,b). They measure from 4¾ to 7½ inches in length. Kidder believes these instruments are late in time.[35]

Four reed flutes were found at Tularosa Cave. They were made of a section of cane, with two or three holes in each. Two examples had bands about ⅜ inch wide burned around them. Six flageolets of varying sizes were found by Pepper at Pueblo Bonito. One had quite a curve in it, and another had an attractive design of steps, circles, and encircling lines painted over most of its length. Still another flute, from a different room, is very interesting as it is square throughout most of its length and is decorated with diamonds.[36]

In an article on "Basketmaker Flutes from the Prayer Rock District, Arizona," Morris describes several of these instruments.

The instruments are long, uniformly constructed tubes. The length of the four complete specimens varies between 68.5 and 74.1 cm., and the outside diameter between 2.4 and 2.6 cm. The exterior surfaces of the barrels are highly polished. The hollowing out of the cylindrical bore reflects extremely skillful manufacturing techniques.... The interiors are smooth and even, and must represent some closely controlled process of drilling. This would have been facilitated by the presence of a large corky pith in elder wood [the material of which these flutes were made].[37]

In four of these flutes there are two sets of three holes each, and they are spaced quite the same in each of the instruments (Fig. 6.22c). These and "other well-defined specifications" led Morris to conclude that here are indications of "a precise recognition of desired notes and an ideal scale on the part of the manufacturers." Morris had a musician play the flutes and make a tonal analysis. "The sounds were not unlike those produced on modern flutes and had considerably more richness and depth than many of those available in ethnographic recordings."[38] Bird feathers were tied to the ends of two of

these flutes in such a manner that when the player blew, his breath ruffled them. There are many other flutes from the Anasazi similar to these, differing only in small variations of size, number of holes, and decoration, and in the wood of which they were made. This type of Basketmaker flute also persists into the Pueblo III Period, and continues on into historic times.

The flute player's widespread distribution would testify to an equally wide occurrence of the instrument itself. Some of the paintings of flute players are much later in time; this, plus the prominence of the instrument among historic Southwest Indians, would indicate a later prehistoric survival of the flute. Perhaps it existed throughout most of the prehistoric period, in addition to Pueblo III. This, if true, would make it one of the longest-lived musical instruments in this area.

Whistles have also been found in Southwestern archaeological sites in considerable abundance. At Pueblo Bonito and Hawikuh, fragments of comparable bone whistles were recovered. Judd says of the Bonitian examples that "They belong to a class generally described as 'birdcalls,' and vary in length from 2⁵/₁₆ to 3⅛ inches. Each is broken at its vent, cut through one wall at approximately one-half the original length. Immediately beneath the vent on two specimens lesser holes were drilled laterally through both walls as though to support the diaphragm. Three of the five were made from the ulnae of the golden eagle, one from the femur of a bobcat. The fifth fragment is an unidentified mammal bone."[39] These whistles are not unlike some used historically by the Hopi Indians. Morris reports a "bird call" from the Village of the Great Kivas; it is a bone tube about 3 inches long and has one drilled hole about midpoint on one side. Otherwise it is a perfectly plain piece of bone. Two comparable bone whistles were found in a pueblo in west central Arizona; apparently, these were made of the bones of small mammals. Bird bones were the materials of two more whistles from Bear Ruin, both very similar to the above. Twenty bone whistles were found at Pecos;[40] they ranged in length from 1 inch to at least 4½ inches (Fig. 6.23a–e). A single hole appears in each, close to the middle of the piece. Three whistles were found in caves of the Upper Gila, each with a single hole. These are longer than the Pecos examples, one of them being 5 inches in length.

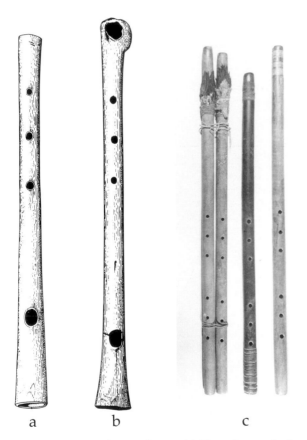

Fig. 6.22 Flageolets or flutes. (a) Flageolet made from the ulna of a golden eagle. From Pecos (Kidder 1932, Fig. 210d). (b) Another flageolet made from the same material as *a*, from Pecos. Both *a* and *b* have three stops near one end and a single larger one at the opposite end (ibid., Fig. 207g). (c) Four flutes from Prayer Rock District. Note two sets of three holes each, and a bit of decoration on the two flutes to the right (by Christy Turner).

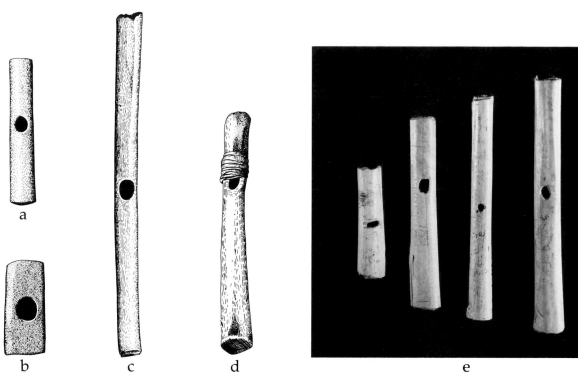

Fig. 6.23 Bone whistles, (a,b, and c from Kidder 1932). (a) A bird bone whistle with a single hole near the middle (211b). (b) A much shorter bone whistle (211d). (c) Fairly long, this bone whistle has the hole close to the center, as was the more common practice (211e). (d) Bone whistle, 4½" long, from White Dog Cave. Note the single hole closer to one end (Guernsey and Kidder 1921, pl. 42i). (e) Four bone whistles, showing variety in size and placement of the single hole. All of these are from Kinishba.

Kidder and Guernsey report finding whistles made of reeds. They were 4 to 4¾ inches long, with a single stop burned into one side.[41] The shaft of one of these was decorated with burned-in bands and longitudinal bands of scroll-like themes created in burned-in dots. They also reported bird-bone whistles that were hollow and had single stops.

Morris reports that there were neither bone whistles nor flageolets in La Plata District sites.[42] From the Prayer Rock District, Elizabeth Morris reports long thin bird bone tubes with a small hole drilled close to one end, probably whistles.[43] Each of two hollow bone tubes found at Tuzigoot had a hole drilled about one-third of the way from one end; it is thought that these were whistles. From the Flagstaff area came a long and a short bone whistle each with a single hole. McGregor notes that "Such whistles are widely distributed throughout the pueblo Culture of the Plateau area of northern Arizona and New Mexico, and so may well have been local, and not introduced from outside cultures."[44]

In the Upper Gila and Hueco areas musical instruments were absent except for what appear to be three reed whistles[45] and several flutes.[46] Holes were cut into two examples, one-half inch from the end of one and about the middle of the other. In the third example a hole was burned 1½ inches above the reed joint. Lengths of the three whistles are 3⅝, 4¾, and 5 inches.

About whistles in the Mogollon, Wheat says that "Bone whistles have a northern distribution. One specimen from Crooked Ridge Village may have been a whistle; if so, this would place a single occurrence in Mogollon 1. Definite whistles are reported only from Forestdale during Mogollon 3 and probably represent an intrusive northern trait."[47]

One of the most amazing of prehistoric musical instruments was the large conch shell trumpet (Fig. 6.24). As is true of other shell objects, this is found in the Hohokam area, close to the source of supply of the material used, but finds of trumpets were also made in the Anasazi. Pepper thought that the Pueblo Bonitians had obtained the Strombus galeatus shell, which they used in some of their trumpets, from the Pacific Coast. Further, he says, "In making this trumpet, the upper end of the columnella was ground off to form a mouthpiece. About 8 cms. of the lid of the shell was

Fig. 6.24 Although few in number, conch shell trumpets have been found in several widely distributed sites in the Southwest. The small photograph demonstrates the manner in which this trumpet was probably played by prehistoric people.

cut away and two holes were drilled near the edge of the remaining portion. These holes were no doubt used for the attachment of a cord by means of which the trumpet was carried."[48] Haury dates the large shell trumpets in the north as Pueblo III and IV, while the only datable one found at Snaketown would be earlier for it was associated with a Sacaton cremation (900–1100).[49] A trumpet was found at Jackrabbit Ruin, a Desert Hohokam site. In addition to the two larger trumpets found at Pueblo Bonito and the one at Snaketown, more were discovered in at least three other sites in

northern Arizona, while no less than six other sites revealed additional trumpets in southern Arizona.

Judd describes another trumpet from Pueblo Bonito made of a different species, Phyllonotus nitidus Broderip. Like the aforementioned, its spire had been ground off, and the outer lip of the shell was drilled, perhaps as in the above example, for a suspension cord.[50] Two other fragments of the same type of shell were found at this pueblo, one of them with bits of pitch still adhering to the lip portion. Pepper found five additional trumpets at this same site, all made from Murex shell, and, along with them, fragments of others. Further examples from the Hohokam include: Two trumpets of Strombus galeatus found at Los Muertos; one of these was a 6½ inch shell. A third smaller shell, a 3 inch Melongena patual, was difficult to blow and it gave a high pitched sound. At Las Acequias, larger examples of this last shell were used for making trumpets, two of which were recovered.

In summary of musical instruments it would seem that whistles, flutes, and simple tinklers appeared first, possibly before 600. Within the next 400 years, rattles were developed, and possibly the foot drum. Shortly after 1000 the conch shell trumpet put in its appearance, as did the Conus tinkler. Copper and clay bells and rasps appeared about the same time. Possibly the spread of some of these instruments started in the years before 1300; certainly after this date many musical instruments spread throughout the Southwest.

Palettes

"Palettes show the gradual rise, the flowering, and the decline of the Hohokam Culture more graphically than any of the other traits of long duration." In these words Haury indicates the importance of this most unusual expression.[51] Not only is the palette distinctive of the Hohokam but also it seems to have been of native growth and development, for there is no indication that it came out of Mexico. It was used from the Vahki Phase through the Sedentary Period at Snaketown (Fig. 6.25).

A pallete is a rectangular stone device, usually with raised borders, which was apparently employed for the grinding of paint. Bits of red, white, or yellow paint have been found on the grinding surfaces of many of these pieces;

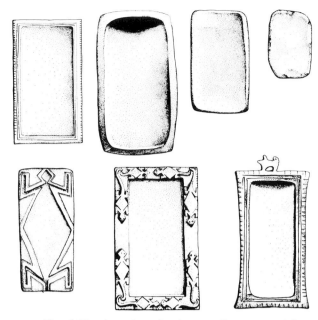

Fig. 6.25 A series of palettes, illustrating different styles from the simplest and undecorated to the most elaborately carved pieces (Gladwin et al. 1937, pls. XCVII a,b,c; CIa; CII c,d).

therefore its use can hardly be doubted. As the palette was found most frequently in cremations at Snaketown, several questions may be asked: Was the paint prepared for the decoration of the body of the deceased before cremation occurred? Or was the palette one its owner had used in his lifetime? Certainly ceremonial painting of the body is of great antiquity in the Southwest.

Materials used in the manufacture of the palette are of interest. The earlier pieces and some later ones, too, were of a hard, crystalline rock, while a later change to a softer schistose material occurred and became important for the production of the finest palettes. Interestingly, the shift to the softer stone inspired the Hohokam artists to do more refined and more decorative work. It is likely, too, that this change was responsible for the thinner palette as well. A high peak in all these traits was reached and persisted throughout the Santa Cruz Phase, to degenerate during the Sedentary Period, and to be virtually nonimportant in the Classic Period.

A simple, thick, flat or nearly flat-surfaced stone without any borders, and oval or rectangular in form, was the original style of the palette (Fig. 6.26). This type appeared in the Vahki Phase and remained through the Sedentary. However, in the Snaketown Phase, borders appeared on the sides or sides and ends of an otherwise still plain piece. Decoration thus seems to have been inspired by the use of both the border and softer stone. The bordered style remained popular to the end of the production of the palette. One other change occurred in shape: during the Sedentary Period, some of these pieces became stubbier in proportions, displacing the longer, thinner rectangular style.

As was true of the basic form changes with the utilization of the softer material, so too with

Fig. 6.26 A series of palettes which shows the same general sequence as in Fig. 6.25. *From top left* are the very early simple side-ridged style, to those with plain or simply engraved border, to styles with figures at the end and the "sandwich man" type. *Second row*, the palette cut in the form of an animal, and then borders ornamented with relief figures or elaborate incising, and last, back to simpler incising or no work on borders.

decoration. Palettes in the harder stone were undecorated as noted; with the use of schistose material, decoration started and developed to fine artistry. Incising, sculpturing, and painting were the techniques used; certainly the first two were, and possibly the last was, developed to very high points. Several of these decorative methods were sometimes combined to make a single palette an exceptional work of art.

In producing palettes of the Pioneer Period the Hohokam artist seemed to have been pre-occupied with problems of form and finish. Although basically rectangular in form, there are longer and shorter pieces; there are thicker and thinner examples; and borders may be lacking, or just barely indicated and blended, or they may be deep, or they were rounded or flat and definitive, particularly on the inner side in the last quality. By the Santa Cruz Phase, the palette was thin and well made, borders were flat and decorated in one of several styles. Sides of palettes were straight or gently curved. Some were grooved, with one to several lines paralleling both sides and ends; some had shorter, oblique, zigzag, or scroll incisions between the long lines; or they had edge notching, or some other simple additions. Life forms were sometimes carved in low relief along the top of the entire border. There were, sometimes, additions to the first style in the form of sculptured figures at one or both ends, in bas relief, or nearly full round; subjects for the added decoration might include birds, snakes, or mammals, or frequently, a bird-snake combination. Perhaps the artistic peak was reached in instances where the entire palette was modeled in life forms, such as a human, horned toad, or lizard, the figure either completely enclosing the rectangular palette proper or with head projecting from one end, feet from the other. In one example of the latter, a human looks like a "sandwich man." Less often the creature's form, such as a lizard, is cut into the rectangle of schist, the back forming the grinding surface. Whether in conventional or more realistic life forms, or in geometric designs, the workmanship is usually precise, careful, vigorous, and with some detail.

In late Santa Cruz and into Sacaton times, evidences of decline begin to appear in workmanship on palettes. First, there is less decoration, or it is stilted and more generalized. Then form became more irregular; some pieces were thicker and unfinished on the under side; borders became low and broad with shallow incised patterns. Notches and grooves disappeared; forms became shorter in proportion to width. All in all, the palette had lost its vigor and beauty.

This description and sequence of events in the development of palettes is based on the first excavation of Snaketown. The second excavation revealed additional examples of these paint grinders. One has a grooved border with notched edges, the entire rectangle of the palette resting on the back of a well-sculptured horned toad. Another has a slight concavity in the sides of its outline, the raised border has multiple and parallel grooves all the way around, and there are two charming curled-tailed quadrupeds adorning each end. A third palette is diamond shaped, has a grooved and notched border, and a carved design jutting out from each of its four sides.[52]

Although not as abundant as the examples from Snaketown, palettes have been excavated at other Hohokam sites. Several were found in Los Muertos area. From Los Hornos came three with bevelled edges and with scratched geometric designs on the raised borders; the designs indicate that the pieces belonged to the Sacaton Phase. From Los Muertos proper were two more with raised borders, one complete palette with an incised design, and fourteen pieces of others, one of which has a notched border. Interestingly there were also several pieces of miniature palettes at this site. An almost square palette, with rather poor scratched decoration, was found at Los Guanacos; it is thought to be Sedentary in time, as are Los Hornos examples. The belief that palettes became unimportant in Classic times is borne out by the scarcity of this item at Los Muertos and Las Acequias.

At Ventana there were no palettes comparable with those from Snaketown. Rather there is a thin schist slab without a border or decoration. In fact, it is not even rectangular in form, for it is narrow at one end and wider at the opposite end. However, it bears paint stains. It does show further variety in form of this important item of the Hohokam culture. From another Desert Hohokam site, Valshni Village, came quite a different palette in the form of a frog effigy.

At the eastern Hohokam site, Roosevelt 9:6, several palettes were unearthed; they were in cremations as were many from Snaketown.[53]

They ranged in size from 2 inches by 3½ inches to 4 by 8 inches, and were about ¼ inch thick. Borders were decorated with incised lines, including parallel lines, zigzags, filled triangles, frets, scrolls, and a few other geometrics.

Palettes are found in both the Mogollon and the Anasazi areas, but they did not enjoy the high development noted at Snaketown. In fact, they are, perhaps, more paint dishes than palettes, or even, something halfway between. For example, at Pueblo Bonito there is a palettelike item that has a depression in the center. Some others, however, are really palettes. A fairly plain one of sandstone was excavated in the pit house level at Kiatuthlanna, and in its simplicity it illustrates a general type not unusual in other sites (Fig. 6.27). "The upper surface of this stone has a shallow concavity, there are small grooves around the corners, and there is a groove completely encircling it around the sides, or perhaps better the edges."[54] The paint grinders from Pecos are crude, and most of them are of "flat, water-worn pebbles of sandstone and silicious schist into the upper surfaces of which have been worked depressions of round, oval, or rectangular forms."[55]

At Pueblo Bonito it seems that any flat stone surface available was used for grinding paint—jar covers, slabs to fit into doorways, a sandal-shaped stone—but seemingly no true palettes were found here.

From Mogollon sites in southwestern New Mexico have been recovered several palettes. Of two of these, one was made from a fine grained stone, the second from schist. Both have incised borders and medial grooves about the edges. Slate palettes have been reported from Three Circle and Mimbres phases, the latter showing strong Hohokam influences. Wheat summarizes the Mogollon style in general as "small flat stone slabs, sometimes with a shallow depression in one face...."[56]

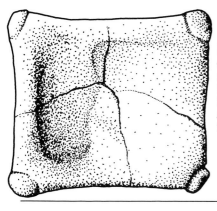

Fig. 6.27 A paint dish or palette. A piece of sandstone made into a bowl or paint palette, from the pithouse level at Kiatuthlanna (Roberts 1931, pl. 35c).

In summary of palettes, it can be said that this was a well-developed complex in the Hohokam area, but the piece was not as highly expressed among the Anasazi and Mogollon peoples. The evolution of the palette is so complete in the first area that there seems little doubt in the minds of some that it evolved there, at the hands of the Hohokam people. Certainly painting of the body was a common practice in pre-Columbian times in the Southwest as it has been historically; not only are there the actual palettes or small mortars, all with paint stains within them in many instances, but also there are balls or wads of the paint itself found in many Southwestern ruins. Pictographs reveal body and facial painting. This subject, as others, may be left with a question or two: Was body and facial painting strictly ceremonial? Or was it also done on a day-to-day basis? Did young and old follow this practice, priests and others as well?

Stone Bowls

Stone dishes are found widely throughout the Southwest. They are either plain or ornamented, the latter including decoration painted on, incising, or carving in high or low relief. Plain bowls are more widely distributed and more common in the north, while the carved or incised pieces are found largely in the Hohokam area with some few in the Mogollon. What the use of these pieces was is impossible to determine in many instances; possibly some were for everyday utility purposes such as mixing or holding some ordinary substances, while others may have had some ceremonial usage such as for paint grinding or for holding special materials. One author refers to them as medicine cups or incense burners. It is quite likely that they were used as mortars in some areas, at some times; however, they are better formed and often of better material than was the mortar, and frequently the latter is not decorated. However, in some of the archaeological literature, these pieces may be interchangeably referred to as mortars and stone bowls, while in other references the latter term is used exclusively. A true mortar has a conical interior working area while the stone bowl has a flatter or slightly rounded interior surface for grinding.

At the site of Kiatuthlanna there were found a number of stone bowls, ranging in workmanship from very crude to finely shaped and finished pieces. All belonged to the pithouses at this village. They were pecked and ground, with several stones represented, including lava, gray sandstone, and granitic boulders. In La Plata, "stone mortars and bowls were used to some extent during all periods, but they were much more plentiful during Basket Maker III than at any other time."[57] Here they were made of sandstone, and in rough shapes; however, one piece, a very rounded form, has its surfaces ground smooth. Paint was found in another bowl from La Plata, a not uncommon situation in other areas as well. From Nantack Village come both well-made and not so well-made stone bowls; tuff is the major material used in forming the bowls, whose sides are more or less rounded. One bowl from Nantack is hemispherical, with a flat base; it is painted with vertical bands in black, red, and yellow, leaving the natural tone of the stone in the areas between the colors.

Other examples from this area and about Pueblo II in time, include a bowl made of tuff and several pieces of them made of pumice. The tuff example is 4⅛ inches in diameter and about 3⅛ inches high; it is rounded in form and rough over the entire exterior. There is no decoration. At Tuzigoot were found 21 small mortars, or bowls, of a fine basalt or rhyolite, or black or red pumice, which varied in size from 1¼ to 3¼ inches in diameter, and about 1 inch high. Most of them are plain but several are of zoomorphic form.

From the Mogollon area come both plain and decorated stone dishes. Mogollon Village yielded rounded- and flat-bottomed and rounded- or straight-sided bowls made of andesite, tuff, or sandstone. They are rather large, from 4 to 8 inches in diameter. Both zoomorphic and painted decoration are found in these pieces. All belong to the San Francisco and Three Circle phases. Wheat reports that in the Mogollon, in general, stone dishes are made of more durable materials than are mortars but have the same use, that possibly the dishes are more carefully finished, and that they are better formed.[58] Further, he says that they occur throughout the Mogollon at one time or another, at one place or another, but that they tend to be late in the north and are more common in the south of the overall Mogollon area. He says, too, that it is possible that they originated in the south and moved to the north.

In the far southwest of the Mogollon, specifically in the San Simon Valley and Cave Creek, Sayles found a variety of stone dishes that run

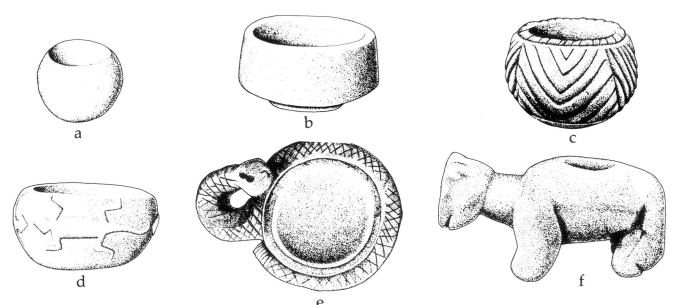

Fig. 6.28 A sequence of Hohokam stone bowl carving, from simple to complex (all examples from Gladwin et al. 1937, plate numbers only given). (a) The simplest of stone bowls, this rounded example is from the Snaketown Phase (LVId). (b) Also Snaketown Phase in time, this bowl has a ringlike pedestal or foot (LVIa). Both *a* and *b* are highly polished. (c) An incised ring at the rim and four sets of chevrons on the sides decorate this Santa Cruz Phase bowl (LVIIa). (d) Low relief figures of lizards pleasingly ornament this bowl, another Santa Cruz example (LXXa). (e) A small rhyolite dish, surrounded by a carved rattlesnake. The head is in full relief while scales and rattles are incisions on the rounded body. Sedentary Period (LXVb). (f) Fully modeled figure of an animal, with the bowl depression carved into its back. Of fine lava stone it is carved with ears in slight relief, with the mouth slightly open and the tongue showing, and with incised eyes and nostril (LXIId).

Fig. 6.29 Four rather different bowls. Two are more familiar, one with two snakes' heads (*top left*), and the other with a head and rattles, the reptile's body surrounding the bowl (*top right*). In the other two pieces full round animals are carved with bowls in their backs; one (*on the left*) appears a bit pugnacious, the other, crude in carving, is barely an animal.

the gamut from crude and coarse pieces made with little work on rough natural pebbles other than the basin itself, to several barrel-shaped, pleasingly formed bowls.[59] Some of these are better formed, are deeper or more shallow, and have rounded or flat bottoms and rounded or straight sides, and they are incised or carved. One incised piece has zigzags at the rim; another has nested chevrons, alternating with points up or down, on the upper part of sides; and a third bowl has zigzags just below the rim and more elaborate ones just below this. Still another bowl has three frogs carved in relief on the sides of a deep-basined piece. At Forestdale, a round-bottomed, flat-sided, limestone bowl was undecorated. From this area also came a very symmetrical quartzite pebble bowl. A stone bowl from Point of Pines village is hemispherical and flat-based. It has vertical stripes in red, yellow,

and black.[60] Fragments of a carved stone bowl came from the Jornada Branch area.

Unquestionably, the Hohokam area was the center of the highest development of stone bowls, and Snaketown reveals a fine sequence of this work (Figs. 6.28, 6.29, 6.30). In the second excavation of Snaketown, Haury located a cache of 50 of these vessels, all broken. Among others were beautifully high relief, carved figures clinging to the sides of the bowl, one a lizard, another a toad, while a dog's figure formed the bowl in a third example, and a full-round figure of a man (possibly another opposite him) held another bowl between his hands.

In other instances, there were a great many elaborately decorated bowls. For example, of 83 pieces of the Colonial Period, the majority were decorated, most of them in carving. Life themes were very prominent in the Hohokam area in

Fig. 6.30 A variety of stone bowls showing different styles of carving and finishing. In the upper row are plain bowls, while the bottom row illustrates incising of the exterior, using simple geometric designs. Bas–relief carving of life forms is represented on the walls of vessels in the second row from the bottom. Almost full round carving appears on the three bowls in the second from the top row.

general, with both realistic and conventional treatment to be noted. A wide variety of materials was used here also, including, among others, rhyolite, steatite, sandstone, lava, quartzite, and granite. Shape ran the gamut from very rough to beautifully finished, from straight-sided and flat-bottomed to hemispherical; they were decorated with incised or carved figures on the sides or the entire dish was formed of an animal or bird, with a small depression on the back to serve as the bowl. In decoration, the craftsmanship varied from extremely rude and barely delineated generalized figures to creatures which could be identified as to species. Details varied too, from none or few to the feathers of birds or markings of the rattlesnake.

Stone dishes are found in every phase at Snaketown, from the four divisions of the Pioneer Period on through the entire develop-

ment of this culture. In the earliest pieces of the Pioneer at Snaketown, softer stones were used, but by the Snaketown Phase, harder material was employed; too, the workmanship was better by this later phase. There were both rounded and flat-bottomed pieces, both straight and round-sided bowls during the Pioneer Period. A few pieces have a slightly overhanging rim. Incised decoration was used in this early period: one fragment had steps and line patterns, perhaps allover in the original, and filled with paint; a second had four zigzags arranged in horizontal, parallel rows; and over the entire side wall of a third was cross-hatching, which was repeated in a single row on the gently out-sloping rim of the piece. One vessel in both the Sweetwater and the Snaketown Phases had carved decoration. In both instances it was bas-relief, in fairly naturalistic style. Two plain dippers or bowls with handles attached were produced in the Snake-town Phase, one of highly polished diorite and the second of a fine schist.

During the Colonial Period, a great deal of decorative work appears in the form of stone bowls. Of the 83 aforementioned bowls dated in this period, only 7 belonged to the Gila Butte Phase, the rest apparently made in the Santa Cruz Phase. About 66 percent of the bowls were carved; fewer than 1 percent were incised, and the remainder were undecorated. Several innovations occurred at this time, one in particular being the forming of the base as an animal or bird and putting a small circular hole in the back for the bowl depression. Among these were a bearlike creature, a swimming duck figure, and a form appearing to be a mountain sheep. Details such as eyes, nostrils, mouth, hooves, and so on are incised. And there is much revealing detail in many of these figures. Then there are bowls with life forms encircling them about the vessel side; these may be very beautifully done or crudely executed. A few Santa Cruz Phase bowls are poorly formed, with conventionalized life forms simply presented. One of these shows a frog with the head, tail, and legs of the creature more suggested than otherwise and with the sides of the vessel serving as the body; this bowl is done in low relief. Also conventionalized but of better craftsmanship is a bowl decorated with two rattlesnakes, their heads crossed on one side, their tails on the opposite side. Tails and heads are carved in full round, while the main parts of the bodies are represented by incised markings around the vessels. Thus, in this Colonial Period, the carving of stone dishes varies considerably, from incising and flat relief to full round, from conventional to realistic, from crude to refined. Thus, the peak was reached in this period, with some of the finest stone carvings of all Hohokam times executed during these years on stone bowls.

Deterioration in stone bowl workmanship seems to have started fairly early in the Sacaton Phase, and by the middle of this period very little in the way of carving appeared on bowls; incising was more important and apparently it replaced the more elaborate form of decoration. Great conventionalization contributed to the seeming decadence of this art. Steatite is the chief material used. There are plain stone vessels in this last Hohokam period, with both crude and fine examples of craftsmanship.

Straight-sided forms seem to predominate, but some are well finished. Incising is sometimes deeper and it is often all over the side of the vessel. Some vessels are carved in the desired life form, a horned toad, a bird, or some other creature, so conventionalized as to be unidentifiable. These are done in more shallow forms than are the earlier pieces, and this along with the high conventionalization seems to rob them of the warm realism found in pieces created in earlier years.

In summary of stone bowls, it must be noted first that, at least in the Hohokam area, they represent a high artistic expression. Even plain pieces throughout the Southwest are attractive in their smooth lines, symmetry, and fine craftsmanship in hard stones. Plain dishes are found all over the Southwest; decorated ones are limited largely to painting in the Anasazi, a little carving in the Mogollon, and a great deal of carving and incising in the Hohokam. Certainly the peak of attainment was reached in the Hohokam area, wherein some of the highest artistry of the Southwest is expressed. Actually there was little local variation in shapes until the life form styles were found, for the majority of stone bowls are simple, rounded, fairly deep dishes. One of the appealing parts of these pieces is the tremendous variety of materials used, some employing local stones and some importing them from other areas. Certainly these bowls reflect the abilities of the native Southwesterners in handling a variety of materials, several methods of workmanship, and an imaginative quality in decoration.

Pipes

Pipes were made throughout the Southwest but were more limited in some areas than in others. In the Hohokam they are very rare, while in the Anasazi they tend to be rather common, and they are quite widely found in the Mogollon. It is likely that certain ceremonial usage could be correlated with this distribution, for in many cases the pipe seems to have been basically for religious purposes; however, it is also probable that it had less religious significance in other instances. Although a "cloud blower" was fundamentally religious among the Hopi Indians in late historic times, certain individuals have been known to sit about the kiva after the ritual to smoke the pipe in a strictly social manner. For the latter reason, it is included herein. Strictly speaking, the "cloud blower" has a straight or nearly straight form, while other pipes might be of elbow type, with a bowl upright to the stem (Figs. 6.31, 6.32). In the straight or nearly straight style, "smoke was blown through the stem and out the bit end rather than drawn into the mouth of the smoker and then expelled."[61]

The prehistoric Southwestern pipe was made of clay or stone, with a fairly wide variety of the latter used in various parts of the three areas. The clay used was generally ordinary pottery clay, often with the temper omitted, but sometimes pipes were made of a finer material. They were finished in a rough manner, or were carefully smoothed, or highly polished. Some were slipped. Clay pipes were baked or unbaked. Stone pipes were made of a variety of materials, from coarse lavas to fine-grained stones. They were left in a rough stage or were highly polished. Rarely pipes were decorated with color.

No pipes are recorded for Snaketown, but one whole pipe and fragments of three others came from Ventana Cave.[62] In these finds it is indicated that pipe smoking goes back to very early times, before sedentary farmers came into the area. All examples are of tubular forms; the one whole pipe is exceptional in that it is very large, almost 7¼ inches long, and because it has a bowl at each end. It is made of sandstone, and seems to be very late prehistoric in time. An

ultra-violet light examination revealed a simple design on the pipe, but it had been absorbed by the porous stone and was not visible to the naked eye. Despite the general lack of pipes in the Hohokam area, tobacco-filled cane tubes, like cigarettes, have been found.

Pipes are not uncommon in the Mogollon area. Both the bowl type, which necessitated a stem, and the combined bowl-stem style in one piece were found. Wheat says that the tubular style is found in most central sites;[63] although they vary in size, they were made to use with a bone or wooden stem. Three styles are found; one is a short, ovoid or cylindrical form and is found early and survives into late times; a second is a longer ovoid or cylindrical style and appears a little later in time in the southwestern part of the area; the latter spreads and survives into fairly late times. The third pipe of the Mogollon is an elongate, truncate, and conical form and is widespread from earliest times but does not last to the end of the Mogollon as do the other two styles.

A few examples of Mogollon styles will further define this pipe. In the Forestdale area, Haury reports the presence of the short clay pipe; this is of the "cloud blower" type used by the Anasazi. It is indicated that this pipe, made of stone and found in eastern sites of the area, is a strong characteristic of the Mogollon.[64] Three examples of the latter are of vesicular lava; one is

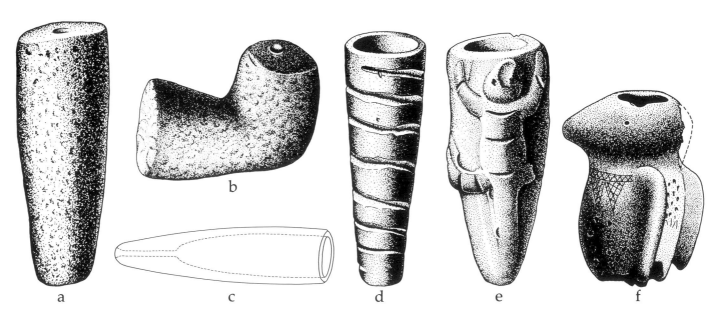

Fig. 6.31 Stone and clay pipes (all examples are from Kidder 1932). (a) A roughed out beginning of a tubular pipe (Fig. 60a). (b) An unfinished elbow pipe of stone (Fig. 61a). (c) This sketch shows the common proportions of bowl and smoke tube in clay pipes (Fig. 136 and based on pipes from Pecos). (d) An interesting decoration on a pipe (Fig. 150b). (e) Another interestingly decorated pipe, with a figure (lizard?) carved on its side (Fig. 150e). (f) An unusual pipe (referred to as an aberrant type) in the form of a bird (Fig. 151d).

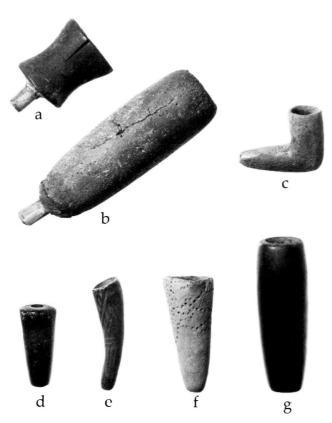

Fig. 6.32   A group of pipes which illustrate several features of this item. Two (a and b) have stems remaining; (c) is an elbow pipe; (e) is slightly decorated. Several materials are represented: lava, *b*; steatite, *d*; hardwood, *a*; and clay, *f*.

just under 2¾ inches in length, and is a very little smaller at one end than at the other. At Harris Village, in southwestern New Mexico, were found both the style that required a stem and the one with a built-in stem, the former of a slipped and highly polished red ware material, and the second of brown clay and unslipped. A third plain, tubular, painted pipe of lava was also found at this site. From both the Upper Gila and the Hueco areas, Cosgrove recovered tubular pipes, all but one of stone and the exception of black walnut. The stone styles are of basalt, tuff, a fine-grained sandstone, or a red clay called halloysite. The stone pieces ranged from 2⅛ to 2⅞ inches in length, while the wooden example was 7½ inches long. Haury found a stone pipe about the same length as the last, also in the Mogollon. The latter example had a tubular bone stem set in pitch at the small end. The sandstone example was painted all over with yellow and had added longitudinal panels of red, green, and black. The tuff example had an

encircling channel cut about midway of the smoothed sides.

In the Anasazi, pipes are found which are made of varied materials, sizes, and forms; however, the short type prevails. From Basketmaker sites come pipes of wood, stone, and clay. Two which are made of the first material measure about 2½ inches in length and 1⅛ inches in diameter; both have tubular bone stems fastened in pitch. Kidder and Guernsey found in sites of the same age both stone and clay pipes.[65] Of stone are the following: one of red sandstone has squat, thick walls and a wooden mouthpiece. Two others, of limestone, have polished outer surfaces. Apparently these stone pipes were first roughed out with a pecking tool, then finished by polishing, as in the last example. A clay pipe was also found in these northeastern early sites; it has a rough, bumpy surface and is slightly longer and thinner in proportions than are the stone pieces. Gum remained in several of these pipes, indicating the placement of a stem in such examples.

From a Basketmaker III site near Durango, Colorado, came a complete pipe and part of a second one, both made of well-polished steatite. The complete pipe is just a shade more than 1¾ inches long; its bore was made by drilling, which is indicated by concentric striations on the interior. Two pottery pipes were found at this same site; one has a very outflaring end and is decorated with three faint encircling lines.[66]

In a late kiva at Pueblo del Arroyo, in the windblown sand and rubble, was found a clay pipe fragment; it has an unusual punctate design in the form of zigzags on its surface. An inch-long piece of a second pipe was also found at this ruin; it is made of a piece of steatite and is polished.

Both stone and clay pipes were found at Pueblo Bonito.[67] Both a tubular type and one with a bowl slightly at right angles to the stem were found; some are short while others are long. Many are decorated. One, a short but broken tube, is of clay, and it has a punctate band completely encircling the larger end. Three examples with the larger bowl slightly bent up from the stem are undecorated; a fourth of this same type combines alternated encircling bands of black stripes with horizontal black stripes in between. Another of these "cloud blowers" is 1⅝ inches across the bowl, which is wider than usual. A clay elbow pipe, which looks very modern, came from a kiva; it was slipped with white paint, then had a black design painted on it, with chevrons at the bowl rim, and wide bands and triangles on the stem. A second clay example of the elbow style has the same white slip over the entire pipe, with a black, undulating snake painted the length of the stem. A third example of this same style and material is decorated with parallel zigzags the length of the stem and a band enclosing the design at each end. Some stone pipes from Pueblo Bonito are also interesting; they range from a yellow claystone of simple, slightly elongate (1 11/16 inches long) cone shape, to a steatite elbow style, with quite a high bowl. A third stone pipe, of travertine, has an unusual disc-like collar about the top of the bowl.

Inasmuch as the pipes at Pueblo Bonito were found in various places, it might be reiterated that they may have been used for purposes in addition to ceremonial cloud blowing. Actually, they were found in kivas, in residence and store rooms, and in rubbish beyond these structures.

From Pecos came a large number of pipes, including everything from a roughed-out tubular pipe to pieces carved with life forms (see Fig. 6.31). Interior construction is revealed in examples from this site. Some pieces from Pecos are incised; one is carved in a bird form, and another with a lizardlike design in relief. One example of an elbow-type pipe was excavated here also. Many are decorated with incised designs.

In summary of pipes, it can be said that they were varied in materials, form, and decoration. The majority are small and cone-shaped, or slightly so, but there is variation into up-tilted and elbow styles. The majority are plain, but some are decorated with painting, a few with punctate, incised, or cut designs. Many have

stems of wood or bone, although many do not. The most common interior construction is a narrow bore for the greater length, with a wider area reamed out for the bowl, this most generally in the conical pipe. Pipes were made throughout the prehistoric period and have survived into the present. There are sites where no pipes have been found, and there are areas, such as the Hohokam, where, seemingly, they were not common. The importance of pipes is indicated in their longevity and in their wide distribution.

In the foregoing pages a number of the major miscellaneous crafts have been discussed. Although some were largely regional, they are of great importance relative to the complete story of prehistoric Southwestern craft arts; excellent examples of this include Hohokam stone palettes and their beautifully carved stone bowls. Everyday pieces in the way of tools, weapons, and implements, although less significant decoratively, nonetheless perpetuated such basics in art as symmetry, repetition, rhythm, and superior craftsmanship, as is often and well exemplified in points, axes, and many lesser pieces. Also, decoration was often applied in surprising spots, such as on an arrow shaft, a flute, an awl, among others of these crafts.

These miscellaneous crafts, as do the major crafts, reflect that ever-present trait in humans, the great desire to express an innate artistic feeling. This is reflected in everything from the beautiful symmetry in form of an arrow point to the delicacy of carving of a lizard on a stone bowl.

Chapter 7

Prehistoric Legacy

THERE DEVELOPED in the Southwestern portion of the United States a culture which had certain internal similarities and differences. Within this area there developed a slow, progressive series of stages from hunting-gathering through the late stone age of cultural attainment, or what might be compared to the Old World Paleolithic, into the new stone age, or Neolithic. Certain aspects of new stone age culture of the Old World are lacking in all New World cultures, such as domesticated cattle, horses, and sheep, but in the particular traits that are comparable, the Southwesterners excelled.

Early Man laid foundation stones for later developments, foundations which were substantial and sound and upon which the later occupants of the same areas built cultures of great substance. The first hunters perfected stone tools in many directions; in the process of so doing, they equipped the right hand to accomplish much more in the centuries to come. They learned to live off the land, another feat which became pertinent to survival in parts of the Southwest that were far from lush. To be sure, it is not known how much in the way of such traits was really handed down from one generation to the next, but surely a modicum of such adaptation was passed on.

Hunters, too, became wily in the ways of obtaining food from the native animal life, a trait never lost among Southwestern Indians. To this day, certain native peoples still run down a deer if they wish to use any part of the animal for religious purposes. Hunting is still practiced and the ways of the past in this area of learning have not been completely lost. Undoubtedly there were many additional lessons passed on by the earliest hunters, such as preparing meat for food, tanning hides for various uses, and working bone for many purposes.

Then there were the food gatherers who were so vitally important to the later occupants of the Southwest. It was they who learned to follow the paths of successively ripening seeds and nuts; it was they who learned the habits of plants to the extent of their growth patterns. In the light of much of this knowledge, they were able to take advantage of the cultivation of corn when this vital plant first appeared in the Southwest. Their seed-grinding tools were adapted to the new product. It was the food gatherer, too, who seemingly did the first weaving, perhaps spurred on by necessity for containers for the small seeds which became essential to their diet, and the fact that, in transit, they had to have a lightweight and efficient device to hold the seeds. Too, they had to cook the seeds, and, in this state of limited development, what was there short of a well-woven basket into which the seeds could be put with water and hot rocks? Weaving of fur robes from skins of small animals also eventuated from necessity, for among the gatherers there were not always the large animals whose skins could be tanned as they may have been by Big Game Hunters for garments.

The inhabitants of the more easterly parts of the Southwest were almost forced to hunt the big game of this area if they were to survive. In like manner, the peoples to the northwest and west had to adapt to the more limited fare, in terms of animal size, but they had a more varied diet as they adopted vegetable foods as well.

And it was the westerners, with their skill and knowledge of plants and their ways of preparing by grinding and cooking these vegetal products, who made the transition into the new stone age.

And that transition was slow, probably painfully slow, but it was realized long before Europeans arrived in this part of the New World. In fact, they advanced, some retrogressed, and some of the latter rose again, not once but several times, and with it all, these natives left a rich inheritance which has become one of the deep roots of native American culture.

The cultures that evolved in the Southwest as permanent village-dwelling societies were knit together with common traits, yet it must be said in the same breath they evolved individual expressions which made for many local cultures within the greater one. First, some of the traits that set these peoples apart from other North American groups would include the following, among others. They built up a tight dependence on corn, beans, and squash, with religious expressions tied in with the cultivation of the fields and, quite naturally, with the worship of the sun, earth, and rain in particular, a feeling of great rapport with nature, with myths and tales related to the animals and various environmental features of the area in which they lived. Basic too were basketry, textile weaving, ceramics, and other crafts. There are some similarities here between the Southwest and some other parts of North America, but in the small intimacies of all these things, and the melding together of them, a distinctive Southwestern culture evolved. Other traits peculiar to this area can be noted in the kiva and the small ball court, in Spider Woman, Turquoise and Shell Woman, in dry farming, in the stepped-cloud pattern, and many other aspects of native expression.

As to the individual traits which were developed along local lines, these deserve a little more space in terms of looking back over them, for it was these parts of culture that were to carry on and serve as a foundation for the surviving Indians of historic years, the traits that enjoyed several millennia of evolution before European contact and that would enjoy several centuries of continued development after the arrival of the Spaniards in the Southwest in 1540. And let it not be ignored that many of the traits developed here were to touch directly upon the lives of the Anglo-Americans, who came to the Southwest in such great numbers and who became the dominant culture of this area.

Basketry surely evolved to high points in the prehistoric Southwest, in terms of variety of form, beautiful weaving, and design—particularly in the Anasazi area. Perhaps the delayed development of ceramics in the Anasazi served as a spur to this attainment, for pottery was well established from the beginning in the other two cultures, the Mogollon and Hohokam, where seemingly less was achieved in their basketry craft. Exchanges of ideas back and forth among these varied peoples can be noted in the common two-rod-and-bundle foundation, which was so widespread, and in comparable shapes. Yet individual attainment within one area is to be noted in the brilliant design developments of the Anasazi with no indication of equal expression in the other two areas. Textile weaving is very reflective of areal variation, with the striped styles of the Anasazi, and the greater width of the Anasazi product as against the greater length of the Hohokam blanket. Much more elaborated designing seems to have prevailed in the Hohokam and even in the southern Anasazi areas than in the Anasazi proper.

Pottery certainly is one of the most important if not *the* most important of all the individual craft arts developed in the Southwest; it is doubly significant because it is both well preserved and is a vital key to the cultural fluctuations within groups and to artistic expression. As discussed in Chapter 4, this craft art reflects not only the differences between the three basic cultures but also the many local variations within each of these areas. The latter is particularly demonstrable in the Anasazi. Further, there are the base wares for each area, the Hohokam red-on-buff, the Anasazi black-on-white and polychrome wares, and the textured wares of the Mogollon, each not to be confused with the others. When found in other areas, a given style would be reflective of trade. This, too, is an important aspect of ceramic studies to the archaeologist. The polychrome wares of the Anasazi are so individual in the composite of their traits that this feature can be used to distinguish many locales, for example, the three Little Colorado polychromes mentioned, which are distinctive in their exterior decorations, Pinedale, with its small and spotted black and white designs, St. Johns with its all-white and usually continuous patterns, and Four Mile with a distinctive black and white, continuous motif. In specific design elements and motifs there are many differences, too. One style might be pointed out for each major area, but it is well to remember that there are many more. The precisely drawn, geometric decoration of the Anasazi contrasts vividly with the quick but expressive strokes of the Hohokam, particularly in life forms; and both are very different from the combined geometric and life themes of the Mimbres people of the Mogollon area.

Even in the lesser arts one can see the importance of local developments. One fine example of this would be the splendid paint palettes from Snaketown, a Hohokam trait but one so highly developed at this particular site. Shell work, too, was a significant Hohokam trait, perhaps because this culture was located closer to the main sources of supply, the Gulf of California. Legs on stone vessels in the same area may be a reflection of a stronger Mexican influence than is felt in the other two areas where this feature is not in evidence. Perhaps reflective of this same southern influence are the coffee bean eyes of Hohokam figurines.

Internal growth accounts for many of the changes in culture; or exchange of ideas or trade between the several groups may have affected cultural growth and development. Too, the environment played a significant part. Perhaps the custom of building in caves with limited space encouraged several-storied structures of the Puebloans . . . or was it the cultural climate, particularly social structure, which became more tight-knit with the passage of years? Too, did the same social structure channel the feeling of reserve in design in Anasazi pottery and other decoration?

Not all cultures reached a peak of attainment simultaneously, nor did any one culture reach peaks in all of its expressions at one and the same time. The Anasazi crested in basketry production as a whole in Basketmaker III times; in pottery the highest attainments of the Chaco were in Pueblo III, while in the Hopi area certain styles were earlier and some later, the latter well illustrated by the late prehistoric and early historic Sikyatki ware of Pueblo IV and V times.

If judged by the apparent stage of attainment of textiles, which was seemingly very high in Pueblo IV times, one can conjecture that it might have continued in its natural growth had it not been interrupted by the arrival of the Spaniards.

Too, many of the pueblos had consolidated, creating larger villages during Pueblo IV. What might this have contributed to a higher development in the arts? Greater strength, more centralized organization, perhaps the beginning of some type of higher specialization . . . these trends might well have contributed to an efflorescence in the arts.

It is difficult to summarize the overall artistry of so greatly different crafts such as are found in the prehistoric Southwest. However, a few general remarks can be made in relation to the total art qualities, with more specific application of them to the individual crafts. Something of the influences exerted upon this art will also be brought into focus.

Artistry began on the Early Man level, with harmony in form and fine symmetry in workmanship in the points produced by the big game hunters. By no means are these qualities essential to the task at hand, nor to the use of the objects produced; the very differences which can be noted between a Folsom and a Yuma point used by hunters of the same animal, the mammoth, would indicate strictly local preferences and artistic trends in the form and finish of the weapon. But that unfathomable quality in man which seems to demand of him something in the way of the esthetic came to the fore in the early stages of human existence and has remained for all time. The sense of artistry may diminish, or, perhaps, wear itself down, but only to be born again. Perhaps in this very situation did the old adage, art is a reflection of culture, manifest itself most profoundly, for it is more a situation in which culture as a whole has "run down," and art, as a breathing part of culture, is likewise depressed.

For a long time after the peak attainments of the Early Man stages of development, there was a hiatus, or perhaps more properly, a pedestrian phase when arts and crafts seem to have suffered a prolonged period of nothing more than a day-by-day production of necessities. Perhaps it took culture a long time to readjust after the great Pleistocene animals disappeared; perhaps the conditions of a shift from gathering to cultivation were such as to demand too much time. Whatever the circumstances, there seems to have been little produced of high artistic value until the Hohokams and the Mogollones caught their breath and started on the long path up the neolithic trail. Certainly agriculture shed quite a different light on matters cultural; art began to respond to this new stimulus. New avenues for expression appeared with the introduction of pottery; artistic inspiration came with growing religious and social concepts, as groups came together on a more permanent basis and for continuous association. All of these circumstances, and more, are exaggerated through the succeeding years and as a result, there were ever more stimuli for the expression of artistic feelings. The response was remarkable, as has been seen in the foregoing chapters. It is possible, too, that new peoples came into the Southwest, that there were ever more mixtures between the established populations of the Southwest, and, as in other parts of the world, these mixtures added their share in terms of renewed vigor that revitalized the artistic feelings of the Indians of this part of the world.

More specifically, some of the traits were so far reaching in their effect on the arts and crafts of these ancient people that further mention of some of these channels of extension should be explored to explain aspects of this art. One of the most significant of all was, of course, the influences and ramifications of agriculture. Economy has always and everywhere been a most vitalizing force in the lives of men. Generally it has served as the base of religious expression: in a hunting society, animal deities are pre-eminent; if cultivation of the fields dominates, that which concerns agriculture is dominant, whether it be a river, rain, or snow, and always, or almost always, the sun. It is not surprising to find the combination of sun, clouds, rain, and lightning, and often lesser things relating to water, such as frogs, used in the mythology and design development of these early cultures. The profound importance of myths and legends among historic tribes testifies to their longevity in native religion, and designs on early crafts support this idea.

Inasmuch as man today is so wrapped up in specialists and ever greater specialization, it may be of interest to stress the importance of all individuals in connection with the production of craft arts. Most women provided their households with the necessities of life, the pots and pans and other household equipment, and whatever clothing the family wore. In like manner, the men made their own agricultural and hunting tools and weapons, and their religious equipment. In addition, they cultivated their foodstuffs, and later most of the material for textile weaving. In some communities, it is possible that women assisted in the fields; and, of course, they gathered the wild materials they used in weaving, all basket materials, and the clay for their pots. Obviously, then, there was little time left over in the lives of these early Indians and much of that may well have been spent in religious ceremonies.

Prehistoric art was a decorative art, for there was no time for art for art's sake. This is, of course, a basic characteristic of much primitive art. Being a decorative art contributed to the continuity of styles over what might seem like prolonged periods of time. The fact that all participated in art expressions, through the utility crafts, and that there were few or no specialists, added to the sameness or strong similarities of the expressions of limited locales. Specialists contribute another dimension unknown to these arts, namely, quick change and limited styles and as noted quite the contrary is true in the Southwest.

Despite the fact that the Southwest is a semi-arid land, it has many natural resources, and these were widely explored by the natives. Reflective of this in their arts and crafts are the varied clays used in pottery, the many materials employed in baskets and textiles, the vegetal and mineral sources for color in all three crafts, the tremendous variety of stone used in tools, weapons, jewelry, and for other purposes. And for their religious objects, the items collected for the medicine man's pouch or to place on the altar or at the shrine, frequently they turned to natural substances which they found near and far, such as quartz crystals, concretions, the flowerlets of a special tree, a special wood for a wand, a particular source for a body paint. Thus many of the specific trends in their arts were directed or controlled by the available materials that the native knew and used. Some change is reflective of a widening knowledge of such matters, such as when they learned to cultivate cotton, or found new clays or different minerals that contributed to greater variety in color.

Techniques of production in the crafts and the development of technical skill also contributed to artistry. Development of coiled basketry made for greater variety in shapes, and finer weaving contributed to more complicated designing. Weft-wrap and twill tapestry opened the doors for greater variety in texture and design in textiles. Open and closed burning techniques in ceramics affected both quality of surface and color in clay vessels. And certainly the prehistoric Southwesterners became expert in these and other matters relative to neolithic technologies.

As described in the foregoing chapters, the prehistoric Southwestern artists expressed themselves in just about every possible manner in connection with the craft arts. Form was a first concern; color was explored reasonably far for a neolithic people; other surface decoration, such as carving, incising, modeling, embroidery, and a few other techniques added to the variety in artistry. And design left little to be desired, for these people had a keen urgency to decorate and a matching ability to do so.

Form was explored far beyond satisfying a definite need. A water jar or storage vessel, whether of clay or basketry, fulfilled obvious needs in a small mouth and a full body; artistic feelings carried these craftsmen beyond into longer and shorter necks, rounded or pointed bottoms, elongate or bulbous bodies, a round or sharply turned shoulder. The loom dictated a square or rectangular cloth, but the weaver's artistic bent dictated a greater dimension by warps or by wefts; warps were strung in a straight line but they could be drawn in at the top by the weaver to create a shaped sleeve. Decoration during the weaving process was explored widely and the weavers also discovered that they could add embroidery or paint a design on the fabric after it was removed from the loom.

A bowl was basically an open-mouthed shallow or deeper-bodied form; artistry made it very wide and shallow, with a gentle rim-to-bottom curved wall; a burden basket required a wide mouth and a deep body but dictated nothing as to whether the body was to be conical or bucket-shaped. A pendant needed a hole near the edge, but the artist in the maker of the piece could produce a simple circle, a keystone shape, a human or animal form. And the latter could be in full front or in profile; it could be naturalistic or conventionalized or highly abstract, according to the whim of the artist or the dictates of society.

The ways in which the prehistoric Southwesterners decorated their crafts almost exhausted possibilities in this direction. Color was of first and foremost importance, whether in baskets, textiles, or pottery, and in some lesser crafts as well. There was greater limitation in basketry, with red and black the major colors. The same preferences are shown in textile decoration, but there is the popular addition of brown, with rare use of other colors such as blue or green. Pottery was most varied in color usage, with various combinations of black, white, red, buff, and yellow; too, there were shades and tones of unbelievable variety.

Above both form and color was design; it ran the gamut from simple to complex geometricity, from realistic to abstract treatment, from basic geometric forms to combinations essentially Southwestern. Some claim that these native Indians exhausted the possibilities of geometric design before Europeans arrived; certainly little was added to their repertoire after the whites came, and that precious little was fused with what was already established, to become essentially Indian.

It was this rich heritage, then, that became the basis of the arts and crafts of historic Southwestern Indians. In fact, in many instances there was such a continuum that any changes or additions are no more discernible than others were in the prehistoric past. It would seem that the Indians took the new gifts in stride, whatever they might have been . . . new design elements, new materials such as silver, or whatever, and quickly turned them to their purposes. What is more Indian than a Navajo cast silver bracelet, a Zuñi turquoise, shell, and coral mosaic held in place by silver, a Navajo "naja" pendant on a necklace, which evolved out of the Moorish crescent moon and star design, "bayeta," an imported cloth raveled and woven into a Navajo rug, Spanish embroidery designs integrated comfortably with cloud themes in ceramic decoration?

Connecting links between the past and the present are frequently missing, but that they are there cannot be doubted. The historic crafts themselves are the same, basketry, textiles pottery, jewelry, everyday tools, weapons, implements. Basically, the same technologies persisted, too, so that it may be noted that in the main the native crafts today are produced in essentially the same way as they were 1,500 years, or more, ago. Coiled, wicker, and plaited baskets are still made; the upright loom has not been displaced; no potter's wheel is used except by a few students in institutions of higher learning; and with the exception of silver and its obviously different techniques of working, some of the finest stone and shell beads are still made with a hand manipulated device.

In many craft arts of the Southwest, material has not changed at all in the shift into historic years. Pottery and basketry still utilize their age-old and familiar native clays and plants; even coloring media are more frequently local than introduced. Wool has been added to cotton in the textile art, and aniline dyes frequently replace native and natural colors. The most significant European addition to all the crafts has been silver in the field of adornment; it may be used alone or in combination with the age-old turquoise and shell or historically introduced coral.

Except where the Indian has catered to the tastes of the white man, forms of native craft arts remain the same. Candlesticks in clay and hand-bags in basketry have replaced nothing; they have merely been added to the already long list of native shapes. Commercialization has taken its heaviest toll in diminished sizes; basically, native forms or simplified versions of the same prevail in both ceramics and basketry. Certainly all of this is in the natural sequence of events; when ancient Mexicans influenced the prehistoric cultures, the southerners left their mark in footed vessels, in the feathered serpent motif, in coffee bean eyes for figurines. As the same loom is in use today as in the past, there has been no change in textile form, not even when the blanket became a rug at the turn into this century. Basic forms in ornaments were established too many centuries ago for much change to transpire; then and now bracelets may be narrow or wider, thick or thinner, simple or more ornate; beads were and are vari-shaped; more has happened to pendants in material than in form; a ring is still a band, plain or decorated. And thus the inventory of forms in ornament repeats itself.

Along with all of these continuities in the crafts field has been the inheritance of the rich and cherished mass of decorative design. Design did not become burdensome in the past, for the native artisans had a profound ability to arrange and rearrange the basic elements and units into ever new and fresh motifs; the addition of a few more ideas along the way gave new vigor to design as a whole. A happy facility to combine the old and the new has resulted in many fine works of art by historic natives of the Southwest.

With the exception of easel painting, which was introduced to the Indian by the white man at the turn of this century, and a limited quantity of true sculpture developed in the second half of the twentieth century, Southwest Indian art has remained a decorative art; hence the long continued use of this style has frequently produced fine and artistic results. Inasmuch as the utility value of pottery and basketry in particular rarely survived, it may be surprising that old forms have continued, even in simplified styles. Perhaps it is the decorative factor that has contributed to this continuity, for design was highly adapted to established forms through the centuries.

A significant change has occurred, which may have profound influences in the future. This is the gradual emergence of individuals who may be called specialists. Little in the way of true guilds of the traditional historic type have developed and continued where experimentation and exchange of ideas would contribute to the furtherance of artistic effort. Perhaps the special school, such as the Institute of American Indian Art, Santa Fe, New Mexico, would be the closest approach to such a situation; however, it has reached a limited number of individual craftsmen and has affected the main flow of craft arts but slightly, and not at all in many areas.

Thus, in a final word, it may be said that the mainstream of Southwest Indian art continues in channels carved out by the prehistoric people. So deeply cut were they, so well adapted to maintain a proper flow of artistry, that the rivulets of historic times that have cut into the mainstream have not diverted the placid waters of prehistoric origins.

Notes

CHAPTER 1

1. Wormington 1957. See also Haury, et al., 1959.
2. Wheat 1972.
3. Jennings 1957: 7.
4. Kidder 1962: 1–56; Wormington 1970; Colton 1946.
5. Gladwin, et al., 1937; Haury 1945a; Kidder 1962.
6. Wheat 1955.

CHAPTER 2

1. Jennings 1957: 7.
2. Rudy in Jennings 1957: 235–65.
3. Carlson 1963: 43–44.
4. Morris, Earl 1939: 117.
5. Judd 1954: 316–20.
6. Martin, et al., 1964: 106.
7. Haury 1934: 72.
8. Morris, Elizabeth 1959a: 466.
9. Morris and Burgh 1941: 20.
10. Ibid: Figs. 35–38.
11. Pepper 1920: 107.
12. Haury 1950: 402.
13. Haury 1945a: 163.
14. Haury 1934: 72–73.
15. Loud and Harrington 1929: 60–64.
16. Haury 1934: 80.
17. Ibid: 73–75.
18. Guernsey and Kidder 1921: 61–62.
19. Ibid.
20. Morris and Burgh 1941: Figure 15b.
21. Ibid: Fig. 14d.
22. Dixon 1956: 60.
23. Haury 1945b: 44–48.
24. Fewkes 1911: 29 and Plates 19, 20, 21.
25. Judd 1954: 312.
26. Pepper 1920: Fig. 71.
27. McGregor 1943: 275 and 277.
28. Haury 1945a: 171.
29. Morris and Burgh 1941: 51 and Fig. 31f; Culin 1908: Frontispiece.
30. Judd 1954: 306.
31. McGregor 1943: 278.
32. Morris, Earl 1928b: 194.
33. Cosgrove 1947: 99–113.
34. Tanner 1968: Chapter II.

CHAPTER 3

1. Kidder and Guernsey 1919: 175.
2. Ibid: 174.
3. Martin, et al., 1952: Fig. 74, 207.
4. Kent 1957: 465.
5. Ibid: 472.
6. Ibid: 479.
7. Colton, Mary Russell, et al., 1951: 12.
8. Kent 1957: 493.
9. Ibid: 603.
10. Martin, et al., 1952: 237ff.
11. Morris, Elizabeth 1959a: 215.
12. Guernsey and Kidder 1921: 66, 71.
13. Morris, Elizabeth 1959a: Fig. 96.
14. Ibid: 316–22.
15. Kent 1957: 488 and 715.
16. Ibid: 488 (loomed cloth from P. III sites, 1100–1300).
17. Ibid: 489.
18. Morris, Elizabeth 1959a: 370.
19. Haury 1945b: 48.
20. Haury 1934: 68–69, and Plate XLIII.
21. Guernsey and Kidder 1921: 54–59.
22. Kent 1957: 476.
23. Ibid: 522, 525.
24. Dixon 1956: 29.
25. Kent 1957: 618–19.
26. Haury 1934: 97.
27. Kent 1957: 602.
28. Ibid: 621.
29. Haury 1945b: 39–40.
30. Haury 1934: 63.
31. Kent 1957: 617.
32. Haury 1950: 429.
33. Dixon 1956: 14.
34. Ibid: 13.
35. Smith 1952: Fig. 25.
36. Ibid: Plate I.
37. Kent 1957: 564–65.
38. Cosgrove and Cosgrove 1932: Plate 227e.
39. Kidder and Guernsey 1919: 100.
40. Cosgrove and Cosgrove 1932: Plate 227d.
41. Bradfield 1929: Plate LXXIX.
42. Kent 1957: 631.
43. Ibid: 635.

CHAPTER 4

 1. Cheney 1937: 13.
 2. Roberts 1930: 79.
 3. Vaillant 1939: 30.
 4. Cosgrove and Cosgrove 1932: 72–73.
 5. Leavitt 1962: Fig. 12.
 6. Ibid: Fig. 13.
 7. Ibid: 23.
 8. Gladwin, et al., 1937: Fig. 112.
 9. Ibid: 211.
10. Wormington 1970: 26.
11. Roberts 1930: 83.
12. Ibid: 110.
13. Ibid.
14. Hayes 1964: Figs. 31, 32, 34, 35, 36.
15. Swannack 1969: 69–71.
16. Judd 1954: Plates 63 and 66.
17. Kidder and Guernsey 1919: 133.
18. Judd 1954.
19. Swannack 1969: 97, Fig. 76.
20. Amsden 1936: 44.
21. Gladwin, et al., 1937: 188.
22. Cosgrove and Cosgrove 1932: 76 and Plates 108–20.
23. Kidder in Cosgrove and Cosgrove 1932: xxi.
24. Cosgrove and Cosgrove 1932: Plate108ff.
25. Ibid: 74.
26. Kabotie 1949.

CHAPTER 5

 1. Smith 1952: Figure 78b.
 2. Judd 1954: 101–02.
 3. Haury 1967: 680–81.
 4. Haury in Gladwin, et al., 1937: 131.
 5. Sims 1950: Plate VII.
 6. Dixon 1956: 9.
 7. Guernsey and Kidder 1921: 47.
 8. Ibid.
 9. Ibid: 48–49.
10. Kidder and Guernsey 1919: 161ff.
11. Morris, Earl H. 1939: Plates 173–77, 141–42.
12. Fewkes 1904: 86–87, Fig. 44, Plate XLIV.
13. Judd 1954: 80–109.
14. Pepper 1920: 134.
15. Judd 1954: 93.
16. Ibid: 106.
17. McGregor 1943: 270–98.
18. Ibid: 289.
19. Clark 1967.
20. Cummings 1940: 60.
21. Roberts 1932: 139 and Plate 48.
22. Wheat 1955: 147.
23. Haury 1936: 46 and Plate XIX.
24. Ibid: 78.
25. Cosgrove 1947: 150.
26. Wendorf 1950: 83.
27. Bradfield 1931: 58, 59; Cosgrove and Cosgrove 1932: 65–66; Smith 1952.
28. Haury 1936: Fig. 30 and Plate XIX.
29. Martin, et al., 1952: 105.
30. Lehmer 1948.
31. Robinson 1959.
32. Haury 1945a: 158.
33. Ibid.
34. Gladwin, et al., 1937: 142.
35. Woodward 1931: 19.
36. Haury 1945a: 158.
37. Woodward 1931: 19.
38. Scantling 1940: 58.
39. Withers 1941: 70.
40. Smith 1952: Fig. 81b.
41. Ibid: Fig. 78b.

CHAPTER 6

 1. Judd 1954: 147–49 and Plate 36.
 2. Lehmer 1948: 33.
 3. Judd 1954: 239.
 4. Lehmer 1948: 62.
 5. Morss 1954, and 1–8.
 6. Kidder 1932: 133.
 7. Rohn 1971: 242, (Illus.) 288.
 8. Ibid: 246.
 9. Judd 1954: 295.
10. Roberts 1932: 147–49.
11. Wendorf 1950: 68.
12. Haury 1934: Plate LXXVI.
13. Caywood and Spicer 1935: 64–65.
14. Sayles 1945: Plate XLVII.
15. Lehmer 1948: 69.
16. Gladwin, et al., 1937: 233–45.
17. Ibid: 234–35 and Plates CXCV and CXCVI.
18. Haury 1967: 671 and 690.
19. Brown 1967: 72.
20. Roberts 1932: 58–60.
21. Lambert 1954: 132.
22. Judd 1959: 130.
23. Wendorf 1950: 81.
24. Brown 1967: 72.
25. Smith 1952: 286–87 and Figs. 26k and 71a.
26. Sinclair 1951: Illus. f.p. 207.
27. Smith 1952: Fig. 61b.
28. Guernsey and Kidder 1921: 50.
29. Judd 1954: 279.
30. Cosgrove 1947: 120.
31. Brown 1967: 76–77.
32. Kidder 1932: 293.
33. Martin, et al., 1952: 429.
34. Wheat 1955: 151.
35. Kidder 1932: 250–51, Figs. 209–10.
36. Pepper 1920: 279.
37. Morris, Elizabeth 1959b: 407.
38. Ibid: 408.
39. Judd 1954: 304–05.
40. Kidder 1932: 252.
41. Kidder and Guernsey 1919: 186.
42. Morris, Earl 1939: 123.
43. Morris, Elizabeth 1959a: 294.
44. McGregor 1941: 230–32.
45. Cosgrove 1947: 120–21.
46. Ibid: 121.
47. Wheat 1955: 144.
48. Pepper 1920: 69.
49. Haury in Gladwin, et al., 1937: 147.
50. Judd 1954: 305–06.
51. Haury in Gladwin, et al., 1937: 125.
52. Haury 1967: 684.
53. Haury 1932: 101–05.
54. Roberts 1931: 157.
55. Kidder 1932: Fig. 48.
56. Wheat 1955: 117.
57. Morris, Earl 1939: 132.
58. Wheat 1955: 120.
59. Sayles 1945: Plate XXXIX.
60. Breternitz 1959: 42.
61. Judd 1954: 299.
62. Haury 1950: 329–32.
63. Wheat 1955: 124.
64. Haury 1940: 117; Haury 1936: 106–07.
65. Kidder and Guernsey 1919: 187–88.
66. Carlson 1963: 33 and Plate 24.
67. Judd 1954: 299–304.

Bibliography

AMSDEN, CHARLES AVERY
1936 An Analysis of Hohokam Pottery Design. *Medallion Papers* No. XXIII, Gila Pueblo, Globe, Arizona.

BOURKE, JOHN G.
1884 *The Snake-Dance of the Moquis of Arizona.* Charles Scribner's Sons, New York.

BRADFIELD, WESLEY
1929 *Cameron Creek Village, a Site in the Mimbres Area in Grant County, New Mexico.* School of American Research, Santa Fe, New Mexico.

BRETERNITZ, DAVID A.
1959 Excavations at Nantack Village, Point of Pines, Arizona. *Anthropological Papers of the University of Arizona*, Number 1, Tucson.

BROWN, DONALD NELSON
1967 "The Distribution of Sound Instruments in the Prehistoric Southwestern United States". *Ethnomusicology*, Vol. XI, No. 1.

CARLSON, ROY L.
1963 Basket Maker III Sites Near Durango, Colorado. *University of Colorado Studies, Series in Anthropology*, No. 8, Boulder.

CAYWOOD, LOUIS R. and EDWARD H. SPICER
1935 *Tuzigoot, The Excavation and Repair of a Ruin on the Verde River near Clarkdale, Arizona.* Field Division of Education National Park Service, Berkeley, California.

CHENEY, SHELDON
1937 *A World History of Art.* The Viking Press, New York.

CLARK GEOFFREY ANDERSON
1967 *A Preliminary Analysis of Burial Clusters at the Grasshopper Site, East-Central Arizona.* Thesis (M.A.) University of Arizona, Tucson.

COLTON, HAROLD S.
1941 Winona and Ridge Ruin, Part II. *Museum of Northern Arizona, Bulletin 19*, Northern Arizona Society of Science and Art, Flagstaff.
1946 The Sinagua: A Summary of the Archaeology of the Region of Flagstaff, Arizona. *Museum of Northern Arizona*, Bulletin 22, Northern Arizona Society of Science and Art, Flagstaff.

COLTON, MARY-RUSSELL F. et al
1951 Hopi Indian Arts and Crafts. *Museum of Northern Arizona*, Reprint Series Number 3. Northern Arizona Society of Science and Art, Flagstaff.

COSGROVE, C. B.
1947 Caves of the Upper Gila and Hueco Areas in New Mexico and Texas. *Papers of the Peabody Museum of American Archaeology and Ethnology*, Harvard University, Vol. XXIV, No. 2., Cambridge, Massachusetts.

COSGROVE, H. S. and C. B. COSGROVE
1932 The Swarts Ruin, A Typical Mimbres Site in Southwestern New Mexico. *Papers of the Peabody Museum of American Archaeology and Ethnology*, Harvard University, Vol. XV, No. 1, Cambridge, Massachusetts.

CULIN, STEWART
1908 Games of the North American Indian. *Bureau of American Ethnology* Annual Report 24, Washington, D.C.

CUMMINGS, BYRON
1940 *Kinishba*—A Prehistoric Pueblo of the Great Pueblo Period. Hohokam Museum Association and The University of Arizona, Tucson.
1953 *The First Inhabitants of Arizona and the Southwest.* Cummings Publication Council, Tucson, Arizona.

DENSMORE, FRANCES
1957 Music of Acoma, Isleta, Cochiti, and Zuñi Pueblos. *Bureau of American Ethnology*, Bulletin 165, Washington, D.C.

DI PESO, CHARLES and Collaborators
1956 The Upper Pima of San Cayetano del Tumacacori. No. 7, *The Amerind Foundation, Inc.*, Dragoon, Arizona.

DIXON, KEITH A.
1956 Hidden House—A Cliff Ruin in Sycamore Canyon, Central Arizona. *Museum of Northern Arizona*, Bulletin 29. Northern Arizona Society of Science and Art Inc., Flagstaff.

FEWKES, JESSE WALTER
1904 Two Summers' Work in Pueblo Ruins. *Bureau of American Ethnology*, Annual Report 22, Washington, D.C.
1911 Preliminary Report on a Visit to the Navajo National Monument, Arizona. *Bureau of American Ethnology*, Bulletin 50, Washington, D.C.

GLADWIN, HAROLD STERLING
1945 The Chaco Branch, Excavations at White Mound and in the Red Mesa Valley. *Medallion Papers* No. XXXIII, Gila Pueblo, Globe, Arizona.

GLADWIN, HAROLD S., EMIL W. HAURY, E. B. SAYLES, and NORA GLADWIN
1937 Excavations at Snaketown, Material Culture. *Medallion Papers* No. XXV, Gila Pueblo, Globe, Arizona.

GUERNSEY, SAMUEL JAMES and ALFRED VINCENT KIDDER
1921 Basket-Maker Caves of Northeastern Arizona. *Papers of the Peabody Museum of American Archaeology and Ethnology*, Harvard University, Vol. VIII, No. 2, Cambridge, Massachusetts.

GUTHE, CARL E.
1925 *Pueblo Pottery Making*. Yale University Press, Andover, Massachusetts.

HAURY, EMIL W.
1932 Roosevelt: 9:6, a Hohokam Site of the Colonial Period. *Medallion Papers*, No. XI, Gila Pueblo, Globe, Arizona.
1934 The Canyon Creek Ruin and the Cliff Dwellings of the Sierra Ancha. *Medallion Papers*, No. XIV, Gila Pueblo, Globe, Arizona.
1936 The Mogollon Culture of Southwestern New Mexico. *Medallion Papers*, No. XX, Gila Pueblo, Globe, Arizona.
1940 Excavations in the Forestdale Valley, East-Central Arizona. *Social Science Bulletin No. 12*, University of Arizona Bulletin, Vol. XI, No. 4, Tucson.
1945a The Excavation of Los Muertos and Neighboring Ruins in the Salt River Valley, Southern Arizona. *Papers of the Peabody Museum of American Archaeology and Ethnology*, Vol. XXIV, No. 1, Harvard University, Cambridge, Massachusetts.
1945b Painted Cave Northeastern Arizona. No. 3, *The Amerind Foundation Inc.*, Dragoon, Arizona.
1967 The Hohokam, First Masters of the American Desert. *National Geographic*, May, Washington, D.C.

HAURY, EMIL W. and Collaborators
1950 *The Stratigraphy and Archaeology of Ventana Cave, Arizona*. The University of Arizona Press, Tucson. The University of New Mexico Press, Albuquerque.

HAURY, EMIL W. and CAROL A. GIFFORD
1959 A Thirteenth Century "Strongbox". *The Kiva*, Volume 24, Number 4, Arizona Archaeological and Historical Society, Tucson.

HAURY, EMIL W. and E. B. SAYLES
1947 An Early Pit House Village of the Mogollon Culture, Forestdale Valley, Arizona. *University of Arizona Bulletin*, Volume XVIII, Number 4. Social Science Bulletin No. 16. Tucson.

HAURY, EMIL W., E. B. SAYLES, and WILLIAM W. WASLEY
1959 "The Lehner Mammoth Site, Southeastern Arizona". *American Antiquity* Volume 25, No. 1.

HAYES, ALDEN C.
1964 The Archaeological Survey of Wetherill Mesa, Mesa Verde National Park, Colorado. *Archaeological Research Series*, Number Seven A, National Park Service, U.S. Department of the Interior, Washington.

JENNINGS, JESSE D.
1957 Danger Cave. *American Antiquity*, Volume XXIII, Number 2 Part 2. The University of Utah Press. The Society for American Archaeology.

JOHNSON, ALFRED E. and WILLIAM W. WASLEY
1960 Hohokam Archaeology of the Painted Rocks Reservoir Area Near Gila Bend, Western Arizona. Ms. (under contract with the *National Park Service*).

JUDD, NEIL M.
1954 The Material Culture of Pueblo Bonito. *Smithsonian Miscellaneous Collections*, Volume 124. Smithsonian Institution, Washington, D.C.
1959 Pueblo del Arroyo, Chaco Canyon, New Mexico. *Smithsonian Miscellaneous Collections*, Volume 138, No. 1, Smithsonian Institution, Washington, D.C.

KABOTIE, FRED
    1949 *Designs from the Ancient Mimbreños* with a Hopi Interpretation. The Grabhorn Press, San Francisco.

KENT, KATE PECK
    1957 The Cultivation and Weaving of Cotton in the Prehistoric Southwestern United States. *Transactions of the American Philosophical Society*, New Series, Vol. 47, Part 3, Philadelphia.

KIDDER, ALFRED VINCENT
    1932 *The Artifacts of Pecos*. Phillips Academy. Yale University Press, New Haven, Connecticut.
    1962 *An Introduction to the Study of Southwestern Archaeology* (with an Introduction on Southwestern Archaeology Today, by Irving Rouse). Yale University Press, New Haven, Connecticut.

KIDDER, ALFRED VINCENT and SAMUEL J. GUERNSEY
    1919 Archaeological Explorations in Northeastern Arizona. *Bureau of American Ethnology*, Bulletin 65, Washington, D.C.

KNOBLOCK, BYRON W.
    1939 *Banner-stones of the North American Indians*. Published by the Author, LaGrange, Illinois.

LAMBERT, MARJORIE F.
    1954 Paa-Ko: Archaeological Chronicle of an Indian Village in North Central New Mexico. *School of American Research* Monograph No. 19, Parts I-V, School of American Research, Santa Fe, New Mexico.

LEAVITT, ERNEST EASTMAN
    1962 *Technical Differences in the Painted Decoration of Anasazi and Hohokam Pottery*. Thesis (M.A.) University of Arizona, Tucson.

LEHMER, DONALD J.
    1948 The Jornado Branch of the Mogollon. *The University of Arizona Bulletin*, Vol. XIX, No. 2. Social Science Bulletin No. 17, The University of Arizona, Tucson.

LOUD, LLEWELLYN L. and M. R. HARRINGTON
    1929 Lovelock Cave. *University of California Publications in American Archaeology and Ethnology*, Volume 25, No. 1. University of California Press, Berkeley.

MARTIN, PAUL S. and ELIZABETH S. WILLIS
    1940 Anasazi Painted Pottery in the Field Museum of Natural History. *Field Museum of Natural History Publications*, Anthropology, Memoirs, Vol. 5, Chicago.

MARTIN, PAUL S. et al
    1952 Mogollon Cultural Continuity and Change. The Stratigraphic Analysis of Tularosa and Cordova Caves. *Fieldiana*, Anthropology Vol. 40, Chicago Natural History Museum, Chicago.
    1964 Chapters in the Prehistory of Eastern Arizona II. *Fieldiana*, Anthropology Volume 55, Chicago Natural History Museum, Chicago.

McGREGOR, JOHN C.
    1941 Winona and Ridge Ruin, Part I. *Museum of Northern Arizona*, Bulletin 18, Northern Arizona Society of Science and Art, Flagstaff.
    1943 Burial of an Early American Magician. *American Philosophical Society Proceedings*, Vol. 86, No. 2, Philadelphia.

MORRIS, EARL H.
    1928a The Aztec Ruin. *Anthropological Papers of The American Museum of Natural History*, Volume XXVI, Part 1, New York.
    1928b Burials in the Aztec Ruin: The Aztec Ruin Annex. *Anthropological Papers of The American Museum of Natural History*, Volume XXVI, Parts III & IV, New York.
    1939 Archaeological Studies in the La Plata District, Southwestern Colorado and Northwestern New Mexico. *Carnegie Institution of Washington* Publication 519, Washington, D.C.

MORRIS, EARL H. and ROBERT F. BURGH
    1941 Anasazi Basketry, Basket Maker II through Pueblo III. Publication 533, *Carnegie Institution of Washington*, Washington, D.C.

MORRIS, ELIZABETH A.
    1959a *Basketmaker Caves in the Prayer Rock District, Northeastern Arizona*. Thesis (Ph.D.) University of Arizona, Tucson.
    1959b "Basketmaker Flutes from the Prayer Rock District, Arizona". *American Antiquity*, Vol. XXIV, No. 4, Part 1.

MORSS, NOEL
    1954 Clay Figurines of the American Southwest. Papers of the *Peabody Museum of American Archaeology and Ethnology*, Harvard University, Vol. XLIX, No. 1, Cambridge, Massachusetts.

NESBITT, PAUL H.
    1931 The Ancient Mimbreños. *Logan Museum*, Bulletin Number Four, The Logan Museum, Beloit College, Beloit, Wisconsin.

PEPPER, GEORGE H.
    1902 The Ancient Basket Makers of Southeastern Utah. *American Museum of Natural History* Guide Leaflet No. 6, New York.
    1920 Pueblo Bonito. Anthropological Papers of the *American Museum of Natural History* Vol. XXVII, New York.

ROBERTS, F. H. H. JR.
1929 Shabik'eshchee Village, A Late Basket Maker Site in the Chaco Canyon, New Mexico. *Bureau of American Ethnology* Bulletin 92, Washington, D.C.
1930 Early Pueblo Ruins in the Piedra District Southwestern Colorado. *Bureau of American Ethnology*, Bulletin 96, Washington, D.C.
1931 The Ruins at Kiatuthlanna, Eastern Arizona. *Bureau of American Ethnology* Bulletin 100, Washington, D.C.
1932 The Village of the Great Kivas on the Zuñi Reservation, New Mexico. *Bureau of American Ethnology*, Bulletin 111, Washington, D.C.

ROBINSON, WILLIAM J.
1959 *Burial Customs at the Point of Pines Ruin.* Thesis (M.A.) University of Arizona, Tucson.

ROHN, ARTHUR H.
1971 Wetherill Mesa Excavations—Mug House, Mesa Verde National Park—Colorado. *Archaeological Research Series* Number Seven–D, National Park Service, U.S. Department of the Interior, Washington, D.C.

RUSSELL, FRANK
1908 The Pima Indians. *Bureau of American Ethnology* Annual Report 26, Washington, D.C.

SAYLES, E. B.
1945 The San Simon Branch Excavations at Cave Creek and in the San Simon Valley–I. Material Culture. *Medallion Papers* No. XXXIV, Gila Pueblo, Globe, Arizona.

SCANTLING, FREDERICK H.
1940 *Excavations at Jack Rabbit Ruin, Papago Indian Reservation, Arizona.* Thesis (M.A.) University of Arizona, Tucson.

SIMS, AGNES C.
1950 *San Cristobal Petroglyphs.* Southwest Editions, Santa Fe, New Mexico.

SINCLAIR, JOHN L.
1951 "The Pueblo of Kuaua". *El Palacio*, Vol. 58, No. 7, School of American Research and others, Santa Fe, New Mexico.

SMITH, WATSON
1952 Kiva Mural Decoration at Awatovi and Kawaika-a. Papers of the *Peabody Museum of American Archaeology and Ethnology*, Harvard University, Vol. XXXVII, Cambridge, Massachusetts.

SWANNACK, JERVIS D. JR.
1969 Big Juniper House, Mesa Verde National Park, Colorado. *Archaeological Research Series* Number Seven-C, National Park Service, U.S. Department of the Interior, Washington, D.C.

TANNER, CLARA LEE
1968 *Southwest Indian Craft Arts.* University of Arizona Press, Tucson.

VAILLANT, GEORGE C.
1939 *Indian Arts in North America.* Harper and Brothers, New York.

WENDORF, FRED
1950 A Report on the Excavation of a Small Ruin Near Point of Pines, East Central Arizona. *University of Arizona Bulletin*, Vol. XXI, No. 3, Social Science Bulletin No. 19, University of Arizona, Tucson.

WHEAT, JOE BEN
1955 Mogollon Culture Prior to A.D. 1000. *American Antiquity*, Vol. XX, Number 4, Part 2, Salt Lake City, Utah.
1972 The Olsen-Chubbuck Site, a Paleo-Indian Bison Kill. Memoirs, *Society for American Archaeology*, Number 26.

WITHERS, ARNOLD MOORE
1941 *Excavations at Valshni Village, Papago Indian Reservation, Arizona.* Thesis (M.A.) University of Arizona, Tucson.

WOODWARD, ARTHUR
1931 The Grewe Site, Gila Valley, Arizona. *Los Angeles Museum of History, Science, and Art*, Occasional Papers Number 1, Los Angeles.

WORMINGTON, H. M.
1957 Ancient Man in North America. *Denver Museum of Natural History* Popular Series No. 4, Fourth Edition, Denver, Colorado.
1970 Prehistoric Indians of the Southwest. *Denver Museum of Natural History.* Popular Series No. 7, 4th Edition, Denver, Colorado.

Index